STOURHEAD

Henry Hoare's Paradise Revisited

For Henry Cadogan Hoare

CONTENTS

FOREWORD

Everybody has their own idea of paradise, but for most Englishmen it will resemble the view across the lake and towards the Pantheon at Stourhead. The creators of this Elysium, several generations of the Hoare family, were exceptionally gifted, for though they excelled in finance they also had a brilliant creative streak. Collectively they must take the credit for the great work of art that is Stourhead, the cumulative effect of the house, art collection, and above all, the garden. Each generation has made its distinctive contribution to the present maturity. But as Dudley Dodd reminds us, the garden at Stourhead is enduring rather than timeless – it is and always has been subject to change and development.

Before the Hoare family created these pleasure grounds, the estate belonged to the Stourton family for as far back as records go, and in legend very much further. It was at the heart of the Stourton family's identity – not only did it share their name (as it was then called Stourton) but it appeared on the family coat of arms, which is effectively a map of the estate: 'sable, a bend or between six fountaines', or in layman's language, the River Stour with the six springs from which once it rose. Those mostly defunct springs are still commemorated with a Hoare monument in the meadow at Six Wells Bottom.

The story of the demesne begins in 1448 when the 1st Lord Stourton was granted a licence to enclose 1,000 acres of pasture: 'To impale and make thereof a park'. At around this time the family commissioned the heralds to write the family history, and must have paid them well for it, for they came up with a fabulous concoction, taking the family back to Alfred the Great and providing a dazzling Saxon story that was never told more engagingly than by Richard Colt Hoare in his history of Wiltshire. The Stourton family has always been grateful to him for supporting these agreeable and romantic myths, but myths they almost certainly are.

Nobody is certain where the old house at Stourton was situated, the best guess being the present stabling area. Things went well for the family until Charles 8th Lord Stourton called for the murder of his father's steward, William Hartgill, in Kilmington church nearby, for which crime he was hung by a silken halter in Salisbury marketplace in 1556. He has been the subject of two plays and a novel. The family estates were attainted by the Crown, and this marks the beginning of the family's long decline. This was accelerated by their staunch adherence to Catholicism: during the Civil War Stourton House was sacked and was probably left uninhabitable. It was described and drawn in its fall by John Aubrey. As royalists,

Catholics, and supporters of James II, the family was on the wrong side of history for most of the seventeenth century, and Edward 13th baron followed King James into exile in France. Their estate was sold and acquired by 'Good' Henry Hoare in 1717. Memory of the Stourtons is that of the black sheep, the murderous 8th baron, of whom National Trust signage constantly reminds us.

The Hoares were by any standard gifted patrons. 'Good' Henry's first act was to pull down the old mediaeval house and replace it with a Palladian villa designed by the brilliant Scottish architect, Colen Campbell. His son, Henry Hoare 'The Magnificent' (1705–85) was, as Dudley Dodd tells us, a cultivated lover of the arts who acquired Poussin's *Rape of the Sabine Women* – Claude Lorrain was a favourite painter and Virgil, a favourite author. He went to live at Stourhead in 1742 and almost immediately began to place garden buildings on the hillside that runs down from the house to the village. It was Henry who made the inspired decision to flood the valley, creating the 18-acre lake around which the garden and the architectural adornments are wrapped. Paramount among them has always been the view of the Pantheon, which Dudley Dodd describes as a knock-out visual punch. However, at this stage Stourhead was far from being a purely classical garden: Dodd reminds us that there was a Turkish tent, a Chinese alcove and elements to which he refers as 'fairground surprises'. Interestingly, he speculates that it was the marriage of Henry's daughter, Susanna, to Lord Dungarven that may have spurred him 'to transform Stourhead from a minor to a major landscape garden'.

Henry dedicated the grounds to pagan river deities, and to ancient heroes, among them Aeneas, Hercules and King Alfred. As a gardener, he was an improviser, working *con spirito* – as the spirit moved him – in the words of his grandson. Stourhead was already recognised as one of the great gardens of Britain by the 1760s, and the garden buildings he left behind are among the most memorable and successful ever created. He was something of a genius in the way he placed them, and the Pantheon across the water has become by far the most famous garden view in England. Henry was ahead of his time in recognising the picturesque qualities of the church and village – rather than ignore them he brought them into the landscape, which he enhanced by adding the bridge and the Bristol Cross, so creating the second of the great views in a composition that he described as 'a charming Gaspard picture at that end of that water'. Henry positioned one of his most ambitious creations out of view, hidden in the woods above the pleasure grounds. Alfred's Tower is all the more potent for being on the putative site where the King raised his standard before the fateful Battle of Edington in 878.

The second family member of outstanding interest is Henry's grandson, Sir Richard Colt Hoare (1758–1838), the historian of Wiltshire. I am presently gazing at six folio volumes of his great work and marvelling at his industry. If Henry the Magnificent's vision was that of a classicist who enjoyed colourful garden ornaments, Colt Hoare was more antiquarian in spirit, and it is to him that we owe much of what we see today, for he altered the look of the garden and brought it to its present Augustan magnificence, partly by removing his predecessor's exotica. Dudley Dodd rather laments this loss. However, Colt Hoare is responsible for the introduction of the Gothic element. He enjoyed ruined abbeys, but without one to preserve he had to improvise, so he introduced his Gothic effects by a subtle crenelation of the village.

Colt Hoare was a collector of old master paintings. He could not afford masterpieces, nor indeed antique sculpture, although he did have enough money to put together a superb library. Much of the fruit of his patronage remains at Stourhead, notably the furniture of Thomas Chippendale and the landscape watercolours of Louis Ducros. It was Colt Hoare who built the two flanking pavilions onto the house, one to contain his library, which became the most admired room in the house, and the other to hold the picture collection. Even in the Hoare family there was a black sheep, the 5th baronet, who caused the library and much of the art collection to be sold – he was a gambler, an unusual thing to find in a banking family.

The last baronet, Sir Henry Hoare and his wife Alda, affectionately described in the writings of James Lees-Milne, had to cope with two tragedies: the first was a fire, which gutted the centre of the house in 1902. Water has been both a creator and the destructor at Stourhead. Without it there would have been no lake or pleasure gardens, but the problem of pumping it 150 feet up the hill to the house defeated the attempts at rescue. The pressure was insufficient to quench the blaze, which gutted the central portion of the house. Unfortunately, the restoration was entrusted to a mediocrity, Doran Webb, who, as Dodd writes, made a botched job of it. The second tragedy was the death of their only son in 1917, which precipitated the eventual gift of the house and grounds to the National Trust. Stourhead has sometimes been called an English garden based on a French painting of an Italian landscape, but it is so much more than that. It is a place where Ancient Rome and English history meet on equal terms, and above all it is a work of incomparable beauty, the perfect expression of the English landscape garden; which, as Kenneth Clark reminds us, was the most pervasive influence the English ever had on the look of things.

How grateful we are to Dudley Dodd for revealing the story behind this masterpiece.

James Stourton, Stour Provost

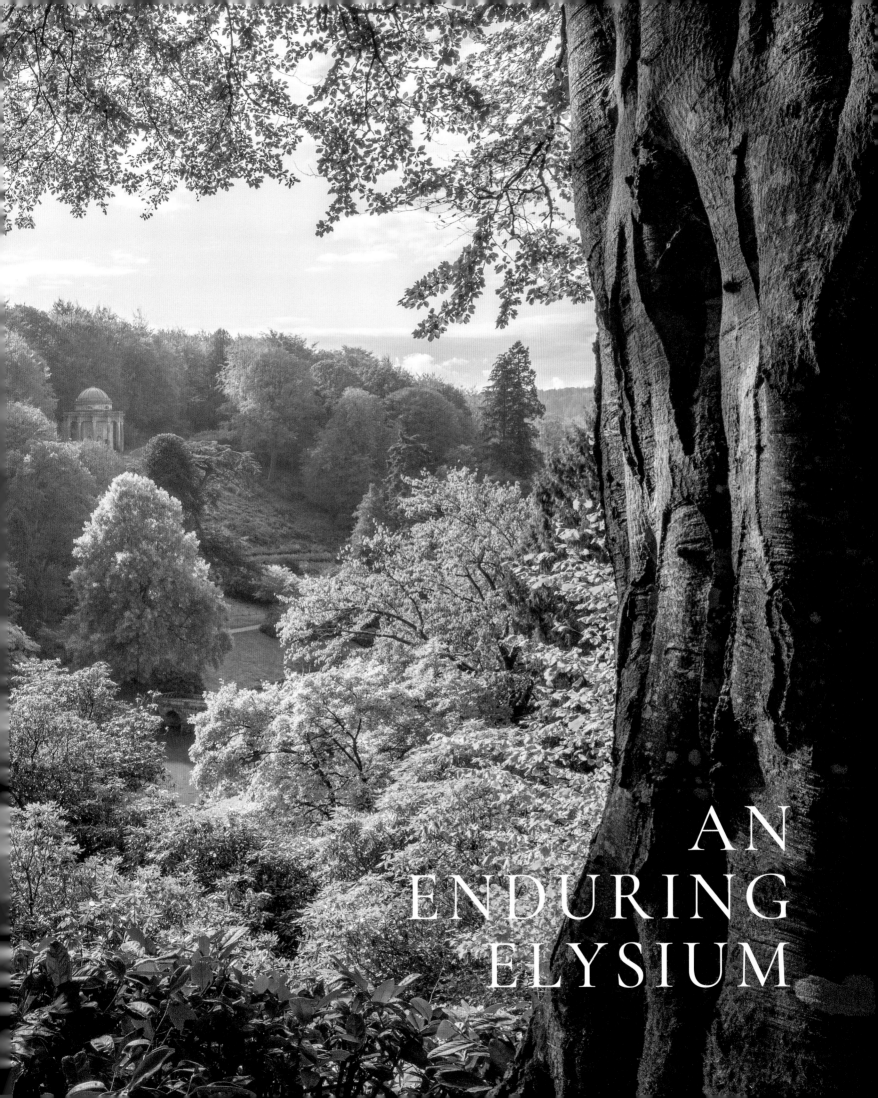

AN
ENDURING
ELYSIUM

ON THE MAP

Stourhead lies some 27 miles west of Salisbury. The old road from the city rises to White Sheet Hill at the south-western boundary of Salisbury Plain. From that vantage point the spectator glimpses the estate spread on the plateau ahead: the house set in parkland, fringed by farms and, beyond, abundant woods. The prospect encompasses an obelisk and Alfred's Tower on the horizon. The upper part of Stourton village stands on this level land, before the road sweeps abruptly downhill to the heart of the residence where the church, inn and cottages cluster. Since the mid-eighteenth century this once sequestered enclave has been a bustle of villagers, gardeners, foresters, tradesmen, worshippers and trippers. Here the newcomer is rewarded with one of the most memorable views in Britain: the Stourhead landscape garden.

The garden is set at the convergence of three valleys: an eastern arm dipping from the flat lands; a second valley, descending from the north-west, where the River Stour rises; and a third shallow valley, down which the river flows southwards passing through man-made lakes.

The house stands about 650 feet above sea level at the meeting point of Wiltshire, Somerset and Dorset. The geology is various. The chalk terrain of Salisbury Plain peters out on the eastern fringes of the estate. Here the soil becomes richer and below lies light-coloured sandstone, quarried in the early nineteenth century near Search Farm. Moving west, a stratum emerges of greensand stone which was quarried on the estate, principally at Bonham, and was first choice for building material in the neighbourhood. Below the stone lies gault clay which emerges in the valley bottoms, providing puddling for lakes and building material.[1] There were once brick kilns in Tucking Mill. Further west at Gasper the soil becomes sandy and gravelly, best suited to forestry. This variety lent appeal to the estate when the first Henry Hoare contemplated its purchase in 1717. The abundant springs of the Stour, rising at the interface of the permeable stone and impermeable clay, were an over-arching attraction. The plateau was farmed as pasture with some arable fields.

Stourhead comprises the house and art collection, the landscape garden and kitchen garden, each of which is labour-intensive and expensive to maintain. By contrast the tenants, woods and tourists generate income. Each component merits attention but because the landscape garden is world-famous it must occupy centre stage.

At first encounter, gardens are among the least-demanding forms of pleasure. They deliver a punch visually. In this respect Stourhead scores a knockout, and that

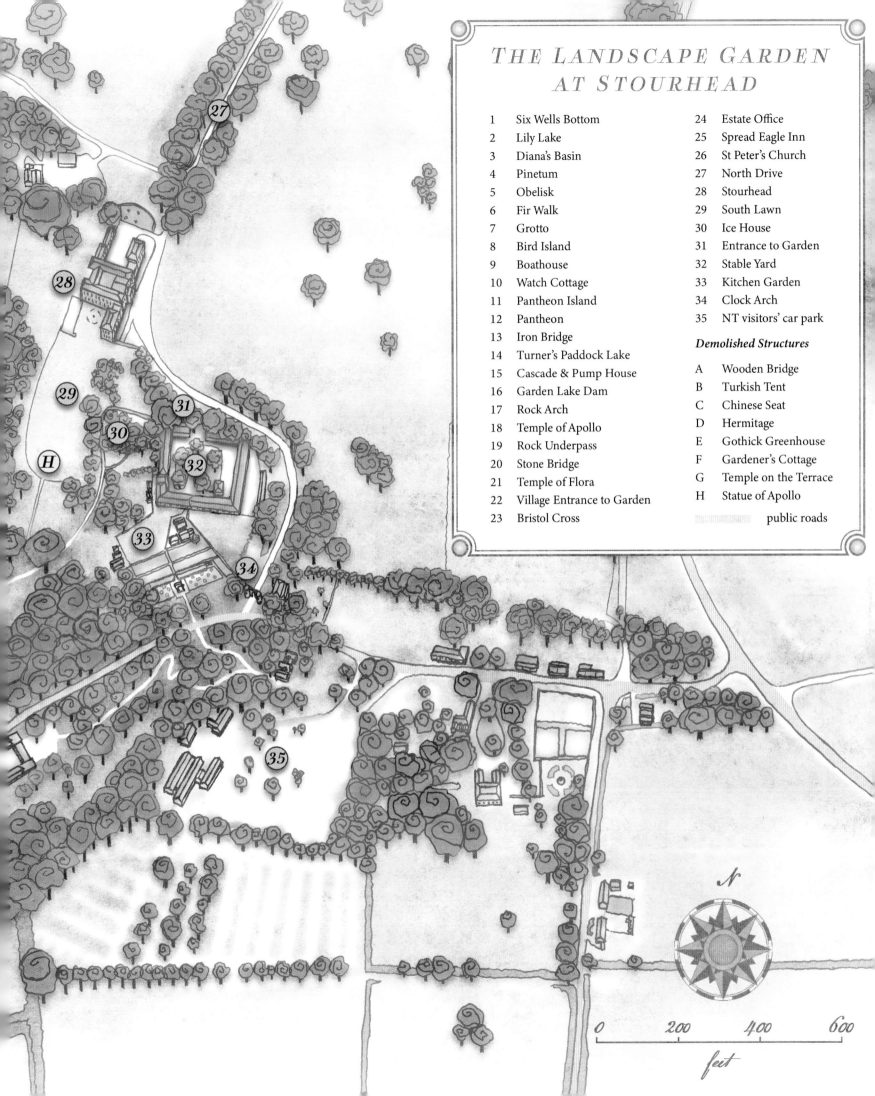

THE LANDSCAPE GARDEN AT STOURHEAD

1   Six Wells Bottom
2   Lily Lake
3   Diana's Basin
4   Pinetum
5   Obelisk
6   Fir Walk
7   Grotto
8   Bird Island
9   Boathouse
10 Watch Cottage
11 Pantheon Island
12 Pantheon
13 Iron Bridge
14 Turner's Paddock Lake
15 Cascade & Pump House
16 Garden Lake Dam
17 Rock Arch
18 Temple of Apollo
19 Rock Underpass
20 Stone Bridge
21 Temple of Flora
22 Village Entrance to Garden
23 Bristol Cross

24 Estate Office
25 Spread Eagle Inn
26 St Peter's Church
27 North Drive
28 Stourhead
29 South Lawn
30 Ice House
31 Entrance to Garden
32 Stable Yard
33 Kitchen Garden
34 Clock Arch
35 NT visitors' car park

Demolished Structures

A   Wooden Bridge
B   Turkish Tent
C   Chinese Seat
D   Hermitage
E   Gothick Greenhouse
F   Gardener's Cottage
G   Temple on the Terrace
H   Statue of Apollo

                    public roads

is best taken on the spot. Photographs demonstrate the particular; they record and remind. Questions bubble up rapidly: who created the garden? Why? And when?

The garden at Stourhead is enduring rather than timeless and it has been subject to both the vicissitudes of the changing fortunes among its owners and to external threats; in the 1960s Dutch elm disease struck and, today, *Phytophthora ramorum* menaces the trees and shrubs. That the garden survived through history is thanks to succeeding generations of the Hoare family.

Bankers, such as the Hoares, seldom sought the limelight while plying their trade, and aspired to be upright and honest and wealthy. It is sad that these laudable characteristics on their own are flat soda water to today's biographers and readers. We must explore Stourhead to discover among its occupants contrasting measures of happiness and sadness; wealth and debt; creative acts and destruction; care and neglect; tragic lives endured and lives cut tragically short.

The Hoare family

Henry Hoare (1677–1724/5) was a second-generation goldsmith and banker, famed as much for his charitable work as his business acumen so that subsequently he became known as 'Good Henry'. He acquired Stourhead in 1717 for £14,000 (above £1.5 million today) and built the Palladian house.[2] At his death, his widow, Jane, moved there permanently becoming the first chatelaine and imprinting her devout personality on the house. After she died in 1742, their son, Henry Hoare (1705–85), took over Stourhead; the first of only two occasions when son followed father. Throughout his life this second Henry worked in London, permitting himself summers in Wiltshire. As a partner at the family bank, his share of the annual profits ranged from £803 to £17,841, aside from personal dealings and rental income. During his long tenure at Stourhead, Henry assembled his art collection and created the landscape garden. It is unsurprising that he became 'Henry the Magnificent' in family circles. He built classical temples and follies inspired by faraway cultures. Henry intended visitors to enjoy the garden and he gave them fairground surprises.

Sir Richard Colt Hoare, 2nd Baronet, (1758–1838) was a grandson of Henry the Magnificent. He was a traveller, archaeologist and county historian and will henceforth be referred to as Colt Hoare. Widowed after two years of marriage, he settled at Stourhead in 1791. Colt enjoyed an annual income estimated at £10,170 from rents on land acquired by his grandfather.[3] On the strength of this he enlarged the house and purchased pictures and furniture. Colt introduced new varieties of trees and shrubs, initiating its progress from landscape garden to arboretum. But he was as much a destroyer as creator in the garden. His was an Augustan vision for Stourhead and he demolished Henry the Magnificent's follies so that today we see the garden through the eyes of Colt rather than his grandfather.

Colt, pale squire of Stourhead, made his reputation in the wider world as an author. He outlived his only son and under his will Stourhead was placed in trust for his successors in tail male.

Sir Henry Hugh Hoare, 3rd Baronet (1762–1841) followed his half-brother, Colt Hoare. He was a wealthy man and senior partner at Hoare's Bank. During his three years at Stourhead he added the portico to the house. His son, Sir Hugh Richard

Hoare, 4th Baronet (1799–1857), was also a banker. When he succeeded to the baronetcy and Stourhead he was the second, and last, son to follow his father. He improved the estate, adding modern buildings, but made no fundamental changes to the house and garden.

Stourhead received a jolt at the death of the childless 4th baronet and the succession of his nephew, Henry Ainslie Hoare (1824–94), henceforth referred to as Ainslie or the 5th baronet. Expelled from Hoare's Bank for misconduct, Ainslie led a peripatetic life flitting between Paris and London. He was ill-suited to the role of landowner but his attention to Stourhead only faltered when the money ran out. Then he was compelled to obtain a private Act of Parliament in order to sell the best of the art collection and Colt Hoare's prized library, raising over £40,000.[4] In 1885 he quit Stourhead, leaving the house in the charge of a caretaker. Ainslie and his wife represent the landed gentry in its decadence.

Rescue arrived with his cousin and successor, Sir Henry Hugh Arthur Hoare, 6th Baronet (1865–1947). He did not work in the family bank but was wealthy in his own right having inherited two estates in addition to Stourhead, which is where Sir Henry settled, making the place his life's work. After the house was gutted by fire in 1902, he rebuilt it and restored the interiors. He was a typical countryman: a shrewd judge of horses, and passionate about hunting, forestry and farming. At Stourhead he planted ornamental trees, hybrid rhododendrons and azaleas. The garden had never been more colourful than when Sir Henry gave the property to the National Trust in 1946, his only son having died from war wounds in 1917. Sir Henry had married a distant cousin, Alda Weston. This remarkable woman, unwavering in her support of her husband, imposed her constricted personality on Stourhead and became its second memorable chatelaine.

The national stage

Because no owner of Stourhead received political or diplomatic appointments, made a career in the armed services or held positions at court, the house offers little evidence of the nation's past. It possesses neither a gallery of portraits nor drawers of mementoes to evoke our political history as found, for instance, at Melbourne Hall in Derbyshire, Mount Stewart in Co. Down or, until recently, at Clandon Park in Surrey. Colt Hoare saw history, ancient and modern, through the prism of Wiltshire. Filaments of British history spread beyond the Stourhead library and emerge infrequently. When they do, they are monarchical: outdoors, the Bristol Cross, St Peter's Pump and Alfred's Tower; indoors, a gold Armada medal, with a portrait of Queen Elizabeth I, was displayed with the Sixtus Cabinet until the medal was sold in the 1880s. There remain busts of *Alfred the Great* and *Charles I*. A copy of Van Dyck's portrait of the royal children once hung above the Saloon chimneypiece.[5] Among house guests recorded, David Garrick, J. M. W. Turner and Thomas Hardy have enduring reputations. The art collection commenced by Henry the Magnificent was enriched by his nephew the first baronet and Colt Hoare. They made informed, if unadventurous, purchases in the fine arts and in the applied arts, notably the furniture; they consistently acquired the best so that Stourhead became a cynosure of Georgian and Regency gentlemen's taste. It has always been a connoisseur's house.

THE HOARES
OF STOURHEAD

Owners of Stourhead are in **bold**

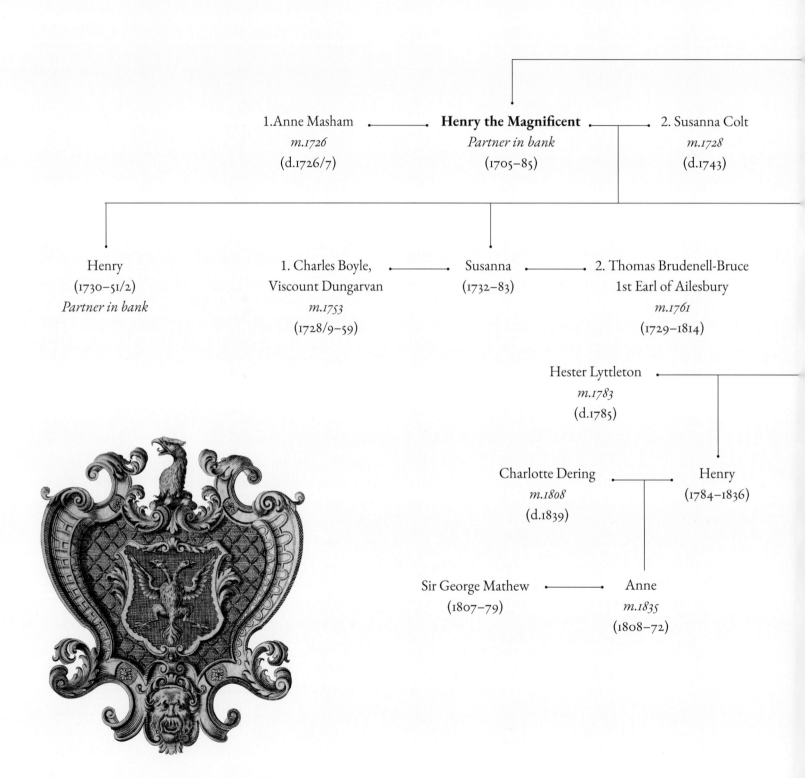

1.Anne Masham ●━━━━━━▶ **Henry the Magnificent** ●━━━▶ 2. Susanna Colt
m.1726 *Partner in bank* *m.1728*
(d.1726/7) (1705–85) (d.1743)

Henry   1. Charles Boyle, ◀━━━●　Susanna　●━━━▶ 2. Thomas Brudenell-Bruce
(1730–51/2)   Viscount Dungarvan   (1732–83)   1st Earl of Ailesbury
Partner in bank   *m.1753* *m.1761*
(1728/9–59) (1729–1814)

Hester Lyttleton ●
m.1783
(d.1785)

Charlotte Dering ●   Henry
m.1808   (1784–1836)
(d.1839)

Sir George Mathew ●━━━━━● Anne
(1807–79) *m.1835*
(1808–72)

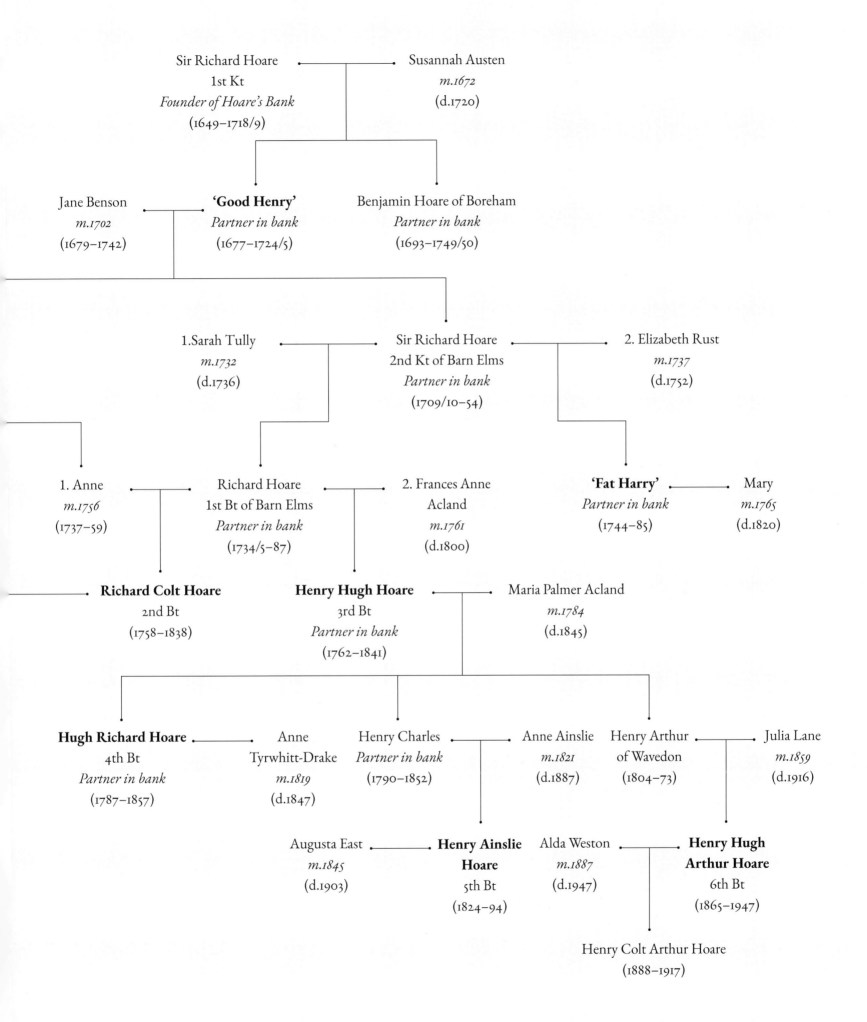

Sir Richard Hoare
1st Kt
Founder of Hoare's Bank
(1649–1718/9)

Susannah Austen
m.1672
(d.1720)

Jane Benson
m.1702
(1679–1742)

'Good Henry'
Partner in bank
(1677–1724/5)

Benjamin Hoare of Boreham
Partner in bank
(1693–1749/50)

1.Sarah Tully
m.1732
(d.1736)

Sir Richard Hoare
2nd Kt of Barn Elms
Partner in bank
(1709/10–54)

2. Elizabeth Rust
m.1737
(d.1752)

1. Anne
m.1756
(1737–59)

Richard Hoare
1st Bt of Barn Elms
Partner in bank
(1734/5–87)

2. Frances Anne
Acland
m.1761
(d.1800)

'Fat Harry'
Partner in bank
(1744–85)

Mary
m.1765
(d.1820)

Richard Colt Hoare
2nd Bt
(1758–1838)

Henry Hugh Hoare
3rd Bt
Partner in bank
(1762–1841)

Maria Palmer Acland
m.1784
(d.1845)

Hugh Richard Hoare
4th Bt
Partner in bank
(1787–1857)

Anne
Tyrwhitt-Drake
m.1819
(d.1847)

Henry Charles
Partner in bank
(1790–1852)

Anne Ainslie
m.1821
(d.1887)

Henry Arthur
of Wavedon
(1804–73)

Julia Lane
m.1859
(d.1916)

Augusta East
m.1845
(d.1903)

**Henry Ainslie
Hoare**
5th Bt
(1824–94)

Alda Weston
m.1887
(d.1947)

**Henry Hugh
Arthur Hoare**
6th Bt
(1865–1947)

Henry Colt Arthur Hoare
(1888–1917)

The garden

The landscape garden enjoys international fame. It lies south of the house, centred upon an artificial lake. Henry the Magnificent owned up to spending a minimum of £20,000 (over £2 million today) on improvements at Stourhead; in truth he laid out perhaps ten times that sum and, in 1773, Mrs Rishton claimed Henry expended at least £300,000 in making the garden.[6] He exploited the topography, developing a sequence of views from the valley-tops, across the water, focused on temples and structures that were both vantage points and eye-catchers.

In the valleys Henry the Magnificent contrived the most beautiful walk in Britain. He set out from the house, crossed the South Lawn and entered the Shades, then descended to the lake. His path, skirting the shore, led to the Grotto and Pantheon, traversed the dam and continued up to the Temple of Apollo before finally reaching the village. Along the way are pausing points to enjoy the view; thus, in 1783, Mrs Boscawen had time to 'to sit, and tarry at the different stations' without, unfortunately, identifying their whereabouts.[7] But visiting the garden four years previously, the Swedish architect, Frederik Magnus Piper, plotted the paths and the sight lines he discovered from the viewing stations as shown in illustrations on pages 136–7, 169 and 193. Since his day several stations have vanished and new ones have been created.

1. The pre-eminent view from either the Bristol Cross or the graveyard, across the Stone Bridge and lake to the Pantheon. For the companions of Henry the Magnificent, this was the finale and climax to the garden. For those approaching from the village, it has always provided a foretaste. (pages 162–3)

2. From the clearing at the top of the Shades, with views down towards St Peter's Church to the left, and the Temple of Apollo to the right. (pages 12–3)

3. In the Shades, a clearing at the fork in the path provides a view across the lake towards the Pantheon. (page 6)

4. On the lower path, the view from the Temple of Flora to the Rock Arch, the great dam and the Pantheon. (pages 2–3)

5. From the Pantheon to the Stone Bridge, the Bristol Cross and the village. (The reverse of the first view.) (pages 28–9)

6. From the Temple of Apollo, the view to the northern end of the lake where the Wooden Bridge once stood. (pages 198–9)

Colt Hoare laid paths from the village and around the lake. Keeping to level ground robs the visitor of the dramatic *coups d'oeil* of his grandfather's walk from the hill-top viewing stations.

'Procul, o procul este profani'

There exists impressive documentation of the Hoares at Stourhead in archives at the house, at C. Hoare & Co. and in the Wiltshire and Swindon History Centre. However, evidence concerning the creation of the landscape garden is fragmentary. Henry the Magnificent's account books survive as do a handful of bills but the correspondence and accounts of Francis Faugoin, his head gardener from 1747, no longer exist. Henry was in London for most of the year so he would have written regularly to Faugoin and entrusted him to hire and pay builders and labourers in the grounds. Letters from 1760 onwards, written by Henry to his son-in-law, Lord Bruce, are a bonus, imparting a breath of life to dry-as-dust bank ledgers. Henry the Magnificent may have covered his own tracks by destroying paperwork because his successor, Colt Hoare, no slouch with archives, lamented how little he could discover.

The garden awakens a wealth of perceptions among visitors, triggered according to their interests and knowledge. How far any interpretation matches the intentions of Henry the Magnificent is impossible to judge because he left too few clues. Like the *Tempesta*, by Giorgione, Stourhead's garden presents a paradox and has become prey to interpreters. Kenneth Woodbridge, doyen of Stourhead studies, conferred the glamour of the *Aeneid* on the garden. His thesis fanned speculation on meanings supposedly locked in the landscape. Some of these interpretations and meditations can be found in the Further Reading (page 312). Their elegant arguments blend fact, classical knowledge, conjecture and imagination. Whether the garden evokes Aeneas, a new Troy, the choice of Hercules, a harbour sheltered from storms, or a mourning patriarch, is a matter of choice for their readers. Few academics have echoed the perceptions of the first commentators, who responded in tune with their outlook and education: a local clergyman imagined the Garden Lake as the Styx and the Grotto as guarded by Cerberus,[8] while John Wesley was affronted by naked pagan gods.[9]

In his surviving letters, Henry the Magnificent proves himself well-versed in literature and knowledgeable about the arts. How far he was influenced by the landscape paintings of Claude Lorrain or Gaspard Dughet will be discussed (pages 39–41). Henry spiced his letters with Latin quotations and he added inscriptions in the garden. He would have expected his readers to recognise these and would have taken pleasure when visitors made their own riffs on his garden.

This book explores advice Henry received from professionals and friends as the garden evolved, and draws on descriptions of Stourhead written by visitors in the eighteenth and early nineteenth centuries and whose pocket biographies feature in Appendix II. The history concludes after the Second World War when the garden was approaching a technicolour zenith and was given to the National Trust. For the past seventy-five years the Trust has looked after Stourhead. This period merits a discrete history, which promises a steeper roller-coaster ride of care and neglect than the place experienced during centuries of family ownership. Happily, along the way the Trust has accumulated an archive. This story will mesh with the growth of the Trust as it became first a part of the establishment and latterly a national treasure.

Since 1947 the organisation has juggled its ambitions, if not its core aims. In recent years it has possessed the resources to follow fashions in curating, conservation, gardening, green initiatives and virtue signalling. That much was inevitable. The statutory duties of the Trust – to preserve and provide public access at its properties – are fundamentally incompatible with each other, the more so when 'access' is stretched to embrace education shading into entertainment. We may ponder how often on this mission the Trust has placed its national agenda above the specific needs of Stourhead and at which moments a satisfactory balance was achieved.

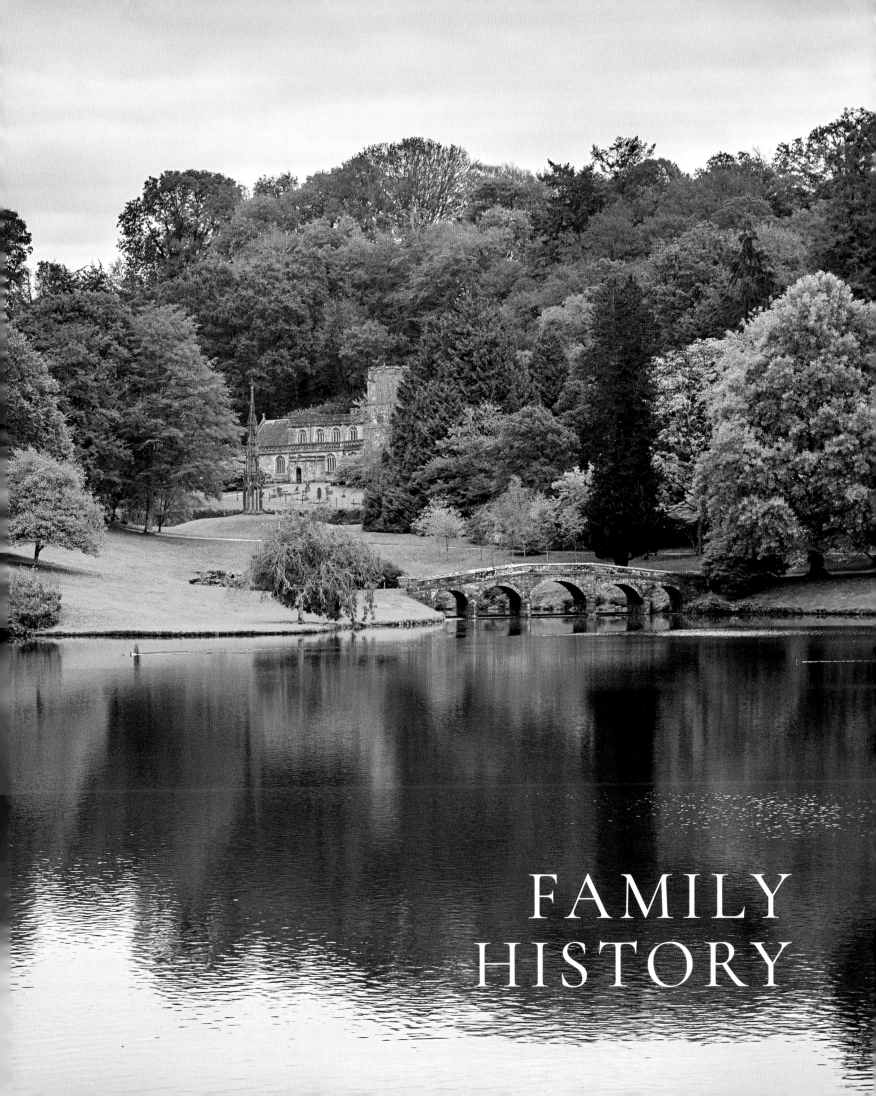

FAMILY
HISTORY

HOW THE HOARE FAMILY ACQUIRED STOURHEAD

Sir Richard Hoare (1649–1718/19)

Sir Richard Hoare was the founder of the family bank. He succeeded in business and, through energy and acumen, became a leader in the City of London. In these achievements he eclipsed his descendants. Sir Richard had trained as a goldsmith and opened a business at Cheapside in 1673. Some of his sparkle came from diamonds in which he invested. But their value fell, indeed they proved his single ill-chosen venture. Nevertheless, in 1719, jewellery represented almost a third of the bank's assets.[1] Lending money was an important aspect of the trade and Sir Richard, with his sons, developed accompanying services for customers, the germ of private banking today.

Sir Richard married Susannah, daughter of a fellow goldsmith, John Austen. In 1690 the family moved from Cheapside to Fleet Street, the site of the present Hoare's Bank. Of their seventeen children, seven survived. The bank premises were confined and Sir Richard acquired a country retreat at Hendon. In 1700 he purchased as an investment 242 acres at Staplehurst in Kent.

The Nine Years War, followed by the War of the Spanish Succession, drained the country's resources and sent the government in search of loans and other means of raising money. Sir Richard, along with Francis Child and Charles Duncombe, galvanised support in the City. As a reward he was knighted at the accession of Queen Anne. He entered Parliament as Tory MP for the City (1710–15) and served in succession as alderman, sheriff and Lord Mayor of London. Further lucrative positions came his way, notably his appointment as a director of the South Sea Company in 1711. When the Whigs returned to power Sir Richard's political career ended. This was a decade of speculation, infamously in the South Sea Company from which Hoare's Bank profited; others, less prudent, failed.

'Good Henry', Henry Hoare (1677–1724/5)

Of Sir Richard's many children he admitted two into the bank: his second son, Henry, was promoted to the partnership in 1698 and the younger son Benjamin, in 1718.[2] The former had a reputation for philanthropy and was subsequently known in the family as 'Good Henry'.[3] In his will Good Henry gave generously to London schools, hospitals and Christian causes.[4] He was a successful banker working in tandem with his father during the eventful years following the accession of George I.

Good Henry married his first cousin, Jane Benson, in 1702 and they lived *en famille* at the Fleet Street premises; Benjamin lodged nearby in St Martin's Lane.

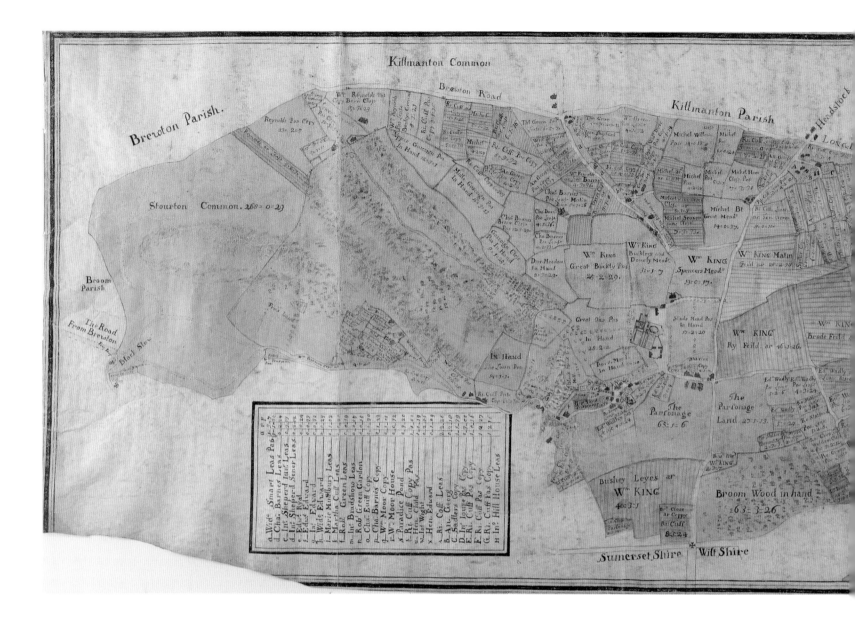

Returns from government stock decreased after 1717 making land an attractive alternative investment. Both sons acquired property outside London: Benjamin at Boreham near Chelmsford while Henry purchased Stourton and Stourton Caundle for £23,000. This fulfilled the pledge in the latter's marriage settlement that at least £10,000 be invested in property. Henry exceeded this; indeed, by 1725 he had laid out £37,150 on land in the south-west.[5] His brother-in-law, William Benson (1682–1754), had already make his presence felt in Wiltshire and probably encouraged Henry in these purchases.[6]

Benson is infamous for his brief and controversial spell as Surveyor-General of the Office of Works, 1718–19, in succession to Sir Christopher Wren.[7] Hitherto he had enjoyed a career on the fringes of politics as the friend of Whig potentates such as John Aislabie, appointed Chancellor in 1717. Thanks to their support, Benson secured the reversion of the Auditor of the Imprests that year. He would have to wait a further eighteen years before claiming this lucrative sinecure so the Office of Works was a stop-gap. In 1707 Benson married Eleanor, daughter of a wealthy Bristol merchant, Joseph Earle. The following year he took a lease of Amesbury House

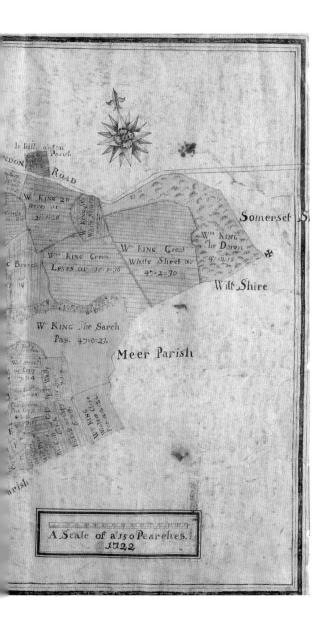

A Scale of a 150 Pearches.
1722

(later, Abbey) and in 1709–10 served as Sheriff for Wiltshire. In 1715 Benson was elected Whig MP for Shaftesbury and aspired to court circles. With Earle's money he purchased land at Newton Toney where he built Wilbury, an elegant villa in the style of Inigo Jones, illustrated by Colen Campbell in the first volume of *Vitruvius Britannicus*.[8] Benson was an early proponent of classical architecture exemplified by Palladio. He installed a Venetian window at the east end of St Michael's Church at Quarley in Hampshire, where Good Henry had property. They added inscriptions to this window, 'Gulielmus Benson et Henricus Hoare F. A. D. 1723'. These amateur ventures did not qualify Benson for the job of Surveyor-General and he was fortunate to appoint Colen Campbell (1676–1729) as his Chief Clerk and deputy. Benson will re-emerge as *cicerone* to the young Henry the Magnificent (page 43).

The Stourton estate

In 1703 Stourton comprised about two thousand acres of farms, woods and common land.[9] The Leicestershire politician Sir Thomas Meres acquired the property from Edward, 13th Baron Stourton, in 1714 and Meres's son sold it three years later for £14,000 to lawyers acting for Good Henry. The estate had been in decline since Charles, the 8th Baron, was hanged in 1557 for the murder of his neighbours, the Hartgills, father and son. In the seventeenth century the Stourtons were Catholic and Royalist. John Aubrey described their estate:

> The Park is large, but bald for timber trees, only some old stagge-headed trees remayning. This tract of country was heretofore all horrid and woody; it bordereth on the Forests of Bruton and Gillingham. In the Parke on a hill is the Toft, they say, of the Castle of Stourton: nothing now remayning but trenches.[10]

The timber was valued at £4,000 in 1704.[11] Unsurprisingly, Lord Stourton promptly felled trees in sufficient numbers to jeopardise his mortgage so that, by 1717, Stourton would have appeared somewhat woebegone.[12] The River Stour, rising from springs at the heart of the estate, filled the fish ponds and powered the mills. The 1722 plan of Stourhead indicates predominantly arable farms to the east and pasture mingled with woods lying to the west. It also identified occupancy: the fields surrounding the house are shown in hand; land east of the house was let to farmer King; to the south, the parson had substantial holdings and the remaining estate was apportioned between some twenty tenants. Stourton Caundle, in Dorset, had belonged to the Stourton family since the fifteenth century.[13] It comprised agricultural land lying between Shaftesbury and Sherborne in Dorset and returned good rents until it was sold in 1911.[14]

Old Stourton house is a lost demesne, dimly apprehended from a description and sketch by John Aubrey in 1685:

> Stourton House... is of gothique building, and standeth on a great deal of ground... Here is a great open-roofed hall, and an extraordinary large and high open-roofed kitchen... In the Court over the Parlour windowe is, in stone,

this quartered scutcheon Stourton... In the buttery is preserved a huge and monstrous bone, which the tradition of the howse would have to be of a mighty man or rather gyant, of this Family... In the Chappell, in the howse, the pavement is of brick annealed or painted with their coate, and Rebus.[15]

William Benson supervised the demolition of the principal buildings, a task performed so thoroughly that, to this day, archaeologists have not discovered the footings of the old house although the entrance and outer courtyard probably occupied the space where the stable yard now stands.[16] Good Henry kept some outlying buildings and reused masonry when possible; indeed, a few stones incorporated in Campbell's house have medieval carving on the inner face.[17]

The new house

If Good Henry needed encouragement to build a new house, this would have come from Benson who would have suggested Campbell as architect. The new house was named Stourhead and was habitable in the spring of 1724.[18] In recent years 'Stourhead House' has found its way to the head of the National Trust's writing paper, but without precedent. 'Stourhead' it remains in this book, with the occasional 'Stourhead house' where clarity demands.

Henry could afford to be extravagant in building Stourhead because the bank was earning profits of over £39,000 during 1720–2, a bonanza for the partners which ended in 1723 and was unmatched until the next century.[19] The architectural evolution of the house is explored later (page 233) while the interior and contents, which concern social history, are touched on in the family biographies.

Good Henry died in 1724/5 leaving Stourhead and his London property to his eldest son and namesake, subject to his widow's right to occupy the house of her choice.[20] Jane Hoare opted for Stourhead where she resided until 1742.

The ground floor of the house was given over to domestic offices spreading into outbuildings along the North Court. The first floor and attics were bedrooms for guests and servants (page 54).

The *piano nobile* comprised a central spine with a two-storey entrance hall and staircase opening into a chapel (now the Saloon). To the south of the entrance hall lay the dining room (Music Room) and beyond, a breakfast room (Small Dining Room) and bedroom (South Apartment); to the north of the entrance hall were a parlour (Cabinet Room) and two further bedrooms (Italian and Column rooms). The chapel was built on two levels permitting the household to worship on the *piano nobile* and the servants on the ground floor.[21]

Good Henry entered in his account books the money spent to equip Stourhead.[22] Textiles dominate: he paid the London upholsterer Robert North the elder over £500.[23] Henry was an opportunist in acquiring a mohair bed at the Duchess of Kingston's sale in 1722 and the gilt-bronze bust of *King Charles I* from a Mrs Gratnick, which survives at the house.[24]

Good Henry mentioned furniture in the accounts infrequently because he bequeathed his wife the contents of the house at Hendon in order to equip Stourhead. An inventory taken in 1742 recorded no gilded furniture, aside

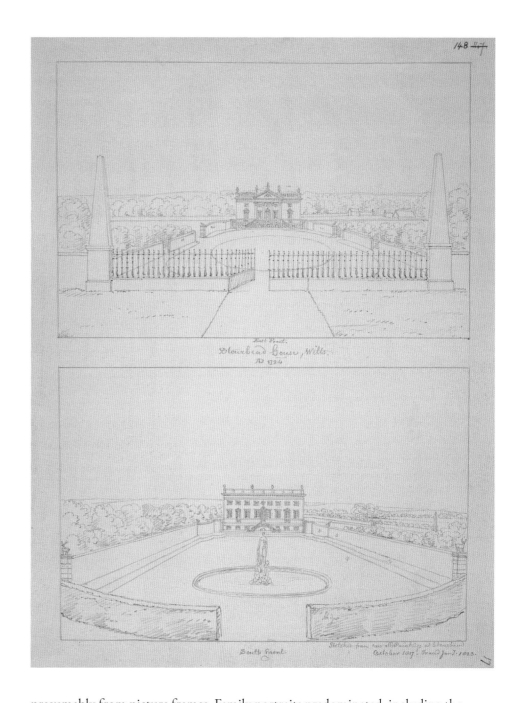

presumably from picture frames. Family portraits predominated, including the vast *Henry Hoare on horseback*, the likeness of the elder son and heir, a sporting picture and two flower pieces.[25] The inventory named one Old Master, *Elijah raising the widow's son*, by Rembrandt, which left the house in 1883.[26] Few furnishings mentioned in its pages are recognisable today with the exception of a marble cistern and a pair of naturalistically carved 'fox' tables.[27] Jane Hoare's energetically Christian widowhood was enlivened by her five children and thirteen grandchildren who visited her with sufficient frequency for the house to have a nursery.

At that time the immediate surroundings of the house mirrored the symmetry of Campbell's designs. Good Henry consulted Stephen Switzer about the garden but we do not know whether he followed this advice. The layout is recorded in the 1722 plan of Stourhead and illustrations by John Buckler taken from two long-vanished paintings at Stourhead.[28]

HENRY THE MAGNIFICENT (1705–85)

The second Henry Hoare, henceforth referred to as Henry the Magnificent where there is room for confusion, imposed his own graceful vision of a landscape garden upon the valleys adjacent to Stourhead. He possessed imagination and wealth sufficient to turn his dreams into reality. This creativity sets Henry apart from the rank of wealthy businessmen who appreciated the arts primarily through possession, although Henry was no slouch in forming his own art collection. He was cultured and well-read in the classics; Claude Lorrain was a favourite painter and Virgil a favourite author. Henry did not accomplish Stourhead alone; rather he was the presiding impresario summoning friends and professionals to design, build and embellish the place.

Henry was educated at Westminster School where Charles Hamilton, creator of the garden at Painshill, was a near-contemporary; they would remain acquainted throughout their lives.[1] Henry grew up in Fleet Street and at Hendon. By will and codicils Good Henry required his son to complete Stourhead and obliged his brother and banking partner, Benjamin, to quantify the private fortune that he had sunk into the partnership and remit this sum to Henry, giving the latter the option to quit banking. Indeed Good Henry may have contemplated his eldest son living as a country gentleman. In Wootton's svelte equestrian portrait, Henry the Magnificent is splendidly arrayed.[2] He enjoyed the sporting life and used the house and stables at Quarley as his hunting headquarters until his mother died.

In April 1726 Henry married Anne, daughter of Queen Anne's favourite, Abigail Masham. The bride died in the following March leaving a daughter who lived until 1735. The following year Henry married Susan Colt (*c.*1709–43). The marriages brought him £28,000 which he invested in purchasing the manor of West Knoyle, close to Stourton.[3] The cash was welcome because the family bank distributed no profits in 1725 and under £2,000 the year following.

At Good Henry's death, Benjamin Hoare (1693–1749/50) was left as sole partner at the bank. He persuaded Henry the Magnificent to leave his fortune in the business. At the same time he invited the bank employee Christopher Arnold to join the partnership and in 1731 Henry's younger brother Richard was promoted as junior partner. Assets were held in these proportions: Henry the Magnificent had 50 per cent, Benjamin 25 per cent and the remainder was split equally between Arnold and Richard.[4] Partners shared the annual profits in the same ratios. These recovered in 1727, rose above £17,000 in 1731, but did not exceed £20,000 until 1762.[5]

Henry the Magnificent became a hard-working, cautious and trusting employer. During his tenure the family bank ticked over, making respectable profits but none as spectacular as his predecessors had achieved. Unlike his brother Richard, Henry sought no public office, except by serving as an unmemorable Tory MP for Salisbury, 1734–41 and as a reluctant trustee of Sexey's Hospital at Bruton from 1776.[6]

Artists and craftsmen

Between 1727 and 1733 Henry held additional bank accounts in his own name: one for building, the second for furnishing. The ledger entries do not specify where the craftsmen worked.[7] Henry was responsible for completing Stourhead but how much this entailed is speculation. In 1726 Henry and his uncle bought number 41 Lincoln's Inn Fields which Henry rebuilt. This could explain the craftsmen and artists recurring in his accounts during these years. At the same time, Benjamin was building Boreham House and the artistic tastes of the two men overlapped. Henry was the first to patronise the painter John Wootton in 1726 and Benjamin did so in 1732;[8] Benjamin paid the portraitist Jeremiah Davison in 1725, Henry, in 1728.[9] Arthur Pond received his first payment from Henry in January 1727/8 and from

Benjamin in May.[10] All three artists honed Henry's sensibilities.

John Wootton (*c*.1682–1764) is remembered today for his sporting pictures and battle scenes. He also produced copies, or pastiches, of landscapes by Claude and Gaspard Dughet, both artists then in high demand. An entry in Henry's ledger for 1746 records a payment to 'M[r] Wootton for a Picture a comp[n] to my Claude L'.[11] The artist had banked with the Hoares since 1708 and Henry the Magnificent became a regular purchaser of his work, paying Wootton almost £800 between 1728 and 1762.[12] Of the nine paintings by Wootton at Stourhead, six were landscapes so he may take some of the credit for enticing Henry to the genre.[13]

Arthur Pond (1701–58), the artist–dealer, was famous for the prints he published in collaboration with Charles Knapton. Their *Italian Landscapes* (1740–48) comprised engravings after Claude and Gaspard Dughet while, in *Roman Antiquities* (1745–51), they reproduced work by G. P. Panini. Henry owned engravings by Pond, perhaps from the first-mentioned publication.[14] In 1727/8 Henry Hoare paid the artist for:

> Two Views of Venice at 16 Guineas each | Two Views of Rome at 8 Guineas each | Cascade of Tivoli by Horizonti £12–12s | Ruins of Rome by Gio: Paolo Pannini £31–10s.[15]

The elusive arcadia of Claude Lorrain

Henry was an *aficionado* of Claude, eager to possess pictures by the artist or his imitators. Originals sold at a premium so he was fortunate to secure one purported example recorded in the Stourhead Catalogue of 1784 as 'A Landscape by Claude' when it hung in the Skylight Room. Henry placed copies of the two Pamphili Claudes in the Cabinet Room (now the Small Dining Room), and a landscape by Gaspard Dughet in the dressing room beyond. He kept a large pair of landscapes by Dughet at his Clapham villa; these later came to Stourhead.[16] During the 1770s Henry bought Boydell's editions of Claude's *Liber Veritatis*.[17] Such visions of arcadia haunted Henry so that he could write of Stourhead, 'The View of the Bridge, Village & Church alltogether will be a Charm[g] Gasp[d] picture at the end of that Water.'[18] Twenty years previously Henry had remarked to Joseph Spence that, in gardening, 'The greens should be ranged together in large masses as the shades are in painting', a comment echoing Alexander Pope's analogy between landscape painting and gardening.[19]

Eighteenth-century tourists recalled landscape paintings by Claude Lorrain when visiting Stourhead's garden. The editor of Defoe's *Tour* wrote in 1779:

> the principal part of the gardens, near a beautiful stone bridge… is an assemblage of beautiful objects both near and distant, and such, indeed, as would demand the pencil of a Claude to delineate with any tolerable degree of perfection…[20]

Baron van Spaen van Biljoen praised the garden as equal to Claude's imaginary landscapes.[21] John Skinner admired:

The view from the colonnade [of the Temple of Apollo] is indeed delightful…
The variegating foliage of the surrounding groves, reflected in the clear mirror
of the lake; the broad masses of shade which gradually increased as the Sune
declined; the contracted light, still heightened by the autumnal tints, gave a
luxuriant tone of colouring to the picture, which Claude might have viewed
with delight and imitated so as to rival many of the paintings he has taken
from the scenery of his own country.[22]

These were broad analogies. To suggest specific paintings influenced Henry as he
planned the garden is supposition; when historians name pictures as precedents, the
disparities, as much as similarities, between the paintings and landscape are apparent.[23]

Most educated visitors would have known the work of Claude and Dughet
if not from originals, from prints. Towards the end of the century tourists carried
'Claude Glasses', pocket-size tinted mirrors, to better appreciate the landscape
by flattening the view and reducing the colours to different shades of a single

*Procession to the Temple of
Apollo at Delos*, 1759–60, by
John Plimmer (1722–60) after
Claude Lorrain (?1604/5–82),
oil on canvas, 149.8 × 200.6 cm.
Stourhead.

tint, like an engraving.[24] When visiting gardens the author and artist William Gilpin carried a Claude Glass and, judging from his sketches, probably used it at Stourhead.[25]

Family, banking and a Grand Tour

Henry the Magnificent's growing interest in art sharpened his desire to take the Grand Tour but he had business to occupy him at Fleet Street and a young family. His first son was born and died in 1729; Henry, the second son, was born the following year, Susanna in 1732, Colt (1733–40), Anne in 1737 and Mary, who

died at five months, in 1743.[26] Meanwhile Jane Hoare, the matriarch, continued at Stourhead. In 1734 Henry bought Wilbury from William Benson. He kept the house for five years and sold it at a profit of £4,000.[27]

Benson was twenty-three years senior to his nephew and, aside from the accomplishments already mentioned, aspired to be a classical scholar.[28] Henry may have learned from Benson the pleasure, in his own words, 'of looking into Books and the pursuit of that knowledge which distinguishes only the Gentleman from the Vulgar'.[29] An inventory taken at Benson's death listed two thousand volumes in his possession. He published *Virgil's husbandry, or an essay on the Georgics* (London, 1724). In *Letters concerning poetical translations, and Virgil's and Milton's arts of verse* (London, 1738), Benson argued that Milton was the heir to Virgil. To commemorate Milton he erected a monument in Westminster Abbey with a second-hand bust of the poet by Rysbrack. By placing his own name on the monument as prominently as the poet's, Benson earned the ridicule of Pope in the *Dunciad.* Benson later commissioned the sculptor to carve busts of Milton in youth and old age for his own collection. These reached Stourhead before the close of the century.[30]

Unrest abroad did not deter Henry from setting out for France and Italy in 1739.[31] His Grand Tour was unusual in that his wife, Susan, joined him in France and they spent a year together at Aix-en-Provence. From that city Henry continued alone to Italy on two occasions. By his own admission he was a relentless letter-writer so it is tantalising that none survive from these years abroad. Account books record Henry's spending and from these an outline itinerary may be deduced.[32] In late March he left England with a servant, but without his wife, travelled to Paris and down through France to Aix, then to Italy, reaching Venice in June where he met the British consul, Joseph Smith (*c.*1674–1770) (illustration page 62).[33] Henry then proceeded south to Florence and Rome.[34] By October he was back at Aix to greet his wife and, having settled her in a rented house, returned to Rome where he remained until the following spring. After twelve months' residence at Aix, the Hoares travelled to Paris where they parted, Susan returning to England in June 1741, Henry lingering in Paris until autumn.[35]

Henry made useful contacts abroad. He probably met Sir Horace Mann when he called at Florence in 1739. Nineteen years later Sir Horace bid successfully for Henry to acquire Maratti's painting of the *Marchese Pallavicini* and the two landscapes by Gaspard Dughet.[36] However, he was unable to purchase paintings by Claude on Henry's behalf.[37] Henry's first Roman banker, Girolamo Belloni, died in 1760. By then he was employing, as agent, Thomas Jenkins, who negotiated with Mengs for *Octavian and Cleopatra*, as a companion to the Marrati.[38]

In Paris, Sir John Lambert was both banker and agent to Henry. He bought the *Judgement of Midas* by Sébastien Bourdon for the Stourhead Saloon.[39]

In France Henry would have visited Versailles to admire the grounds and, in Paris, the picture collection formed by the duc d'Orléans at the Palais-Royal. The Italian High Renaissance and Baroque in that collection appealed to Henry and he spent time studying the paintings and their settings which he would attempt to emulate at Stourhead.

No bills survive from Henry's years abroad and the ledger entries do not specify what he purchased. Henry's expenditure amounted to £6,300, a considerable sum which places him in the upper echelons of spenders on the Grand Tour. Payments to Edward Fowler for shipping and customs included 'figures' (statues) and 'cabinets'.[40] The former may include the *Livia Augusta* now in the Pantheon at Stourhead (page 145) and two antique statuettes at the house.[41] 'Cabinets' probably involved the mighty Sixtus Cabinet which had reached London by 1742 and is the subject of a recent monograph.[42] While the 1742 Inventory of the house included a single Old Master painting, the Stourhead Catalogue of 1754 listed 29, indicating the putative extent of Henry's purchases.

If documentary evidence is sparse for Henry's continental tour, his peregrinations in Britain went unrecorded for the most part and are possible only to surmise.[43] Places where he had an entrée are more-than-conjectural, if less-than-proven, excursions. In the vicinity of Stourhead, he was on friendly terms with Stephen Fox, 1st Earl of Ilchester, who was landscaping the park at Redlynch, with Charles Hamilton and Henry Flitcroft at his elbow. The 5th Earl of Cork and Orrery was altering the grounds of Marston in the wake of Stephen Switzer's improvements for his father.[44] Richard Pococke described Marston in 1754 with which several structures would have counterparts at Stourhead.[45] After Susanna Hoare married

The Sixtus Cabinet, Rome, c.1585, pietre dure, ebony veneers, pine carcase, 214 × 126.2 × 84.9 cm. Pedestal, 1742, by John Boson, mahogany veneers on oak carcase, 108 × 134 × 90 cm. Stourhead.

Lord Bruce of Tottenham Park in 1761, Henry got to know Savernake Forest and followed his activities there. When his son-in-law summoned Capability Brown to landscape the park, Henry wrote:

> I am glad Your Lordship has got Mr Browne. He has undoubtedly the best taste of any body for improving Nature by what I have seen of His Works, He paints as He plants; I doubt not that He will remove Damps & the too great regularity of Your Garden, far better to be turned into a park.[46]

At Cirencester the first Lord Bathurst, a customer at Hoare's Bank, was erecting follies and planting avenues on a royal scale.[47] Henry would have known Alexander Pope's villa at Twickenham. The garden, created by the poet and William Kent, was popular with tourists and supremely influential in gardening circles. From 1720 to 1743 the poet developed his grotto which was one inspiration for Stourhead. Painshill landscape garden in Surrey also has a special relationship with Stourhead because Henry knew the creator, Charles Hamilton, and acted as one of his bankers. On a single occasion Henry specifically acknowledged Hamilton's help at Stourhead (page 201).[48] We may speculate whether William Benson encouraged Henry to visit Studley Royal, the famous garden in Yorkshire, created by Benson's mentor, John Aislabie.

Hoare's Bank held accounts on behalf of several noblemen with important

ABOVE
Architectural capriccio with the Pantheon and the Maison Carrée, *c*.1745–54, attr. Francis Harding (fl. *c*.1730–60) oil on canvas, 72.4 × 47 cm. Stourhead. In the distance stands the Stourhead Pantheon which did not exist in 1745. The artist may have added it later.

OPPOSITE
Choice of Hercules, 1636–7, by Nicolas Poussin (1594–1665), oil on canvas, 88.3 × 71.8 cm. Stourhead. Purchased by Henry the Magnificent in 1747 at the sale of the 1st Duke of Chandos.

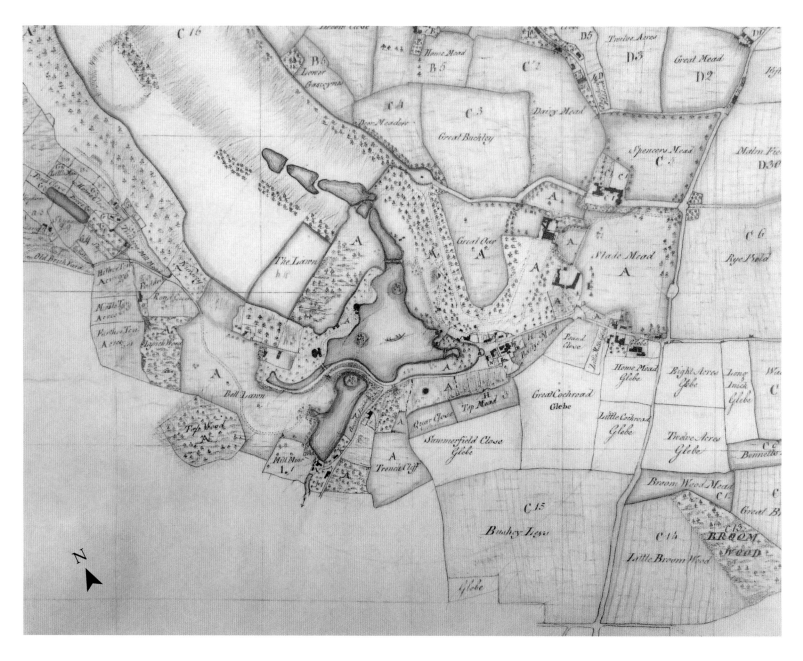

gardens, notably the 3rd Earl of Burlington, the 1st Duke of Newcastle and George Lyttelton. Lord Burlington encouraged his protégé William Kent to transform the formal grounds at Chiswick Villa, softening the rigid geometry of the layout into the pictorial style favoured by Kent.[49] The Duke of Newcastle, a leading politician of the mid-eighteenth century, owned Claremont in Surrey where the most famous garden designers all worked. He borrowed substantial sums from Hoare's Bank, Henry insisting Claremont stood as security for the loan.[50] At Stowe in Buckinghamshire, grandest of contemporary landscape gardens, Viscount Cobham seethed in political exile and encouraged his nephews to make trouble for the duke when he was prime minister. One such 'cub' was George Lyttelton, a frequent visitor to Stowe, secretary to Frederick, Prince of Wales, a friend of Pope and creator of the landscape garden at Hagley Hall in Worcestershire. He opened an account with Hoare's Bank and was on cordial terms with Henry.[51] If the latter visited Hagley he would surely have called at the Leasowes, nearby in Shropshire.

'A Plan of the Manor of Stourton in the County of Wilts. belonging to Richard Colt Hoare Esqr.', 1785, by John Charlton, ink and colour wash on parchment, 680 × 965 mm. Wiltshire and Swindon History Centre.

Fields are named and colour-fringed to indicate their uses defined in the legend. The plan records occupancy. 'A' are fields in hand but the list of tenants is lost.

Stourhead after 1742

Henry the Magnificent made Stourhead his residence after his mother died there in 1742. The jingle-jangle of banking kept him in London for ten months of the year but he yearned for country life. His arrival at Stourhead coincided with the resignation of Sir Robert Walpole as Prime Minister. Four years later the Duke of Cumberland defeated the Jacobites at Culloden Moor. At the outset of the Seven Years War, Hoare's Bank's annual profits stood below £6,000 but recovered with news of the British and Prussian victories and reached £22,759 in 1762.[52]

Long hours at the bank in London sharpened Henry's appetite for sporting pursuits. As a young man, he hunted and shot from horseback.[53] In mid-life he delighted in galloping a thoroughbred and in old age he saddled up gleefully to ride with his youngest grandchild, so that Hester Lyttelton, the fiancée of his eldest grandchild, found Henry 'surprisingly active & stout considering he is fourscore'.[54] Henry took care of himself and his letters are tinged with hypochondria.

Charting how Henry created the Stourhead landscape garden, we might suppose that bursts of activity matched rises in the bank's profits as those in turn mirrored events, national and international. But there is a closer relationship with family circumstances and, come the 1750s, Henry faced financial commitments beyond Stourhead.

There were highs and lows in the Hoare family. Henry's wife died in 1743, leaving him with three children: Henry, Susanna and Anne. Henry the younger died at Naples in 1751/2, a sadness mitigated by Susanna's marriage the following year to Charles Boyle, Viscount Dungarvan, elder son of the 5th Earl of Cork and Orrery, Henry's neighbour at Marston. The young couple were contented enough, living at Henry's house in Lincoln's Inn Fields, but trouble erupted between the in-laws to which we will return. In 1756 Anne married her cousin Richard, son and namesake of Henry's brother. Both marriages were dynastic: Susanna acquired social status while young Richard's betrothal established him as the potential heir to Henry. In 1759 deaths once again blighted the family: Anne died in May and Lord Dungarvan that September. Under the marriage arrangements for his daughters Henry had laid out £36,000 for Susanna and £20,000 for Anne.[55] Around 1755 Henry moved from Lincoln's Inn Fields to Clapham Common, incurring further expenditure.

Once established at Stourhead Henry began to place garden buildings on the hillside leading down to Stourton village, known as the Shades. He did not do so in a measured fashion; indeed the genesis of the landscape garden was akin to a box of fireworks set alight by accident: as Colt Hoare wrote, he proceeded '*con spirito*'.[56]

At the valley floor, Henry celebrated the two most active springs: to the east in a cascade below the Temple of Flora (1744–5); to the west in the Grotto (*c*.1748). A stretch of formal water opened from the temple cascade while water from the Grotto tumbled outside into a pool. Henry linked them with paths through the woods and by the Wooden Bridge (1749).

Pococke, visiting Stourhead in 1754, witnessed the construction of the dam impounding the Garden Lake. He confided that Henry intended to form a large lake

with 'three islands in it, with different kinds of buildings in them, one of which is to be a Mosque with a Minaret'.[57]

The Garden Lake, a *coup de foudre*, coincided with the marriage of Susanna Hoare and Lord Dungarvan, an event which may have spurred Henry to transform Stourhead from a minor to a major landscape garden. The mosque remained a pipe dream. Nevertheless, Henry had set his heart on a wide repertoire of garden buildings; supreme among them would be the Pantheon whose prolonged construction, 1753–62, may be down to the dynastic marriages.

Henry was helped and encouraged by a coterie of friends and professionals: the architect Henry Flitcroft, the gardener Francis Faugoin, the polymath C. W. Bampfylde, the sculptor Michael Rysbrack and the artist William Hoare of Bath.

Henry Flitcroft (1697–1769) opened an account with Hoare's Bank in 1724, so he was acquainted with Henry the Magnificent years before the summons to Stourhead.[58] Their association continued until the architect's death; indeed he designed the majority of the garden buildings. Flitcroft was grounded in the

Stourhead Pleasure Grounds, Wiltshire, view to the Pantheon, c.1775, by C. W. Bampfylde (1720–91), watercolour, 360 × 546 mm. Stourhead.

Palladian tradition and had a reputation for competence as he progressed on the ladder of promotion in the Office of Works to his appointment as Comptroller in 1758. However, he was responsible for no important public buildings and his reputation rests on private commissions, notably Wentworth Woodhouse in Yorkshire from 1735, Wimpole Hall in Cambridgeshire 1742–5, and Woburn Abbey in Bedfordshire 1748–61. He was involved at Windsor Great Park where the Duke of Cumberland, bathed in post-Culloden glory, busied himself with the Great Lodge and its surroundings. Flitcroft had served as architectural tutor to the duke and designed buildings for the park including a circular Doric temple (c.1748) and a single-span wooden bridge (c.1752–4).[59] The first lake at Virginia Water was almost contemporary with the Garden Lake at Stourhead.

The three surviving letters written by Flitcroft to Henry during August and September 1744 document the Temple on the Terrace and Temple of Flora. Flitcroft also referred to an existing building:

> a great Deal of yᵉ old Entablature will come in (as Stone) but I believe must be entirely new wrought, for I much doubt if any part be tolerably Exact... pray let them take care to Make yᵉ pediment true pitch, which in yᵉ present portico is to high.[60]

The building was evidently classical but its purpose and appearance are beyond surmise. Flitcroft also alluded to an open circular Ionic temple and specified stone for its construction.[61] In the second letter he continued, 'I... have inclosd the Section & Construction of yᵉ Masonry for yᵉ Entablature & dome of the round Temple.'[62] These drawings do not survive and Flitcroft gave no hint where it would stand, nor do any visitors mention it. We may speculate whether Henry's brother, Sir Richard Hoare, took over Flitcroft's design for Barn Elms where, in 1817, Nattes drew a circular Ionic temple surmounted by a hemispherical dome.[63]

Flitcroft's documented work at Stourhead comprises: the Saloon (1743–6), the Temple on the Terrace (demolished), the Temple of Flora, the Obelisk (1746), the Pantheon (1753), Alfred's Tower (1762) and the Temple of Apollo (1765).[64] Flitcroft also designed Henry Hoare's Clapham villa (1752). Between 1745 and 1769 Henry paid Flitcroft £1,047. It is arguable that the architect did more at Stourhead; he was probably responsible for the design of the pedestal for the Sixtus Cabinet (1742), Clock Arch, the Grotto, Wooden Bridge and Garden Lake dam. That he understood hydraulics and ornamental water features is evident from his designs for Wimpole Hall in Cambridgeshire, 1741–67.[65] Among a clutch of Stourhead drawings in the Bodleian Library is a pencil sketch of an elaborate three-storey open temple, resembling a gigantic ciborium, and set close to the Wooden Bridge.[66] The temple is depicted in detail whereas an obelisk and bridge are lightly sketched, perhaps by another hand. Candidates as draughtsmen of the temple include Flitcroft and Bampfylde.

Coplestone Warre Bampfylde (1720–91) was a Somerset landowner with an artist's eye and the money to create a landscape garden at Hestercombe. He was also an amateur architect credited with designing the Market House (1770) in Taunton.[67]

Bampfylde married Mary, the daughter of Edward Knight, a wealthy iron-founder. The marriage was childless and Mary's ill health took the couple to Bath on regular visits. Mary was a skilled needlewoman and an example of her work survives at Stourhead.[68]

In 1753 Bampfylde made a careful drawing of the Temple of Flora with its cascade and canal (page 144).[69] He became a close friend of Henry Hoare; they visited each other regularly and compared gardens.[70] Specifically, Bampfylde was party to the design of Alfred's Tower (page 256) and the Stourhead Cascade (1766), inspired by Hestercombe. Bampfylde was also a friend of his neighbour Sir Charles Kemeys-Tynte (1710–85) who was developing an ambitious landscape garden at Halswell. The gardens created by these three wealthy men were pleasingly diverse. Henry Hoare was acquainted with Sir Charles.[71] But, while the latter drew ideas from Bampfylde, he gleaned more from the circle of the 4th Duke and Duchess of Beaufort at Badminton and Stoke Gifford, guided by their designer, Thomas Wright.

Bampfylde the artist practised a variety of styles. The oil paintings and decorative watercolours include romantic soufflés in the style of Claude Lorrain and Vernet.[72] His book illustrations veer from the satirical in *An Election Ball* to the whimsical frontispiece in each volume of *Columella*.[73] The topographical views are competent souvenirs of his tours in Britain. It was as recorder of Stourhead that Bampfylde excelled: his two watercolour drawings of the *Pleasure Grounds*, *c*.1775, are unchallenged as sophisticated renderings of his friend's arcadia.[74] One of these, *View to the Pantheon*, is as encyclopaedic as a Breughel painting in showing different ways to enjoy the garden: walking, boating, fishing, riding, driving and sitting (page 50).

Francis Faugoin (1716–88)

The first mention of Faugoin occurs in Henry's ledger for 1736 when he was 'the gardener', presumably working at Quarley, having acquired expertise from his father.[75] After Henry departed for the Continent in 1739, he found work elsewhere. But when Susan Hoare died in 1743 Faugoin's wife, Mary, who had also worked for Henry, came to the rescue by temporarily taking charge of his younger daughter, Anne Hoare.[76] In 1747 Faugoin succeeded Roger Helliker as head gardener at Stourhead and continued in the post for the remainder of Henry's life.[77] While the latter was in London, Faugoin was resident at Stourton and acted as gardener, buildings overseer and agent. A visitor in 1766 claimed that the garden and estate cost 4,000 guineas annually to maintain.[78] Ten years later Mrs Powys counted fifty workers in the grounds.[79] Henry's ledgers record payments to Faugoin without particulars; whereas entries in the Customer Ledgers specify the individuals whom Faugoin paid on behalf of Henry. The sums involved were substantial and indicate that Faugoin was trusted to do business with tenants and contractors on Henry's behalf. Appendix 1 lists these payments, which exceeded £50,000. Faugoin's garden accounts are lost but one letter to Henry Hoare has survived and demonstrates his attention to detail (page 215).[80]

As head gardener Faugoin was called upon to accompany important visitors around Stourhead. He was sufficiently well-known to feature in the poem, *A ride and a walk through Stourhead*:

Me weary Faugoin, silver'd o'er by Care,
Conducts to Flora's; latent, modest Fane.[81]

His substantial family tomb chest stands close to the porch of St Peter's Church, while a marble memorial tablet inside described him as 'Steward to the late Henry Hoare Esq: forty eight years'.

'The most desirable House for a man from 2000 to 10000 a year I Ever was shewn'

Thus wrote Sir John Parnell in 1769 and certainly Henry had worked his magnificence on the house.[82] To stray into Stourhead during Jane Hoare's day we might be entering a conversation piece by Arthur Devis, so sparse, polite and formal were the rooms.[83] By 1760 Henry the Magnificent had transformed them into settings recalling British interiors by Zoffany. Soon after his mother's death Henry made structural alterations to the house. He replaced her chapel with the Saloon.[84] To give this grand space pleasing proportions, Flitcroft extended the house westwards and rebuilt the façade. Francis Cartwright, the carver-architect

'The Saloon at Stourhead Wilts. The Seat of Sir Richard Colt Hoare Bart. May 26 1824', by John Buckler (1770–1851), pencil, ink and watercolour, 265 × 355 mm. The British Library.

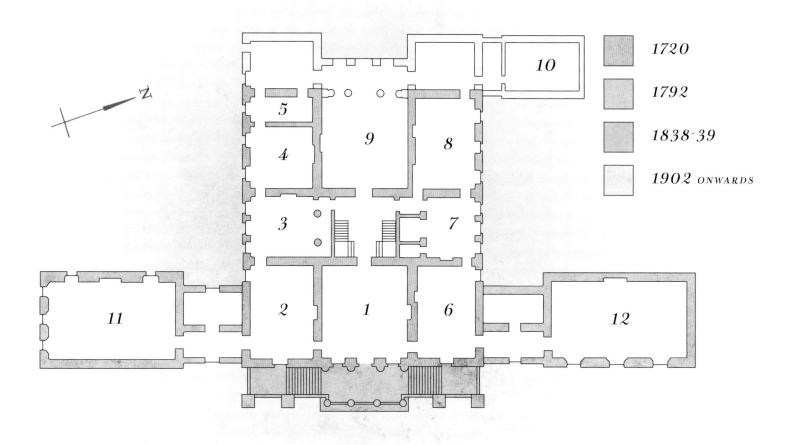

1720
1792
1838-39
1902 ONWARDS

STOURHEAD ROOM KEY

	1742 Inventory	1784 Catalogue	1838 Inventory	1908 Inventory
1	Great Hall	Hall	Entrance Hall	Entrance Hall
2	Great Dining Room	Parlour	Music Room	Music Room
3	Breakfast Room	Cabinet Room	Dining Room	Small [Little] Dining Room
4	Picture Room	Damask Bed Chamber	South Apartments	South [Apartment] Room
5	Mr Hoare's Dressing Room	Dressing Room	Small Room in South Apartments	Capt. Hoare's Room or Terrace Room
6	Little Parlour	Library	Cabinet Room	Cabinet Room
7	Best Alcove	Painted Alcove	Sir Richard Colt Hoare's Room	Italian Room
8	Mrs Hoare's Room	Column Bed Chamber	North Apartments	Column Room
9	Chapel	Saloon	Saloon	Grand Dining Room [Saloon]
10		Skylight Room	North Apartments	Billiard Room
11			Grand Library	Library
12			Picture Gallery	Picture Gallery

from Blandford Forum, fitted out this, the grandest room at Stourhead.[85] At the centre of the south front stood the breakfast room (now the Small Dining Room) which Henry adapted for the Sixtus Cabinet, displayed behind a screen of columns. Around 1758 he added the Picture or Skylight Room to the *piano nobile* at the north-west corner of the house (later rebuilt).

When Horace Walpole visited Stourhead in 1762 he found the rooms, 'in general too low, but richly furnished'.[86] His tour began in the hall, dominated by three large paintings; *Henry Hoare on horseback*, *The Marchese Pallavicini* by Maratti and *Octavian and Cleopatra* by Mengs.[87] Henry used the hall as the family living room. Jonas Hanway described, 'the stone floor of Mr H[oare's] hall is covered with a thick Turky carpet, by the assistance of which it is rendered very habitable even in the winter'.[88] And thirteen years later Parnell noted the family, 'Breakfast & spend all the morning in this Hall, the Prospect lovely from the Door'.[89] Rysbrack's *Bacchus* stood in the parlour (now the Music Room). Next came the breakfast room, now rechristened, dominated by the Sixtus Cabinet and hung with Old Master paintings. Continuing down the south side, Walpole encountered the red damask bedroom (South Apartment) and dressing room displaying more Old Masters. On the north side of the house he found similar progress westwards from restraint to opulence: the library (Colt Hoare's Cabinet Room) with family portraits and, beyond, two bedrooms, the last with Rembrandt's *Elijah raising the widow's son* (page 35). Finally he reached the Skylight Room, close hung with pictures. The Saloon displayed copies after Old Master paintings. Today, two artists befriended by Henry Hoare remain conspicuous at Stourhead: Michael Rysbrack and William Hoare of Bath.

Michael Rysbrack (1694–1770) was the leading sculptor in Britain between 1720 and 1740 and, despite competition from two other immigrants, Roubiliac and Scheemakers, he remained eminent up to his death. He had a talent for catching a sitter's likeness so that portrait busts and funerary monuments became his staple commissions; indeed the marble bust of Good Henry in St Peter's Church, Stourton, is attributed to him. Henry the Magnificent was twenty-two when he purchased a marble bust of *Inigo Jones* by Rysbrack together with a plaster statuette of the architect and one of *Palladio*, all three deriving from Lord Burlington's commissions for Chiswick Villa.[90] Their whereabouts is unknown but two plaster statuettes survive at Stourhead from the set comprising *Duquesnoy*, *Rubens* and *Van Dyck* which Henry purchased in 1744.[91] Three years later he commissioned Rysbrack to carve the large marble *Hercules* for the Pantheon (pages 173–7), following this up by purchasing his marble *à l'antique* of *Bacchus*. In 1759 Henry ordered a marble *Flora* as companion to *Hercules*.[92] He toyed with the idea of acquiring a large stone statue of *Fame* from Rysbrack, now at Longford Castle in Wiltshire.[93] Instead he commissioned the sculptor to carve a marble bust of *King Alfred* (1764) and subsequently purchased reliefs and drawings at Rysbrack's auction.[94] In gratitude for Henry's friendship and support, the sculptor bequeathed him the terracotta model of *Hercules*.[95]

Rysbrack, the prime exponent of classical sculpture, never visited Italy and relied on models, drawings and prints of antique sculpture. Over the years he assembled an extensive library.[96] Adapting a small two-dimensional image into a life-size sculpture came readily to Rysbrack. Several of Henry's commissions to other sculptors derived

Alfred the Great, 1764, by Michael Rysbrack (1694 –1770), marble, H 91 cm. Stourhead.

from engravings which Rysbrack could have suggested and indeed have supplied, so his taste extended beyond the documented work at Stourhead (pages 156–9).

A new king and a new son-in-law

In 1760 George III ascended the throne, marking a fresh beginning for Britain. That same year Henry the Magnificent's life was changed by the betrothal of Susanna to Lord Bruce of Tottenham Park. The Treaty of Paris ending the Seven Years War was approved by Parliament in December 1762 and signed the following February. Henry welcomed peace because of the cost of war when the country's average annual expenditure had risen to £13.7 million.[97] During the next twenty years George III struggled to govern through hand-picked ministers who in turn sought to control hostile parliaments. Ministries rose and fell like yoyos and the years were filled with measures regulating trade and hiking taxes to speed recovery from the war. The Stamp Act passed in March 1765 with little controversy in Parliament; however, protests from colonial representatives led to its repeal the following March. At home the poor harvest in 1766 prompted a ban on exporting grain. Henry the Magnificent was concerned about crime and complained:

> Thieves steal all our poultry Young & old, by which They will annihilate the breed, as They have near accomplished that of Hares and Partridge, that Game being near up with Us. Not A Farmer in the Land but must return Thanks for this as well as the poor Cottagers who lose all Their Geese & Ducks. Lord Ilchester's Tenant at Maddington near Shrewton lost 100 poultry in one night. They held matches under Them as they sit at Roost & it suffocates Them, & they drop down & then They fill the Sacks with Them & away to The Higlers. We cannot now get any sort of Poultry without applying to Them & submitting to give them Bath prices.[98]

Henry had little inclination to participate in public life or gain ennoblement, recognising perhaps that a banker would be rash to advertise his politics and foolhardy to compete socially with his customers. By contrast he was single-minded in the advancement of his surviving daughter.

To outward appearances Susanna Hoare (1732–83) had a gilded life, blessed with titles aplenty and a father willing to bankroll two expensive husbands. In 1753 she had married Charles Boyle, Viscount Dungarvan, the elder son of the impecunious 5th Earl of Cork and Orrery who lived at Marston, close to Stourhead. The termagant Lady Cork complained that Susanna:

> was of Birth far inferior to the Ladys of those Noble Houses from whom both my Lord & his Son were descended... while in our House We Endeavour'd to make so Agreeable to Lady Dungarvan as it was in our Power by Treating her with more Indulgence than We had ever Shewn to any Child of Our Own.[99]

Henry the Magnificent and Lord Dungarvan watched in dismay as the Corks' extravagance and business entanglements worsened until they persuaded the

Susanna Hoare, Lady Bruce (1732–83), 1757, by Arthur Pond (1701–58), oil on canvas, 76.2 × 63.5cm. Stourhead.

spendthrifts to relinquish management of their financial affairs. Henry and his son-in-law became trustees to recover income from the Boyle estates in Ireland, pay off creditors in an orderly fashion and provide an allowance for the Corks. Henry was enraged to discover Lady Cork was diverting Irish rents to pay undeclared debts. Henry temporarily stopped their allowance. Matters cooled down after Lady Cork's death in 1758. Susanna's first child, Henry, died an infant in December 1755; her daughter Henrietta Boyle, known as 'Harriot' was born *c*.1756. Lord Dungarvan, himself a sick man, died in September 1759. Soon after that Henry offered Susanna to his neighbour the 9th Duke of Somerset. Negotiations stalled over the terms of a marriage settlement and the match was scuppered.[100] How Henry tracked down Lord Bruce, the second bridegroom, is unrecorded; they had mutual friends in Lord Masham, and the Reverend Cutts Barton.

Susanna's second marriage, celebrated in February 1761, was successful on most levels: Lord Bruce needed ready cash, and Susanna acquired enhanced status. He was the hereditary warden of Savernake Forest and a gentleman of the bedchamber to George III. Their first child, George Brudenell-Bruce, was born in 1762 and grew

into a sickly youth. Susanna continued with Caroline, born in 1763, and Frances, in 1765. Eight years later she gave birth to a healthy son christened Charles Brudenell-Bruce. Walpole branded Susanna as 'mad' when Lord Bruce resigned as governor to the Prince of Wales days after accepting the appointment: 'It is said, that his mad wife, Mr Hoare's daughter, had written a piteous letter, promising she should die if deprived of her dear Lord'.[101] Mrs Boscawen agreed that Susanna had caused the resignation but did not consider her deranged: 'Lady Bruce has done all this mischief, though parading about Bath in good health'.[102]

At the bank Henry the Magnificent courted the well-born for astute commercial reasons; the aristocracy and landed gentry offered sound security for loans in their land holdings. Yet he was not socially at ease in their company and his confidence deserted him when confronted by the likes of Lady Cork. Henry wrote to his second son-in-law in obsequious terms, although he grew fond of the man. He was relaxed with his own class and the newly ennobled, such as the Bensons, Beckfords, and Fox families. To those who did him good service he was a loyal and generous friend, notably to John Rust, the parasitic and impoverished tutor of his long-deceased son. The 'coxcomical' Rust returned to Stourhead year after year to the increasing exasperation of his host.[103]

Henry was gregarious to the point of disliking his own company; he invited his widowed niece, Martha Hoare (née Cornelisen), to live with him at Clapham and he badgered the Bruce family to holiday at Stourhead. Around 1777 Frances Bruce, the youngest granddaughter, wrote to her brother George, 'You will be surprized to hear that we arrived at Stourhead last Tuesday on account of My Grandpapa being but indifferent, and quite alone, we propose staying about a week'.[104]

Henry had an engaging nephew and namesake, Henry Hoare of Beckenham (1744–85), known among the family as 'Fat Harry'.

The Infants Christ and St John with angels, c.1762–3, by William Hoare RA (1707–92) after a picture by Sir Peter Paul Rubens at Wilton House, pastel, 94 × 124.5 cm. Stourhead.

Judged by his portrait this was a sobriquet well earned.[105] At the family bank he became a partner in 1770 and also operated a separate account offering personal loans, predominantly to oblige friends.[106] In 1765 Fat Harry married Mary, daughter of William Hoare of Bath. This must have been a love match because Mary was neither blue-blooded nor an heiress. Their only son, Henry James, was born in 1767; he was a febrile child who died in 1779.[107] Fat Harry delighted in *pulcinello* traits; his uncle applauded when 'Harry goes out with all the pomp & circumstance of War against the Game but never brings home even a Rabit'.[108] If Fat Harry was a social animal he was no pussycat: he had claws and used them when Henry the Magnificent proposed to settle his affairs in a way that he considered unfair to himself and his elder brother. He played hard and died young in February 1785. His widow lived until 1820.

Stourhead society

Each summer Henry the Magnificent delighted in filling the house with friends, relatives and neighbours. The entertainment was lavish: in 1776 he wrote to his son-in-law, newly promoted as Earl of Ailesbury, 'very many Thanks for Your Lordships kind & bountifull remembrance of Us in fine Venison & Trout today. We dine on a Turtle of 146 pounds, a present sent me by The Flying Coach fresh & lively'.[109]

Close neighbours, Lord Stourton from Bonham, William Chafyn Grove of Zeals House and Montagu Barton, the rector of Stourton, regularly took their places at Henry's table. Richard Hoare and his son Colt called during the summer.[110] Fat Harry was a frequent visitor. He befriended David Garrick, whom he took to Stourhead in 1776 to the delight of their host who wrote:

> Gracious what a Figure of Fun is here: Mr Garrick has not His fellow for
> Private as well as Publick entertainment. He is active and strong & feelingly
> alive to each fine impulse. I have held both my sides with laughing till I can
> hold no longer like Falstaff.[111]

Perhaps only a royal visit would have capped this social highlight. But when George III was staying with Lord Pembroke at Wilton in 1778, the King chose to return to Windsor via Stonehenge, rather than divert to Stourhead.[112]

Henry's favourite guests were Susanna and her family. Harriot Boyle, Susanna's daughter by her first marriage, returned as a teenager to Stourhead, where she had spent much of her infancy.[113] She re-awoke the peacock in Henry as he wrote:

> tell Miss H.F.B [Harriot] that you saw me to day in my 8 spangle Button hole
> Coat & Waistcoat which I shall soon lay up in Lavender till the Xning of Her
> first Child.[114]

George Bruce, her sickly elder half-brother, was an occasional visitor while her stepsisters thoroughly enjoyed summers at Stourhead exploring the garden and playing the house organ.[115] The younger brother, Charles (1773–1856), was a favourite with Henry and from early childhood made the Clapham villa a second home. By

1776 Charles was old enough to visit Stourhead without his mother, a holiday which became an annual treat. The imp pandered to Henry who wrote:

> In our passage to [Maiden] Bradley I saw a poor man breaking stones on The Road. I told Charles He was struck dumb with the Palsey but was as laborious, as ever with His Hands, so I flung him a Shilling. Charles looked me in the face & said Grandpapa if I had a Shilling I would give Him one also. What a good heart![116]

When Henry the Magnificent met the artist William Hoare of Bath RA (1707–92) is unknown but he made a first payment to the artist in 1754.[117] They had several common bonds of which the coincidence of name was the most slender – they were not blood relatives. They shared a love of the Continent and classical authors; both possessed first-hand knowledge of Renaissance and Baroque art and a familiarity with antique sculpture. This is evident in a single surviving letter from William to Henry which exudes connoisseurship, at the same time cadging an invitation to Stourhead and promising a picture of 'a favourite Sleeping Nymph in your Garden'.[118] This materialised as a jewel-like, if blatant, pastel.

William Hoare was soon a regular guest at Stourhead and, with his paint box and network of contacts, became indispensable to Henry who handed him £1,777 between 1754 and 1772, which would have included the purchase of nine pictures by the artist, recorded by the Stourhead Catalogue of 1784.[119] His portraits are competent if unadventurous. However, William Hoare was versatile and bubbled with ideas to embellish the garden; he decorated benches for the Pantheon and Temple of Apollo (pages 177 and 197).

Today, Stourhead is among the best places to enjoy William Hoare. Arrayed in the Small Dining Room are twelve pastel portraits in oval frames with elastic attributions to the artist (and some by his daughter Mary) depicting Sir Richard Hoare, 1st Baronet and his second family. These may have come from the 1st baronet's collection at Barn Elms or were bequeathed to Colt Hoare by William Hoare's son, Prince Hoare (1755–1834). However, the latter seems unlikely because they are first recorded at Stourhead in the inventory of 1908.[120]

William Hoare may have encouraged Henry the Magnificent to acquire work by a new generation of artists. During the winter 1760–1 Henry took delivery of *Octavian and Cleopatra*, a neoclassical foray by Mengs (page 43).[121] In the same decade he bought paintings by Marlow, Vernet, Wilson and Zuccarelli, while John Plimmer copied a second Claude from the Palazzo Doria Pamphilj.[122] From the early 1770s Henry showed further enterprise in purchasing living artists, spurred on by his experiences in Paris.

In 1771 Henry returned to France for a few months accompanied by his nephew, Richard Hoare, and Richard's second wife, Frances Anne.[123] The trip was intended as a rest-cure and change of air.[124] Of the £1,272 Henry spent abroad, a third went on acquisitions.[125] He purchased a pair of bronze greyhounds as a present for Richard and two small paintings by Vernet for Lord Bruce.[126] He also acquired paintings by Jean Louis François Lagrenée, the elder, seven of which remain at Stourhead.[127]

Henry enjoyed sentimental neoclassical confections by Lagrenée and in 1773 he

acquired two paintings in a similar vein by Angelica Kauffman.[128] Richard Hoare also commissioned Kauffman to paint an overmantel and a portrait of Frances Anne (both reached Stourhead in 1895).[129] Henry acquired a landscape by Thomas Gainsborough in 1773 which was sold in 1883.[130] Paintings by Kauffman went in the same auction and their absence makes it easy to overlook this late flowering of Henry's taste. In 1772 he declined Sir John Lambert's offer of a pair of Claude landscapes but he did not turn his back on the Old Masters and bought paintings by Neffs, Cuyp and a version of Dughet's *Jonah and the Whale* by William Taverner.[131]

The landscape garden after 1762

In the garden Henry the Magnificent turned his attention to the southern and eastern shores of the lake where they met the village; in other words, the view from the Pantheon. An account of the hot summer in 1765 is among his most beguiling descriptions of Stourhead:

> 'It is a piping hot Sum[r] indeed & We are forced to resort to our Riding House under the Trees for an Umbrello such & so small as it is when compared to Your Noble Forest. I had a delicious souse into the Cold Bath this morn[g].[132]

Henry dabbled in a variety of styles which gives an impression that he was enjoying himself. Gothic architecture and history had caught his imagination. His pride in British history was deep-seated as was his loyalty to George III, while his patriotism was enhanced by friendship with Lord Bruce who was a habitué of the court. Henry was also impressed by Walpole's connoisseurship at Strawberry Hill which he visited in 1763 and he remarked to Lord Bruce:

Sleeping nymph of the Grotto, 1760, by William Hoare RA (1707–92), pastel, oval, 60.3 × 81.3 cm. Stourhead.

I was highly entertaind at Mr Walpole's last Saturday with the finest painted Glass Windows & Gothick Taste in the best man^r that it can be employ'd in so small a Space. He has added a Gallery of 50 feet Long which leads to the most Beautifull Cabinet a Room of 16 Square with 4 Circles that Break from the Center lighted from the Top by a Flaming Star in painted Glass which makes all the objects in the room look like a Glory & it is full of Virtu intaglios Cameos, Statues Bronzes miniatures Antique Urns & Lamps in short most exquisite & will please Lady Bruce beyond all imagination. It is a Sanctum Sanctorum, & the Gothick dissolves the Soul in Extasy.[133]

In Henry's mind gothic and classical styles could mingle. On 23 October 1762 he sent Susanna a chatty letter describing the construction of the Stone Bridge.[134] Midway through the decade he built the Temple of Apollo (1765) and acquired

A Pastoral Landscape, 1730–45, by Francesco Zuccarelli, RA (1702–88), oil on canvas, 101 × 134 cm. Stourhead. Probably purchased by Henry the Magnificent through Joseph Smith. The inner frame is Venetian; the outer, English.

the Bristol Cross (1765).[135] In December 1765 he placed a sculpture of *Neptune* in the lake.[136] Bampfylde and William Hoare designed the Cascade.[137] To explore the wider estate on horseback or by carriage Henry created a perimeter drive which commenced at the Obelisk with a spectacular Terrace Ride, while further along the way he introduced architectural excitements: St Peter's Pump (1767), Alfred's Tower (1772) and the Convent (1767).[138] Henry described his grandchildren enjoying the garden in 1776:

> they are all fine & well & now make nothing of walking round the Gardens & I mounted The Tower Thursday with the Dear Children & They are vastly delighted with this spot. The Temple of The Nymph [the Grotto] is all enchantment to Them, & The Cross now new painted fills Them with rapture.[139]

Earlier that year Henry had painted the monarchs on the Bristol Cross in bright colours to the indignation of Mrs Powys: did he do this to please the young?[140] Even before the perimeter drive was complete Stourhead had become famous. As a banker Henry Hoare fought shy of the public eye; yet – and this is a paradox – he made every effort to place Stourhead in the public domain. Indeed it became a tourist attraction, featuring in *The New Bath Guide* from 1762 onwards, the only private estate listed among popular destinations.[141] Henry converted Stourton Inn into a hotel and, for connoisseurs, he commissioned engravings of highlights from the picture collection.[142]

'Damn'd Hypocrisy compleated this diabolical Declaration': Henry the Magnificent bows out

Henry was keen to purchase land and, perhaps from the outset, he had it in mind that the estate should remit sufficient rents to support Stourhead independently from the bank. Before 1774 he spent over £70,000 in purchasing property.[143] This comprised farms and land at West Knoyle, acquired in 1732 for £31,360; land at South Brewham bought for £13,000; at Norton and Kilmington for £15,480; at Henstridge for £6,600; and at Hollwell for £6,350.[144]

The American War of Independence and unrest at home, culminating with the Gordon Riots, weighed heavily on Henry's mind as he pondered the succession at the bank and Stourhead. He was determined both should survive; but if the bank failed, what would become of Stourhead? He resolved to make the estate self-sufficient and in 1777 invested £44,000, purchasing Lord Berkeley's estate at Bruton, a holding of about 2,300 acres.[145]

Family life fractured when Susanna, now Lady Ailesbury, long an invalid, died on 4 February 1783. Henry Hoare cannot have been surprised by the news but it brought with it recognition that he had now outlived all his children. His spirits were not lifted with the news that Colt Hoare was to marry. An undated manuscript written by Fat Harry opens with the author and Richard Hoare arriving at Stourhead to discuss the impending marriage.[146] Lord Ailesbury was already ensconced at the house to mourn Susanna. Mention in the narrative of George

Brudenell-Bruce places the encounter shortly before his death on 28 March. Henry received his nephews hospitably but declined to discuss family business when Lord Ailesbury was present, a situation eased by the latter who kept to his room except at mealtimes. Nevertheless Stourhead was a small house, which would have added to the tension. Henry did not take the announcement of the impending match well. He had in mind potential fiancées for Colt Hoare. Top of his list was his granddaughter, Lady Frances Brudenell-Bruce, then seventeen. Alternatively Henry hoped his grandson could have 'attach'd himself to some Lady of 40 or 50 fortune which he might have done with an equal Prospect of Happiness'.[147] Hester Lyttelton, the bride-to-be, would not do. She was about twenty and without significant means, being the daughter of a younger son, William, Lord Westcote.[148]

Henry confided his intention to hand Stourhead to his grandson with a single constraint. The announcement stunned his listeners because Richard Hoare had reasonable expectations of becoming Henry's heir. Worse would follow. Henry was pessimistic about the future. Britain, he perceived, was on the brink of chaos, without stable government, perhaps without a king, and with financial ruin impending. He foresaw the family bank swept away and the partners' wealth consumed in the fall. His overarching ambition was to secure the future of Stourhead. Richard and Fat Harry were enmeshed in the bank and essential to its business but Colt Hoare had only recently begun his career there, was not yet a partner, and could be extracted without harming the business in the short term. If he would agree to quit the bank forever, he should have Stourhead. Henry knew that the estate and the satellite land holdings would not produce an income to sustain the house and garden in the style he himself had adopted. This explains why Henry wished Colt Hoare to marry an heiress, as he himself had done. If Hester was *fait accompli*, Henry would supplement his gift with his freehold London properties, including the bank premises. When Henry informed Richard and Fat Harry they were aghast; their kaleidoscope had been unexpectedly shaken up and they found the new pattern distasteful. At that moment the supper bell sounded, Lord Ailesbury appeared and they joined the unnamed ladies and proceeded to dinner. Nobody can

'Villa of the late James Brogden Esq. M.P.' Henry the Magnificent's villa at Clapham, c.1800, anonymous lithograph.

have slept easily. Richard Hoare thought his uncle had taken leave of his senses. Fat Harry wrote:

> I was obliged to give him [Henry the Magnificent] full Credit for Understanding what he had said and equal Credit for the most base & treacherous Conduct to my B[rother] in particular and ye Partnership in general. It was contrary to Faith, Honor and Justice - Damn'd Hypocrisy compleated this diabolical Declaration, and Transaction. for had not the Business we went upon obliged him to confess the contents of his last Will… nothing would have appeared till his Death.[149]

The following morning Richard left the talking to his brother; neither would behave with conspicuous gallantry. Fat Harry might have argued that his uncle was unduly pessimistic about the state of the nation, that the bank was sound. Instead he dwelled on the slight to his brother: Richard was to be passed over as heir to Stourhead and would simultaneously become his son's tenant in London. Moreover, the brothers considered that the bank premises should belong to the partners, not to an outsider. Henry listened attentively, recapitulated his reasons and assured his nephews of his affection for them. On the future of Stourhead he was unswayed and he remained adamant Colt Hoare should quit the bank. But he agreed the London property portfolio should pass to Richard, including the bank premises, subject to a life interest awarded his fellow partners, Fat Harry and Henry Hoare of Mitcham Grove.[150] Seldom can a house party have ended so dismally. The brothers departed; nobody was satisfied. Henry the Magnificent felt his nephews had been small-minded; Richard was denied Stourhead and Fat Harry had clashed irreparably with his uncle. Colt Hoare abandoned his career as a banker and took on Stourhead without the resources which he considered sufficient to enjoy it to the full. He rose to the challenge but the enforced departure from banking blighted his life. Hester would receive a polite but frosty welcome at Stourhead when she met the patriarch.[151] Lord Ailesbury returned to Tottenham Park where he learned that his eldest son had died abroad.

Colt Hoare married at Barnes in August 1783. Henry's seemingly inexhaustible vitality dwindled and that October he settled for the last time with Faugoin; the shadows lengthened and he took leave of Stourhead, his Camelot, for the last time at Christmas.[152] He signed the family settlement on 27 January 1784.[153] His home was now the Clapham villa where, judged by the wine merchants' bills, he continued to entertain.[154] If there was coldness among the Hoare tribe, Lord Ailesbury and his children were attentive and dutiful. Henry left the earl his largest legacy of £10,000.[155]

SIR RICHARD COLT HOARE, 2ND BARONET (1758–1838)

Sir Richard, henceforth Colt Hoare, presided at Stourhead for half a century during which he made changes to the gardens which culminated in their transformation. At the house his alterations were radical from the outset.

His marble effigy surmounts a tall plinth in the north transept of Salisbury Cathedral; to some Colt Hoare appeared equally aloof in life.[1] He may be portrayed as a self-centred person, immersed in his own interests, accustomed to getting his own way, an inscrutable father and a cold fish. In later years deafness exacerbated his shyness in the company of strangers.

But there was another man, fiercely loyal to his family, friends and servants who in turn repaid him with their devotion. In 1827 Joseph Hunter, who we will meet shortly, considered Colt 'kindness and good humour personified' and, visiting Stourhead some years later, remarked, 'everybody in the neighbourhood speaks [of] his great kindness'.[2]

Colt had wide interests but these touched neither politics nor commerce. In pursuit of his chosen subjects he was unremittingly curious. He absorbed facts and statistics with sponge-like capacity. When compiling *Modern Wiltshire*, his final endeavour, he scarcely had time to filter data as it flowed from his pen. He is seldom easy reading; nevertheless, it is as an author that he won renown.

His ghostly pen is forever scratching away to deafen the biographer. Colt was an inveterate letter-writer. In 1836 he lamented, 'Time was, when my hand was never tired, but gout in it *now* has put a stop to my penmanship, and, till very lately, I could not indite a legible epistle.'[3] He was chronically hard-working and delighted in detail; here he orders a tablecloth from France & Banting:

> The dark blue will not suit my room – it being painted light color. You must therefore make the cover of the strongest cloth of the patterns sent – but as the two yards are not quite wide enough you must add a border of black cloth to lap over the edge – which will accord with the linen of my room i.e. blue & black there is to be no drapery hanging down – the cloth to fit neatly all around – as the corners of the table have sharp angles, I wish you to insert a piece of leather at each corner that the angles of the cloth may not be burst.[4]

By training at the family bank and by temperament Colt relished paperwork. Like the scorer at a cricket match, he recorded activities around him objectively, seldom touching on his emotions so that, at the close of his inky life, he left a formidable archive; in addition to his publications and drawings were the written paraphernalia of the estate, letters received, bills, receipts and laundry lists.

On a good day Colt could write, 'I have always considered money, as to be spent, for the benefit of the community: not to be hoarded.'[5] He lived in style and Hunter assessed Stourhead as 'befitting the Baron rather than the Baronet'.[6] Nevertheless money was a preoccupation. Colt resented his exclusion from Hoare's Bank; writing in 1828 he recalled:

> Had the 'auri sacra fames' been my ruling passion, this event [his enforced retirement from the Family Bank] would have been a severe mortification: and if I had been imprudent in engaging in a <u>second</u> marriage, & had a large family like two of my brothers, I should have been the poorest man of my family.[7]

Sir Richard Colt Hoare, 2nd Baronet, (1758–1838), c.1783, by Prince Hoare RA (1755–1834) oil on canvas, 125.7 × 100.3cm. Stourhead.

He kept neither a mistress nor racehorses but he spent prodigiously on his library and publications. His income depended on rents and when short of funds he called on the family bank for loans secured on his bond or mortgage. By 1836 he also owed his half-brother, Henry Hugh, £13,150, a sum repaid by his executors who took out a mortgage on the estate.[8]

The early years

Colt Hoare was five months old when his mother died; thereafter he was brought up at Barn Elms by his stepmother with her children. He attended Mr Davis's school at Wandsworth and later a seminary at Greenford, near Harrow.[9] During the summer holidays the family visited Stourhead where Colt learned to shoot and fish and to enjoy the country. His grandfather, Henry the Magnificent, described him as a boisterous twenty-one-year-old, impatient on a carriage journey from Marlborough to London:

> in the 2^d Gate field [we] saw a fine Covey of Birds which called Colt to Arms & I thought He would have bounced thro the fore Glass after Them... I believe They have had Salt laid on Their Tails.[10]

By 1779, the year this was written, Colt had joined the family bank while continuing to study the classics with a private tutor.[11] He received an annual allowance of £2,000 from his grandfather, enabling him to rent a house in Lincoln's Inn Fields which Thomas Chippendale the younger furnished.[12]

Colt Hoare had an uneasy relationship with his father, Richard Hoare, 1st Baronet (1734/5–87) although there is no reason to doubt his devotion. They were both potential heirs to Stourhead. Richard, the father, was fortunate by birth and inheritance, yet in the family history he is ill-defined because he left an elusive paper trail. Henry the Magnificent was his mentor, promoting him to the banking partnership in 1754 and marrying him to his daughter, Anne, who died in 1759.[13] Henry had lost his only surviving son seven years previously so Richard had expectations of inheriting both the bank and Stourhead. In 1761 he married Frances Anne Acland. Of their numerous children, four boys and one girl survived to adulthood.

Richard had inherited Barn Elms from his father in 1754. The house stood on level ground extending from Barnes village eastwards to the Thames. The elder Richard had landscaped the grounds, doubtless consulting Henry the Magnificent.[14] Richard, the younger, continued by turning the formal canal into an ornamental lake with serpentine banks.[15]

In 1783 shares in the family bank were apportioned in this manner: Henry the Magnificent 6,000; Richard 3,000; Fat Harry 2,000; and Henry of Mitcham 1,000.[16] At the time of the family showdown, Henry the Magnificent promised Richard his London property but gave Stourhead to Colt Hoare.[17] After Henry's death, Richard acquired a smart house in St James's Square and engaged Chippendale the younger to furnish it. He also purchased a baronetcy.[18] But the preening was short-lived and he died at Bath in October 1787. Sir Richard had probably intended a rapprochement with Colt because he acquired land at Stavordale, immediately to the west of Stourhead, and took the lesser house, New Park, as a country retreat.[19] His son welcomed the news, 'I hope on my return that we shall be very good neighbours'.[20] But Sir Richard had died before Colt resumed residence at Stourhead.

There are several portraits of the 1st baronet at Stourhead. Furniture and paintings from his houses in St James's Square and Barnes arrived at Stourhead in 1895 so that today he enjoys a presence in the house where he was forever a guest.

Soon after settling into banking Colt Hoare was betrothed to Hester Hoare, née Lyttelton (c.1763–85), the daughter of William Lyttelton, Baron Westcote, whose elder brother had been a friend of Henry the Magnificent. Richard Hoare, mindful that his mentor might not approve the match, travelled to Stourhead with his half-brother, Fat Harry, to alert their uncle. The debacle which ensued is recounted elsewhere (pages 63–5). Henry the Magnificent acquiesced in the match and the young couple married at Barnes in 1783. They took a house in the Adam brothers' development Adelphi Terrace where Chippendale the younger again supplied furniture.

Hester was high-spirited and sociable.[21] In London she consorted merrily with the young among the Hoare family and enjoyed the opera and theatre.[22] Her love of music and literature is celebrated in a magnificent and mysterious commode probably made for the house in Adelphi Terrace, and now at Stourhead.[23]

Hester delighted in Stourhead and her new role as chatelaine. Having given birth to a male heir she set about the house: confiding in Lady Bisshopp,

The Hon. Hester Lyttelton, Mrs Hoare (d.1785), by Samuel Woodforde RA (1763–1817), oil on canvas, 127 × 101.6 cm. Stourhead.

We are new papering the Rooms upstairs and have almost completed one, with a White paper and broad bordering of Yellow, the bed is to be White Dimity lined with yellow Callico and trimmed with borders of a Chintz pattern dye'd yellow the effect is <u>beauteous</u>, the next room...[24]

The flurry of activity ended at the birth of a second son, his swift demise, and her own death on 22 August 1785. Within weeks Henry the Magnificent had breathed his last and Colt had departed for the Continent. He was now a man of means and of leisure but had yet to find a purpose in life. From 1785 to 1791 Colt roamed the Continent. He had few commitments to hold him in England; against his will he had retired from the family bank and, furthermore, Stourhead was in the capable hands of the agent, Thomas Charlton. Much is known about his travels because in middle life he revised his continental journals and printed them in four volumes as *Recollections Abroad* intended 'not to challenge the criticising pen of the public but for the partial gratification of a few friends and relations'.[25]

The first journey: Rome, 'the most rewarding place in the Universe'
With these words Colt Hoare praised the city to his half-brother, Henry Hugh.[26] When Colt embarked in September 1785, he travelled through France, crossed the Alps and progressed swiftly through Turin, Florence and Rome to reach Naples in November, where he passed the winter.

Satinwood commode, c.1780–85, attr. Thomas Chippendale the younger (1749–1822), veneers and marquetry of harewood, satinwood and purplewood; mahogany and oak carcase, 87.5 × 168 × 66.3 cm. Stourhead.

Family and friends kept an eye on Colt. He left England with one Captain Meyrick who accompanied him to Naples where he died in December 1785.[27] Recent family deaths had hardened Colt's rind and he continued his travels. His brother-in-law, George Lyttelton, joined him in Naples where they met the Reverend John Warner (a future rector of Stourton).[28] In the spring Colt went sightseeing in Rome with the veteran *cicerone* Colin Morison. In July 1786 he travelled leisurely to Switzerland where he was reunited with George and met Henry Hugh Hoare and his wife. That autumn Colt took George to Spain where they were entertained by the British consul and Spanish governor in Barcelona.[29] Returning to France Colt encountered James Greville who had been among the Swiss party and the pair sailed down the coast of Italy in time to celebrate Christmas in Florence. In the new year Colt returned to Rome to join the young artist, Samuel Woodforde.[30] When the weather improved they set out for Venice before making the journey homewards across the Alps, travelling via Lyon and Paris before reaching England in July 1787.

On his continental tours Colt was accompanied by Robert Davis, who was appointed his valet in 1778, and remained in his employment for the remainder of his life.[31] Colt recruited a second servant, Girolamo, shortened to 'Giro'.[32] So, on the homeward journey his entourage comprised Woodforde, Davis, Giro, 'Michael' (the footman), and a postilion.

Colt quickly became a robust and inquisitive traveller. The *Recollections* hint at his bravura as he scaled the Alps or drew pistols on sharp-dealing Spaniards.[33] His letters to Henry Hugh tell of a lively social life:

> I got acquainted with many Florentines, to whom I spouted Italian very boldly – I played at Whist every Evening & strange to tell you for once good fortune favor'd me for I departed the Winner of one hundred Pounds by playing Guinea Whist.[34]

Colt enjoyed playing cards, winning and losing considerable sums.[35] In Siena he was taken up by the engagingly named Steddy Grinfield:

> who is settled there & Captn Rowley, sister to the Miss Rowley whose Cap you once disconcerted ... then to the Opera where Grinfield introduced me to half the Women in the house to all of whom I was obliged to chat away [in] bad Italian.[36]

Whilst in Italy Colt Hoare purchased thirty-five Old Master paintings. With the exception of an Andrea del Sarto, priced at £115, he paid no more than £50 for a picture, an economy which disadvantaged the Stourhead collection.[37] In May 1787 he had the luck to buy ten drawings of Venice by Canaletto from a Venetian bookseller.[38] These hung in the Library at Stourhead until sold in 1883.

Antique sculpture was beyond his means. Colt took trouble in commissioning a colourful memorial to Hester from the stonemason and sculptor, Pisani of Florence.[39] Pisani also supplied reductions of famous Roman marbles, notably three *Niobe* figures and several vases, including three for Henry Hugh.[40]

Colt's preoccupation with landscape paintings drew criticism from the artistic community in Rome.[41] On his first tour Colt acquired four topographical drawings from Louis Ducros, four from Philipp Hackert and eight from Carlo Labruzzi, supplementing his own sketches.[42] However, his interest was not exclusively in landscapes. Colt commissioned the English artist John James Rouby to make studies of High Renaissance and Baroque paintings.

Colt Hoare reached England on 13 July 1787. He returned to satisfy himself that Stourhead was ticking over and his son adequately cared for. That summer was a

time for reunions with family and friends and enjoyable visits to London and Hagley Hall in Worcestershire with the Lytteltons. His father was head of Hoare's Bank. Come autumn Sir Richard's health declined beyond any cure Bath had to offer and he died there, bequeathing Colt the house in St James's Square. Barn Elms went to Henry Hugh along with a half-share of the bank premises split with his brother Charles as tenants-in-common of the remainder.[43] This melancholy turn of events delayed Colt's return to Italy until the following summer. He decided to sell the town house and, in the interim, borrowed £14,000 from the family bank, which he repaid when the sale went through in January 1789.[44]

The second journey: 'At length I breathe the air of my beloved Italy'
Several reasons for returning to Italy played across Colt Hoare's mind in addition to his affection for the country which is apparent in the quotation above.[45] He relished the freedom of travelling abroad where he had only himself to please. The climate suited him. He had learned to speak Italian and could enter society, his status boosted by the baronetcy. Colt also nursed an ambition to explore Etruscan cities and the Via Appia. Accomplishing this would take years rather than months. Colt embarked on 30 June 1788 and returned to England in the summer of 1791.[46]

France was now volatile. That June rioting had broken out in Grenoble, a foretaste of the revolution. Colt avoided the country by travelling to the Netherlands, then down though the German states and Austria, sightseeing on the way and reaching Trieste by late October. Henceforth, his itinerary had a rhythm of vigorous expeditions and periods of repose. During the winter months he settled in a comfortable provincial city and mingled in local society. The first winter Colt spent in Florence where he took lodgings and often dined in before venturing on the town for a concert, play or game of cards. In the new year he moved to Siena. Evenings he passed with the Bucci family in whose company Colt, hitherto not rated a heartbreaker, seems to have discovered a *tendresse*. His days fell into a relaxed pattern of mornings writing letters, compiling his journal or drawing, followed by a carriage-drive, dinner at home then, in his words, 'as usual in Evening' often with an '×' appended.[47] So Italy may not have been a sexual Sahara for Colt. Kenneth Woodbridge noted that he wrote more letters to Teresina Bucci than to any other correspondent while he was abroad.[48] Lothario or *cicisbeo*, Colt relished Siena and it became his base to explore the nearby Etruscan ruins.

The classical authors remained in the forefront of Colt's mind and he was excited to visit places described by Virgil and Horace. They prompted his journey along the Via Appia undertaken with the artist Labruzzi in October 1789. That winter Colt sailed to Sicily to begin a nine-month exploration of the island. In Palermo Colt was taken up by the Prince of Trabbia and lionised in Sicilian society.[49] His diary filled with visits to the opera, theatre, cards and *conversazioni*. Sicily became a popular destination for travellers in the 1770s and several authors published accounts of the island.[50] Having struggled to Paestum on the mainland, Colt was keen to inspect the Greek temples at Segesta and Agrigento. Like the majority of tourists he was impressed by the setting and scale of the ruined buildings which he dutifully sketched. He paid little attention to baroque architecture. But

The Adoration of the Magi, 1605, by Lodovico Cardi, 'il Cigoli' (1559–1613), oil on canvas, 345.4 × 233.7 cm. Stourhead.

he delighted in the natural beauty of the island and determined to enjoy it from the summit of Mount Etna. As it turned out plumes of smoke obscured his view but the crater awed him.

On the mainland Colt travelled with two coaches and a retinue of servants. To explore Sicily where the roads and tracks were primitive he exchanged his carriages for mules. His entourage comprised a driver, two servants and two *campieri* travelling on six mules: one laden with his litter, bed, baggage and 'kitchen furniture'.[51] Sleeping in remote inns, Colt had complained of flea bites, making a travelling mattress a necessity.[52] For the most part, in Sicily he found private accommodation, with letters of introduction passing him from one landowner to another. These included monasteries, most of which he found comfortable. There were disagreeable exceptions during his earlier exploration of northern Italy. In Pula, south of Trieste, he lodged at a Franciscan monastery where a monk invited visiting servants for a night on the town with the local girls. The servants refused but two monks enjoyed the spree, returned drunk and, as Colt observed, were shriven at the confessional the following morning.[53]

In autumn 1790 Colt returned to Naples then travelled north to Siena. That winter he pulled off a coup in purchasing *The Adoration of the Magi*, by Cigoli, which had been the altarpiece of the Albizzi Chapel in San Pier Maggiore, a recently demolished church in Florence (page 74).[54] Colt travelled from Siena in

*The Falls of Tivoli, c.*1786, by Abraham Louis Ducros (1748–1810), watercolour, 660 × 1016 mm. Stourhead.

February 1791 to clinch the deal.[55] His receipt for 300 zecchini (about £150) is dated 19 February.[56] The large painting dominates the Picture Gallery at Stourhead.

In the spring of 1791 Colt visited Rome and once more met up with Woodforde who accompanied him on the homeward journey.[57] They had a month in Siena where Colt parted from his Italian friends in late June. Thereafter he and Woodforde travelled rapidly through Europe, avoiding France and reaching England at the end of July.

Colt's account at the family bank records payments to bankers and agents made while he was abroad, indicating that his expenditure during the two continental tours was about £6,000.[58] On both trips he commissioned work by the artists Ducros, Hackert, Labruzzi and Rouby.

Abraham Louis Ducros (1748–1810), the Swiss artist, enjoys a commanding presence at Stourhead where thirteen of his spectacular watercolours hang in the Column Room. They depict landscapes dear to Colt Hoare: five in Umbria, four around Tivoli and four in Rome.[59] The pictures are remarkable on account of their size and the intensity of colours. In *Modern Wiltshire* Colt puffed up Ducros's influence on British artists.

Jakob Philipp Hackert (1737–1807) was an established and popular landscape painter when he encountered Colt Hoare in Rome during the spring of 1786. That year he was appointed court painter at Naples where his large canvases now make a

welcome interlude from the portraits crowding the royal palace and the state rooms at Caserta. Colt bought an oil painting and four drawings by Hackert which remain at Stourhead (page 73).[60] The artist and the Englishman became well-acquainted and in autumn 1790 they made two excursions from Naples.[61] The first was to Isernia, in Molise, where they attended a festival deemed a survival of the pagan cult of Priapus; the second was to admire the natural phenomena at Piedimonte Matese.[62]

Carlo Labruzzi (1748–1817) was born and trained at Rome where he earned a reputation for landscape drawing and painting. Colt Hoare had met Labruzzi on his first tour when he purchased a painting and two drawings.[63] Their mutual interest in topography and antiquity sparked a plan to examine Roman monuments as they travelled together along the Via Appia from Rome to Brindisi. They set out on 31 October 1789 on a journey that was less one of discovery than of recognition because Colt was steeped in the literature, both contemporary and classical. Intoning Horace (*Satires* 1.5) and other Roman authors, he travelled the road pausing to copy Latin epigraphs while Labruzzi drew.[64] Early on they deviated from the road to visit Sperlonga and Gaeta where Colt admired a Greek marble vase used as a font.[65] When the weather and days closed in, Labruzzi fell ill and the travellers were compelled to abandon the journey at Benevento.

Labruzzi returned from the expedition with many *plein air* sketches, sixty-seven of which are now at the British Museum, while a further one hundred were

PREVIOUS PAGES
The Grotto.

ABOVE
*Angel from the expulsion of Heliodorus, c.*1787, by J. C. Seydelmann, (1750–1829), after Raphael, bistre on paper, tondo H 87.1 cm. Stourhead.

dispersed at a London gallery sale in 1960.[66] In Rome Labruzzi worked up his sketches as finished drawings, incorporating Colt's transcriptions. These drawings are now at the Accademia di San Luca, Rome. The artist made a second, more refined, set of 226 drawings with captions in English. These remained at Stourhead until Sotheby's auctioned them in 1883 for seventeen guineas.[67] They are now in the Vatican Apostolic Library.[68] Labruzzi etched twenty-four plates published in Italy and England with a dedication to Colt who paid for the printing in 1794–95.[69]

John James Rouby (1750–1812), although born at Plymouth, spent his working life in Rome where he was resident from 1776.[70] He styled himself a history painter but is remembered for his versions of Old Master paintings drawn in bistre on large sheets of paper, a technique also practised by his contemporary J. C. Seydelmann (1750–1829) of Dresden. Today there are 33 drawings by Rouby at Stourhead and two by Seydelmann who traced one directly from Raphael's fresco in the Vatican with Colt in attendance.[71]

In Italy he put to practical use his studies of classical literature. He immersed himself in Italian publications: guides, histories, biographies or art-orientated texts, ancient and contemporary. In these he found the information to better appreciate his surroundings. By the time he returned to Stourhead, he had amassed some two thousand volumes. He was sufficiently proud to publish a catalogue and, when his library filled with British books, he gave the British Museum the pick of his Italian collection.[72]

To what extent did experiences abroad influence Colt's attitude towards Stourhead's garden? The *Recollections* touch lightly on gardens and horticulture. At Chantilly Colt found the English Garden distinctly un-English; at Caserta he visited the celebrated English Garden without comment.[73] In the grounds of Versailles he mentioned neither the formal gardens nor the fountains but remarked upon the copies of antique sculpture.[74] In the Boboli Garden at Florence he commented on the modern sculpture. Colt was critical of most Sicilian gardens, deploring the vogue for planting fruit trees in pleasure grounds. He admired the oaks, pines and cypresses in the convent at Nicosia, conceding it 'might be rendered a most delicious garden'.[75] Above all, Colt relished the natural scenery of Italy and that is what Ducros and Hackert drew for him.

Colt never intended a third visit to Italy; he was keen to explore Spain and Portugal but was thwarted by Napoleon.[76]

'I wish to preserve my Liberty & Independence': Stourhead 1791–1800

Returning to Stourhead in August 1791 Colt Hoare greeted his steward with a head full of plans. A good deal is known about his ensuing activities because in 1792 he began the 'Stourhead Annals', as an annual record of key events at the property, including the trees planted and entries from the game book. It was kept by Colt and his successors until 1947 with a gap between 1861 and 1894 left by the improvident 5th Baronet.

In 1799 Colt had the opportunity to extend the estate westwards by purchasing the Manor of Gasper.[77] The soil was poor, best suited to forestry. With this addition the woods on the estate then comprised 77 acres in the landscape garden, 959 forest-acres surrounding, and another 1,178 acres at outlying properties.[78] Henry the Magnificent had kept the landscape garden pristine, the lawns tended, the edges clipped and glimpses of the village and country beyond carefully stage-managed. Colt, in picturesque frame of mind, preferred to blur the distinction between the garden and perimeter drive, opening views from one to the other. He allowed trees to spread and mature so that the sward around the lake shrank during his tenure. Whether for aesthetic or financial reasons the garden was less well-manicured than in his predecessor's day when it had purred with labourers.[79]

Colt removed the exotic garden buildings of which he disapproved.[80] Their demolition robbed the garden of the architectural variety that Henry the Magnificent had created. Kenneth Woodbridge largely absolved him for cleansing the garden in this way so that today Stourhead is lauded as a classical landscape garden par excellence. Colt laid paths around the Garden Lake, rerouted the main drive and moved Clock Arch to its present position. At the house he engaged Moulton and Atkinson, the Salisbury partnership of architect-builders, to refurbish the domestic offices and built two wings although he did not complete the latter until the new century.[81]

Colt kept on the move: 1796 is typical of the decade.[82] From January to the end of May, he was socialising in London. He then set off for Wales where he fished, explored and sketched. On the homeward journey he stayed with Sir John Leicester at Tabley House near Knutsford and George Lyttelton at Hagley Hall in Worcestershire. Colt reached Stourhead by early September for the shooting season. In November he visited his half-sister, Henrietta Fortescue, at Holnicote in North Somerset.[83]

The newly established squire was in no hurry to embark on public commitments. When Lord Ailesbury offered him a seat in Parliament, he declined: 'I wish to preserve my Liberty & Independence without any Incumbrance whatever. My time is pleasantly occupied with my favorite Pursuits of reading & drawing'.[84] Happily his insouciance was not a portent of the future.

Between 1793 and 1810 Colt Hoare visited Wales each summer for about two months.[85] On the early excursions he was content sketching the scenery and making brief entries in a journal. His friend William Coxe, the sharp-eyed and glutinous clergyman, sensed his lack of focus so introduced him to Welsh history and the pleasures of writing. For Colt it was an epiphany.

Archdeacon William Coxe (1748–1828) was educated at Eton and King's College, Cambridge where he was made a fellow, ordained and appointed tutor to the eldest son of the 3rd Duke of Marlborough. It was an auspicious beginning for a prelate remembered less for spreading the word of God than for a steady stream of publications. Coxe wrote biographies of Sir Robert Walpole (1798), Horace Walpole (1802) and the 1st Duke of Marlborough (1818). Released from Blenheim, he had accompanied George Herbert, heir to the 10th Earl of Pembroke, on a tour of Russia, Scandinavia, Poland and Italy from 1775 to 1779. Six years later he escorted Samuel Whitbread to the Continent. Come the French Revolution, Coxe resumed a career in the church. Lord Pembroke appointed him rector of Bemerton and, in

THE NANNAU OAK.
fell to the ground
27th of July 1813.
This frame is made of the real wood.

*Sketched by Sir Rich.d C. Hoare.
on the morning preceding
the night on which it fell.*

·209·

The Nannau Oak, 1813, by
Sir Richard Colt Hoare, 2nd
Baronet (1758–1838), watercolour,
470 × 349 mm. Stourhead.

1800, Colt made him rector of Stourton (1800–12). He was raised to Archdeacon of Wiltshire in 1805.

Coxe and Colt Hoare were fellows of the Society of Antiquaries and shared a love of travelling. In 1798 he invited Colt to collaborate in his *Historical tour in Monmouthshire*.[86] Coxe would write the text while Colt would provide illustrations and finance the publication. Colt made ninety-six drawings of which thirty-six were engraved for the book.[87] In the course of their expedition they encountered prehistoric monuments and commissioned Thomas Morrice to survey these sites. The experience awoke in Colt an interest in archaeology and an appetite to write: in the future he could be illustrator *and* author. Coxe was polished, learned and popular; arriving at Stourhead with a six-course appetite, Colt remarked how Coxe tucked into venison daily. [88]

Colt Hoare grew to love Lake Bala in Gwynedd where the landscape and fishing surpassed his expectations and he took a bungalow named Fach Ddeilliog (Leafy Nook) on its shores.[89]

In Italy Colt had classical authors as guides to the ruins of antiquity; in Wales he seized upon Archbishop Baldwin's tour, undertaken in 1188 and described by Giraldus de Barri. Colt followed the itinerary faithfully, visiting what remained of the ecclesiastical buildings, castles and towns described. He published the Latin text of Giraldus in 1804 and two years later issued his own translation, accompanied by generous scholarly apparatus. *The itinerary of Archbishop Baldwin through Wales* (London, 1806) filled two imposing volumes. John Carter, the antiquarian architect and proponent of gothic architecture, drew the maps, ground plans and architectural studies. Colt himself made 144 drawings in sepia and blue wash from which he selected less than half to engrave for publication.[90]

In the commentary Colt commended Welsh scenery to artists, admonishing them to look hard and learn 'the *grammar* of weeds, rocks, and trees in order to become a good painter', a prescription unlikely to convey the romance and picturesque qualities he himself so ardently admired.[91] Without doubt the mountains and valleys, the ruined abbeys and lakes of Wales fired Colt's imagination, yet he failed to convey this delight either by his pen or his brush.

Having taken over Giraldus, Colt pursued his conquest of Wales, planning further publications with his friend Richard Fenton. By then his interest was waning because of the new-found appetite for archaeology in Wiltshire. He did, however, make time to illustrate Fenton's *Historical tour through Pembrokeshire* (London, 1811).

Few reminders exist at Stourhead of these happy interludes in Wales. Colt's own sketches were sold in 1883 and 1887.[92] An oil painting of Llangollen by Callcott and Colt's drawing of *The Nannau Oak* do not convey his affection for the principality (previous page).[93]

Richard Fenton (1747–1821), the Welsh author and poet, trained as a lawyer in London where he associated with writers, painters and company that bubbled with wit. Fenton returned to Wales as a practising barrister where he also occupied himself with local history and archaeology. Fenton possessed an engaging personality and enquiring mind; he was soufflé to Colt Hoare's suet. They met in 1793, the year after money from his father and his marriage enabled Fenton to retire. From an uncle, Fenton inherited property in Fishguard, in Pembrokeshire, where he built a new house, Plas Glynamel.

In *A tour in quest of genealogy* Fenton described a visit to Stourhead. He arrived at the inn on 7 November 1807 and in his polite fiction recounted first meeting Colt and gave a detailed account of the house and grounds.[94]

Journeying to and from Wales, Colt Hoare would call on relatives and friends. Each year Sir John Leicester invited him to Tabley. His brother-in-law, George Lyttelton, always welcomed him at Hagley. Meanwhile Colt's half-brother, Henry Hugh, had acquired a sporting estate at Wavendon in Buckinghamshire, which Colt visited for the first time in 1798.[95] Colt also called on relatives in the south-west: Charles Hoare at Luscombe Castle in Devonshire, and his half-sister, Henrietta Anne, at Holnicote in North Somerset. Colt did not describe their houses and gardens in his journals. He did, however, write about other houses and gardens.

Gothic appealed to Colt for several reasons: ruined abbeys and castles were picturesque and their architecture spoke to him of history. The *Itinerary* closes with

a twenty-three-page essay on medieval architecture. He admired Fountains Abbey
in Yorkshire, and remarked elsewhere that landowners should incorporate ruins in
their parks as eye-catchers and, more importantly, preserve them.[96] He deplored the
want of care in Wales where year by year he witnessed the decay of Margam Abbey
and Beaumaris Castle.[97] When it came to interior decorating, Colt inclined to the
austere and formal. He admired Adam's Kedleston Hall in Derbyshire but found the
state rooms at Harewood House in Yorkshire 'gawdy and expensive'.[98] At Downton
Castle in Herefordshire he praised the dining room, modelled, as he remarked, on
the rotunda of the Pantheon at Stourhead; as to the rest of the mansion, it was a
mish-mash of styles.

   Colt admired, as historical survivals, the garden terraces at Powis Castle in
Wales and the cascade in the garden at Chatsworth in Derbyshire as 'a specimen
of the old English taste'.[99] Landscape gardens, he opined, should look natural, not
man-made. He acknowledged that such an effect was achieved by tactful planting,
the subtle turn in a path and so on, but this should be unobtrusive without overt
artistry. Colt disliked the formal water at Studley Royal in Yorkshire because it
looked contrived.[100] He was suspicious of parks designed by Capability Brown whose
signature clumps and sculpted lakes had become clichés. At Burleigh House in
Lincolnshire Colt was distressed by the sinuous and bald shoreline which betrayed
Brown's lake as artificial.[101] Colt admired the landscape gardens at Downton
Castle and Foxley, both in Herefordshire, created by two lions of the Picturesque,
respectively, Richard Payne Knight and Sir Uvedale Price, 1st Baronet. Their gardens
impressed Colt because they were set in strong natural scenery.[102] Bridges, mills
and cottages added to the variety in a pleasing way if useful and not merely
ornamental. He admired Price's attractive farm buildings which were prominent,
not concealed by belts of trees as Brown had favoured. Colt followed the baronet's

example at Stourhead by opening views from the garden into the estate and building attractive lodges and cottages. Francis Nicholson's watercolours captured their bucolic charm.

Europe at war: Colt Hoare at work 1800–10

During the first decade of the new century Europe was convulsed by war and Britain was poised to repel a French invasion but this had little impact on the purposeful doings of Colt Hoare. Wanderlust, and a wish to absent himself during building work at home, kept Colt on the move; indeed he passed no more than seven months of each year at Stourhead.[103] At home he was busy translating Giraldus and cultivating William Cunnington whose archaeological exploits would form the basis of *Ancient Wiltshire*. In 1805–6 Colt served as High Sheriff of the county which, he noted, cost £265 19s.[104]

For ten years Colt had lived among his grandfather's possessions: the silk wall hangings had faded, the furniture was well-worn and the pictures were in a muddle.[105] The two new pavilions stood proud, but empty until the builders fitted them out early in the new century.[106] In addition to equipping them Colt renovated the *piano nobile* (page 54). The parade rooms stretched along the east façade while the family apartments occupied the rear of the building as it extended westwards. The new Library filled the southern pavilion. In the adjoining Music Room he would display contemporary art. To the west of this room Colt created the Small Dining Room (where the Sixtus Cabinet had formerly stood) and, beyond, the private South Rooms, hung with drawings by Rouby. He accumulated enough family portraits to people the Entrance Hall and on the north side he converted the old library into a room to display the Sixtus Cabinet, surrounded with landscape paintings, ancient and modern. Beyond lay the new Picture Gallery housing the largest and best Old Masters in the collection. The west door from the new Cabinet Room was sealed because it led directly to Colt's bedroom (Italian Room) and thence to the North Apartments (Column Room), hung with watercolours by Ducros and Turner.[107]

Colt entrusted the decorating and furnishing to Thomas Chippendale the younger: the Picture Gallery, Ante Room, Cabinet Room and Small Dining Room undertaken from 1801 to 1804; the Library, from 1805 to 1806, campaigns described by Judith Goodison.[108]

Chippendale offered a range of finishes and quality for his furniture, from opulent pieces loaded with fatty deposits of ormolu, as found at Harewood House, to the simple painted furniture which Colt had ordered for Lincoln's Inn Fields. The Stourhead commissions lie midway in terms of finish: few items are gilded but the veneering and joinery are superb; furthermore the designs are dazzlingly original. Colt was a discerning customer with an appetite for detail. In the Library the carved Egyptian heads, in *nemes*, a striped headcloth, are the recurring motif, perhaps celebrating Britain's defeat of Napoleon in Egypt. Chippendale may have copied these from Wedgwood's Egyptian ceramics, produced from 1769 (Colt purchased examples in 1806).[109] They in turn may have derived from Montfaucon's *L'antiquité expliquée*.[110] Or perhaps the cabinetmaker took Egyptian motifs from Piranesi's etchings.[111]

Library armchair, 1805, by Thomas Chippendale the younger (1749–1822), mahogany, 83.3 × 68 × 51 cm. Stourhead.

Colt and Chippendale would have enjoyed such esoteric discussions but sadly their correspondence is lost. Chippendale also supplied curtains and carpets, making the house glow in a full-blooded Regency palette. The Picture Gallery was furnished in satinwood with ebony banding, the curtains and upholstery shone in sulphur-yellow sown with black stars. The Cabinet Room was hung with royal-blue curtains.

Chippendale's bills have survived as a holy grail for furniture historians and they disclose, among the wayside pleasures, that the cabinet maker billed Colt Hoare for nine jardinières which stood in the window embrasures.[112] When filled with plants, they suffused the house with fragrance. Colt was a keen plantsman but it was not until 1809 that he purchased geraniums from the well-known Bristol nurserymen, Miller and Sweet.[113] He was elected a fellow of the Linnean Society in 1812, probably at the behest of his friend, the botanist, Aylmer Bourke Lambert (1761–1842). Colt took to cultivation with characteristic thoroughness. In 1820 Robert Sweet, brother of the nursery man, published *Geraniaceæ, the natural order of gerania* and included in the first volume illustrations of six species propagated at Stourhead.[114] A year later Colt himself printed a list of 600 varieties growing in his glasshouses.[115]

'Antiquarian Confectionary'

The phrase was coined in an anonymous review of *Modern Wiltshire* and reflects Colt Hoare's enthusiasm for local archaeology.[116] In the new century, this became his dominant passion, reaching fulfilment in *The Ancient History of Wiltshire*. It was inspired by *Nenia Britannica*, produced by his friend James Douglas and issued in instalments between 1786 and 1793. Douglas described and illustrated prehistoric burial customs discovered from relics extracted from barrows, mostly in south-east England.[117] After Douglas died his widow gave his archaeological finds to Colt.[118]

As an adventurous young man Reverend James Douglas (1753–1819) is reputed to have enlisted with the Austrian Army. After returning to England he worked as a military engineer. In the 1780s his career took several unexpected twists: he was married, ordained, and elected a fellow of the Society of Antiquaries. After a stint in Northamptonshire, he moved to Sussex where the 3rd Earl of Egremont appointed him rector of Middleton. He was also a chaplain-in-ordinary to the Prince of Wales. The illustrations set *Nenia Britannica* apart from *Ancient Wiltshire*. In the latter Philip Crocker's survey-drawings were faithfully rendered by distinguished engravers, including James Basire the younger. Douglas's aquatints lack this precision but were more adventurous in amalgamating plans and images in *trompe l'oeil* plates.

In Wiltshire Colt Hoare found himself in the company of a friend, an antiquarian-minded clergyman and an inquisitive landowner with time on his hands, each happy to mull over the rich archaeology of the county. They were William Coxe, Colt's mentor in Monmouthshire, and Thomas Leman who had studied and walked the Roman roads in the county. The third, Henry Penruddocke Wyndham, was obsessed by the long barrows which he believed were ancient battle burials. Meanwhile a remarkable tradesman living in Heytesbury was excavating fragments of bone, pottery and metalwork belonging to this early history.

William Cunnington (1754–1810), a retired clothier, welcomed the well-connected

historians for their knowledge of literary sources and for their easy relations with fellow landowners whose permissions were needed for his excavations. Cunnington trained Stephen Parker and his son John to open barrows and took advice from Leman on how to document and label the finds which were valued not for their aesthetic merit but as evidence of ancient customs. The excavators sank shafts and sliced into burial mounds with a crudeness distressing to modern archaeologists. Cunnington displayed the archaeological finds in his Moss House at Heytesbury.[119] This curious outbuilding was constructed in rough timber and clad in dried heather, the interior, according to his daughter, as intriguing as any hermitage.[120] Colt would later acquire this archaeological collection for Stourhead where it was locked into cupboards and glass-topped cases to languish in his museum beneath the Picture Gallery.[121] Thomas Dibdin admired the array of finds at Stourhead, musing, 'one would think that their owner had handled the beard of every Druid in the realm'.[122]

Coxe and Wyndham had introduced Colt to Cunnington in 1801. Colt grasped the importance of the excavations and himself became an enthusiastic barrow-opener. Coxe intended to publish the discoveries but withdrew after his marriage in 1802; thereafter Colt took over the coordinating role with Crocker the surveyor at his side.

Philip Crocker (1780–1840) of Frome was trained by his father as a land surveyor and worked for the Ordnance Survey. He moonlighted with Colt Hoare from 1802 and became his surveyor and draughtsman for *Ancient Wiltshire*. By about 1810 he was employed fulltime at Stourhead as land steward, a job inherited by his son, John.

Each summer Colt and Crocker explored the county, scouting out inviting-looking barrows to excavate and compiling lists for Cunnington's annual 'campaigns'. Colt was always keen to inspect the finds and keener still to read Cunnington's descriptions of the work. Two copies of these letters survive, one sent to Colt (now at the Society of Antiquaries) and another kept by Cunnington (now at the Wiltshire Museum, Devizes). Colt incorporated Cunnington's reports, often verbatim, into his text, while Crocker produced accurate and elegant surveys of the sites and drew eye-catching finds.

The first volume of *The Ancient History of Wiltshire*, covering the south county, was issued in three folios, 1810–12. *North Wiltshire* appeared in 1819 followed two years later by a final folio, *The Roman Æra*. Few could deny the sensual pleasure of the books in the large-paper printing, measuring 57 × 42 cm with broad borders, elegant typography and a wealth of informative illustrations. Leather-bound and finished with top-edge gilt, each volume weighed nearly twelve kilograms making it a lectern-worthy read. The laurels for presentation belong equally to Colt Hoare and the printer, William Bulmer.

In 1811 *The Quarterly Review* reviewed the first volume.[123] The editor, William Gifford, was noted for his acerbity so it is no surprise that the articles began by attacking Colt as a snob. The reviewer dismissed the introductory history as speculation, then calmed down enough to praise the author's assiduity in describing the excavations. There was substance in the criticism although Colt side-stepped the folklore surrounding Stonehenge and used the term 'druid' sparingly. He was unable to date finds and wisely omitted a chronology. Many contemporaries accepted 4004 BC as the date of the Creation which cramped any prehistoric timeline.[124] Leman theorised that stone implements preceded bronze and that iron finds were Roman; recognition of the Stone, Bronze and Iron ages came later.

In *Ancient Wiltshire* Colt described about a quarter of the two thousand barrows identified in the county today and was noticeably sketchy in the north.[125] The text is encumbered by lengthy quotations from earlier historians. Colt spiced his descriptions by quoting poetry; in this snatch the Reverend William Bowles imagined himself as the defunct chieftain:

> O'er my moulder'd ashes cold
> Many a century slow hath roll'd,
> Many a race hath disappear'd
> Since my giant form I rear'd:
> Since my flinted arrow flew.[126]

Colt Hoare in sickness and in health 1810–20

The decade was momentous for Britain, pivoting midway with the victory at Waterloo and closing with the death of George III. The defeat of Napoleon ushered in a spell of reaction and repression at home and abroad. Against this backdrop, Colt Hoare pursued his own interests with customary energy despite failing health and his troublesome son.

Henry Hoare (1784–1836), this prodigal son, had the distinction of greeting a reigning monarch at Stourhead: in 1789, George III and Queen Charlotte called when travelling from Weymouth to Longleat. The Queen glimpsed the five-year old boy at her carriage door.[127] Visitors to Stourhead today encounter three portraits of Henry in the Entrance Hall, two as a blond-haired schoolboy, the third as a man in his jaded prime.[128] Henry was less than a year old when his mother died and his father took off for the Continent, leaving him in the care of servants. When Colt Hoare

returned, he dispatched Henry to boarding-school and then to Eton where the boy showed no academic aptitude. Like his father he was restless. He accompanied Colt to Wales on several occasions and to Ireland in 1806; however, a bucolic life did not appeal to him and he gravitated to London.[129] When he fell for Charlotte Dering, his father opposed the match but could not bring himself to forbid it. Later Colt indulged himself in a jeremiad:

> How little does he [Henry] know... what an alliance I could have made for him for on telling my old friend Sir Abraham Hume of my son's intended marriage, he expressed a wish that an alliance should have been made with his daughter a most accomplished young woman afterwards married to Lord Brownlow by which Marriage His son will inherit the Duke of Bridgewater's immense property and so might my posterity have done.[130]

On 20 February 1808 Henry and Charlotte married at St George's, Hanover Square. Colt had made a settlement securing an annual allowance of £1,500 for Henry, a jointure for Charlotte and provision for their children.[131] The young

Henry Hoare (1784–1836), 1829, by Margaret Carpenter (1793–1872), oil on canvas, 127 × 101.6 cm. Stourhead.

couple embarked on married life at a rented house near Shaftesbury before moving to a farm at West Knoyle belonging to Colt.[132] Both yearned for pavements. In December 1808 Anne, their only daughter, was born. Henry, jobless, rudderless and unable to finance his wife's extravagance, collapsed with a nervous breakdown in 1811.[133] Thereafter the couple lived apart and by 1819 Henry had moved to Paris and was running short of money.[134] The following year Colt increased his annual allowance to £2,000.[135] Some form of reconciliation occurred and the errant son returned at intervals to Stourhead.[136] Hunter met Henry in 1827 and described him as a handsome man despite 'suffering the consequences of an irregular life'. But, he opined, 'Stourhead will be a different place when he is proprietor'.[137] Colt, who had the measure of his son, intended to bequeath Stourhead, the estate and works of art to trustees so that Henry and his heirs would inherit life interests without the right to sell.[138]

In 1835 Anne married George Mathew; it proved a disastrous match. The following year Henry died at Hastings. Colt shrank from commemorating his son but did allot him space in the new family vault. Anne placed the brass memorial tablet to her father in Stourton church. Colt paid debts run up independently by the unloving couple. London tradesmen and servants claimed £1,767 and £2,450, owed respectively by Henry and Charlotte, with a further £900 for decorating Charlotte's house in South Audley Street.[139] In Wiltshire, Henry left an overdraft of £9,000 with the local bank, a debt which his uncle eventually settled.[140]

During the decade 1810–1820 Colt did much to prettify Stourton village. He was a practical man and added new stables and a coach house at the inn, built a new rectory at the upper end of the village and improved the graveyard. In 1818 expenditure on the estate amounted to:[141]

House	£99–19s–6d
Garden	£361–10s–6d
Game	£309–9s–6d
Stables	£219–17s–0d

Colt had always been a nimrod. The game bag for 1818–19, not a particularly good season, amounted to:[142]

Partridge	327
Pheasant	341
Hare	548
Woodcock	136
Rabbit	2,155

The gamekeeper's house and kennels, close to Turner's Paddock Lake, were a showplace.[143] Trophies reached Stourhead where the 1838 inventory recorded 'fifteen cases of Stuffed Birds' in the Saloon. Sporting Stourhead has been airbrushed from the house in recent years. Colt had first complained of gout in 1801 and Chippendale supplied a scurry of gout stools.[144] The illness returned in 1806 and limited his attendance at Cunnington's excavations. Like his fellow archaeologist he also became a victim to headaches for which he sought a cure in Bath where he was prescribed doses of arsenic.[145] Nevertheless Colt continued to shoot and fish.[146] Woodforde remarked in 1814 that his patron was greatly aged from the rheumatism brought on by long hours enjoying his favourite sport of salmon fishing.[147]

By 1822 Thomas Dibdin found Colt 'in the full enjoyment of his mental faculties, although the gout now and then crippled his feet, and a deafness prevents a very quick colloquial intercourse'.[148] Gout enforced Colt's confinement at Stourhead and afforded the opportunity to write. In the second decade of the new century he completed *Ancient Wiltshire* and began the sequel.

The history of Modern Wiltshire was Colt Hoare's most ambitious self-imposed assignment. It was published in fourteen parts, or Hundreds, and covered the southern county because that insatiable bibliophile and manuscript hunter, Sir Thomas Phillipps, 1st Baronet, reneged on an agreement to tackle the north.

The first county histories had appeared in the seventeenth century, notably *The antiquities of Warwickshire* (1656) by William Dugdale. In Colt's lifetime John Hutchins had published *The history and antiquities of the county of Dorset* (1774) and John Collinson, *The history and antiquities of the county of Somerset* (1791). John Nichols compiled a scholarly four-volume *The history and antiquities of the county of Leicester* (1795–1815) which was a model to Colt.

The 'Hundred of Mere' was published in 1822 and the last two volumes of the juggernaut appeared posthumously. The Nichols dynasty was the publisher and each Hundred was printed separately with a recommendation to bind the set into six volumes.

Modern Wiltshire was a collaborative venture; the Hundreds followed along the river courses of the county. To summarise the authors and titles:

> vol. I
> 'Hundred of Mere', by Hoare, 1822
> 'Hundred of Heytesbury', by Hoare, 1824
>
> vol. II
> 'Hundred of Branch and Dole', by Reverend John Offer and Hoare, 1825
> 'Hundreds of Everley, Ambresbury, and Underditch', by Hoare, 1826
> vol. III
> 'Hundred of Westbury', by Richard Harris and Hoare, 1830
> 'Hundred of Warminster', by Henry Wansey and Hoare, 1831
> 'Hundred of South Damerham', by William Henry Black and Hoare, 1835
> 'Hundred of Downton', by George Matcham and Hoare, 1834
> 'Hundred of Cawden', by Hoare, 1835
>
> vol. IV
> 'Hundred of Dunworth', by James Everard Arundell, 10th Baron Arundell and Hoare, 1829
> 'Hundred of Chalk', by Charles Bowles and Hoare, 1833

vol. V
'Hundred of Alderbury', by John Gough Nichols and Hoare, 1837
'Hundred of Frustfield', by George Matcham, 1844
'Addenda to vols I–IV', 1844

vol. VI, pts I and II
'Old and New Sarum', by Robert Benson and Henry Hatcher, 1843

J. B. Nichols printed 150 large-paper copies of the 'Hundred of Mere' and 250 in the standard format. For later Hundreds he reduced the quantities to one hundred and 150 respectively. The large-paper editions sold at six guineas in limp bindings.[149] Around 1835, halfway through the series, Nichols totted up the printing costs to £3,115 and the sales at £2,238.[150] Colt made up the difference. These figures omitted the cost of the illustrations.

The design and typography of *Modern Wiltshire* is impressive. Unlike *Ancient Wiltshire*, however, the new volumes were sparingly illustrated and as the Hundreds progress the plates almost dry up. In the text, Colt quoted at length from public and parish records and manorial and ecclesiastical documents. He seldom synthesised information and long passages are indigestible. He supplied genealogies of fearful complexity, histories of the leading landowners and data compiled from questionnaires sent to parishes. Architecture, ecclesiastical and secular, found its place in the text. The 'Hundred of Mere' (1822) shows up the strengths of *Modern Wiltshire*. It has elegant maps and plans by Crocker and illustrations by a variety of artists, including John Buckler. Colt devoted fifty pages to Stourhead with a list of the pictures identifying, with initials, those he inherited and those he purchased. He passed on tips for planting trees, illustrating his favourite implement. Special pleading also accounts for the six pages allotted to the herbarium of his friend and fellow Linnean, Aylmer Lambert, at Boynton House in the 'Hundred of Heytesbury'.

The gallery of authors and researchers assembled to marshal useful facts and a few fictions is peopled by clergymen, schoolmasters and lawyers, professions requiring Latin and familiarity with historical documents. John Offer (d. 1822) was a stipendiary curate at Warminster and later at Kingston Deverill. He discovered and translated documents for Colt before expiring at Stourhead. His successor as librarian-researcher was the argumentative Stephen Hyde Cassan (d. 1841) a high church stipendiary curate at Mere, West Knoyle and subsequently perpetual curate at Wyke Champflower, Bruton. All these livings were in gift of Colt Hoare. Henry Hatcher (d. 1846) began his career as a school teacher, before being appointed assistant to William Coxe and later to Colt. Hatcher was an energetic historian and a linguist who ran a private school in Salisbury. After Colt's death he quarrelled publically with Robert Benson, co-author of 'Old and New Sarum', the final volume of *Modern Wiltshire*. William Henry Black (d. 1872), a distinguished librarian and antiquary, was also an assistant keeper of the Public Records and, in his spare time, a minister of the Seventh Day Baptists in Whitechapel. Three authors had a legal training: George Matcham (d. 1877) served as chairman of Wiltshire quarter sessions,

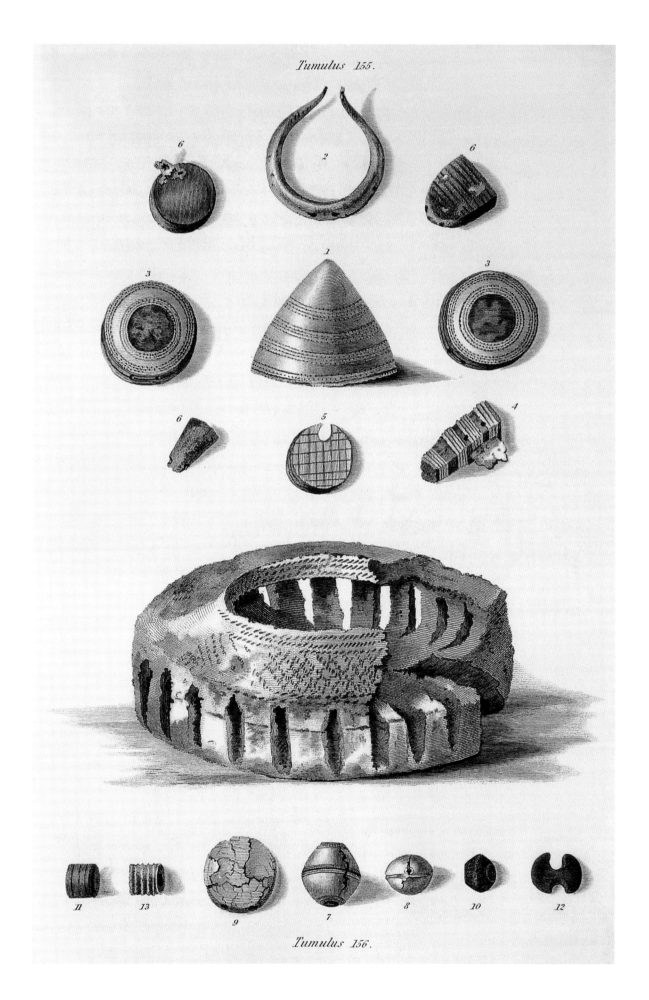

Tumulus 155.

Tumulus 156.

Charles Bowles (d. 1837) was Recorder of Shaftesbury and Robert Benson (d. 1844) was Deputy Recorder of Salisbury. Two wealthy merchant-traders contributed: Richard Harris (d. *c.*1837) was a clothier, or wool-merchant, from Westbury while Henry Wansey (d. 1827) was a clothier, a globetrotter and fellow of the Society of Antiquities. The Roman Catholic James Everard Arundell, 10th Baron Arundell (d. 1834) alone outranked Colt.

Colt had gained confidence from *Ancient Wiltshire* and learned how to dragoon and organise his authors. He was always the centrifugal force of *Modern Wiltshire*. Robert Benson described how:

> In readiness for our arrival, Sir Richard had caused the outer wrapper, as well as the title-page, of our respective portions to be printed; and these he presented to Lord Arundell, Mr. C. Bowles and Mr. Wansey, as well as to myself... These wrappers and title-pages were the badges of our fellowship. [151]

A prospect of seeing their work in print was a powerful lure, especially when Colt picked up the bills. To encourage Benson and his co-authors, Colt held annual court at Stourhead for four or five days, usually in the autumn. Authors were encouraged

Castello di Ardea, Lazio, 1785–91, by Sir Richard Colt Hoare, 2nd Baronet, (1758–1838), pen and sepia wash, 325 x 219 mm.

to use his library and to hobnob with likeminded men, mostly fellows of the Society of Antiquaries. Joseph Hunter (d. 1861) was an archivist, an able historian and, for a spell, a Presbyterian minister in Bath. Hunter was a regular at the Stourhead gatherings and chronicled the occasions.[152] Participants sat to Stephen Catterson Smith whose sketch portraits now hang in the Library at Stourhead. Hunter had unstinting admiration for Colt.[153] No women seem to have attended the occasions and Hunter indicated his host often withdrew to his own quarters.[154] The broad spectrum of society and of religious belief did not impede the authors' work but may have caused ripples during mealtimes.[155] At dinner, the near-resident bore, John Skinner, rector of Camerton, could be relied upon to dilate on his parish as the site of *Camulodunum* or drone on interminably about the etymology. Skinner, ever stalwart and self-pitying, shot himself the year after Colt Hoare died.

In the Stourhead library Colt amassed all the printed material he could lay hands on to facilitate his research. J. B. Nichols's catalogue of the collection, published in 1840, recorded approximately 14,000 books. The library also housed drawings by Buckler, Nicholson and Turner as well as Colt's own artistic endeavours. Nichols's catalogue is the enduring record of the library before Sotheby's auctioned the entirety in the 1880s.

Colt Hoare, aesthete and connoisseur

Colt was a pupil of John 'Warwick' Smith (1749–1831), six of whose Italian watercolours hang in the Library Ante Room at Stourhead.[156] In Italy Colt had ample leisure to practise and to learn from Ducros and Labruzzi. The 1840 library catalogue mentioned over 800 drawings and sketches by Colt. This continental work was bound in fifteen elephant folios of which four returned to Stourhead after the auctions.[157] He was a competent and conscientious draughtsman but he never aspired to being an artist. In 1812 Skinner:

> accompanied S[r] R Hoare and M[r] Crocker his draughtsman into the [*pleasure* inserted] grounds to see A Camera Obscura on a new Construction it is formed of canvas so light that it may with care be wheeled about to any part of the premises. The views replicated on the paper from the different stations of this magnificent Panorama are indeed most striking S[r] R is about making a collection of them, which will be unrivalled as to richness and effect.[158]

Colt Hoare enjoyed commissioning draughtsmen and topographic artists. John Carter (1748–1817), expert in gothic architecture, made 208 drawings of the ecclesiastical buildings in South Wales and a further 61 in Wiltshire.[159] For *Ancient Wiltshire*, Philip Crocker had produced the 52 beautiful watercolours of prehistoric finds.[160] John Buckler (1770–1851) surpassed them all with 690 watercolours of buildings in Wiltshire and 199 elsewhere.[161] Turner's views of Salisbury are in a class apart. All these were sold in 1883.

Francis Nicholson (1753–1844) completed 33 large watercolours of Stourhead for Colt Hoare who bound them in an atlas-size volume for his library where they remained until 1883.[162] Twenty-five from the collection are now at the British Museum together with an album of Nicholson's preliminary sketches for these compositions.[163]

At the time of the commission Nicholson was midway in his career. He was born and trained in Yorkshire before moving to London in 1803.[164] He developed a method of enriching watercolours by stopping out the light areas and applying repeated washes to the mid and dark tones to emulate the richness of oil paints.

Nicholson became acquainted with the Hoare family in the early nineteenth century. Henrietta Anne Fortescue (1763–1841), Colt's half-sister, was married to Sir Thomas Dyke Acland, 9th Baronet, who died in 1794 leaving a seven-year-old heir to the Killerton and Holnicote estates. With her second husband, Captain Matthew Fortescue (1754–1842), she settled at Holnicote in North Somerset. Here Nicholson enjoyed summers coaching Henrietta.[165] He was acquainted with Colt who commissioned him to work up watercolours from his own sketches of Italy. These Nicholson exhibited at the Society of Painters in Water-Colours in 1810 and 1812. His finished pictures of Stourhead are not dated, but the first sketches are inscribed June 1812 and the latest dated June 1816. Nicholson charged seven guineas a watercolour.[166]

Colt considered himself an *arbiter elegantiae*; others disagreed. William Hazlitt dismissed the majority of the pictures at Stourhead as *trash*, awarding light praise to the Canaletto drawings, and copies after Guido Reni.[167] William Beckford went further and pronounced that Colt Hoare had no taste.[168] Both critics ignored Colt's predilection for topographic art. When it came to contemporary art he was not in the same league as Lord Egremont but then, he enjoyed one tenth of the latter's annual income.[169]

Regency patrons of British art are often assessed by their response to Turner and in such company boycotting Constable was the norm. The latter visited Stourhead in 1811 and made a sketch of the garden.[170] At Petworth, Lord Egremont offered opportunities to Turner who took advantage of the setting, the hospitality and his host's indulgence. Sir John Leicester, the boon-companion of Colt Hoare, was also an enlightened patron of Turner, refreshing his collections in London and Cheshire by exchanging Turner's early work for his latest pictures. By contrast Sir George Beaumont, doyen of the art establishment, disapproved of Turner's pictures and thereby alienated young British artists. Colt occupied a space between Beaumont and Leicester. He commissioned topographical watercolours of Salisbury from Turner but had little appetite for his more personal landscapes.

It is easier to set in context than to admire Colt Hoare's acquisition of contemporary 'fancy paintings' hung in the Music Room and Picture Gallery where *Distress by Sea* (exhibited at the Royal Academy in 1804) and *Distress by Land* (1811) by Henry Thomson loom immense and ominously on the window wall (overleaf).[171] Colt was proud of the pair, appending verses and displaying them in Kent-revival frames. Eight of Colt's fancy paintings by artists such as Collins, Hilton, Morland and Northcote left Stourhead in the 1880s. The finest of these was Reynolds's portrait of Colt's son, Henry, as a fledgling gardener in a pristine white smock.[172] Their loss weakens the flavour that contemporary paintings gave the collection.

Thomson was among the artists collected by Sir John Leicester, 5th Baronet (1762–1827). The latter was a life-long friend to Colt. As a crony of the Prince of Wales, Sir John had a raffish side to his character; his pretty mistress, Emily St Clare, modelled for Hoppner (in the nude) and for Northcote (clothed, in a painting acquired by Colt Hoare).[173] Leicester, four years younger than Colt, inherited Tabley House in 1770. The estate provided an annual income of about £12,000, a little above Colt's wealth. Both men took drawing lessons, both made the Grand Tour. Back in England they met in London and at their country houses. Callcott, Thomson and Turner were guests at Tabley. Leicester purchased their work both for his country house and London residence in Hill Street where he admitted the public to the gallery. He achieved a lifelong ambition when he was created Baron de Tabley the year before he died.

Colt Hoare and Leicester were among the early subscribers to the British Institution, founded in 1805. It exhibited works for sale by living artists and also held exhibitions of Old Masters lent by subscribers, as exemplars to young artists.[174] The institution, mistrusted by the Royal Academy, proved divisive among artists some of whom considered that originality went unrewarded. These rebels deplored the fashion for buying Old Masters in preference to their work. Colt was stung by the controversy and reached for his pen in defence of the institution.[175] Certainly the early nineteenth century witnessed a bonanza of masterpieces flooding from the Continent and snapped up by collectors.

Outside the Hoare family few men were better acquainted with Colt Hoare than the painter Samuel Woodforde RA (1763–1817), nephew of the diarist, Parson Woodforde. Around 1778 another uncle showed Henry the Magnificent drawings by the young artist.[176] Henry invited him to study the pictures at Stourhead. Evidently Samuel was a hit with the family because, in 1783, Hester Hoare described, 'a Young Man being constantly painting in it [the old library], he is a protégé of Mr Hoares a self-taught painter and a wonderful genius, he is now copying a charming picture of the Holy Family'.[177] Henry paid for Woodforde to attend the Royal Academy schools and bequeathed him £100.[178] Richard Hoare and Fat Harry commissioned copies of Stourhead pictures and continued as his patrons enabling Woodforde to go to Italy in 1785 where he lived for six years, returning with Colt on his homeward journeys in 1787 and 1791.[179] Woodforde then settled in London, making a living from portrait commissions and history painting. He was elected an associate RA in 1800 and academician seven years later. The artist married in middle life, his health deteriorated and the couple travelled to Italy where he died in 1817.

Assessing his paintings at Stourhead, where he should have excelled, Woodforde falls somewhat flat; his portraits of the Hoare dynasty lack the glamour of those by Sir Thomas Lawrence or even by Prince Hoare. Stourhead Library is dominated by Woodforde's large variations on Raphael's *The School of Athens* and *Parnassus*, *c*.1804, the first a cartoon for the painted glass, the second on canvas, both competent decorative works in colours enriching the room.[180]

J. M. W. Turner RA (1775–1851) at Stourhead

Although Turner's pictures are long gone from Stourhead, a ghostly rainbow lingers thanks to the survival elsewhere of the commissions he received from Colt Hoare. The latter was among the first to admire Turner's command of perspective and architectural detail evident in drawings exhibited at the Royal Academy. Turner visited Stourhead in 1795 or 1796, where his host was eager to show off watercolours by Ducros. Turner also enjoyed the Venetian drawings by Canaletto, the copies of Claude and *Landscape with the rest on the flight into Egypt* by Rembrandt, a painting which he singled out for admiration in a lecture delivered fifteen years later.[181] The garden provided inspiration for Turner although his watercolour sketches of the grounds may have been intended as demonstrations of his technique.[182]

Colt was interested in architectural subjects and commissioned Turner to make twenty watercolours of the city of Salisbury and the cathedral. He was fast off the mark: Turner's great patrons, Sir John Leicester and Lord Egremont, purchased his work *after* 1800. The Salisbury commission began in 1795 and ended ten years later when Turner had completed eight views of the cathedral and nine of city buildings.[183] Turner exhibited the cathedral views at the Royal Academy. Colt framed and hung them next to his bedroom, in the North

Distress by Land, 1811, by Henry Thomson RA (1773–1843), oil on canvas, 237.5 × 145.4 cm. Stourhead.

Apartments (Column Room). They were sold in 1883. The city series he bound
in a folio. This was omitted from Sotheby's catalogues because it was at Stourton
rectory. J. A. Ellis, rector from 1874 to 1887, could have 'acquired' the folio from
the impecunious 5th Baronet and it remained in private hands until sold and
dispersed in 1927.[184]

Although Turner was in high demand and diversifying into art far ahead of his
own time, in 1814, Colt commissioned *Lake Avernus: Aeneas and the Cumaean Sibyl*,
based on a drawing which Colt had made in 1786. He intended it as a companion
to *The Lake of Nemi with Diana and Callisto* by Richard Wilson which his
grandfather had acquired in 1760. Both oil paintings were sold in 1883. Wilson's
Nemi has returned to Stourhead on loan while Turner's *Avernus* is at the Yale
Center for British Art.[185]

That Stourhead lodged in Turner's memory is proven by a luminous
watercolour, *Rise of the River Stour at Stourhead (The swan's nest)*. It was exhibited
at the Royal Academy in 1825 but never belonged to Colt Hoare.[186]

Rise of the River Stour at Stourhead (The Swan's Nest), 1825, by J. M. W. Turner RA (1775–1851), watercolour, 763 × 1022 mm. Trustees of the Walter Morrison Collection, Sudeley Castle.

'All locomotion at an end': Colt Hoare in old age

The surly advance of decrepitude kept Colt Hoare at Stourhead for long periods.
He was a regular patient at Bath spa and in 1822 he toiled to Weymouth for the
saltwater cures. These were efficacious and he returned to the resort one or twice a
year for month-long treatments.[187] When gout permitted, he continued to travel for
pleasure. In the 1820s he visited his half-brother at Luscombe and Samuel Hasell
who was excavating Roman villas near Somerton.[188] Hasell was flattered by Colt's
attendance but apprehensive that he would steal his thunder by rushing into print.
Colt did precisely that, sweetening the takeover by bringing Crocker to survey the
sites and inviting Hasell to Stourhead.[189]

On the estate Colt created New Lake at Gasper. He continued to add ornamental
trees and shrubs around the Garden Lake and planted rhododendrons on the north
shore, 1828–31. In the village he laid out a flower garden beside the Bristol Cross.
Colt entered his final decade sound of mind but physically frail. In 1835 he wrote
dolefully to his protégé Robert Benson:

> I have indeed been a great invalid of late, but am now tolerably well, after
> a confinement of four months to my house, and eight repeated attacks

*Sir Richard Colt Hoare, 2nd
Baronet, aged 73–4 (1758–1838),
1832, by Stephen Catterson Smith
the elder (1806–72), chalk, 190 ×
170 mm. Stourhead.*

of rheumatism, but I fear my legs are past recovery, and all locomotion at an end.[190]

Colt published a further three Hundreds of *Modern Wiltshire*. He was well cared for; during the 1830s he retained five men and six women as indoor staff.[191] Bereavements encircled Colt and in 1836 his son Henry died. He recorded in the annals for 1834–35 the deaths of his head gardener, Bartholomew Lapham, and of his servant Robert Davis. He had employed both men for over half a century.

Colt Hoare lived to see Victoria succeed as Queen and expired on 19 May 1838, a few weeks before her coronation. Under the terms of Colt's will the property was placed in trust for his half-brother, Henry Hugh, as tenant-for-life and then to his son; in default the life interest would pass in turn to Colt Hoare's younger half-brothers and their eldest sons.[192] The inheritance as it played out may be followed in the Hoare family genealogy (pages 20–1).

The baronetcy and Stourhead Colt Hoare had inherited. In mid-life he set out to make a name as an author and from this ambition stemmed the publications: some beautiful, some informative, others obscure; there were enough to fill a shelf and earn him national status as a pioneer archaeologist and a place in the pantheon of Wiltshire luminaries. He handed on Stourhead enriched. The garden was a paradox: he added variety in the planting yet shrank its appeal by expunging his grandfather's exotic and whimsical follies.

Sir Henry Hugh Hoare, 3rd Baronet (1762–1841)

Sir Henry Hugh Hoare reunited Stourhead with the family bank where he had been a partner from 1785 and senior partner since 1828. At the death of his half-brother, Colt Hoare, he succeeded to Stourhead and the baronetcy. He was already a man of property having inherited Barn Elms from his father. He later purchased a house in St James's Square and a sporting estate at Wavendon in Buckinghamshire, where he enjoyed his leisure hours. These were plentiful: in 1809 he devoted eleven weeks to business.[1] His obituary described him as 'tall and of a fine manly form' and 'when not laid up by gout, he was to the last able to enjoy hunting, and other country amusements'.[2] His wife, Maria Palmer Acland, presented him with sixteen children, seven of whom were living in 1838.

When he moved to Stourhead, the 3rd baronet was in his late seventies and, with commendable energy, began to put the place in good order. He repaired the Pantheon, rebuilt the Obelisk and added the projecting portico to the house. He also placed the monument to Colt Hoare in Salisbury Cathedral. In the house the 3rd baronet modernised the service quarters but did not add to the collection; his portraits arrived there in 1895.[3] He was more concerned with securing the contents of Wavendon which included furniture and pictures from Barn Elms which he had sold in 1825.[4]

With the knowledge that Stourhead would pass to his son and his male heirs, Henry Hugh made a will leaving Wavendon to his second son and, in default, he prescribed a formula to preclude a future heir from inheriting both estates.[5]

Sir Hugh Richard Hoare, 4th Baronet (1787–1857)

Step inside Stourhead and the single reminder of the 4th baronet is his portrait depicting a benign old man, tubby and seated, gazing out under bushy eyebrows.[6] He is remembered for his improvements to the forestry and farms on the estate.

Hugh Richard grew up in London and at Wavendon and, like his father, he enjoyed the sporting life in Buckinghamshire. He married Anne, daughter of a county family, the Tyrwhitt-Drakes of Shardeloes. Hugh Richard rented Lillingstone near Buckingham to enjoy this affluent hunting society. The family bank also beckoned and in 1828 he was made a partner.[7]

He inherited the baronetcy and Stourhead in 1841 when he was in his mid-fifties and childless. The 4th baronet was rich enough to keep Lillingstone and he continued at the family bank until 1845 when he retired with an annuity of £5,200, later raised to £8,000.[8] Lady Hoare did not impinge on Stourhead though she probably derived comfort from the appointment of a relative, John Drake of Amersham, as rector of Stourton. She died in 1847 at 118 Eaton Terrace. Two years previously she had entertained her husband's nephew and heir, Henry Ainslie Hoare, at Stourhead.[9] The occasion marked the first leg of his honeymoon. The bride, Augusta East, delighted in everything about Stourhead; nevertheless the newlyweds were not invited to return because Ainslie was dismissed from Hoare's Bank for misconduct.[10]

This posed a problem for the 4th baronet. Stourhead would never be self-sufficient. In preparation for lean years ahead, he resolved to set the property in good order. He installed Cooper Cardwell from Buckinghamshire at the home farm, making him bailiff for the estate and, around 1851, he appointed another Buckinghamshire man, John Clarke, as land agent.[11]

The 4th baronet re-established the tree nursery on the plateau behind the Temple of Apollo.[12] He planted annually an average of 34,767 trees as a commercial crop. Whenever agricultural land on the estate became vacant he took it in hand. In the landscape garden he repaired buildings and planted new species of ornamental trees.

At the house the 4th baronet refurbished bedrooms and redesigned the domestic offices.[13] In 1847 he renovated the parish church. In the Stable Yard he replaced thatched roofs with tiles and, in the Kitchen Garden, remodelled the geranium glasshouse to grow pineapples, melons and grapes.

Sir Henry Ainslie Hoare, 5th Baronet (1824–94)

This Sir Henry possessed faults on a generous scale. He is vilified at Stourhead for selling Colt Hoare's library and the best pictures. His reputation stands equally low at the family bank from which he was dismissed thanks to his addiction to horseracing and gambling. During his lifetime this complex man was known as Henry, later, Sir Henry; subsequently he was referred to as Henry Ainslie or just Ainslie to differentiate him from his forebears and contemporaries.

Can we punch through this ice-crust of disapproval? Alone among the owners of Stourhead, Ainslie was a figure in the public eye, featuring frequently in the national and local press. He stood for Parliament on four occasions and was twice elected as a Liberal MP. He became an early champion of the Primrose League, formed in 1883 as a patriotic organisation pledged to support the Conservative Party to which Ainslie had defected.[14] Ainslie was energetic, egocentric and an accomplished public speaker. Two portraits of the man hang at Stourhead.[15] He was raised in London and at the family house at Wavendon where he acquired a lifelong passion for hunting from his father, Henry Charles Hoare. The latter was a none-too-active partner at the family bank, attending to business during lulls in the sporting calendar. Ainslie joined the bank in 1845, the year of his marriage to Augusta East (c.1821–1903).

The young couple settled into family accommodation in Fleet Street where they remained until his dismissal in 1848.[16] He then removed the family to France where the regime of Napoleon III held many excitements, not least for Ainslie who had a taste for the *douceur de vivre* and fast horses. His idyll was interrupted by the death

Sir Hugh Richard Hoare, 4th Baronet (1787–1857), c.1850, British School, oil on canvas, 127 × 101.6 cm. Stourhead.

of his father in 1852 and the loss of his only son two years later. Augusta preferred London, the security of her own family and a small circle of friends. The charms of the domestic hearth held no attraction for Ainslie and the couple led separate lives.

At the death of his uncle, Hugh Richard, in 1857 Ainslie inherited the life interest in Stourhead and the baronetcy. He was part of the establishment, if not the nobility, keen to enjoy, and take advantage of, the privileges this status afforded him. His restlessness came from enormous physical energy and precarious finances. His handwriting betrays this impatience and he was unable to settle anywhere for more than a few weeks at a time. He continued to frequent France where, away from family, he could resume his saturnalia. From Paris, Ainslie wrote regularly to his mother. His letters prove him nimble-minded, entertaining and popular.[17] He was welcome in ambassadorial circles and a habitué of Longchamp and Chantilly.

In the 1860s Ainslie became interested in British politics and was elected Liberal MP for New Windsor in 1865, although promptly unseated for bribing the electors. He had better luck three years later when he became one of the two Liberal MPs returned to Parliament by the new constituency of Chelsea.[18] He was an assertive public speaker; nevertheless he was defeated in the 1874 election and returned to Paris. His jaded character might have qualified him for a minor role in the Palliser novels. During the 1880s Ainslie deserted the Liberal Party and stood as Conservative candidate for East Somerset in 1885. Neither local newspapers nor voters were persuaded by this switch of allegiance. He took defeat with a rare lack of grace:

> Sir Henry Hoare, was greeted with a volley of groaning, and it was a minute or two before he could make himself heard. When the noise had a little subsided he said… I am ashamed of you for the way in which you are behaving to a defeated opponent (more hooting)… Many of you have stated I was a turncoat (hear, hear, and 'so you are') now you have got 800 turncoats in Somerset, who have for some reasons promised to vote for me and have voted against me (applause and hooting). I wish you a very good day, gentlemen. [19]

Ainslie's neighbour, Henry Hobhouse of Hadspen, was the victorious Liberal candidate. To the consternation of Augusta, he promptly closed up Stourhead, never to return, and retreated to Paris. At last his superabundant energy was spent; stricken he limped home to his wife and expired at their London house in July 1894.

When Ainslie inherited Stourhead in 1857, he was a stranger to the place. As a sporting man he relished hunting and steeplechasing. The family took up residence in Wiltshire each year from July to early October or, more accurately, Ainslie settled his wife at Stourhead while he came and went. He was not cut out to be a country squire but he began in style making repairs to the house and collection.[20] His printed instructions for sweeping the chimney flues identified those to be climbed and disclosed that there was a Turkish bath in the basement.[21] Early on Ainslie laid out an Italian garden between the library and glasshouse.[22] But he was bored by the vicissitudes of domestic life; his instructions went unheeded and as a consequence chimneys caught fire and the roofs leaked with increasing frequency as the years went by.[23]

In 1863 Robert Shackleton was appointed land agent and continued in the post for the remainder of Ainslie's life, becoming a family friend. Shackleton kept appointment diaries recording daily meetings with Ainslie when he was at Stourhead, often continuing late into the night as they poured over the accounts together.[24] When his master was absent, Shackleton wrote regularly and Ainslie immersed himself in the business of the estate which was well cared for until the 1870s. Unfortunately, after an initial flourish, Ainslie discontinued the Stourhead Annals so that a gap exists from 1861 to 1894. Ainslie had no appetite to alter the fundamentals of the garden; he respected them while deploring the cost of maintenance. Before 1861, the annals record that he planted 124,278 trees in the woods.[25] Forestry was a staple of the estate and, during the lean years ahead, sales of timber provided much-needed income. In the 1870s cheap wheat from the United Sates entered Britain and the price of grain fell. This coincided with a row of summers with bad weather which hit farmers. Stourhead had the timber business and more pasture than arable land so was well placed to endure the agricultural

Sir Henry Ainslie Hoare, 5th Baronet (1824–94) 'a reformed radical', 1883, by 'Spy', Sir Leslie Matthew Ward (1851–1922), chromolithograph from *Vanity Fair*, 359 × 242 mm. Stourhead.

depression ahead. Rents reached a peak of over £18,000 per annum in 1876, then fell by £2,700.[26] Ainslie, perpetually short of money, was in no position to subsidise the estate and was precluded under the settlement from selling land. Shackleton made efforts to economise: throughout 1880 *The Western Gazette* advertised garden produce for sale from Stourhead and, on 24 September, it announced a 10 per cent abatement in rent for Ainslie's tenants ready to pay immediately.[27] In 1885 he let the shooting rights on 4,500 acres of the estate.[28] At this time Ainslie frequently consulted his lawyer, Thomas Stevens of Longbourne, Longbourne and Stevens and, from 1879 onwards, Shackleton took to visiting their office in London. The family bank, itself struggling, held the mortgage on the property and thus had an interest in its financial viability.

Seeking further economies, Ainslie attempted to rent out the house but no tenant stepped forward and he resorted to raising money by selling the most valuable contents of Stourhead. There were two obstacles: Colt Hoare's settlement specifically prohibited a sale of the heirlooms. This could only be broken by Act of Parliament and for that Ainslie would require the cooperation of the heir apparent, his cousin, Henry Hugh Arthur, then a boy of sixteen. So Ainslie had to deal with the guardians who were the young man's mother, Julia Hoare, and his maternal grandfather, Thomas Veale Lane. Correspondence written by the guardians' solicitor, Henry Tylee, exists along with the copies he made of letters from Thomas Stevens, acting for Ainslie.[29]

In December 1881 Ainslie informed the guardians he wished to sell and that he required their consent. The Stourhead Settled Estates Act received the royal assent in August 1882. It set out the terms of the original settlement and recounted how the inheritance had played out. It recorded the mortgage originally taken out to pay the annuities and other obligations left by Colt Hoare. The debt stood at £21,757. The trustees were permitted to sell the heirlooms, valued at £50,000, provided both Ainslie and Henry Hugh Arthur agreed the items available. Finally, the Act laid down that the proceeds could be used to pay the legal costs of the Act and redeem the mortgage. The remainder was to be held in trust under the provisions of the original settlement; in other words it was to be dedicated to Stourhead.

Of course this was not the only estate in trouble at the time. Throughout Britain, the value of agricultural land had declined and rents had fallen into arrears or were reduced. Many estates, like Stourhead, were held in trust which impeded change of ownership. Parliament addressed this problem with the Settled Land Act in 1882 (passed eight days prior to the Stourhead Act). The new law gave tenants for life wider powers of dealing with land without the need for applications to court or private Acts. Henceforth they could sell entailed land provided the proceeds were paid into court or to trustees, thus protecting the property of the beneficiaries. In this respect the powers it gave were wider than those granted by the Stourhead Settled Estates Act, but the public Act related to land, not chattels. That did not stop Stevens arguing, on behalf of Ainslie, that he could proceed without the guardians' consent, as empowered by the public Act. Happily this threat remained untested.[30]

In November 1882 Stevens sent the guardians a preliminary list of proposed sales comprising paintings, ceramics and flashy furniture, including *pietre dure*, but not the

Sixtus Cabinet.[31] A supplemental list followed with more pictures.[32] Both sides agreed that family portraits were sacrosanct. Furniture and ceramics sold on 1 June for £2,085 and the pictures on the following day raised a further £9,832.[33] The most valuable picture by far was Gainsborough's *Peasants going to Market* which fetched £2,835.[34]

Meanwhile, a row was brewing over the sale of the library. The guardians consented to the sale in principle on condition they could vet the list of books. Henry Tylee was dismayed therefore to find that the Sotheby printed catalogue included manuscripts and drawings by Colt Hoare which the guardians had specifically requested be omitted.[35] In reply Stevens rehearsed boneless excuses made by Ainslie and offered an assurance that these lots could be bought in.[36] Once again they compromised; the sale went ahead from 30 July to 8 August and some lots were withdrawn.[37] That auction raised £8,066, after commission.[38]

Ainslie also negotiated private sales from Stourhead. Prior to the auctions he sold two Sèvres china vases, and 'the Marie Antoinette Cabinets & the Armada Medal' for £15,000; the purchaser also paid the expenses of the Act.[39] In July 1883 Ainslie disposed of two more paintings for £6,000.[40] These appear to have been a lesser work by Gainsborough, *Two children and a cat,* and Reynolds's sugary portrait of *Master Henry Hoare (1784–1836) as a boy gardening.*[41]

In total Ainslie had raised £40,000.[42] That was not the end of the matter. In July 1884 Christie's auctioned silver from Stourhead in seventy-four lots, raising over £1,500.[43] In December 1887, Sotheby's sold a second instalment from the library comprising 1,313 lots. Among these were more drawings by Colt Hoare including those of Southern Italy and Sicily held back in 1883. In 1887 Ainslie reached agreement with his cousin, Henry Hugh Arthur, to break the entail imposed by Colt Hoare. Under a new compact they both acquired annuities, financed by a new £45,000 mortgage on Stourhead, which took the purr out of the heirloom sales because the debt these should have expunged was thereby regenerated and doubled.[44]

Augusta, Lady Hoare endured as best she could the indignities of her husband's failed careers and the anguish of the heirloom sales. In her daily diary the private Ainslie stands revealed: his restless travelling, his crowded social life in which she played so little part and his occasional indulgences towards her. We learn about her frequent illnesses and recoveries; indeed her resilience is astonishing and she outlived Ainslie and died at the age of eighty-four.

Her father, Sir George Clayton East, 1st Baronet (1794–1851), inherited Hall Place near Hurley. Of his eight children all except Augusta died before 1866. Yachting rather than hunting was the family pastime and Cowes week the high point of their year. Augusta remained closer to her family than to Ainslie's relatives. Of her two children, her daughter Augusta – known as Gussy – survived to adulthood. In 1868 Gussy married William Angerstein whose delinquencies increased with age. They had four children to whom Augusta acted as guardian while her daughter attempted

'Harry C. A. Hoare, Alda Hoare, (Sweep), Henry H. A. Hoare, Barry Phillpotts, Julia Hoare, Percy Philpotts. This photograph of the three generations taken at Stourhead Octr 4th 1912, being Alda & Henry's Silver Wedding Day', photograph, 170 × 210 mm. Stourhead.

to curb Angerstein's excesses. The young brought this simple-hearted woman her greatest happiness, in particular during their annual summer holidays at Stourhead.

Leighton's wistful portrait of Augusta hangs in the Entrance Hall at Stourhead.[45] She fulfilled her role as chatelaine with disturbing charm, attending church and visiting the sick of Stourton. The house was open to the public and Augusta recorded 128 visitors on 23 July 1858. Her diary entry for 9 August 1882 is exceptional:

> the finest day ever seen. I gave tea in front Hall [at Stourhead] to 84 of the school children… They played games on lawn & we walked round Lake to finish – the dear children giving us hearty cheers in Pantheon – one of the happiest days I ever spent.[46]

Inevitably Ainslie and Augusta are remembered at Stourhead for depleting the collection. They made no fundamental change to either the landscape garden or the house: had they the financial resources, might they have done otherwise?

Sir Henry Hoare, 6th Baronet (1865–1947)

The photograph taken at the silver wedding celebration of the 6th baronet and his wife stars Lady Hoare, resplendent in white (previous page); yet there is something disquieting about her appearance – what that might be, will emerge. The couple presided at Stourhead for half a century, steering the property through two world wars and the menace of taxes that threatened to extinguish the landed gentry. Sir Henry and Lady Hoare dedicated themselves to Stourhead: they restored the house twice: once on inheriting in 1894, again after the 1902 fire. They returned the garden to glory in the 1890s, and again after the Great War. Under Sir Henry's management the home farm flourished and the woods produced quantities of timber important in the war efforts and useful as income. At the death of 'Harry', their only son, in 1917, they were bereft; neither recovered emotionally from this cataclysm and their anguish complicated a thirty-year quest for an heir. Tenants and friends spoke no ill-word about Sir Henry and Lady Hoare; their kindness and sense of duty were admired throughout the neighbourhood.

Henry Hugh Arthur Hoare, henceforth referred to as Sir Henry or the 6th baronet, was born in 1865. He was brought up at Wavendon where his mother, Julia Hoare, presided after his father died in 1873. On her son's behalf, Julia had sparred with Ainslie over the heirloom sales but, at some point, mother and son fell out, probably in 1887 when Henry married his cousin, Alda Weston (1861–1947). The newlyweds settled at Wavendon Manor and succeeded Julia at the principal house two years later.[47] Soon after inheriting the baronetcy in July 1894, Sir Henry moved to Stourhead and let the Buckinghamshire houses. He was a countryman with a love of hunting and farming and, as an owner of a respected stable of percherons, was also a popular judge at horse trials and county shows. On moving to Wiltshire he was appointed a director of the Wiltshire and Dorset Banking Company (later Lloyds Bank) in Salisbury where he attended every Wednesday, a commitment he placed above hunting which occupied his winter days. On summer evenings he fished New Lake.

Around 10 a.m. on 16 April 1902 a spark from a bedroom hearth in Stourhead began a fire which burned beyond the servants' control and spread to the attics.[48] Fire fighters summoned lacked an adequate water supply to extinguish the blaze and turned their efforts to removing the pictures and furnishings from the *piano nobile*. They accomplished this before the roof collapsed destroying ceilings and wall decorations in the centre block. Sir Henry and Lady Hoare had separate errands that day and returned to Stourhead as fire crept towards the Picture Gallery and Library to be staunched in the nick of time. The rest of the house was a shell and around it the contents lay strewn across the lawns. The unhappy pair commandeered the agent's house in the village where they had begun seven years previously. Stourhead was fully insured and the following day Sir Henry, the solicitor, Thomas Stevens, and the architect, Edward Doran Webb (1864–1931), met to plan the restoration. Doran Webb was a family friend and had designed the south terrace. His practice was predominantly ecclesiastical with an antiquarian bent; sadly he had neither sufficient experience of country houses, nor the wit to recruit expert help. Harry Hoare laid the first stone on 16 June 1902 and Webb's preferred building firm, Trask

from Norton sub Hamdon, began work.[49] At first Doran Webb could clothe his
lack of experience in arrogance which the Hoares went along with until they moved
back to the southern rooms in July 1904 and discovered the house reverberated like
a drum, with voices and other more ominous sounds, because the architect had
omitted insulation.[50] At this point Sir Henry summoned Sir Aston Webb (1849–
1930), no relative of Doran, but with a national reputation for grand private and
public commissions, notably the Cromwell Road façade of the Victoria and Albert
Museum (1899), the Mall (1901), and subsequently Admiralty Arch (1908) and the
east front of Buckingham Palace (1913). Aston Webb prescribed doubling the joists
and more insulation, a disruptive cure, only partially successful. Worse followed. In
March 1905 a chimney caught fire and the ceilings in the Entrance Hall and Saloon
were found to have sagged more than two inches.[51] At this time of crisis Sir Henry
had taken his son to convalesce in Egypt, leaving Lady Hoare and the solicitor to deal
with the renovation because Doran Webb had became elusive. When Lady Hoare
confronted the architect 'I was not out of temper but firm', she wrote; the interview
was brief and he left 'without adieu'.[52] Stevens struggled to keep the peace and might
have succeeded had not Mrs Doran Webb penned a vaudeville provocation to Lady
Hoare, 'Mr Webb is seriously ill from the effects, & if he is to continue his work
at Stourhead it can only be done by you standing aside; otherwise I must bring all
the influence I can bear on him to throw up the whole thing <u>and at once</u>.'[53] Lady
Hoare, in high dudgeon, accepted his resignation while the luckless architect wrote
defending his record, signing off melodramatically 'I shall leave for France by the last
train from here on Friday'.[54] When Sir Henry returned he engaged Sir Aston Web
and his son Maurice to make good the defects and complete the restoration.

　　Who then 'designed' the new Stourhead? Doran Webb produced few plans
and working drawings, a shortcoming noted by Stevens.[55] The craftsmen seem to
have relied on photographs of the interior taken in 1900 and that may account
for the flat and fleshy appearance of the decorative carving. Sir Henry wished the

'V.A. Hospital, Mere, Wilts.',
photograph, 90 × 140 mm.
Annotated by Alda, Lady Hoare
'Myself in Hat & "my" Soldiers
June 1918'. Stourhead.

house reinstated but not completely replicated; for example, Doran Webb designed the Staircase Hall and Saloon, both botched jobs. The detail too is Edwardian as evidenced by the numerous polished mahogany doors, teak parquet, copper fireplace hoods and predominant white glossy paintwork. Outside, Doran Webb designed the unimposing west front while Maurice Webb added the steps. To enliven this façade Sir Henry moved lead sculpture from the Temple of Apollo (page 197). In a word, the restoration was chaotic, yet by the summer of 1906 the task was accomplished for £35,000 and under budget.[56] Sir Henry learned disparate and valuable lessons: to accept the limitations of local builders; to maintain an up to date inventory of the contents and to guarantee a reliable water supply for fire fighting – hence his preoccupation with the pumping station and private reservoir (page 231). Lady Hoare was not Doran Webb's nemesis; he wended his Catholic way designing religious buildings including Birmingham Oratory (1907) and Blackfriars Priory in Oxford (1929).

Days before 4 August 1914, when Britain declared war on Germany, Sir Henry's son enlisted with the Queen's Own Dorset Yeomanry, while the 6th baronet himself was appointed a military purchasing officer for the army, charged with acquiring horses in the neighbourhood. He was also host to visiting army units. That autumn four officers and twenty men of the 7th Battalion of the Berkshires were billeted at Stourhead. In April 1915 came a brief visit from a division of Cyclists, comprising four officers and 120 men, followed by three companies of Royal Engineers, in several visitations each of eighty men, with an officer. The officers lodged at the house, the men were billeted on the estate.[57] In 1916, Lady Hoare was preoccupied by the fate of her son who was serving in Palestine. Nevertheless she busied herself entertaining soldiers convalescing at the Red Cross hospital in Mere.

On 3 September 1939, at the beginning of the Second World War, Sir Henry was seventy-three and his wife four years his senior. They were failing physically but not in spirit and they struggled to sustain their stately lives. To Stourhead came a succession of army formations, again accommodated in the house and on the estate. A thousand men from the 7th Battalion of the Devonshire Regiment arrived on 5 September and remained on the property until the end of November, twenty officers lodging at the house. There followed detachments of about a hundred men from the 47th Division of the Royal Signals Corps for three months. 'A' squadron of the Liaison Regiment, comprising five officers and fifty men were stationed at Stourhead from March 1941 to October 1942. From 1943 to 1944 the Hoares were hosts to three more units.[58] Sir Henry maintained the troops were no trouble. Not so the domestic staff, with whom Lady Hoare conducted a private war, enforcing obsolete standards of service. The turnover was brisk. Towards the end the elderly and demanding owners were cared for by two or three hostile and transient servants, where formerly the indoor staff had numbered twelve.[59] The house grew shabby in wartime and the laundress recalled heavily darned sheets and window curtains in tatters.[60]

Alda, Lady Hoare, née Weston (1861–1947), the chatelaine of Stourhead, was a diva in everything but name. Her mother, Alda Gertrude Lethbridge, was a granddaughter of Henry Hugh Hoare, 3rd Baronet, and had married W. H. Purcell

Weston in 1857. They lived in Dorset, latterly at Wolfeton House. After ten years of marriage Alda the elder fled with two daughters and her lover, Andrew Quicke. They settled in Paris and later Brussels where Alda the younger was educated, providing her with a grounding in French language and literature. Alda the younger remained a Francophile for the rest of her life, habitually scanning *L'Écho de Paris* at Stourhead. She returned to Britain and was reunited with her father, but her happiest days were spent at Wavendon. She had known the future Sir Henry since early childhood and in 1887 they married.[61]

When Alda, now, Lady Hoare, reached Stourhead she was thirty-four years old and her personality and tastes were defined: she was devoted to her husband and son, teetotal, vain, thirsty for affection, impatient in the company of her own sex and a hoarder of possessions and memories. This we learn from her diaries, which are heavily underscored and peppered with exclamation marks to dramatise her pile-driving prose. Convalescent soldiers at Mere touched her heart. On 26 October 1916 she wrote 'no one can help see my Tommies love me – Henry, & everyone, sees it – and I am so proud of their affection; & love them'. She held regular parties at Stourhead, giving the men the run of the house and garden. On 23 September 1916 she entertained twenty-six convalescents, providing a lavish tea and playing the piano as they sang for her. Rationing, imposed in 1918, put a stop to tea parties on a grand scale. Thereafter Lady Hoare would motor to Mere hospital to play the piano and distribute cigarettes. The men appreciated her *savoir vivre* and she in turn delighted in the adulation, even able to laugh at herself:

> 'What!!!' Said my "Tommy", 'You've been married 30 years, my lady??
> Well!! No one would ever, think it' 'Really!' I Said, 'You ought to be
> ashamed to talk such nonsense!!!' 'No, but I mean it – You look quite
> young to me!' he says, quite earnestly. For one minute I eye him... &
> then, seeing that <u>actually</u> he seems to mean it (!!) I lift my shoulders &
> spreading my hands to the others to express how <u>hopeless</u> he appears
> to me, I go off into an uncontrollable, really hearty, fit of laughing, in
> which every man joins.[62]

After the death of her son, wounded in action in 1917, Lady Hoare met society on revised terms: she shunned weddings, funerals, garden parties, fetes and balls and declined to accompany Sir Henry to county events. She lost her appetite for posing in photographs, hitherto a conspicuous vanity. No record of her appearance seems to exist after 1918 beyond the written word.[63] Lady Hoare detested sleeping a single night away from Stourhead and travelled to London for the day by train to be fitted for new reading spectacles and corsets. Her tailors operated in Bath. But Lady Hoare was no recluse and she welcomed family and friends as guests at Stourhead and entertained them in style. Following success with 'her Tommies' she was keen that the public should visit the house and garden and welcomed in particular pupils from Downside School and the local boy scouts. She frequently set forth with the chauffeur to pay calls around the neighbourhood, visiting tenants and chatelaines of country houses, noting carefully hostesses who were 'in' or 'out' on her arrival. It is untrue to say Lady Hoare disliked all women; she had compassion for those at a disadvantage, specifically the poor of Stourton, dowager duchesses and the wives of Thomas Hardy.

The novelist himself was her prize and his three-day visit to Stourhead in July 1914 marked an apex of happiness for Lady Hoare.[64] A rung below Hardy came Charles Whibley, fellow Francophile, essayist and biographer of Pitt the younger. He was the tenant at Wavendon Manor and a family friend.[65] Lady Hoare was an avid reader, despite weak eyesight: she enjoyed novels and biographies of a conventional nature. The same applied to her taste in pictures. She admired work by Sergent but disdained Augustus John. Among the galaxy of living French artists she bought Théophile Steinlen. Sir Henry and Lady Hoare were patrons of several artists, each an appreciative house guest, none with an enduring reputation. The collection of

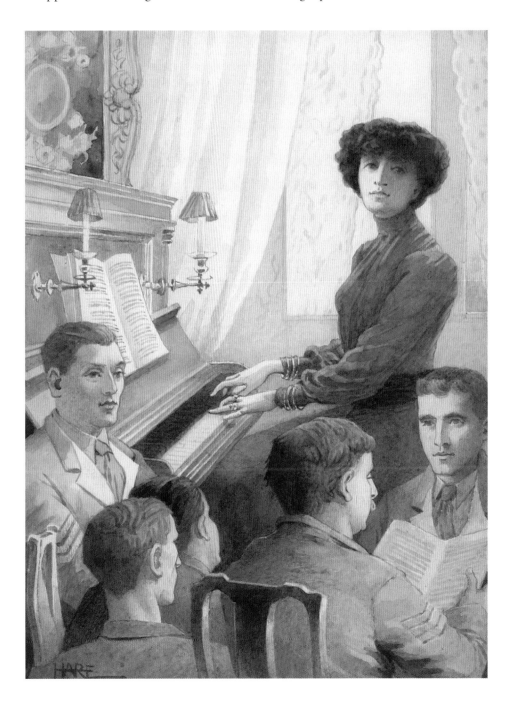

'Lady Hoare at the piano with her 'boys', c.1917, by St George Hare (1857–1933), pen and sepia wash, 270 × 200 mm. Stourhead.

paintings by St George Hare is a social rather than aesthetic phenomenon and stirs controversy to this day. Although his female nudes are once again banished to the storeroom at Stourhead, there remain his portraits: disquieting likenesses of Lady Hoare or men wreathed in tobacco smoke.

Sir Henry and Lady Hoare welcomed museum curators and were delighted by their discoveries at Stourhead; thus Ralph Edwards, from the Victoria and Albert Museum, visited Stourhead in 1923. He identified furniture made by Chippendale the younger whose bills Lady Hoare had looked out for him and he illustrated fifteen pieces from the house in the *Dictionary of English Furniture*.[66] Mrs Esdaile, expert on Roubiliac, struck up a friendship with Lady Hoare who, it must be hoped, saw the comic side of the scholar's overture, 'Dear Lady Hoare, I really am thrilled over your bust!!'[67] (She referred to a plaster portrait-bust of Alexander Pope.)

Lady Hoare's predilections in architecture were also conservative. She deplored Clouds and Bryanston House, two mansions completed in the 1890s, and was charmed by old houses such as Brympton d'Evercy. She found much to admire at Wardour, that Georgian barracks, where the Dowager Lady Arundell entertained her in 'the huge room wherein all still was arranged in the style of 60 years ago'.[68] Photographs of the principal rooms at Stourhead *c.*1900 show walls crowded by pictures and floors congested with furniture on which regiments of china ornaments paraded. Chairs were upholstered in multiple patterns while a forest of palms reared ceiling-wards.

After the fire Lady Hoare reinstated these ensembles, which survived up to 1947. Rooms were never shut up or shrouded by dust-sheets because Lady Hoare preferred to keep the house in readiness for visitors and guests. She moved 'her headquarters' from room to room according to the seasons; her sanctum was a boudoir adjoining her bedroom and overlooking the main drive. Lady Hoare preserved her son's study and bedroom as he left them after being home on sick leave in July 1916. They remained untouched until her death.

Sir Henry had inherited Stourhead and its satellite properties, comprising 11,262 acres (4,557 hectares).[69] From his father he acquired estates at Wavendon and Oxenham in Devonshire. The prospect of a land tax in 1909 frightened Sir Henry into selling his outlying land to consolidate at Stourhead. In the annals he recorded the prices achieved over a period of twenty years.[70]

1911	Oxenham 1,000 acres[71]	£12,305
1911	Stourton Caundle & Purse Caundle, 2,912 acres[72]	£34,824
1912–13	West Knoyle, 1,782 acres[73]	£30,000
1913–14	Oxenham Manor, 336 acres[74]	£6,935
1918	Bruton, Castle Cary and portions of Brewham, 2,869 acres[75]	£78,784
1919	Wavendon, 1,018 acres[76]	£45,000
1920	Brewham	£25,465
1932	Oxenham, remnant	£3,305

The 1911 sales repaid the mortgage placed upon the property by his predecessor and altogether these disposals raised £236,618 which Sir Henry could devote to Stourhead.

On his arrival there in 1895 he faced the task of taming the landscape garden by clearing laurels and pruning back trees and rhododendrons which threatened to engulf the buildings and shoreline. On the eve of the Great War he completed the task only to watch as the garden slipped backwards again. After 1918 Sir Henry recommenced the process.

There is a long-held belief that, while Lady Hoare reigned at the house, Sir Henry ruled the garden and estate. But, given the closeness of the marriage, it is no surprise that Lady Hoare's influence was universal in all but sporting matters. Almost daily she walked the grounds and when entertaining house guests led them down through the Shades to the lake shore where they might board a boat or stroll to the village. Indeed, when the Hoares had trouble with the land agent in 1920, Lady Hoare temporarily took charge in the gardens.[77]

Among Sir Henry's early purchases for Stourhead was a saw bench to supply posts and rails for tenants willing to replace barbed wire fencing which impeded the hunt.[78] He was interested in forestry for commercial and aesthetic reasons and recorded in the Stourhead Annals each year new trees and their locations. During his fifty years in residence he planted over a million forest trees. The woods lie predominantly on the western side of the estate towards Penselwood in the south, and up to King's Wood Warren at Brewham in the north. In 1895 the plantations were depleted and a great storm three years later hastened the task of renewal. Sir Henry's favourite commercial crops were Douglas fir and Japanese larch which flourish on the estate. He experimented successfully with natural regeneration of ash trees on Park Hill. During the Great War the Admiralty Collieries at Cwmtillery purchased quantities of larch as pitwood.[79] After the war landowners were encouraged to lease the Forestry Commission woodland and, in the light of tax advantages, Sir Henry and his neighbour, the Marquis of Bath, sold the government long leases on land. At Stourhead these comprised: King's Wood and King's Wood Warren to the north, and Newpark Wood to the south-west.[80] Come the Second World War, Sir Henry once more stepped up timber sales.

In 1917 Sir Henry had taken the Home Farm in hand and purchased a herd of dairy shorthorn cattle.[81] The breed proved an asset: during the Second World War profits at the farm rose from £1,026 to £6,404.[82]

Sir Henry was less successful in providing water to the estate. It was not for want of trying and the annals record the purchase of larger pumps and new pipework (page 132). Despite the drop in population from around 650 in 1831 to below 400 in 1931, the system could not keep up with demand.[83]

Lady Hoare doted on her only son, Captain Henry Colt Arthur Hoare (1888–1917), known in the family as Harry. In July 1909 his twenty-first birthday was celebrated by his parents, the tenants and employees. After graduating from Cambridge he was made land agent at Stourhead working under the watchful eyes of his father and the family solicitor.[84] The Duchess of Somerset deemed Harry eligible for two nieces

but neither won his heart and prompted his remark 'Somehow I've an idea I'll never marry – that there'll be no children of mine, here'.[85] It would be a bold fiancée who measured up to Lady Hoare.

At the outbreak of the Great War, Harry joined the Dorset Yeomanry, fighting in the Dardanelles with valour and distinction until wounded. He was invalided home in 1916, recovered, rejoined the regiment, was posted to Palestine and wounded again. Already in poor health, Harry died in the military hospital at Alexandria on 20 December 1917, at the age of twenty-nine. The news reached his parents on Christmas Eve. Dark ripples of bereavement convulsed them.

His death was indeed a cruel blow. Henceforth Lady Hoare's leisure moments were consumed in tearful retrospection. Over fifty, she could not hope for a second child and the quest for an heir to Stourhead began among the relatives. Next in line for the baronetcy stood Peter Hoare of Luscombe, then his son and namesake. But Sir Henry and Lady Hoare had taken umbrage at the Luscombe family's inadequate response to Harry's death.[86] The Hoares at Ellisfield Manor near Basingstoke made themselves agreeable and invited Sir Henry and Lady Hoare to stay in 1920. They accepted, despite Lady Hoare's aversion to sleeping away from home.[87] That year their son, Henry Peregrine Rennie Hoare (1901–81), made a favourable impression at Stourhead.[88] Sir Henry remained undecided. Three years later Lady Hoare was much taken by the young Peter of Luscombe when he visited Stourhead but she maintained a glacial hostility towards the parents.[89] Both Rennie and Peter had careers in the family bank. In the 1920s Sir Henry had wished to leave the estate to the bank for use by the partners but upon conditions which precluded acceptance.[90]

Finances, as much as lineage, played a part in determining the future of Stourhead. Taxation was rising. In 1919 death duties were charged at 40 per cent

on estates valued over two million pounds and, by 1946, rose to 75 per cent and the threshold lowered. During the Second World War the highest rate of income tax reached 99 per cent. Against this background the National Trust had announced its Country House Scheme in 1936. In return for giving an estate to the Trust, with sufficient land or investments to endow the place, the previous owner could continue to live there under the terms of a memorandum of wishes.[91] The property itself must be of outstanding national importance, a matter decided by the Trust's governing committee, and in return the Trust would declare the property

Henry Colt Arthur Hoare (1888– 1917), 1909, by St George Hare (1857–1933), oil on canvas, 161.9 × 95.3 cm. Stourhead.

inalienable, so that it could be disposed of only by Act of Parliament. Under successive finance Acts, gifts of property and of endowment funds to the Trust were exempted from death duty. As a charity, the Trust paid no taxes. Thus an estate's income, freed from taxation, had a better chance of matching expenditure. Sir Henry took up the Trust's invitation to join the scheme; indeed Stourhead was the first country house and garden assessed, and approved, by its committee. When war came Trust employees found themselves helping Sir Henry with a variety of estate matters as well as recruiting servants on their behalf.

Sir Henry gave Stourhead to the Trust in 1946. His munificent gift included the garden, house and art together with enough land to endow the property. In practice this meant dividing the estate in two, the eastern half, comprising 3,002 acres (1,215 hectares) passing to the Trust. Sir Henry left the remaining 2,215 acres to Rennie Hoare.[92] Under his memorandum of wishes Sir Henry requested that his heirs should occupy the house and that the estate should so far as practical continue to be managed as a single entity.[93] He bequeathed the Home Farm pedigree cattle to the Trust after securing a loose-worded pledge that it would continue the herd after his death.[94]

Sir Henry and Lady Hoare died within hours of one another on 25 March 1947. His unsettled estate was valued at £267,090, which was taxed at £116,041. He left legacies to Lady Hoare and long-serving employees.[95] Lady Hoare died intestate; her estate was assessed at under £1,500.[96] Generous, worthy, God-fearing Victorians, they could go forward to meet their maker with clear consciences.

Stourton, meet of the South and West Wilts Hunt, c.1911, photo. Stourhead.

HISTORY OF
THE GARDEN

THE STOURTON
DEMESNE 1700–42

PREVIOUS PAGES
From the Temple of Flora towards
the Temple of Apollo.

OPPOSITE
Houses opposite St Peter's church.

BELOW
Detail from the 1722 plan of
Stourhead, unknown, ink and
tempera on parchment, 340 ×
705 mm. Wiltshire and Swindon
History Centre.

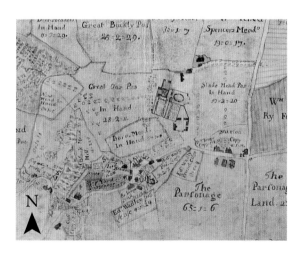

S oon after acquiring the Stourton estate Good Henry made his presence felt by demolishing the old house and replacing it with a Palladian villa set in formal surroundings (page 34). For locals the arrival of the banking dynasty brought much-needed wealth to the estate.[1]

The River Stour rises north-west of Stourton village, in the valley known as Six Wells Bottom. The 1722 plan indicates the sides of this valley clothed in woods which peter out as they reach the village. The Lords Stourton had dammed the stream to form five ponds. The plan depicts three dart-shaped pools followed by two larger expanses of water, the first adjacent to a withy bed. The second, known as the Great Mill Pond, was assessed in 1703 as covering almost four acres.[2] These lower ponds were flanked by two narrow and, one suspects, boggy pastures let to the miller. A third piece of land is identified as arable and assigned to the parson. A spring fed the village water supply which is marked on the plan as a square basin and designated 'Paradice Pond'.

Good Henry purchased unspecified trees but whether for the valley or the plateau is unrecorded.[3] The village itself was strung loosely from St Peter's Church to a smaller group of dwellings on high ground to the east.

St Peter's Church, Stourton

The church at Stourton dates from c.1300 with a north aisle and clerestory added two hundred years later.[4] Good Henry, a devout Protestant, employed Nathaniel Ireson to restore the building, 1722–3, and he presented new Communion plate.[5] His monument, along with his son's, was moved from the chancel to the south aisle when it was built in 1847. In 1808 John Skinner had complained that 'the inside is rendered dark and heavy, by a gloomy wash of lead colour over the walls'.[6] The nave today is equally bleak because in 1910 the plaster was stripped from the walls and in 1937 the east window was immured.

Mills

The Domesday Book recorded two mills at Stourton.[7] In 1651 a 'Grist Mill' (corn) and 'Mault Mill' were leased as one holding by William, 11th Lord Stourton.[8] In 1735 Henry the Magnificent let the 'Cascade Mill beside Black Mead' to Robert Turner.[9] The mill stood close to the site of the Pantheon and is marked on the 1722 plan.[10]

In 1724 Good Henry Hoare enlarged the withy pond by heightening the dam to provide water power for 'Mr Benson's Ingine'. Under the contract for this dam, John Humphry undertook:

> to dig barrow and well lay and ram as many yards of earth to the Wythybed pond head as will raise the same five foot higher than it now is with good Substantiall and proportional side and leat and to be fifteen foot Wyde on yᵉ Top and to be well Ram'd and Substantialy Closed so as hold water from time to time and at all times.[11]

'Mr Benson's Ingine' (demolished)

Stourhead stands about 150 feet above the valley floor where the River Stour rises.[12] The Lords Stourton were content with well-water. Good Henry wished to pump spring water to the house.[13] Switzer had described and illustrated a variety of chain pumps driven by water or horse-power.[14] Henry enlisted help from his brother-in-law, William Benson, who had a penchant for hydraulics and a tame prelate at Amesbury at his disposal. This was Thomas Holland who appeared more interested in hydraulics than parishioners. 'Mr Benson's Ingine' is named in the contract which Henry made in 1724 with a Joseph Andrews to supply water to the house piped from springs in the valley.[15]

Andrews had first to put one of Benson's pumps in working order and build a housing.[16] It probably resembled the contraption installed at Wanstead, in Essex, and described by Desaguliers. This pump was powered by an undershot water wheel 30 feet in diameter and comprised a pump with four barrels or 'forcers'.[17] The Stourhead pump was also powered by a water wheel but operating three barrels.[18] In truth, these were not Benson's invention; they were chain pumps with a refinement patented by Holland.[19]

At Stourhead Andrews quoted for lead piping from the 'Whithybed Pond' to

St Peter's Church, Stourton, 1793, by Lancelot-Henri Roland Turpin de Crissé (1754–c.1800), pencil, 210 × 340 mm. Musées d'Angers.

the top of 'Parradice Coppice', then elm pipes to feed a reservoir and 'Drying Yard' before reaching a cistern in the house. The 1722 plan identifies 'Parradice Pond', the site of the Temple of Flora and, by implication, Paradise Coppice rose up the hill behind.[20] The withy bed or willow pond is not named on the plan; it was probably located close to the Grotto. Good Henry had enlarged the dam to create sufficient force of water to power the wheel. Andrews made adjustments to the system in 1744.[21] In 1749 the rhymer of 'Stourton Gardens' admired:

> See yonder engine! mark each curious part
> Where nature's pow'r is overpower'd by art!
> Water that downward tends its boisterous tide
> Wondrous! ascends a lofty mountain's side.[22]

The disc-like pond on the axis of the south front of Stourhead is probably the tangible evidence of the pump's prowess, or lack of it (page 34).[23] When water reached the house it was undrinkable, as Andrews himself had predicted.[24] By 1756 Henry the Magnificent had lost patience with the pump because he did not relocate it when the Garden Lake dam was built. In default of water piped from the valley, Henry the Magnificent probably drew water from a deep well at the house, raised by a horse-powered pump. Richard Fenton commented in 1807 that drinking water was supplied (by hand?) from a spring near the Temple of Flora.[25] Fresh running water was eventually piped from the Stour's springs to the house in 1848 (page 231).

The Fir Walk and Obelisk.

THE FIRST LANDSCAPE
GARDEN 1742-54

'Design uncommon is in all express'd'

Around 1732 Henry the Magnificent planted an avenue of trees along the crest of the valley closest to the house. It became known as the Fir Walk. Whether he made further alterations to the grounds during his mother's lifetime is unknown. After her death in 1742, he summoned the architect, Henry Flitcroft, to design the Temple on the Terrace (1744), situated close to the commencement of the Fir Walk and, at the opposite end, a stone Obelisk (1746).[1]

Architect and patron also turned their attention to the floor of the valley. They began with two springs. On the east side, at 'Paradice Pond', Flitcroft designed the Temple of Flora (1744-5) with a cascade below. On the western side, at the withy bed, he built the Grotto (c.1748) with a second minor cascade. The 1792 low-water plan of the lake identified pools created for these features which were rediscovered, submerged, by the Nautical Archaeological Society underwater survey of 2004-5 (page 135).[2]

To reach the Temple of Flora and Grotto, Henry laid paths down through the Shades. Then as now, common beech trees predominated on the slopes, underplanted with laurel.

Having admired the Fir Walk from its southern end and taken in the prospect from the Temple on the Terrace, Henry and his guests threaded their way through the Shades into the valley either pursuing a left-hand path which fell abruptly to the Temple of Flora or taking the right fork onto a path running parallel to the Fir Walk before descending to the valley floor and the Grotto.

Joseph Spence considered the Shades to be the 'Bridgman' part of the garden, probably because Henry studded them with exotic attractions, all long gone.[3] Happily these are known from contemporary descriptions, the estate map of 1785 and also from the survey of Stourhead prepared for the King of Sweden, in 1779, by Fredrik Magnus Piper (pages 271-2). A short distance along the right-hand path, it forked again, one branch leading to the Chinese Alcove (1749).[4] The main path continued to Diana's Mount, a viewing station, named after the lead statue of the goddess acquired by Henry in 1744-5.[5] An engraving, c.1773, from the eastern garden recorded the name, although by then the statue had reached the Pantheon and would be replaced by the Turkish Tent (page 167).[6]

From Diana's Mount, the eighteenth-century visitor admired the view before zig-zagging down the incline to the Wooden Bridge (1749), crossing to the further shore,

The Shades.

at Stourton

General — Plan
of f. d. Banquieren Henry Hoares Lustpark vid Stourton i Wiltshire
nära Bristol

N

afstichnad 1779.
af f M Piper.

100   200   300   400   500   1000 Engelske fot

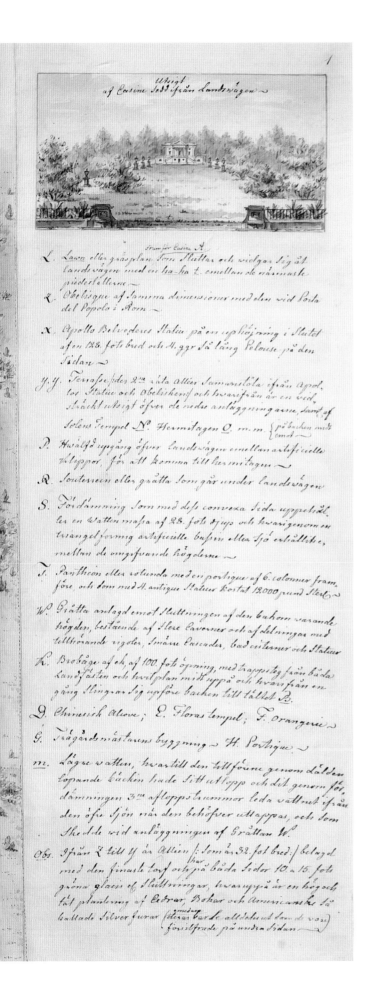

General plan of the former banker Henry Hoare's pleasure park at Stourton in Wiltshire, near Bristol, drawn 1779 by F. M. Piper

Key

L Lawn or grass field in front of house A which slopes and enlarges towards the road and a ha-ha t. between the nearest pedestals.

Z Obelisk of identical dimensions to the one at Porta del Popolo in Rome.

X *Apollo Belvedere* statue on a mound at the end of a lawn 128 feet* wide and four times as long on that side.

y.y Terrace; where two straight walks from the Apollo statue and the Obelisk meet [at the southern end the Temple on the Terrace is marked and identified by the sketch of the temple attached to the reverse of this plan]. From the terrace there is an extensive view over the lower garden and the Sun Temple [of Apollo] N, Hermitage O and the opposite hill.

P Arched crossing [Rock Arch] over the road between artificial rocks to reach the Hermitage.

R Souterrain or grotto passage passing under the road.

S Dam with a concave profile impounding water 28 feet deep to form an artificial triangular lake between the surrounding hills.

T Pantheon or rotunda with a portico of 6 columns in the front and, with four antique statues costing in total £12,000 sterling.

W Grotto built into the hill comprising many caverns and sections with surprises, small cascades, bath-cistern and statues.

K Bridge with a span of 100 feet, steps sprung from two abutments to a level   top, after which a path snakes up to the [Turkish] tent B.

D Chinese Alcove

E Temple of Flora.

F Orangery.

G Gardener's building.

H *Portique.* [Piper marked, but failed to identify, the Bristol Cross]

m Lower Water into which formerly the old streams ran. Now fed by 3 conduits through the dam to channel water from the upper lake when it requires draining and carried out when building the grotto [?]

Obs. [Fir Walk] From z to y the walk (which is 32 feet wide) is covered by the finest turf and has on both sides 10 to 15 feet green embankments on which grow high and dense plantations of Cedars, Beeches and American, so-called Silver Pines (because their needles appear silver-coated on the lower sides).

* Swedish feet approximate British feet.

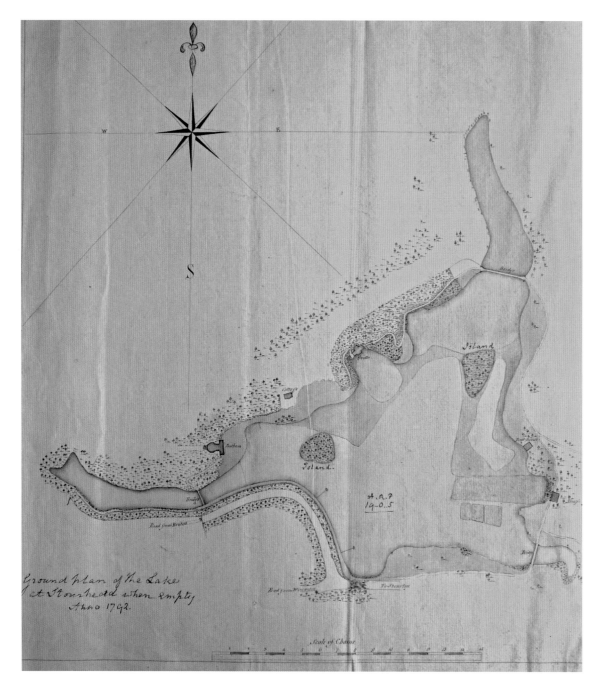

then joining a path through the woods to the Grotto. The bridge was spectacular, leaping the lake in a single span of almost 100 feet. Turpin de Crissé depicted it landing beside a small lawn and a fenced path (page 151).[7] Piper showed the path entering a clearing in the trees where he sketched a stone vase.[8] The approach to the Grotto was thickly planted. Eighteenth-century writers mentioned a variety of trees: the 1749 rhymer saw ash, beech and poplars while, thirty years later, Graves found ancient oak and weeping willows.[9] The same year Piper also noted the willows and ash trees and found a sweet chestnut overhanging the exit from the Grotto (page 155).[10] In 1807 Richard Fenton summed up the planting as a 'matted umbrage'.[11]

Before the Garden Lake was created visitors left the Grotto and returned to the eastern shore either by retracing their steps or taking a boat across the existing lake, marked on the 1722 plan. In 1749 the author of 'Stourton Gardens' set out from the

A View from the Pantheon, in Mr Hoare's Garden at Stourton, in Wiltshire.

village, first encountered the Temple of Flora, then strolled across a lawn bordering this lake and took a ferry to the Grotto (the rhymer did not mention the Wooden Bridge because it was in the process of construction). After admiring the *Nymph* and Benson's pump, the author returned to the Shades, presumably by boat. Five years later, Richard Pococke walked from the Grotto to the Pantheon, then under construction, and admired the view towards the village – but he gave no clue how he returned.[12] Henry Hoare would resolve the dilemma by creating a walk along the southern shore.

The master plan

For how long did Henry Hoare nurse the ambition to create the Garden Lake before he acted? If he conceived it as early as 1743, he would not have troubled with the cascade at the Grotto and canal at the Temple of Flora. On the other hand, the pebble pavement of the Grotto stands above the level of the Garden Lake. The first payments for the Grotto occurred in 1747, the year in which Henry commissioned Michael Rysbrack to carve the marble *Hercules*. By then he would have decided on the Pantheon so we may infer that he planned the Garden Lake around that time.

The Fir Walk

The Fir Walk, which Henry Hoare planted *c*.1732, offered a vista extending northwards

ABOVE

'A View from the Pantheon in Mr Hoare's Garden at Stourton in Wiltshire', *c*.1773, unknown, etching and engraving, 115 × 198 mm. From *A new display of the beauties of England*, 2 vols (London 1774). British Library.

Diana's Mount, on the left, is prominent in the distance as a bare slope and without the Turkish Tent.

OPPOSITE

The Obelisk.

in a straight line for 500 yards and measuring 40 yards wide.[13] Seventeen years later, the author of 'Stourton Gardens' enthused

> See stately firs along the margin stand
> (We seem to walk on soft enchanted land):
> But yonder slopes that terminate the green,
> And to the eye are hence contiguous seen,
> Are distant far --- the village lies between.[14]

The view from the southern end opened onto fields and the distant hills. In 1769 Sir John Parnell enjoyed the same prospect and identified the trees as 'the Spruce firr' which, he claimed, 'takes plashing up to great perfection, feathering out after cutting like a Deciduous tree, and the Branches from tenderness Beautifully weeping.'[15] Piper called them American silver pine (perhaps white spruce, *Picea glauca*).[16]

By 1776 Lady Polwarth considered the Fir Walk old-fashioned.[17] Colt Hoare, displeased by the spikey silhouette which the trees developed, felled the avenue in 1792–3 and replanted with a mixture of beech and fir.[18] This regime continued and by the 1970s the vista was lost in a tangle of laurel and seedlings grown to trees. The avenue is now reinstated.

The Obelisk

The stone Obelisk is a useful means of orientating on the estate, rising 100 feet as the climax of the Fir Walk and visible from the house.[19] In September 1746 William Privett, the quarry owner and builder from Chilmark, was contracted to erect the Obelisk and gave his bond guaranteeing the stone for five years.[20] Henry Hoare annotated the agreement 'for true performance of the Obelisque also all Their Bills & M[r] Flitcrofts remarks on Them as p[d] Dec[r] 11th 1750'. Privett submitted a statement of the cost amounting to £349–17s–4d.[21] In 1748 Mr Norris supplied the final flourish, a metal sunburst, which Jonas Hanway admired as a 'mythra, or sun, of six feet diameter, in gilded copper'.[22]

In 1815 Colt Hoare added the Latin tribute to his grandfather.[23] The 3rd baronet rebuilt the Obelisk in Bath stone and his successor repaired the shaft after a lightning strike in June 1853.[24]

The Temple on the Terrace (demolished)

In 1754 Pococke wrote, 'To the South of the house is a lawn with a piece of water, and from that a winding descent over the above-mentioned valley; in the way is a Dorick open Temple'.[25] Piper sketched the temple (but with Ionic capitals) and marked its position on his plans of the gardens in 1779.[26] Henry Hoare probably intended the temple as a vantage point, with the façade facing the valley.[27] Henry Flitcroft supplied designs in 1744 and termed it 'the Venetian seat'.

The façade comprised a central arch flanked by two lesser rectangular openings, loosely based on a Venetian window or more accurately on a triumphal archway by Serlio.[28] It was also reminiscent of designs by James Gibbs.[29] The builder was

Nathaniel Ireson.[30] Piper shows the temple with a square ground plan and a central indoor feature, the pedestal for the Borghese vase which Henry purchased *c*.1770 (page 148).

Prince Leopold Friedrich Franz von Anhalt-Dessau (1740–1817) built a replica, *c*.1764–5, at Worlitz, in Germany, well before Colt Hoare demolished the Stourhead temple.[31]

The Temple of Flora

The temple presides over springs which provided water to the village. It was designed by Flitcroft, built by William Privett 1744–5 and first dedicated, by Henry Hoare, to Ceres.[32] Flitcroft's letters indicate the temple replaced an earlier structure (page 51). The Doric portico is limestone from the Chilmark quarry while

ABOVE
'Temple on the Terrace', *c*.1779, by F. M. Piper (1746–1824), ink and sepia wash, 155 × 105 mm. The Royal Swedish Academy of Fine Arts, Stockholm. y–y in the inscription refers to the general plan (pages 136–7).

OPPOSITE
Temple of Flora. In the foreground, a stone vase, 1750–51, attributed to Robert Parsons or his son, Thomas.

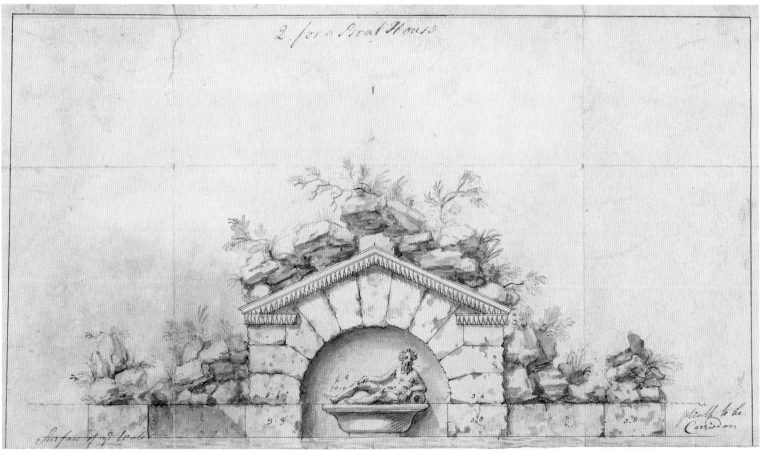

the temple itself is greensand stone, rendered at the sides and exposed at the rear. The tiled roof was renewed in 1842 and the building restored in 1894.[33]

The story of the temple is complex to unravel. It housed the marble statue of *Livia Augusta as Ceres*, Roman goddess of agriculture or, in Greek mythology, Demeter, the mother of Persephone and instigator of the Eleusinian mysteries. After Henry moved her to the Pantheon, *c.*1760, he rededicated the temple to Flora, goddess of fertility and flowers. Above the entrance is inscribed *Procul, o procul este profani* (Begone, you who are uninitiated), resonating nicely with the Eleusinian mysteries, but this well-known quotation from Virgil is first documented at Stourhead in 1787.[34]

Hanway, 1756, described:

> the temple of Ceres, which is on the side of the water nearest to the village...
> Eight or ten feet below, level with the water, in a subterraneous grotto, is
> another figure of the river god.[35]

A drawing attributed to Flitcroft depicted this rock-work archway sheltering a river god who reclines above a basin.[36] Thomas Manning supplied the river god which was drowned when Henry completed the Garden Lake in 1756.[37] Flitcroft's archway was later remodelled as a rock-work cave. Happily, Bampfylde had already drawn the original ensemble, showing a cascade of water tumbling from the basin into the canal.[38] Flitcroft also designed the canal and its retaining dam which were both subsequently inundated.[39] The 1792 low-water plan shows the canal extending in a straight line about a third of the distance towards the present dam and its existence was confirmed in the underwater survey of 2004–5 (page 135).[40]

The life-size marble statue of *Livia Augusta* is Roman, early imperial, a copy of a fourth century BC Greek original.[41] Henry may well have purchased her when he was in Italy but the payments for shipping in his ledgers are not specific.[42] Mark Parker, who acted as Henry's agent in Italy, was granted export licences for sculpture.[43] The licences were deliberately imprecise; nevertheless, they indicate how Henry could have exported *Livia Augusta* by playing down the quality. In 1766 an anonymous author claimed that the marble was purchased for a thousand guineas in the sale of Cardinal Ottoboni (1667–1740).[44] The price quoted should be taken with a pinch of salt: two other Stourhead visitors, neither recognised as authorities, pitched the cost on either side of this figure.[45] John Britton admired *Livia Augusta* in the Pantheon and stated she came from Rome, whereas Baron van Spaen had asserted it was Herculaneum.[46]

After removing *Livia Augusta*, Henry Hoare acquired a statue of *Flora* for the temple. An anonymous, but knowledgeable, visitor described this as a 'good Statue'.[47] James Dallaway suggested *Flora* was acquired at the sale of Doctor Mead. He was writing in 1816, sixteen years after visiting Stourhead and may have erred.[48] The Stourhead Catalogue of 1784, which listed all the marble statuary, omitted this *Flora* (inferring she was lead or plaster). Three years later Count di Rezzònico saw *Flora* in the temple.[49] But in 1800 Richard Warner omitted her from his description but noted the Borghese vase.[50]

Count di Rezzònico also noted the two polychrome busts found in the temple today and thought to represent *Vibia Sabina*, mother of Marcus Aurelius, and

Faustina Minore, the emperor's wife.[51] A second pair *ensuite* with the empresses may have come from the Temple on the Terrace and depict the *Young Marcus Aurelius* and *Alexander the Great*.[52]

Hanway described the furnishings: 'On each side are too [sic] commodious seats, which are made in imitation of the pulvinaria, or little beds which were placed near the altar at the time of sacrifice, on which the pagans were wont to lay the images of their gods in their temples.'[53] Count di Rezzònico saw, 'two altars and two *lectisterni*'.[54] The design of these *pulvinaria* derives from Bernard de Montfaucon's *L'antiquité expliquée*.[55] The count's two altars belong stylistically to a group of furniture associated with William Kent and Flitcroft.[56] All these pieces were grained at a later date and are now stored away from the temple.

A measured drawing dated 1749 and two pencil sketches of the indoor walls suggest Henry Hoare contemplated further embellishments of wall panels with classical reliefs, in paint or plaster, similar to those made later for the Pantheon.[57] The interior of the temple was modified for a third time when Colt Hoare installed the replica *Borghese Vase* from the Temple on the Terrace. This copy in patent artificial stone was supplied, *c*.1770, by Mrs Coade's factory.[58]

Close to the temple stands a stone vase supplied by Robert or Thomas Parsons of Bath; it featured in the latter's *A collection of vases* and is similar to those placed at the entrance to Chiswick Villa, *c*.1728.[59] The design is illustrated in *L'antiquité expliquée*.[60] Francis Nicholson depicted the Stourhead vase standing beside the temple.[61] It was moved to the pedestal at the water's edge by the 6th baronet.[62]

For a decade the Temple of Ceres commanded the cascade and canal and was the dominant feature in the garden until trumped by the Pantheon. From being a destination, the temple became a detour, mentioned by visitors almost as an afterthought. When Colt Hoare laid the path around the lake the temple regained status because it was on the pathway from the village.

The Borghese Vase, 1770–72, by Eleanor Coade (1733–1821) and Daniel Pincot (d.1797), Coade stone, H 124.5 cm. Stourhead.

The Gothick Greenhouse (demolished)

Midway down the hill from the Temple on the Terrace, Henry Hoare erected an ornamental greenhouse which was first described in 1762 but was probably somewhat earlier.[63] Piper marked the position on his general plan and drew an H-shaped ground plan. Visiting in 1769 Parnell noted the greenhouse was 'built in coarse flints with gothic pilasters, at about 25 or thirty feet long'.[64] In 1776 Mrs Powys described it, 'prettily adorn'd on the outside by Stone or Burnt Cinders from the Glasses Houses at Bristol. The Inside Black gravel Stones mixed in the Mortar it looks like pounded flints and has a pretty effect.'[65] A flint finish was evidently popular; William Wrighte, publishing in 1767, included a design for a five-bay greenhouse, 'faced with Flints and irregular Stones'.[66] Bampfylde included the greenhouse on the extreme right of his panoramic view which shows the façade had three pointed arches and a parapet bristling pinnacles (page 139).[67]

The edition of *The Tour through Britain* published in 1779 included a description of the immediate surroundings, 'a small rustic green-house, with parterres and platforms of flowers, and scented shrubs, in a small open garden'.[68] The German author C. C. L. Hirschfeld also noted this flower garden.[69] Flower beds were appropriate in the vicinity of the Temple of Flora; there was another instance at Nuneham Park in Oxfordshire.[70] Colt Hoare demolished the Stourhead greenhouse in the 1790s and later dug flower beds closer to the village entrance.[71]

The Chinese Alcove (demolished)

Henry Hoare was in playful mood when he commissioned the alcove. It stood in the Shades, midway between the Temple on the Terrace and *Diana of Versailles*, the location marked on Piper's general plan. In 1749 the rhymer of 'Stourton Gardens' proceeded:

> To yon strange seat, my friends! we next repair,
> Perhaps a Mandarine inhabits there!
> Design uncommon is in all express'd
> 'Twas surely finish'd in the furthest East.
> The genius thus by foreign nation shown
> (And but for commerce never had been known)
> Deputed there the stately Tartar see,
> Whose greatest princes dare not say they're free:
> His finger points to th' globe beneath his hand;
> He seems to say, All China I command.[72]

In 1762 the Duchess of Beaufort noted a 'Chinese Temple' but Horace Walpole ignored it.[73] Early examples of garden *chinoiserie* include the Chinese house at Stowe in Buckinghamshire, first recorded on the plan of 1739, and at Shugborough in Staffordshire, Thomas Anson built a Chinese house *c.*1747. Stourhead's is contemporary with the Chinese seat at Painshill which Lady Newdigate sketched in 1748.[74] At Barn Elms, Sir Richard Hoare added a Chinese temple *c.*1751, paid for in part by Henry the Magnificent.[75] Henry's Stourhead neighbour, Stephen Fox, 1st Earl of Ilchester, also commissioned a Chinese seat for Redlynch in 1755.[76] Colt Hoare demolished the Stourhead alcove without recording the appearance but Piper could have had it in mind when he included a 'Chinese Alcove' in his 'Description of the idea and general-plan for an English park'.[77]

Diana of Versailles

John Cheere supplied Henry Hoare with a cast of *Diana* in 1744/5 with the copy of the *Apollo Belvedere* for the South Lawn.[78] *Diana* was first recorded in 1749, described stalking in the Shades below the midway point of the Fir Walk:

> Hence thro' the windings of a lovely grove,
> Thro' shady walks, and flow'ry paths we rove;
> The virgin huntress next presents to view;
> Her favourite chace seems eager to pursue.[79]

Cheere's cast derived from *Diane de Versailles,* a Roman copy in marble of a lost bronze, attributed to Leochares, fourth century BC.[80] French *Diane* is accompanied by a stag beside her left leg and she carries no bow. The statue was given to King Henry II of France by Pope Paul IV in 1556. For King Charles I, Hubert Le Sueur made a bronze version (with neither stag nor bow) which is now at Windsor Castle.

By 1762 Henry had removed *Diana* to the Pantheon and would substitute the Turkish Tent.[81].

The Wooden Bridge (demolished)

In 1749 Henry Hoare erected a footbridge vaulting across the water where the northern pond narrowed into a channel. He did so before forming the Garden Lake. It traversed almost 100 feet shore to shore, the crown rising to 11 feet above the water level while the deck was 7 feet broad.[82] The bridge allowed visitors to cross from the base of the Mount of Diana onto a tree-hung path leading to the Grotto. Walpole correctly associated the design with Palladio and, indeed, Henry probably owned Leoni's luxurious edition of the *Quattro Libri* which described its construction.[83] Capability Brown used the same design for a contemporary wooden bridge at Wotton in Buckinghamshire with a span of about 100 feet.[84]

Henry Hoare paid William Privett for a bridge in 1749 although, as a stonemason, he would probably have supplied only the stone footings.[85] Flitcroft may well have provided the working drawings. He is credited with designing a similar single-arch timber bridge for the Duke of Cumberland at Virginia Water in 1753.[86] That bridge carried carriages and spanned 165 feet rising to a height of 20 feet. For Sir Richard

ABOVE
Diana of Versailles, 1745, by John Cheere (1709–87), lead, H 213.5 cm. Stourhead.

OPPOSITE ABOVE
Wooden Bridge, detail from Piper's general plan 1779 (page 136–7). The Royal Swedish Academy of Fine Arts, Stockholm. Annotated in Swedish with the dimensions and 'm. n. stone abutments permanently under water on piles'.

OPPOSITE BELOW
Wooden Bridge at Stourhead, 1793, by Lancelot-Henri Roland Turpin de Crissé (1754–*c.*1800), pencil, 210 × 350 mm. Musées d'Angers.

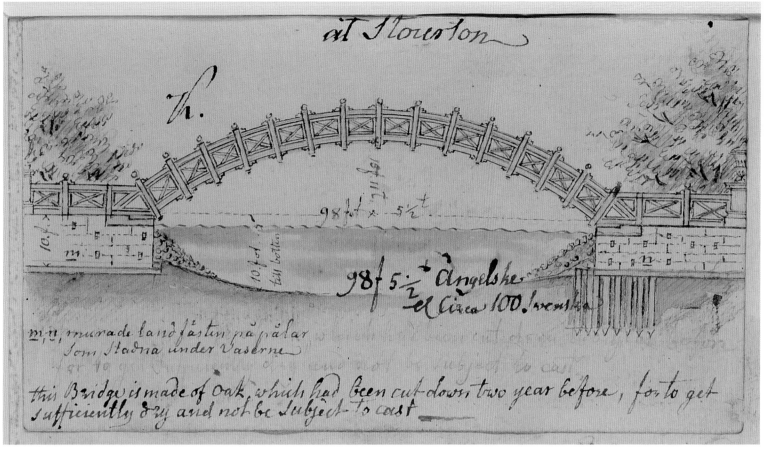

at Stourton

98/5½ Angelske
el Circa 100. svenska

m,n, murade landfästen på pålar
Som stadna under vaserne

this Bridge is made of Oak, which had been cut down two year before, for to get
sufficiently dry and not be Subject to cast

Stourhead.

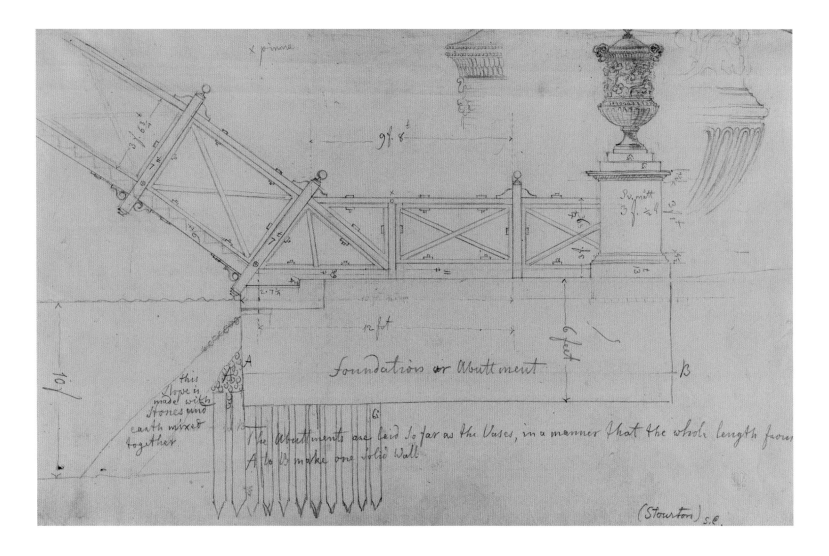

The Wooden Bridge, *c.*1779,
by F. M. Piper (1746–1824),
pencil, 210 × 340 mm.
The Royal Swedish Academy
of Fine Arts, Stockholm.

Hoare, Flitcroft designed a pocket-size 'Chinese' bridge some 52 feet and 6 inches in length across the lake at Barn Elms. Payments made to the carpenter responsible for this bridge, Thomas Spinks, allude to Flitcroft.[87] Spinks also worked for Henry the Magnificent and we may speculate whether he was also responsible for the Wooden Bridge at Stourhead.

Palladio designed stone abutments rising to clasp each end of the framework but, at Stourhead, the abutments were at ground level and horizontal. Triangular timber frames transferred the thrust to balustrades which terminated at four stone pedestals with vases, the latter supplied by Robert or Thomas Parsons of Bath.[88]

In 1779, Piper made a thumbnail sketch of the bridge (previous page). He also prepared eight pencil studies of the bridge annotated with the dimensions of the timbers, evidently with a view to copying, or refining, the design.[89]

The open treads alarmed Mrs Powys:

> The Idea of going over a kind of Ladder only is frightful, another party of company could not bring themselves to venture but return'd back, but 'tis not so bad after you have brought yourself to venture a few of its steps, tho' its perpendicular Appearance and seeing the water through at first looks formidable.[90]

Some eighteenth-century writers termed the bridge 'Palladian'.[91] Seven called it Chinese, including Colt Hoare who dismantled it in 1798 and substituted a ferry operated by pulleys.[92]

The Grotto

The approach to the Grotto has always been exciting. Spence, ever the keen gardener, admired:

a low (mysterious) laurel-arching over the path; which hides all the Front of the Grot, except a part of the Top to the left hand: & a little on to the same side, is a lump or two of stones, with Harts-tongue, some Fern, & much

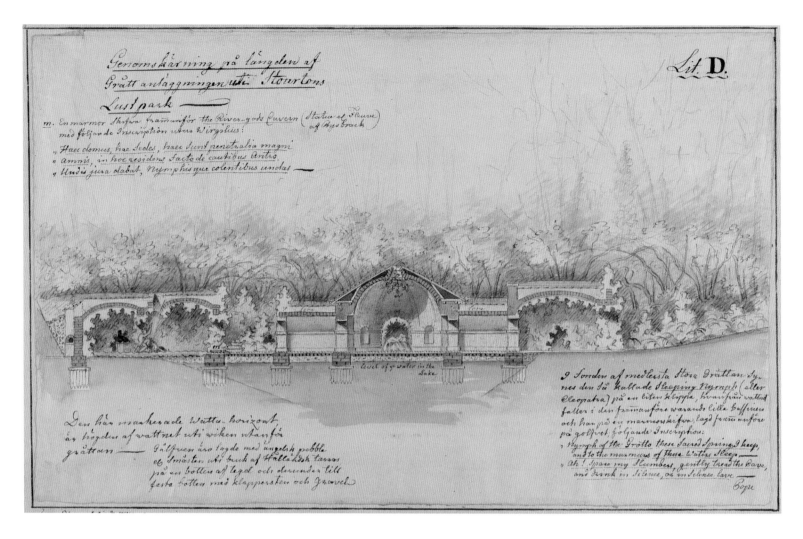

Perriwinkle, growing on & between them.[93]

It is easy to miss the inscription incised in the pediment above the original entrance because the passage was extended in 1776.[94] The quotation derives from the *Aeneid*:

Intus aquæ dulces vivoque sedilia saxo;
Nympharum domus[95]

Escaping a storm, Aeneas sheltered his fleet in a cave inhabited by nymphs before encountering Dido, Queen of Carthage. Hanway referred to 'the grotto of the nymph' and Henry Hoare once described his grandchildren as enjoying 'the Temple of the Nymph'.[96] Elsewhere he referred to 'the Grotto' and other visiting authors followed suit.

Henry began the structure in 1748. The central chamber accommodates a plunge bath where he sluiced, exclaiming to his daughter, Susanna, one hot July, 'I had a delicious souse into the Cold Bath this morn᷎ to The Tunes of French Horns playing Round me all the while belonging to Company who lay at Our Inn'.[97] To his son-in-law, Lord Bruce, he wrote 'a Souse into that delicious Bath & Grot fill'd with fresh Magic'.[98] Even on summer days the experience is bracing rather than relaxing.

The plunge bath lies in front of a deep recess occupied by a lead statue of the sleeping *Nymph* from whose couch the ice-cold water tumbles perpetually. Her cave

'Lit. D., Cross section of the length of the Grotto in Stourton Pleasure Park', *c*.1779, by F. M. Piper (1746–1824), ink and colour wash, 210 × 334 mm. The Royal Swedish Academy of Fine Arts, Stockholm.

Annotated with a Swedish translation of the inscription on the Nymph's basin rim and Ovid's verses from the tablet at the River God's cave, mis-attributed to Virgil. Piper also erroneously ascribed the god to Rysbrack.

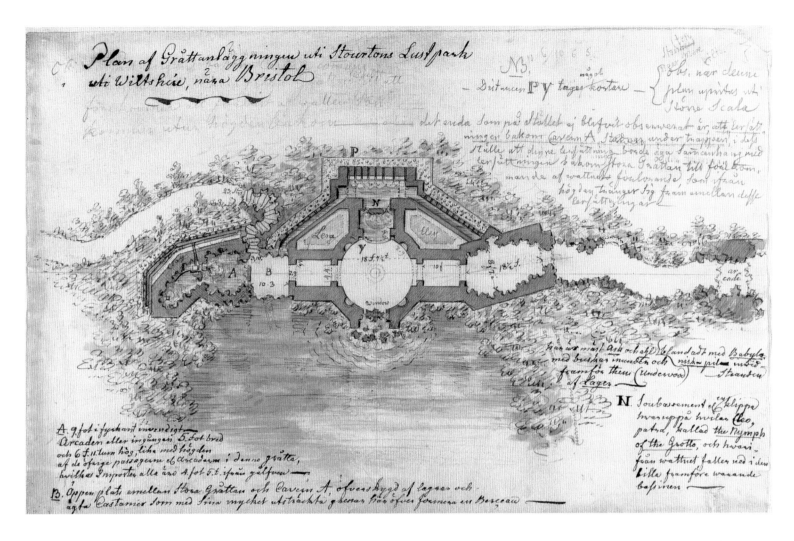

'Plan of Grotto complex at Stourton's Pleasure Park in Wiltshire, near Bristol', c.1779, by F. M. Piper (1746–1824), pencil, ink and colour wash, 205 × 325 mm. The Royal Swedish Academy of Fine Arts, Stockholm.

Annotated, '[at the entrance]... ash and [*alder* inserted] mixed with Babylon willow along the shore, with bushes underneath and in front of [?] underwood [?] laurels' and 'Open place between the Main Cave and Cavern A, overshadowed by laurels and sweet chestnuts, which form a bower with their very extensive branches'. Further notes on the clay lining used to achieve the water effects.

abuts the rotunda of the Grotto. The sponge-stone lining, resembling tufa, belies its architectural sophistication. This circular chamber is intersected by two passageways while, opposite the *Nymph*, is an arched opening looking across the lake towards the village. Niche-seats punctuate the walls and the shallow ribbed dome above is also clad in sponge stone. Beyond the second passage, in a lesser chamber, is a lead figure of the *River God*, top lit and resting against an urn from which spring water gushes; it is as baroque an effect as could be imagined and was added a few years after the main chamber.[99]

The sophistication of the Grotto suggests Henry Flitcroft provided the design. William Privett was the builder.[100] The Reverend Merewether supplied the sponge stone, a porous limestone found near Bath and Cirencester.[101] Visitors perceived the chamber lining in different ways. In 1749 author of 'Stourton Gardens' exclaimed:

> But view the roof! there with amazement gaze,
> If petrefactions have the pow'r to please;
> Strange objects form'd by nature's dædal hand,
> Plac'd here by magic art, our thoughts demand.[102]

Twenty years later Parnell found the *Nymph* 'on a Bank of fossils, shells &c'.[103] In 1773 Mrs Rishton remembered the *River God* in a cave 'composed of the most

beautiful Spas and Fossils'.[104] But by 1776 Lady Polwarth remarked that the Grotto was 'constructed of rough stones, & some of the pointed petrifactions, no shells, nothing gawdy, & glaring.'[105] The Stourhead Grotto was a decade and more earlier than those at Painshill and Oatlands in Surrey, both characterised by dazzling crystal-lined interiors created by Joseph Lane (1717–84) who had previously worked for Privett.[106]

Piper drew fourteen sections and plans of the Grotto as he puzzled over the hydraulics.[107] The lake façade of the Grotto is built in greensand stone; it rises from regular courses to rubble stone at the jagged parapet which masks the shallow stone-clad exterior of the dome. At the footings Piper drew a small cascade tumbling over a rock platform.[108] In this spot the Nautical Archaeological Society survey discovered stone steps below the waterline.[109] The Grotto was repaired in 1852 and 1894–5.[110]

No bill or ledger entry records the purchase of the *Nymph of the Grotto* but the sculpture is usually attributed to John Cheere.[111] True, Rysbrack sketched the *Nymph* in her cave but it does not follow that he supplied a maquette.[112] The reclining figure, all-too-familiar in funerary monuments since Etruscan times, is here an object of desire. She derives from sculptures of Ariadne asleep, such as the well-known marble

ABOVE
Nymph of the Grotto, before 1749, attr. John Cheere (1709–87), lead, 86.5 × 170 cm. Stourhead.

ABOVE
Entrance to the Grotto.

OPPOSITE BELOW
Ariadne, Roman copy of Greek
marble, second century AD,
129 × 226 cm. Uffizi Gallery.
The head and right arm are late
eighteenth century and replace
a sixteenth century restoration
on which the Stourhead cast was
based. This deposed head is also
at the Uffizi.

version in the Vatican.[113] Until the eighteenth century she was known as 'Cleopatra' on account of her serpent bracelet.[114] The Stourhead *Nymph* has no bracelet and she reclines in a more relaxed posture than the Vatican marble.[115] Indeed she has a stronger resemblance to the marble *Ariadne*, as restored in the sixteenth century, formerly at the Villa Medici, in Rome, now at the Uffizi Gallery in Florence.[116]

Lest visitors to the Grotto were in doubt as to her identity, Henry reminded them with lines by Alexander Pope inscribed on the rim of the plunge bath:

> Nymph of the Grot these sacred springs I keep,
> And to the murmur of these waters sleep;
> Ah! Spare my slumbers, gently tread the cave,
> And drink in silence, or in silence lave.[117]

This is the translation of a Latin epigram written in the late fifteenth century in the style of Greek lyric poetry.[118] The same Latin inscription was placed beside a sculpture of a sleeping nymph in the garden of Angelo Colocci, *c*.1513, in Rome, and illustrated in *L'antiquité expliquée*.[119]

The River God was a one-off commission and is arguably the masterpiece of John Cheere who was paid almost £100 for the lead sculpture in 1751.[120] The pose derives from an etching by Salvator Rosa, *The dream of Aeneas*.[121] Michael Rysbrack probably possessed this print.[122] Piper was incorrect when he attributed the *River God* to Rysbrack.[123] However he was accurate in depicting the sculpture with a paddle raised in the right hand.[124] Colt Hoare described the figure as 'holding an urn in his left hand, and in his right a trident', the latter vanishing a long time ago.[125]

At the entrance to his cave a wooden tablet displayed verse noted by some visitors and surviving into the nineteenth century.[126] The verse derived from the *Metamorphoses*:

> Hæc domus, hæc sedes, hæc sunt penetralia magni
> Amnis, in hoc residens facto de cautibus antro,
> Undis iura dabat, nymphisque colentibus undas.[127]

The story tells of the river god Peneas grieving the loss of his daughter Daphne after he had transformed her into a laurel bush so she could escape unwelcome advances from Apollo. However most eighteenth-century writers identified the Stourhead sculpture as the River Stour.[128] A few christened him Neptune.[129]

As the century drew to a close, the Grotto awakened a fresh sense of awe. David Garrick resolved to be buried there.[130] By 1810 John Britton's pulse was racing:

> It will be impossible for me to describe the awful sensations which I experienced on entering its gloomy cells; my fancy was set afloat on the ocean of conjecture, and imagination conjured up thousands of those ideal images that poets have described, and such painters as a Fuselli and Mortimer have delineated[131]

The interior is indeed dank and mysterious. The unimaginative Nicholson drew tendrils drooping from the oculus (page 153).[132] Francis Skurray was spooked:

> Fancy pourtrays the watchful Cerberus
> Guarding the entrance of the nether world.
> With proffer'd cates or music's notes disarm
> The monster's rage, whilst I pursue my way
> To view the beauteous Naiad of the stream,
> Lull'd on her rocky couch by waterfall.[133]

THE GARDEN LAKE AND PANTHEON 1754–62

'My large water was convulsed rose upon a sudden'

Henry the Magnificent took the breath-taking decision to flood the valley and create the Garden Lake in the late 1740s. The Pantheon was an integral part of his ambitious plan. When it was complete in 1762, Stourhead took its place as a world-class garden. At about that date Henry, in carnival mood, erected a Turkish Tent atop the Mount of Diana.

The lake is the dominant feature in the landscape garden. Aesthetes admire the harmony between the natural and the man-made. Historically minded visitors imagine how the valley looked before the dam was built. The technically inquisitive speculate about its construction. The abundance of springs plays a crucial role and so too does geology: beneath the soil and greensand lies Gault clay, ready-made puddling for water features.

The dam

Henry built the dam in 1754–5.[1] It is 722 feet long (220 metres), 33 feet high and 15 feet wide at the crest.[2] Siting the dam was an aesthetic and engineering accomplishment; the construction was a matter of responsible supervision. The profile is conventional: a shallow inner slope and a steep outer face.

A footpath runs along the crest of the dam and a cart track traverses the base of the outer face. The inner face is stone clad where it approaches the crest. In 1994 the dam was heightened by some eight inches.[3] The structure is a matter of surmise. Piper drew a cross-section in 1779, derived from observation and presumably from conversations with Francis Faugoin who witnessed the construction. Piper's research enabled him to sketch the profile and make drawings of three sluices controlling the water level. He described how the dam was built by the tried and tested method, without a clay core which, assuming he was correct, was unnecessary because the earth used was already rich in clay. Piper wrote (translated):

> The actual dam was made of a clayey soil that keeps water out and was dug down somewhat above a quarter below the solid bed of the upper lake or the former dale.* [*If the soil is loose and stony, it should be ploughed up to a depth of one ell or more and all rubble removed; one starts where the bed is lowest and lead the water immediately there through small temporary trenches, inserted] It [the soil] was trampled and compacted by 12 oxen harnessed to carts with fairly broad wheels that performed the same task as rollers; one layer [?] at a

time 9 inches thick, and, moreover, [the soil] was rammed together by 10 to 12 people provided with clubs. In dry weather the layer was moistened before new ones were laid on top. NB the spoil for the dam was used for planting on the side of the dam.[4]

The western arm, known as the backwater, extends a further 459 feet. It is contained by a low dam but, in this instance, with a rammed clay core (page 235).[5]

The costs of building the new dam and forming the Garden Lake were subsumed in payments to Francis Faugoin (Appendix I). Henry Flitcroft was probably the mastermind having already designed the dam for the formal water at the Temple of Flora (page 144). He was responsible for garden buildings in Windsor Park, where up to 500 workers reshaped the landscape for the Duke of Cumberland. There were two dams on the site: one, impounding the Great Meadow Pond, was built *c*.1747. The second dam, at Virginia Water, was designed by the Deputy Ranger, Thomas Sandby, in 1752.[6] It was breached by storm water in 1768 and rebuilt in 1782; a disaster earning Sandby the nickname 'Tommy Sandbank'.[7]

Faugoin owned up to one mishap at Stourhead, *c*.1755:

> Monday was 3 Weeks my Large Water was convulsed rose upon a Sudden that side next y[e] Pantheon & oveflowd the Head in an Instant w[hic]h other side next [*where* inserted] the Waste Water goes off overflowd prodigiously and run down over the Head a Vast Torrent w[hic]h Labourers & Francis [Faugoin] who saw it ran to it with Spades think[g] the [*New* inserted] Head was bursting out & when They came up it was stopt. Francis then let off 2 feet of Water... not knowing what could be y[e] cause & that caused A Report in Dorset[e] that y[e] Head was down.[8]

'Profile of the Great Dam', 1778–80, by F. M. Piper (1746–1824), ink and colour wash, page 330 × 220 mm. From 'Beskrifning öfwer Lustparkerne uti Stourton och Payneshill... 1778–79 1780, par F. M. Piper'. The Royal Swedish Academy of Fine Arts, Stockholm.

Annotated in Swedish, 'de : df [inner gradient of 4:1], and ab : ac [the outer, of 2:1]; x, the country road hidden m planting; p lower water, at the height before the new dam was built.'

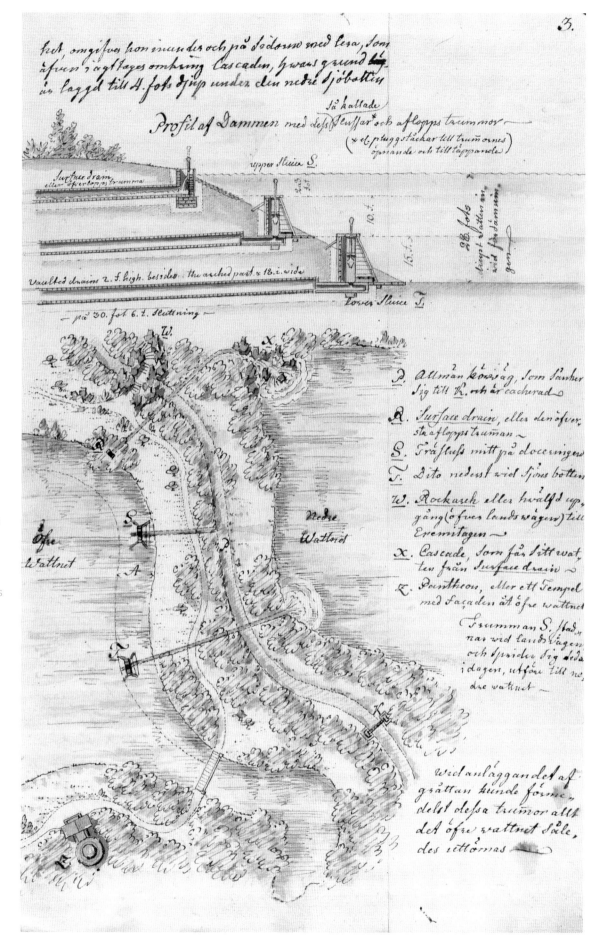

'The Dam, cross-section and plan', 1778–80, by F. M. Piper (1746–1824), pencil, ink and colour wash, 330 × 220 mm. From 'Beskrifning öfwer Lustparkerne uti Stourton och Payneshill... 1778–79 1780, par F. M. Piper'. The Royal Swedish Academy of Fine Arts, Stockholm.

Section headed 'profile of the dam with the sluices* and conduits (* or stop logs controlling the flow)'.

Key:
P. Public road leading down to R and hidden from view.
R. Surface or uppermost conduit.
S. Wooden sluice for the middle regulator.
T. Ditto at the lowest point at the lake bed.
W. Rock Arch or vaulted passage (over the country road) to the Hermitage.
X. Cascade which gets its water from the Surface conduit.
Z. Pantheon, or temple with the façade towards the upper water.
The conduit S ends at the country road and [the water] flows in the open into the lower water.

The Stourhead dam can be compared with others impounding ornamental lakes:[9]

	Date	Length (ft/metres)	Maximum height (ft)	Width of crest (ft)	Lake impounded (acres)
Serpentine, Hyde Park	1730–1	515 (156.7)	17	60	40
Grimsthorpe, Lincs.	1746–8	420 (128)	18	20	36
Virginia Water, Berks.	1782	600 (183)	30	–	59
Petworth, Sussex	1752	540 (164.6)	23	35	15
Stourhead Garden Lake	1754–6	722 (220)	33	15	18.3

The Garden Lake, dam and Cascade, 1812–16, by Francis Nicholson (1753–1844), watercolour, 405 × 552 mm. British Museum.

The dam forming the Serpentine in Hyde Park was built in 1730–1. Charles Bridgeman was responsible for its design and the construction involved 200 labourers.[10] The Serpentine dam contained a clay core estimated to be 18 feet wide. At Grimsthorpe in Lincolnshire, John Grundy the younger (1719–83) designed a dam for the Duke of Ancaster; his drawing and estimate survive.[11] He built a larger version of this dam for the duke in 1746–8.[12] The design shows a similar profile to the Stourhead dam. However, Grundy inserted a central core of compacted clay six feet wide. In the course of his career Capability Brown constructed forty dams, his first at Petworth in Sussex, in 1752. To make it watertight he laid a blanket of clay over the inner face of the dam, protected near the crest by stone pitching.[13]

The Stourhead dam, devoid of architectural ornament, is seen to advantage from the Shades where the view opens to the Garden Lake and Turner's Paddock Lake with Top Wood beyond.[14]

The Garden Lake

The lake covers about 18 acres (7.4 hectares).[15] Piper assessed it at 28 feet deep at the dam face.[16] The underwater survey plotted the shallows at a few feet, depending on the water level.[17] The lake is fed by the infant River Stour whose springs flow from Six Wells Bottom, in the Grotto and below the Temple of Flora.

The 1792 low-water plan suggests how Henry Hoare sculpted the shore (page 138). He excavated along the western bank from the Grotto to Watch Cottage, carving out Pantheon Island in the process and forming the bay preceding that temple. Along the opposite bank, from the Wooden Bridge to the Boathouse, he dug the shallows leaving Bird Island and excavated the shore from the Temple of Flora to the Stone Bridge. The margins of the lake and islands are protected with stone cladding which was relaid in 1974–5.[18]

Before commencing the dam Henry had built the Wooden Bridge which, like the Grotto floor, would have determined the maximum rise in the water level of about three or four feet above the existing ponds.[19] Drawings show how water then lapped inches below the timber springing of the bridge (page 151).

In 1762 Henry extended the lake eastwards towards the village and remodelled the shore when he built the Stone Bridge.[20] Until the twentieth century the two islands were planted with low shrubs and no trees.[21] Piper invented a third island rising between the dam and the village.[22]

The Garden Lake was well stocked with fish. *A ride and a walk through Stourhead* celebrated:

> Huge Carp, like Porpoises, their fatten'd Sides
> And golden Scales in wanton Sport display.[23]

When Colt Hoare drained the lake in 1792 he counted about 2,600 carp and 'an abundance of eels'.[24] In 1807 Richard Fenton found the water, 'most remarkably

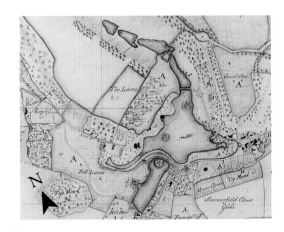

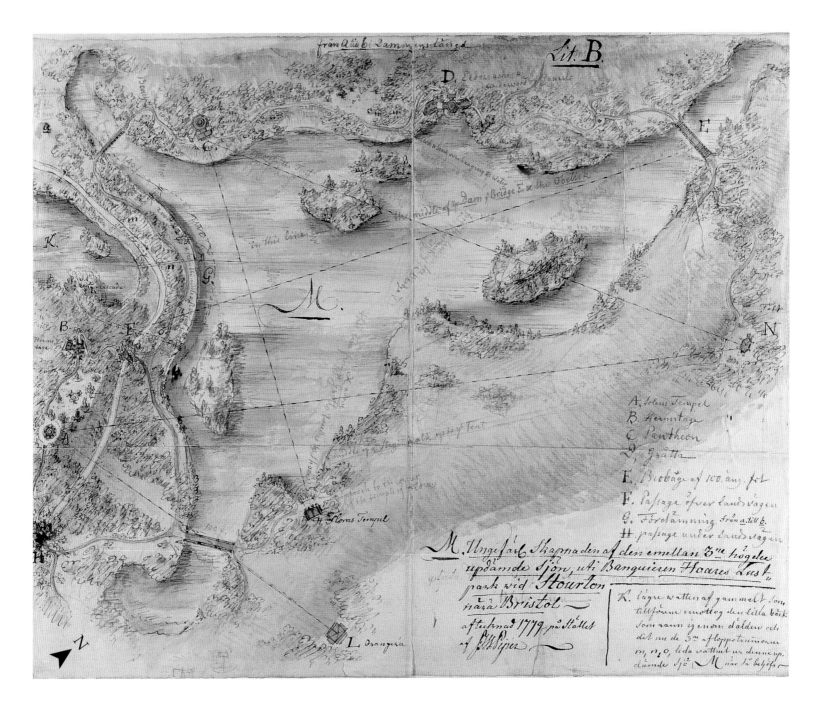

Lit. B.

'Lit. B. Approximate appearance of the lake pent up between three hills in Banker Hoare's pleasure park at Stourton near Bristol, drawn on the spot in 1779 by F.M. Piper', (1746–1824), pencil, ink and colourwash, 333 × 422 mm. The Royal Swedish Academy of Fine Arts, Stockholm. Piper added two fictitious islands.

clear, and free from weeds'.[25] But three years later something had evidently gone wrong; Louis Simond protested during July, 'the water of the lake is dull and muddy, full of reeds and aquatic plants, which mark its stagnation.'[26] In 1824 Colt Hoare also complained about the depth of silt and the dearth of fish in the lake.[27] The remedy, if there was one, is unknown. The practice of netting the lake persisted in the nineteenth century, an event Augusta, wife of the 5th baronet, recorded in her diary.[28] There is no record of attempts to dredge the bottom and the underwater survey encountered deep layers of silt that rose in dense clouds when disturbed.[29]

In 1756 Jonas Hanway made a 'coasting voyage on the little enchanting ocean' in 'a very pretty boat'.[30] The earliest images of the garden show a miniature yacht moored on the Garden Lake (pages 140 and 167).[31] Fanciful or not, a publication

written a few years later described, 'a handsome pleasure-boat'.[32] C. W. Bampfylde depicted rowing boats on the lake in the 1770s. Hester, bride of Colt Hoare, boasted to her friend about a romantic voyage on the lake in 1785.[33] Augusta, Lady Hoare also enjoyed boat trips and Alda, wife of the 6th baronet, encouraged house guests onto the water.[34]

The Pantheon

Henry Hoare commissioned the marble *Hercules* in 1747 which suggests he had in mind a Temple of Hercules, or Pantheon as it is better known. Building was in progress by 1753 and the interior complete by 1762.[35] Sir John Parnell considered it 'the most Elegant Expensive Building I Ever saw in an Improvement, not even the Best at Kew Excepted'.[36] The editor of the *Tour through the island of Great Britain* (1779) claimed that the Pantheon, 'except the temple of Concord in lord Temple's gardens at Stowe, is the most superb garden-building in Great Britain'.[37] By coincidence Charles Hamilton completed the Temple of Bacchus at Painshill in 1762. Henry sniped at this rival temple:

> It is an oblong the Form of The Temple of Fortuna Virilis or the Long Temple of Balbec. The Bacchus a Noble Statue stands in the Center & turns a profile to You as You enter. Windows are on the other end & in my poor opinion the figure (truely Antique) is lost or hurt in a Temple built on purpose for it.[38]

The antique marble *Bacchus* has since lost prestige and is now at Anglesey Abbey in Cambridgeshire while the Painshill temple was demolished *c.*1950.[39] Flitcroft designed the Temple of Hercules for Henry Hoare, taking the Pantheon in Rome as his starting point and evolving a building of independent character.[40]

One drawing, attributable to Flitcroft, shows the Stourhead temple with a blunt pyramidal roof rather than a dome.[41] Henry Hoare paid the builder William Privett directly up to 1755, with further instalments presumably made through Francis Faugoin (Appendix I).[42] To complicate matters, Henry, himself, paid some secondary contractors.[43] According to Piper the Pantheon cost £12,000.[44]

The five-bay Corinthian portico *in antis* is flanked by short screen walls each with niches set at the front and sides. The two forward-facing niches contain lead casts of the *Callipygian Venus* and *Bacchus* while the side niches are empty.[45] In 1787 Count di Rezzònico identified these statues and a lost cast of the *Dancing Faun* on one flank.[46] Above the portico looms the triangular pediment and, behind, the drum and lead-clad dome of the rotunda. The composition works both at water level and from the Shades. The exterior walls of the rotunda form an octagon chamfered as it rises into the squat drum. The entire building is clad in Chilmark stone with an ashlar finish which was an extravagance bearing in mind the rear of the building thrusts into the hillside which has always been densely planted. The inner walls and basement are brick (page 174).

Mounting the shallow steps to the portico, visitors pass through the screen of Corinthian columns into a spacious loggia closed at the ends by square apses

View of the Pantheon across the Garden Lake.

'The Pantheon rose up in front of me with portico and rotunda derived from the building by Agrippa. The former comprises four freestanding Corinthian columns and two pilasters make a dignified front to the vestibule.' Count di Rezzònico 1787.

furnished with a pair of wooden table altars. The apses have enjoyed several
lodgers. Horace Walpole described each 'with a Vase, to imitate porphyry' (he
was probably referring to the pair of vases now in the vestibule to the rotunda).[47]
By 1800 Warner could admire 'two antique busts, that on the right Alexander,
and that on the left Pompey', perhaps those now in the Temple of Flora.[48]
Sweetman's guidebook for 1907 noted 'in niches are busts of Minerva and Ceres'.[49]
Today two handsome eighteenth-century consoles carry stock plaster busts of
Homer and *Horace*.[50] Entering the building is a solemn experience contrasting
with the theatre enjoyed in the Grotto; the double-leaf door opens into a darkened
vestibule, undecorated apart from two plaster vases and an iron screen at the far end.

    Henry Hoare, Flitcroft and Rysbrack had ample time to plan the decoration
of the rotunda whose coffered ceiling recalls the Roman Pantheon.[51] The space
is flooded with light from a central oculus filtered through yellow stained glass.[52]
From this opening spreads the shallow coffered dome reaching down to imposing
plasterwork entablature.[53] The walls are painted to approximate the 'broken-purple'
remarked upon by Joseph Spence and Warner: the further from chocolate brown,

*Reconstruction of the Pantheon in
Rome*, 1553, unknown, engraving
published by Antonio Lafreri
(1512–77), 346 × 473 mm.
The Metropolitan Museum of Art,
New York.

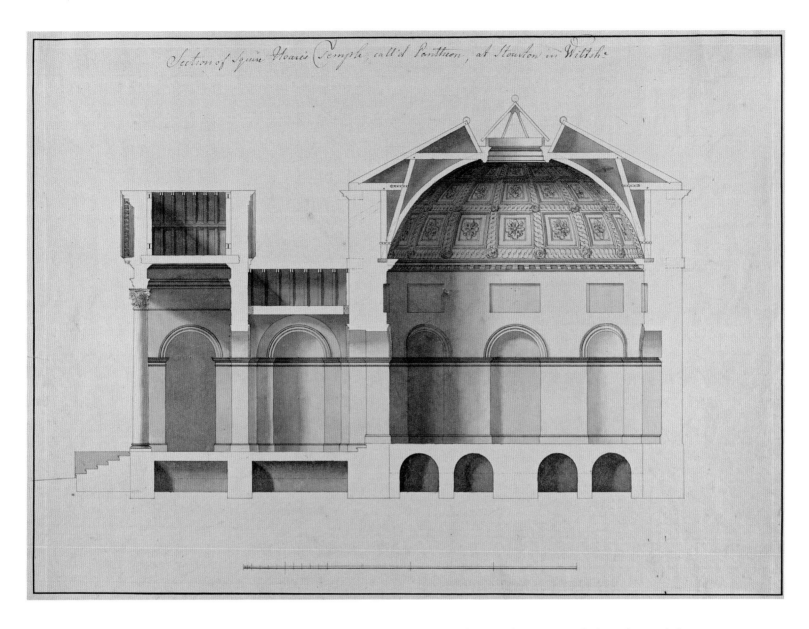

the better.[54] Samuel Woodforde and Francis Nicholson depicted the interior; curiously both transposed the statues of *Diana* and *Meleager*.[55]

Seven round-headed niches house an assembly of life-size sculptures: opposite the entrance is the marble *Hercules* by Rysbrack flanked by the antique *Livia Augusta* (page 145) and a marble *Flora*, also by Rysbrack. At the sides *Diana*, in lead (page 150), confronts a plaster *Meleager* (his hound omitted) while the entrance is guarded by plaster casts representing an antique *Priestess of Isis* and seventeenth-century *Santa Susanna,* after François Duquesnoy (1597–1643).[56] John Cheere supplied *Meleager* and the remainder are usually attributed to him because he had access to the moulds and supplied other sculptures to Henry Hoare.[57] Hunter and huntress chime with a theme in the plaster relief panels above. If Henry or his contemporaries read a symbolic significance in the priestess and saint, that meaning is lost although Isis is thought to personify nature. The two statues were, perhaps, admired as exemplars of drapery carving: the one, ancient; the other, modern.[58]

Rysbrack signed the contract for *Hercules* in 1747.[59] The marble sculpture is inscribed with the date 1756 and Henry gave the sculptor a bonus of £50 the

following July swelling the cost to over £430.[60] The sculptor bequeathed Henry
the terracotta model mentioned in the contract.[61] According to George Vertue,
Rysbrack made the model for *Hercules* early in 1743/4. Vertue described
how the sculptor:

> Finding himself somewhat at leisure. business not being so brisk (as had
> been with him for some years before.) He therefore set himself about a
> Model of Hercules with the intention to show all the skill he was Master of…
> in order to his improvement in this study, he had found out a strong well
> made proportiond man. being one of the famous fighting boxers – [*George
> the Coachman*] – of Broughtons Amphiater – by this man he planted his
> whole figure, and as it is sd of the Antient Greek statuarys – from several
> human bodies they formd an Intire Model best of the proportions the best
> scimetry. & parts accumulated together in one figure. so when Rysbrake
> had well disposd & planted his Model of Clay, in due proportions – he had
> the bodies of several other men stood naked before him in order to form the
> body, Limbs. arms legs &c to chuse the most beautyfull, or the most perfect
> parts. for example – the head [*coachman*] of Hercules he had several antient
> Medals – for the neck & breast [*Taylor*]. for the belly & lower arts another.
> [*broughton*] for the back of the neck & shoulders [*Hussey*] another for the

Armes to the wrist [*Ellis*] for the thighs and legs [*&c*]. the lower part of the back another – besides modelld hands & feet from the best chosen life. or antique – at least seaven or 8 different men – & altogether. is surely an excellent Model for truth correctnes & excellentcy of stile. [*about 2 feet hi.*] truely comparable to the ancient statue of Hercules.[62]

Rysbrack drew inspiration from the *Farnese Hercules*, a vast marble by Glykon, third century AD, which Henry Hoare could have seen in the courtyard of the Palazzo Farnese in Rome. [63] The sculptor never went to Italy and would have relied on drawings, prints and reductions of this famous statue. He took the pose from a lost painting of *Hercules in the Garden of the Hesperides* by Pietro Cortona and known from an engraving.[64] Both the *Farnese Hercules* and Rysbrack's version clasp apples in allusion to his success stealing the golden fruit from their guardians. Walpole maintained Rysbrack copied the head from the *Farnese Hercules* but it is apparent from the terracotta bust, now at the Mellon Center at Yale, that Rysbrack used 'antient Medals'.[65]

In 1759 Rysbrack signed the contract for *Flora* with Henry Hoare who stipulated 'a Figure of Flora in Statuary Marble from the Antique'.[66] His model was the *Flora*, companion to *Hercules* from the Palazzo Farnese, itself a Roman copy of a Greek *Aphrodite* dating from the fifth century BC.[67] Rysbrack would have known the *Farnese Flora* from drawings, engravings and a lead cast at Kensington Palace.[68] The sculptor made a terracotta model for the Stourhead *Flora* which he mentioned to Sir Edward Littleton on 14 December 1758:

> I have made a Model of Flora (which I am glad Every Body approve of) I have followed the Model of Flora which I had by me, and likewise a Flora in Plaster, only altering some Places according to Mr. Hoare's Desire for whom I am going to do it in Marble.[69]

Sir Edward purchased the little terracotta which is now at the Victoria and Albert Museum.[70] John Cheere took a mould to make plaster statuettes.[71]

The head on the terracotta is closer to the *Farnese Flora* than to the Stourhead marble. Walpole had commented in 1762 that the latter was 'much inferior to the Hercules; the head particularly flat & without grace.'[72] He enlarged on this criticism in a letter to Henry Hoare who forwarded it to Lord Bruce with this reaction:

> Mᵣ Rysbrack will return with me... in order to examine & retouch the Head of Ceres [Flora] He left unfinishd till He saw it in its place with the Skylight [in the Pantheon] I beg Yours and Dear Lady Bruce's thoughts on yᵉ enclosed from Mᵣ Walpole wherein He says the features are too short & compressd.[73]

Henry commissioned eight plaster relief panels, painted to resemble stone, placed above the niches and the entrance.[74] Benjamin Carter supplied the set *c.*1760 priced at £16 each, although Henry paid him a total of £162–9s.[75] The sculptor had previously supplied a marble chimneypiece and a pedestal for the Skylight Room. The reliefs were one-offs and taken (with a single exception) from engravings in Montfaucon's *L'antiquité expliquée* or from his source, illustrations by Pietro Santi Bartoli in *Admiranda Romanarum Antiquitatum*, in turn copied from antique marble reliefs in Roman collections.[76] Rysbrack's name has been linked with the Stourhead plasters and he may well have suggested, even lent, the source publications to Carter.[77] Henry, with or without Rysbrack, could have selected the engravings which represent sports, hunting, amorous frolics (reprised in the painted bench backs), nuptials, feasting and drinking. The exuberance of these reliefs contrasts with the serious-minded statues below.

The rotunda is furnished with four seats, the design once more derived in part from *L'antiquité expliquée*. The back panels were painted by William Hoare of Bath with a variety of amorous deities and *putti*, again taken from antique sources.[78]

Flora, 1759–61, by Michael Rysbrack (1694–1770), marble, H 179 cm. Stourhead.

The theme of plaster reliefs and bench backs set a bucolic and hedonistic tone. How tantalising it is that Henry made no mention of his activities at the Pantheon! Walpole observed the rotunda was warmed by a heating apparatus.[79] In 1779 Piper recorded an addition at the rear of the building labelled 'Furnace room' and indicated how hot air was introduced to the rotunda.[80] Hendrik Frans de Cort, with greater accuracy and less imagination, drew an altogether humbler building tacked on at the back (page 174)[81]. This outhouse has gone but the rotunda has an external flue and its flanking walls are scarred with traces of the pitched roof comparable to de Cort's record. In 1804 Thomas Chippendale the younger delivered a stove for the rotunda.[82] Hester, the young bride of Colt Hoare, wrote in 1785 'we have been since dinner on the Water and were amused with Music in the Pantheon, during the whole of the Voyage'.[83]

From the Pantheon steps visitors enjoy the view across the water towards the Temple of Flora, Stourton and once, to the far left, the Turkish Tent.

The Turkish Tent (demolished)

The tent was not for purists in search of a classical Elysium. It stood, indeed, as an antithesis to the Pantheon. Pitched in the Shades, above the Wooden Bridge, it was colourful, decorative and exotic.[84] Piper marked the position on his general plan.[85] A visitor in 1765 described how:

Design for a Turkish tent at Painshill, c.1760, by Henry Keene (1726–76), pencil and colour wash, 137 x 225 mm. Victoria & Albert Museum.

we next walked to the Turkish Tent, a very pretty Invention, It is covered with white Linnen & fringed with Blue, the inside is Painted Blue & White in Stripes like a Sattin, there is three half Moons on the Top which you see at a great distance.[86]

Four years later Parnell sniffed, 'on the Bank opposite the Attic temple is a Turkish tent taken from M[r] Hamiltons, very elegant but rather inferior to his.'[87] George Hamilton had erected his Turkish Tent at Painshill in 1759. It comprised canvas draped around a brick structure with the timber roof covered in lead. This was the model for Henry Hoare. As at Painshill, the Stourhead tent was a viewing station commanding a grassy slope dropping to the water's edge and overlooking the Grotto and Pantheon (page 140).[88] It is seen on a cream bowl and dish cover in Wedgwood's 'Green Frog Service', 1773–4.[89]

In 1776 Henry invited Susanna, Lady Ailesbury, to smarten up the tent which Mrs Powys viewed with approval.[90] In 1780 the rhymer of the *Ride and Walk* willingly took shelter:

> Still we ascend, till the gay Silver Tent
> Of Mussulman th' extended Nerves unbends.
> Here seated I regale luxuriously;
> While three resplendent Crecents o'er my Head
> At Mid-day shine – and Phoebus is obscur'd.[91]

Alas, the tent had gone by 1792 while the Painshill original survived until 1870 and has been replicated.[92]

The Mount of Diana with the Turkish Tent, covered dessert-bowl with views of Stourhead Garden and Lympne Castle in Kent, 1773–4, from the *Green Frog Service*, by Wedgwood Manufactory, Staffordshire, faience and overglaze painting, 17.25 × 17.5 cm. State Hermitage, St Petersburg.

THE GARDEN 1762–72

'A charming Gaspard picture'

From the steps of the Pantheon Henry the Magnificent could relish the view across the Garden Lake. To the left, the Shades reared up behind the Temple of Flora. In the centre stood St Peter's Church and the village (pages 182–3).[1] To the right, the south shores of the lake were hemmed by the public road from which the hill rose abruptly. Close to the Pantheon the prospect encompassed the crest of the dam.

There was no cause to repose and Henry's imagination was already active. He wrote to his daughter, Susanna, in 1762:

> You allways wish'd I would build at the passage into the orchard & the scheme of carrying the Water up & loosing out of sight towards the parish this Bridge is now about. It is simple & plain I took it from palladio's Bridge at Vicenza, 5 arches, & when You stand at the pantheon the Water will be seen thro the Arches & it will look as if the River came down thro the Village & that this was the Village Bridge for publick use. The View of the Bridge, Village & Church alltogether will be a Charm[g] Gasp[d] picture at the end of that Water.[2]

The Stone Bridge (1762) provides a visual link between the lake and the village. Two years after it was erected, a stroke of luck enabled Henry to acquire the medieval high cross, recently dismantled in Bristol. This he placed felicitously between the bridge and the village. Henry let fantasy rip when he placed a sculpture of *Neptune and his horses* (1765) in the lake close to the Temple of Flora. He left the dam unadorned, treating it as a terrace from which to enjoy the Garden Lake and the view of the lower lake (Turner's Paddock Lake). This he enlivened with a Cascade (1765–6) plunging artistically over carefully positioned boulders.

The southern hillside is visible from paths through the Shades so it is surprising that Henry left the slope unadorned until the 1760s. The road was sufficiently busy for him to build a bridge and underpass, allowing visitors to traverse it without interrupting their garden idyll. Both crossings were contrived in a playful and inventive manner. Near the top of the hillside Henry built the Temple of Apollo (1765), his final homage to classical architecture. Henry had long toyed with a circular temple for Stourhead; indeed Henry Flitcroft had drawn up plans for one in 1744 (page 51). The architect returned to the theme twenty years later. Close to hand

From the west shore towards Stourton, the Boathouse, Temple of Flora, Bristol Cross and Stone Bridge.

'Gardens at Stourhead from ye
Pantheon', view of the Temple
of Flora, *Neptune and his horses*,
Stone Bridge, Stourton village and
Temple of Apollo, *c*.1770–80, by
C. W. Bampfylde (1720–91), pencil
and grey wash, 275 × 752 mm.
Victoria & Albert Museum.

Henry placed the Hermitage (1771), both stage-set and viewing station. He joked that he would become the hermit. Temple and Hermitage stood in counterpoint, perhaps echoing the dichotomy between the Temple of Flora and the Bristol Cross.

The Stone Bridge

The bridge was a favourite with artists but prompted relatively few comments from eighteenth-century visitors. Henry acknowledged the design came from Palladio although his bridge has five arches rather than Palladio's three.[3] William Privett provided the facing stone and presumably built the structure, c.1762.[4] It has a turf deck and served no practical purpose; J. C. Loudon, ignoring its visual significance, dismissed it as 'over-conspicuous and superfluous'.[5]

The Bristol High Cross

Henry acquired the Bristol Cross in 1764 and erected it the following year where the garden and village meet.[6] Sir John Parnell admired how the Cross:

> Stands within his grounds but appears as belonging to a little Village with a real parish church just without them. this was the very spot of all others to place this neat Building in, which would have wanted meaning as a mere garden Building. here it appears as the markett cross of a neat Village. On Entering the grounds by This cross are two or three pretty Cottages neatly ornamented with trees, but thatchd, w[ch] I much admire for its simplicity.[7]

The monument had enjoyed a crowded history since its erection c.1400 in Bristol at the intersection of Broad Street and High Street with Wine Street and Corn Street.[8] It is a confection of stone canopies sheltering sculptures; on the first storey stand King John, Henry III, Edward I (?) and Edward III. In 1633 a second tier was added with seated monarchs: Henry VI, Elizabeth I, James I and Charles I.

There matters rested for a century until the structure was taken down in 1733 and re-erected on College Green where it was depicted by Samuel and Nathaniel Buck who described it as 'Guilded and Painted'.[9] In 1762 the Cross was again dismantled and relegated to store. The following year the Reverend Cutts Barton, recently appointed Dean of Bristol, gave Henry permission to remove the fragments of the Cross. The dean was a long-standing friend of Henry Hoare, indeed his younger brother, Montagu, was rector of Stourton.[10] Parnell remarked that Henry had 'paid for the Carriage & putting up about £300' and there is no record in Henry's account book that he purchased the Cross.[11] On 2 October 1764 Henry wrote to Thomas Paty, the Bristol architect and statuary mason:

> The Dean of Bristol is so obliging as to write to me word I may send for the Cross directly. I have therefore ordered my servant, Faugoin, to send out two waggons from Stourhead... as I shall be at Stourhead the end of November or the beginning of December, wish it may be convenient to you to come over, and let me see you and consult with you how to repair and put it up, and what base or support will be required for it.[12]

Paty hired four more waggons and, assuming they arrived at Stourhead that winter, Henry spent the next twelve months repairing the fragments. He wrote to Lord Bruce in December 1765 describing the preparations: 'The Cross is now in hand & there are so many pieces that We must I believe employ Harriot [his granddaughter] to put it together'.[13] And, a few weeks later, 'I also saw the first Story of the Cross put just together & repair'd & now the rest will go on swimingly & be done sooner than We expected. & the foundation of Stones is finished & the mount forming round it'.[14] Henry replaced the original five shafts supporting the structure but, late in the day, took fright and encased the centre pier in a unifying ashlar pillar.

In 1776 Henry painted the monument and topped it with an iron cross.[15] Mrs Powys was critical of this embellishment, 'its Kings & Queens in the Nitches round it would in my opinion have look'd better of the original Stone Color, than so Ornamented with red, Blue & Gilt Clothing; but still 'tis pretty through this profusion of finery'.[16] Count di Rezzònico commented that Queen Elizabeth I 'is skied so that her posture looks indecent and calls to mind Tasso's saying 'Sovra scettri e corone alzi la gonna'.[17] William Gilpin echoed these criticisms: 'The gilt-cross is a very disgusting object'.[18] Henry would have noticed traces of earlier paint and gilding on the statues and may have wished to revive the custom. Its fairground colouring would have delighted his grandchildren. Colt Hoare was content to let the Cross weather without cleaning off the paint, because a watercolour sketch by Nicholson shows the figures coloured.[19] Fragments of paint still adhere to the standing monarchs.

Colt Hoare admired the ancientness of the Cross and during his life it became the most remarked-upon feature of the garden, commended in particular by John Britton.[20] In Victorian times Bristol awoke to the historic significance of the Cross; a newspaper reported a visit by the Mayor in 1879 to assess whether it could return to the city, 'an intimation having, we believe, been received from the present baronet

The Bristol High Cross, 1734, by Samuel (1696–1779) and Nathaniel (fl.1724–59) Buck, engraving, 475 × 300 mm. Stourhead.

RIGHT
The Bristol High Cross, 1812–16,
by Francis Nicholson (1753–1844),
pencil and watercolour,
360 × 210 mm. British Museum.

OVERLEAF
The eastern extremity of the
Garden Lake, the Bristol Cross
and St Peter's church.

[Sir Henry Ainslie Hoare] if the citizens cared to recover the old monument they were welcome to it'.[21] The Mayor concluded it was too fragile – in other words too expensive – to move.[22] The monument, evidently precarious, was dismantled and repaired at Stourhead in 1894–1895.[23] Bristol again requested the return of the Cross in 1975. A few years later the National Trust dismantled the structure, strengthened the five supporting shafts and removed the infill from the base to enhance its filigree appearance. The Trust lent the Victoria and Albert Museum the four standing kings to safeguard the paintwork and in return the museum supplied carved stone replicas for the Cross.[24]

Neptune and his prancing horses (removed)

Henry Hoare wrote to Lord Bruce at Christmas 1765, 'I had the satisfaction of seeing Neptune & His 4 Naggs (& very fine & full of Spirit They are) landed on His Pedestal before the Arch under the Dorick Temple [of Flora]... & it has a fine appearance there.'[25] Captain Barton, the rector's brother, supervised this enjoyably muddy operation.[26]

Neptune, invisible from the village, would have been discernible from the Pantheon and prominent in the view from the Hermitage and Temple of Apollo. It has not survived so its appearance must be surmised from Henry's description and calligraphic squiggles in panoramas by C. W. Bampfylde, c.1770. In one drawing the horse-drawn chariot appears close to the Temple of Flora (page 139).[27] A second drawing also hints that Neptune emerged from the arched cavern below the temple.[28]

Henry recorded neither the name of the sculptor nor the material. A payment in his ledger the following spring might indicate that William Hoare of Bath acted as an intermediary, '2 Statues bought by Mr Hoare & pd by Mr Barton & Mr Webb £31.10s'.[29] Were it not for this entry, John Cheere would be the obvious supplier, although his Neptune fountain at Queluz in Portugal, c.1755, does not match the Stourhead descriptions. The Neptune group proved controversial. In 1769 Parnell wrote:

> a statue of Neptune his carr with sea Horses Just as coming out of his Cave
> & Launching in the Deep. the worse thing in my opinion of Mr Hoare's,
> as having too Little of nature to be admitted into a scene where all appears
> an arcadia or Beautifull spott of an Existing country, not a mere Visionary
> scene where Neptune may be supposed more properly to Exhibit his Ideal
> Chariot.[30]

This criticism was echoed in 1787 by Count di Rezzònico.[31] Colt Hoare was equally disenchanted and expunged Neptune so effectively that the underwater survey in 2004–5 found no trace of it.[32]

Turner's Paddock Lake

The lower lake extends from the foot of the Garden Lake dam and is depicted in the 1773 engraving (page 167).[33] It was known as the 'mill pond' until the twentieth century when it became 'Turner's Paddock Lake'.[34] F. M. Piper included it on his plans and from his annotation we might infer it was earlier than the Garden Lake.[35]

Henry Hoare made the pond into an ornamental feature which Parnell described in 1769 as 'another fine Piece of water not long made, its Head not yett conceald by Plantation as it will be in a few years'.[36] The 1785 plan recorded the lake with an island at the near end and a mill beside the retaining dam.[37] Piper also plotted this island and Turpin de Crissé drew all the features.[38] Colt Hoare demolished the mill in 1812 and at some point the island was scalped.[39]

The Cascade

The Cascade, constructed from 1765–6, was designed by Henry's boon-companions William Hoare and Bampfylde.[40] It was inspired by the artificial waterfall which Bampfylde had created at Hestercombe.[41] The Stourhead version is fed from the Garden Lake and falls about 30 feet.[42] Visiting Stourhead in 1797 John Skinner was lukewarm: 'an artificial cascade, the gardener having previously dispatched a person to open the sluice... it would be injurious to compare it with any of the natural falls in North Wales or Cumberland.'[43] In 1797 John Thelwall found the cascade 'theatrically artificial'.[44]

ABOVE
View from the dam to the Turner's Paddock Lake, detail from the panorama, 1812–16, by Francis Nicholson (1753–1844), pen and wash, 460 × 4600 mm. Stourhead.

RIGHT
The Cascade, Turner's Paddock Lake and the mill at Stourhead, 1793, by Lancelot-Henri Roland Turpin de Crissé (1754–c.1800), pencil, 230 × 370 mm. Musées d'Angers.

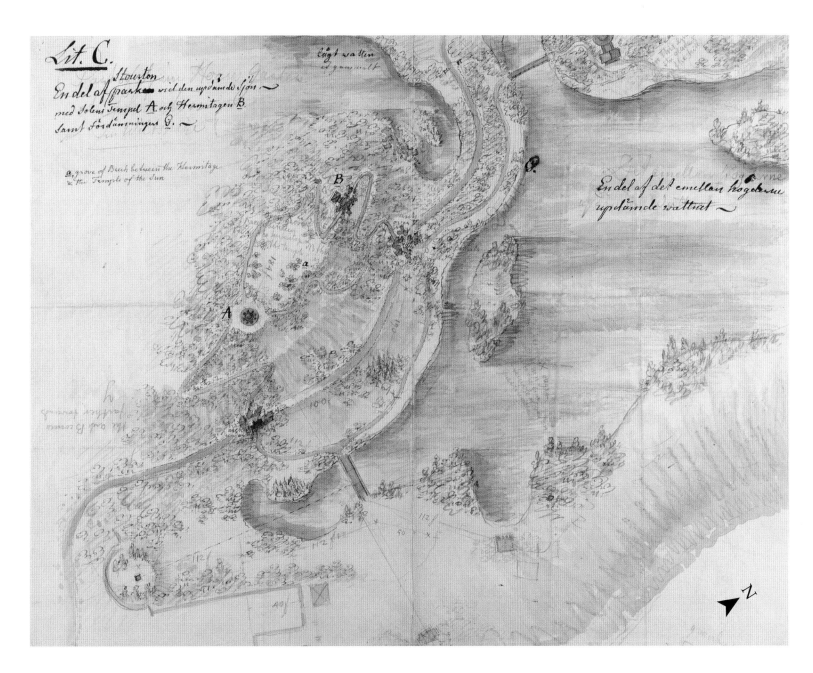

Within the map image (handwritten annotations):

Lit. C.

Stourton
En del af park... vid den updämda Sjön ~
med Solens Tempel A. och Hermitagen B.
samt fördämningen G. ~

a, grove of Beech between the Hermitage
& the Temple of the Sun

B

a

A

lågt wattn
af gammalt

En del af det emellan högderne
updämde wattnet ~

ABOVE

'Lit. C. Part of Stourton Park at
the dammed up Lake', c.1779, by
F. M. Piper (1746–1824), ink, colour
wash and pencil, 336 × 422 mm.
The Royal Swedish Academy of
Fine Arts, Stockholm.

Annotated: 'The Temple of the Sun
A. and the Hermitage B., and also
the dam, G.' Left: 'a, grove of Beech
between the Hermitage and the
Temple of the Sun.' Centre: 'A part
of the water dammed between the
hills.' The island shown opposite
the Hermitage is fictitious.

OPPOSITE
The Cascade.

The southern shore

In the 1760s Henry Hoare turned his attention to the hillside south of the road
from Stourton to Gasper. There he built the Temple of Apollo and the Hermitage,
reached by crossing at the Rock Arch, with the return through an underpass (before
1765). Progressing from the dam, visitors could choose whether to follow the lake
shore or climb the hill to these follies. The level path to the village runs parallel to
the public road. It is visible in Bampfylde's watercolour and marked on Piper's
sketch plan.[45] The strip of ground between the dam and the Stone Bridge is hemmed
by the lake and a low stone wall against the public road.
Parnell described:

> a Rail cutts of[f] this fine Dressd Part of the Banks of the Lake from a Part fed
> with Sheep and open to many sorts of fowl, which being fed here keep on this
> Part when out of the water.[46]

The Rock Arch and souterrain

The arch was described in 1765 by an anonymous commentator and by Joseph Spence.[47] It is a substantial bridge spanning the road. From the garden path it appears as a jumble of moss-covered stones coagulating into caves, reminiscent of Italian grottoes. From the road it appears as a bridge clad in greenstone, enlivened by mysterious hollows and knobbly parapets.[48] In 1769 Parnell described:

> a sort of Ruind castle & winding up one of the turrets goes along a Passage which you find to be over the High Road, as the Passages Round a fortified town are carried over great gateways, only all seems in Ruin, grass &c growingly Extremely Romantickly in Evry Interstice of this Whimsical Building.[49]

And the excitable rhymer of a *Ride and a walk through Stourhead* exclaimed:

> But lo! A dire Impediment compels
> To halt. The tott'ring ruin'd Arch impends,
> Nodding Destruction from its convex Weight.
> gaze – it falls not – Resolution comes.[50]

By 1791 Baron van Spaen found the bridge pleasingly dishevelled and screened by a shrubbery.[51]

Visitors return to the village from the Temple of Apollo through the serpentine *souterrain* which is as ingenious as the arch and may be by Flitcroft.[52] Henry Hoare explained, 'I have made the passage up from the Sousterrain Serpentine & will make it easier of access, facilis descensus Averno'.[53]

The Temple of Apollo

Spence, visiting the temple before its completion, remarked that it was preceded by 'the Walk of the Muses' which may be the grove which Piper described as planted with young beech trees.[54] From this short terrace the ground falls away abruptly to the road. Bampfylde depicted the bare hillside with a fringe of trees along the ridge.[55] Colt Hoare planted up the incline so that in his day the Temple of Apollo emerged amidst a leafy canopy.[56]

The glory of the temple is the view opening from its steps and encompassing the lake and the landscape beyond. Bampfylde drew this prospect *c.*1770 (page 139).[57] Spence listed the buildings visible.[58] Baron van Spaen was enchanted by the prospect and, unusually, mentioned the susurrations rising from the cascade and mill.[59]

In classical mythology Apollo, the sun god, was also god of prophecy, music and poetry. So it is small wonder that Henry Hoare dedicated a temple to Apollo. It was designed by Flitcroft and complete by December 1765.[60] The circular plan derived from the Temples of Vesta in Rome and at Tivoli with a nod to William Kent's Temple of Ancient Virtue (1737) at Stowe. The Stourhead temple has a scalloped entablature and side niches taken from a plate in *The ruins of Balbec* by Robert Wood (1757), a publication which Henry owned.[61] Lady Polwarth, alone

'The Rustic Bridge over the road at Stourhead Wilts June 12 1829', by John Buckler (1770–1851), pencil, 200 × 315 mm. British Library.

Rock Arch crossing the road to Gasper.

among visiting authors, remarked on similarities between the Stourhead temple and the Temple of the Sun at Kew, designed by Sir William Chambers and completed by 1761.[62]

Flitcroft capped his temple with a double-skin dome, and between the entablature and outer shell he interposed a drum pierced by six Diocletian windows so that the inner dome is refulgant, as Richard Warner explained:

> The roof of the temple spreads into a dome, and has a double ceiling, in the lower is the aperture, and in the coving of the other, a splendid gilt representation of the Solar Rays, which, receiving the real light of this orb by an artful construction, throws into the temple below a most splendid reflection when the sun is in its strength.[63]

In 1837, fire damaged the dome which was promptly repaired; two decades later the 4th baronet had to renovate the building.[64] After a period of neglect the dome was replaced by a flat lead roof, which is shown in a 1901 photograph.[65] The 6th

Temple of Apollo from the South, 1812–16, by Francis Nicholson (1753–1844), watercolour, 408 × 563 mm. British Museum.

baronet patched it twice during the 1920s and subsequently replaced the lead skin with a timber structure covered in 'Ruberoid'.[66] The National Trust first placed a hemispherical aluminium dome over the void. In 2009–10 it rebuilt the dome, sheathed in lead, and installed a double ceiling to give an impression of the original.

Chambers had decorated the cove of the Kew temple with the frieze containing the signs of the zodiac. At Stourhead Spence described, 'Niches for Eleven Statues on the outside wall: and the 12 Signs of the Zodiac, are to be over these statues & the Door'; however, the signs were never added.[67] In the niches stood classical statues probably supplied in 1766 by John Cheere who sent a bill for nine lead casts:

'five Drapery Statues of yᵉ Vestal, Ceres, Pomona, Minerva, & Venus Belface [*all most naked* inserted] at 25 Guineas each...
a drapery Statue of Urania [£]21
a Statue of Mercury [£]18–18[s]
a Statue of Apollo [*Very Small* inserted] [£]18–18[s]
Statue of Bacchus [£]21.[68]

Visiting in 1776, the unreliable Samuel Curwen described niches occupied by two busts and five statues, but naming only Venus, Minerva, Apollo and Jupiter. [69] Count di Rezzònico mentioned *Callipygian Venus, Apollino, Mercury,* 'ed altre simili'.[70] In the early twentieth century the statues were removed to decorate the exterior of the house (page 236).[71] Two stone figures occupying niches flanking the entrance represent *Urania* and a *Vestal Virgin* and were commissioned in 1907–8 as copies from the lead casts now at the house.[72] Although Spence hinted that his friend, William Hoare of Bath, doubted a statue befitted the inside of the temple, in 1791 Baron van Spaen admired a cast of the *Apollo Belvedere w*hich filled the interior.[73] Warner also noted his presence.[74] Colt Hoare may well have installed the cast from the South Lawn.[75] It probably succumbed to the fire which destroyed the dome.

Inside the temple Spence opined, 'Guido's Aurora (enlarg'd by the Seasons following the Chariot of Apollo, & Night fleeing from before her) is to be painted round the inside walls by Mr Hoare [of Bath].'[76] There is no trace of this painting on the walls. But there survives a large bench curved to fit the rotunda. The back panel is decorated with a variation of the *Aurora* after Guido Reni and attributed to William Hoare.[77] The bench itself is an inflated version of the Pantheon seats.

Colt Hoare was unnerved by the Baalbek entablature and fretted:

a *defect* in the architecture of the portico which surrounds the building; for one of the chief intents of a portico was to secure a sheltered walk along the building; whereas, in this design, the roof is intersected by excavations of a horse-shoe form between each column, so as to admit every shower of rain in the portico. Here, indeed, there is just reason for criticism: and I wished to have effected such an alteration as to prevent it, by filling up the interstices and cavities in the upper part of the colonnade; but the difficulty was too great to be undertaken.[78]

OVERLEAF
Panorama from the Temple of Apollo towards the north end of the Garden Lake. Compare with Bampfylde's drawing page 139.

He was among several authors referring to The Sun Temple or Temple of the Sun, appellations that linger to the present; but to Henry the Magnificent it was always the 'Temple of Apollo'.[79]

The Hermitage (demolished)

The Hermitage stood to the west of the temple, secluded in a grove of trees. Eighteenth-century visitors found the surroundings melodramatic. Edward Jerningham wrote in 1777, 'passing thro' the gloom of that recess, the burst of light and of the scenery has a most striking effect'.[80] Henry Hoare also provided a viewing station which Piper marked on his plan (page 193).[81] Thus Warner was, 'led [from the Hermitage] to an eminence, when the view becomes more extensive, and the immediate objects being lost, the valley opens to the right and left.[82]

The Hermitage came late to Stourhead. Henry Hoare's friend, Charles Hamilton, had built one for Painshill in 1754, the year Sir Richard Hoare decided to erect one at Barn Elms.[83] The contemporary hermitage at Marston was whimsically equipped with 'a seat or two in it – one is made in the hollow of a tree... a little irregular court, with a fence of horses' heads and bones'.[84] So it was no surprise that, in 1771, Henry disclosed:

> I am building a Hermitage above the Rock [Arch] & when you are about a Quarter part up the walk from the Rock to The Temple of Apollo you turn short to the right & so zig zag up to it & thence go under The Trees to The Temple of Apollo as M[r] Hamilton advised & We stop or plant up in Clumps the old Walk up the Hill to that Temple. It is to be lined inside & out with Old Gouty nobby oakes the Bark on which M[r] [William Chafyn] Grove & my Neighbours are so kind to give me. I am [*quite* inserted] sure it is not ante Diluvian. I believe I shall put in to be myself The Hermit. [85]

Two years later Mrs Rishton found this to be 'a Prodigious fine root-house with Several Cells intended as a hermitage[.] A lamp Always Burning, hour glass, human bones, and several inscriptions'.[86] These inscriptions may have named the Christian hermits whom Count di Rezzònico identified as Saints Mary Magdalene, Paul, Antony, Hilarion and John Climacus.[87]

The hermitage at Painshill sported knobbly tree trunks and rustic materials that Henry would also use but there the resemblance stopped as is apparent from Piper's drawing and description of Stourhead:

> a Hermitage which surpasses everything... with respect to both its well-adapted location and its rustic shape and the Materials there used both externally and internally. These latter consist in reality of large and knobbly Oak stumps, of which the bark sides are cemented together with moss and the upward-turned roots form four pointed archways. One forms the entrance, the 2nd constitutes the entrance to the so called Druid's Cell or hut, the 3rd served as exit and the 4th opens to a view from the Hermitage across the whole Park located below.[88]

The Temple of Apollo.

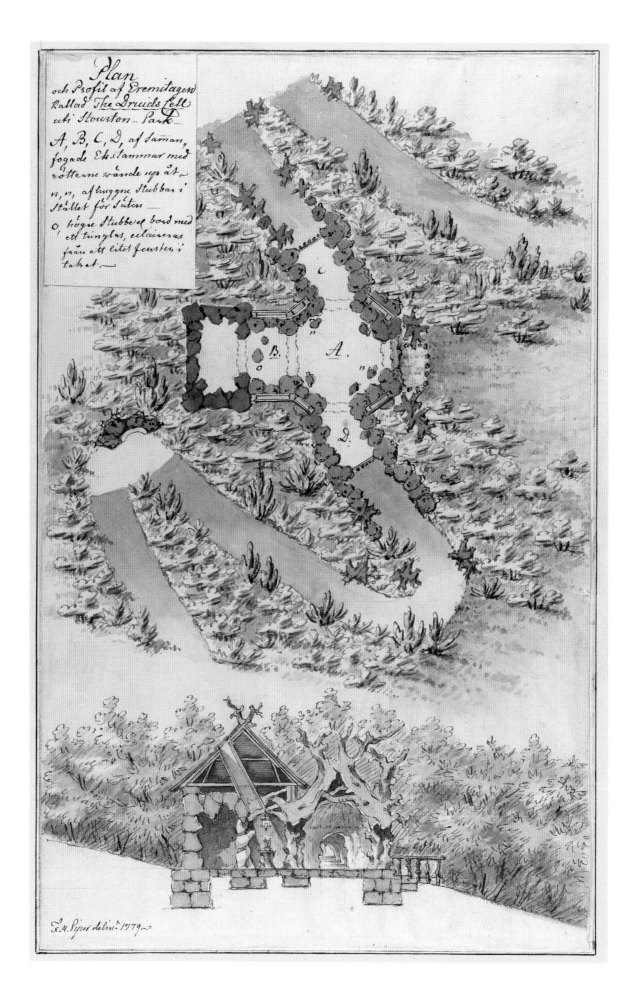

Piper sketched the interior of the Hermitage equipped with furnishings made from tree stumps.[89] In 1767 William Wrighte had published designs for hermitages and their furniture, including, 'Seats attached are intended to be composed of large irregular Stones, Roots of Trees, &c.'[90]

Richard Fenton was the last to describe the Hermitage before Colt Hoare demolished it in 1814–15.[91]

Garden seats

The Pantheon and Temples of Flora and Apollo were equipped with benches and altars derived from Roman precedents. Each suite is remarkable as a bold venture in archaeologically inspired furnishings.[92] For the Convent, Henry Hoare found antiquarian X-frame chairs after Renaissance examples. The Hermitage, as already described, was furnished with chairs and tables made from tree stumps. Was Henry

89
the Best contrived seat I know to take in the
ornaments of a fine situation as by moving
your foot you can take in a new portion of
the Scene when you have sufficiently Examin'd
another it is form'd of a great Butter
Porter Hogshead cutt in the front and a
Seat fixed in With the top Sloped up to
keep off the weather — It is prettiest painted
all green Except the
top which may be Slate
colour, or the Barrel
may be white - if in a
Place where a White object
is desirable it rests
on a pivot below and with a foot may
be turned as the the Person sitting in it pleases
they say Queen Elizabeth was the first
Inventor of these & brittone at Ham

The Iron hoops
are Rivetted on
where they are
not Extended
all Round -
they are Rivetted
where the Dotts are

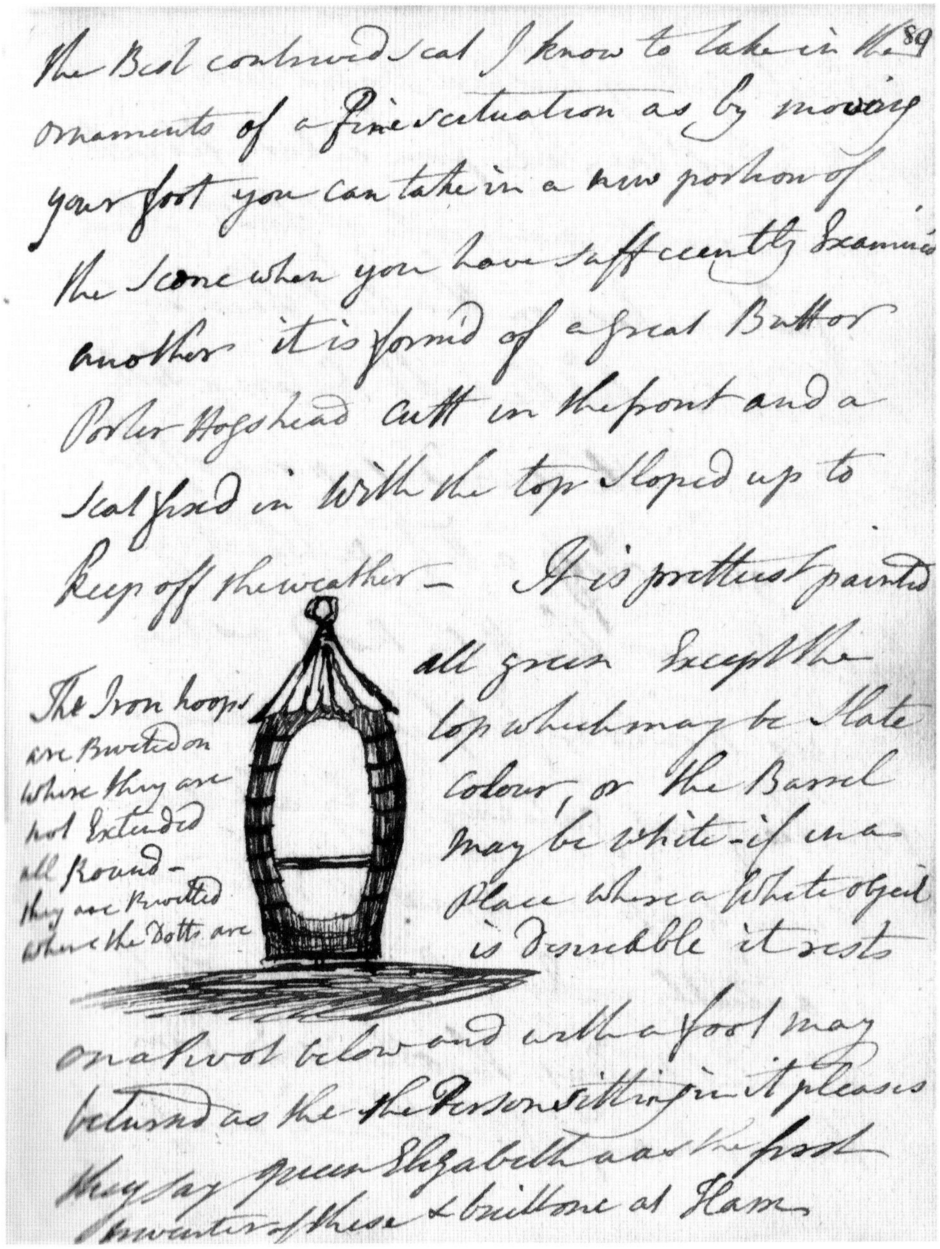

'OPPOSITE
Plan and profile of the Hermitage called the Druid's Cell in Stourton Park, Hermitage', *c.*1779, by F. M. Piper (1746–1824), pencil, ink and colour wash, 432 × 280 mm. The Royal Swedish Academy of Fine Arts, Stockholm.

Annotated: A, B, C, D supports of oak trunks turned upside down. n, n, sawn-off stumps for seats. o, a taller stump for a table with an hourglass and lantern lit from windows above.

RIGHT
Sketch of a garden seat at Stourhead, by Sir John Parnell, 2nd Baronet (1744–1801), ink, 198 × 154 mm. From 'Journal of a Tour thro' Wales and England, anno. 1769' by Sir John Parnell, MS, 4 vols, vol.II, fol. 89. The London School of Economics and Political Science, Archives Collection.

equally innovative out of doors? He placed seats at viewing stations.
 William Clarke mentioned a 'Chinese parasol' close to the Stone Bridge.[93] It was ephemeral but noteworthy because in 1778 Henry Hoare wrote, 'Mr Hoare's picture from The umbrella is here I think it in the Stile of Paul Brill or Brilliant'.[94] Most Chinese umbrellas or parasols in mid-eighteenth century pattern books were elaborate, garnished with tassels and bells. When Piper drew the Stourhead umbrella in 1779 he depicted it as neither fanciful nor exotic.[95]

Henry may have hoisted the umbrella on special occasions; it is absent from the well-known watercolour by Bampfylde (page 50).[96] More idiosyncratic was a barrel seat which so intrigued Parnell in 1769 that he described and drew the feature:

'Druidical Seat in the pleasure Ground of Stourhead Wilts, Augt', 1790, by Samuel Hieronymus Grimm (1733–94), ink, 262 × 185 mm. British Library.

Here [between the Pantheon and dam] stands, level almost with the surface of the Lake, a kind of Seat which, tho' no ornament in itself, is the Best contrived seat I know to take in the ornaments of a fine situation as by moving your foot, you can take in a new portion of the Scene when you have sufficiently Examined another. It is form'd of a great Butt or Porter Hogshead cutt in the front, and a seat fixd in With the top sloped up to keep off the weather. It is prettiest painted, all green, Except the top which may be Slate Colour, or the Barrel may be white, if a Place where a White object is desireable. It rests on a Pivot below, and with a foot may be turned as the Person sitting in it pleases. They say queen Elizabeth was the first inventor of these & built one at Ham.[97]

A similar device is illustrated on the trade card of William Webb, *c*.1785 (along with an X-frame chair).[98]

In contrast to the sophisticated furniture in the Pantheon, Mrs Powys noticed along the path to the Grotto, 'many pretty seats at the Stems of many Trees of Stones piled like rock-work on each other' while S. H. Grimm drew seats placed in hollow tree stumps.[99]

At the Leasowes in Shropshire, Shenstone attached quotations to his seats to nudge the imagination of visitors. Henry may have followed this example. Mrs Rishton, an attentive observer, noted at Stourhead 'there are hundred others [inscriptions] disposed about the gardens'. Would that she, or other visitors, had transcribed these!

'View of the Temple of the Sun, Pantheon &c, in former Banker Hoare's Pleasure Park at Stourton, F M Piper delint 1779', (1746–1824), pencil and ink, 210 × 340 mm. The Royal Swedish Academy of Fine Arts, Stockholm.

THE REGENCY GARDEN

olt Hoare followed a style of gardening closer to nature than that practised by his grandfather. By 1790 the contrast between the bosky Shades and open expanses on the slopes of Diana's Mount and the Temple of Apollo were no more admired than the manicured banks of the Garden Lake. Amos Green echoed this sentiment when he annotated his sketch of the garden in 1792.[1] Compare C. W. Bampfylde's watercolours of the garden with those by Francis Nicholson some fifty years later. The disparities show Colt's planting was extensive.

The Fir Walk was considered old-fashioned before Henry the Magnificent died, so it was no surprise when Colt felled the avenue in 1792 on the pretext of disliking a spikey skyline, preferring broadleaf trees.[2] In addition to beech, oaks and chestnut trees he planted red Virginian cedars, cypresses, maples, sycamores, thorn and flowering specimens such as tulip trees, *Catalpa* and *Chionanthus*.[3] Two venerable tulip trees (*Liriodendron tulipifera*) survive from Colt's day, one at the foot of the South Lawn, a second close to the Rock Arch on the lake shore. His favourite shrub was common laurel which flourished so that, by 1833, J. C. Loudon recommended:

> Two thirds at least of these laurels ought to be removed, and their place

OPPOSITE
Watch Cottage.

RIGHT
The Temple of Apollo from the north end of the lake with the Wooden Bridge, 1792, by Amos Green (1735–1807), pencil and watercolour, 190 × 267 mm. Stourhead.

OVERLEAF
The tulip tree planted by Colt Hoare and the Temple of Apollo.

supplied by rhododendrons and other American shrubs; and by box, holly and yew. This would be nothing more than acting in the spirit of the original planter, laurels being, about the middle of the last century, as choice as rhododendrons are now.[4]

Colt had indeed acquired a single *Rhododendron ponticum* in 1791 and he purchased 200 in 1828.[5] Their mauve flowers gave a new richness to the gardens. Today the path from Diana's Basin to the Grotto is characterised by a mighty *Rhododendron arboreum* which Colt Hoare may well have planted.

Beginning in 1792 Colt laid gravel paths around the lake to make a circuit walk on level ground, and along their borders he planted trees and shrubs.[6] These, or their replacements, lend variety; for example, near the Boathouse: a variegated tulip tree (*Liriodendron tulipifera* 'Aureomarginatum') and pin oak (*Quercus palustris*), and, close to the site of the Wooden Bridge, a London plane (*Plantanus x hispanica*).

After demolishing the bridge in 1798, Colt provided a ferry operated by pulleys (page 153) at the crossing point and also laid a path across the dam separating Diana's Basin from the upper pond, known since Edwardian times as Lily Lake, thus giving visitors a view towards Six Wells Bottom.[7]

By 1810 trees planted by Henry the Magnificent had matured and Colt's new planting was spreading over Diana's Mount and closing in around the Temple of Flora. Colt Hoare considered artificial the sinuous and naked shores of the lake which had delighted Bampfylde. He planted the water's edge with shrubs so that Richard Fenton described 'banks finely fringed with laurel, alder, and the most grotesque growth of every kind.'[8] The lip of the dam remained exposed, however, the northern and western extremities of the Garden Lake were lost among the trees, enhancing the illusion it was a natural sheet of water. In 1810 Louis Simond, already ill-tempered after a perceived slight from a servant, complained:

> The lawns are half covered and belittled by shrubs, planted everywhere,
> particularly endless tufts and thickets of laurels; beautiful in
> themselves, but in too great profusion. The woods are also too close,
> resembling rather an American thicket... there is as much done to spoil,
> as to adorn this fine spot.[9]

War on the follies

Richard Graves had satirised the diversity of garden buildings at Stourhead in 1779:

> In the justly celebrated gardens of Stour, we are led from an hermitage to a
> temple of Venus, and from St. Augustine's cave to the temple of Bacchus and
> thence to a Saxon temple, and so on. *Quelle melange!* We should fix upon
> some particular style of design in laying out our place, whether Roman,
> Gothic, Chinese, or plain English, and in some measure adhere to it.[10]

Colt agreed. He would impose a predominantly classical vision upon Stourhead.[11] In the annals he mentioned removing the Turkish Tent (before 1792),

The Temple of Apollo.

the Wooden Bridge (1798) and the Hermitage (1814–15). In *Modern Wiltshire* he owned up to destroying the Temple on the Terrace (classical) and Gothick Greenhouse and, in a manuscript memoir, banishing the *Apollo Belvedere*.[12] He scuppered the *Neptune* sculpture without comment. Nor did Colt, an avid chronicler and keen draughtsman, pause to record their appearance. He wrote:

> My object in removing them was, to render the design of these gardens as chaste and correct as possible, and to give them the character of an Italian villa; and I think every man of taste will agree with me, that the Turkish and Chinese architecture could never accord with that of Greece and Rome.[13]

It is curious that he gave an aesthetic and not a practical reason. By the 1790s the canvas draping the Turkish Tent would have rotted, as would the timber footings of the Wooden Bridge, dunked in the lake. Structures in wood and ephemeral materials require maintenance and renewal. Very few of these fragile follies have survived with their original materials: the Chinese Tea Pavilion (mid-eighteenth century) at Boughton House in Northamptonshire, and the Chinese House (before 1738) at Stowe are rare examples of canvas-covered structures. At Killerton House in Devon

Lily Lake and Six Wells Bottom.

Diana's Basin.

the timber Bear Hut (*c.*1808) incorporates deer skins, fir cones and deer bones, an ensemble often enjoyed and repaired by the Acland family.

By demolishing such attractions at Stourhead, Colt made it challenging to appreciate his grandfather's finished masterpiece; henceforth the garden was more classical and less exotic, a reflection of his own personality. Happily Colt admired medieval architecture and spared the Bristol Cross, Peter's Pump and the Convent. In 1799 he even toyed with the idea of importing the medieval Conduit House from Wells.[14] This substantial stone structure, like the stump of a bell-tower, comprised two storeys wrapped in blind gothic arcading. Where would Colt have placed this relic at Stourhead?

Colt Hoare's major building campaign occurred in the village and on the estate where he added cottages, kennels, lodges and a rectory. In the landscape garden he put up a new boathouse and brought Watch Cottage into prominence.

The Boathouse

Colt Hoare built the Boathouse close to the Temple of Flora in 1794 and it features in Nicholson's panorama of the lake.[15] The robust water gate comprises two archways faced with greensand stone, as craggy as the façade of the Grotto. The interior

is ashlar-lined and capacious with twin berths, flanked by quays separated by an internal wall.

The Boathouse replaced an earlier shelter; indeed Henry Flitcroft's design for the pedimented rock-work archway is headed '2. For a Boat House', a caption which may refer to a drawing on the missing adjacent sheet (page 144).[16]

Colt owned a fishing boat, a pleasure craft and a ferry.[17] In solitude he cast with rod and line where once Henry the Magnificent enjoyed musicians drifting by the Grotto and blasting away on their instruments.[18] Fenton remarked that the lake 'produces carp, tench and eels of an exquisite flavour, so that the Baronet's bill of fare never need lack fish'.[19]

Watch Cottage

The cottage became a minor feature in 1782 when Henry the Magnificent added the bay window and stone seat. As Faugoin reported:

> [I] have told White the Plaisterer to Begin lathing the Cottage by the Pantheon and to begin the first coat of Plaister – the covering of straw may also be taken from the new Stone seat and the Windows Glass'd but dont know what sort of Form you would have the Glass somewhat Like those at the Convent.[20]

ABOVE
Watch Cottage.
'a picturesque Gothic cottage, covered with various sort of creepers, woodbines and celemates'. Richard Fenton 1811 (1807).

OPPOSITE
The Shades with the Boathouse at the waterline.

Richard Graves had floated the idea of a habitation near the Grotto in 1779.[21] About the same time Bampfylde sketched a view of the Pantheon with the cottage which is also marked on the 1785 estate plan.[22] Colt Hoare made the little building a picturesque feature, naming it the Gardener's Cottage and adding a porch probably designed by John Carter.[23] John Skinner found it occupied by a keeper in 1808.[24] In 1895 the 6th baronet repaired the building, now Watch Cottage, and put it to new use (page 230).

The gardener's house (demolished)

The house stood close to the entrance from the village. Francis Faugoin, Henry the Magnificent's head gardener, probably lived there.[25] In 1776 Mrs Powys commended it as 'a pretty romantic thatch'd cottage'.[26] Skinner, a visitor iron-clad against charm, described a 'humble white cottage embosomed in trees'.[27] Colt Hoare remarked 'it was one of the oldest houses in the parish, and stood within the gardens facing the Bristol Cross'.[28] He remodelled the dwelling in 1808.[29] John Buckler and Nicholson recorded the picturesque effect.[30] The house burned down in 1813 as Colt bemoaned, 'I had lately spent a good deal of money in decorating it, and it became a pretty object.'[31]

Stourton

The eastern sweep of the garden between the temples of Apollo and Flora includes Stourton village or, more accurately, the dwellings grouped around St Peter's. The 1722 plan marked about thirteen free-standing buildings in the lee of the church. The 1785 plan shows the lower village configured much as it is today with the inn, steward's house, the Bristol Cross and a row of cottages opposite the church. Between these cottages and the graveyard stood an L-shaped range of utilitarian buildings which Turpin de Crissé and another artist depicted (page 132).[32] Henry the Magnificent planted to screen them in the view from the Pantheon. Colt Hoare demolished them in 1812–13 and extended lake further towards the village.[33] From 1815 he was busy improving the graveyard, erecting a new stone cross and gothick seat before placing a shelter over the tombs of his forebears and, east of the church, sinking a new family vault surmounted by a gothick stone canopy designed by John Pinch the elder (1769–1827).[34]

At the inn, Colt built new stables, a coach house and two battlemented stone towers flanking the entrance to the courtyard; the complex was drawn by Buckler.[35] Colt renamed the inn 'The Spread Eagle', carving the family's coat of arms on the exterior and planting his crest on the gate piers.[36] Fifteen years later he added the single-storey room.[37]

Near the village entrance to the garden Colt placed a stone seat in the form of a semi-circular bench supported by carved animal feet throbbing with bunions (c.1824).[38] The design derived from *schola* tombs at Pompeii.

Colt laid out a flower garden beside the Bristol Cross and, whether by example or dragooning, persuaded his tenants to grow flowers beside their dwellings.[39] J. P. Neale and Loudon praised the studied charm of the village.[40] The latter remarked in 1833:

the church yard is one of the best kept which are to be seen in England. Roses and other flowering shrubs are planted against the church; cypresses and other trees are sprinkled among the graves, and the grass is kept as smooth as any lawn... What highly gratified us was, to see as much attention paid to the public road, and road-side without the entrance arch, and thence to the inn, the steward's house, the cottages, and the church, as is paid to the grounds within the pleasure-ground fence. The flower-gardens to the line of cottages opposite the church are well planted, and as nicely kept, as the flower beds on any gentleman's lawn.[41]

In 1824 William Hazlitt described the habitation in terms that would have delighted Colt:

you descend into Stourton by a sharp-winding declivity, almost like going under-ground, between high hedges of laurel trees, and with an expanse of woods and water spread beneath. It is a sort of rural Herculaneum, a subterranean retreat... the village-church stands on a lawn without any inclosure; a row of cottages facing it with their white-washed walls and flaunting honey-suckles, are neatness itself. Every thing has an air of elegance, and yet tells a tale of other times.[42]

The Lodges

The Stourhead Annals record fourteen lodges built on the estate between 1799 and 1841.[43] Colt Hoare had met the architectural draughtsman Willey Reveley (1760–99) in Italy and invited him to submit proposals for lodges at Stourhead.[44] Reveley was a classicist and whether or not lodges were built to his designs on the estate is conjecture.[45]

Three stand in the vicinity of the main house, none classical. The lodge beside Clock Arch is conspicuous to visitors today and was built 1802–1803. It is single

LEFT
Distant view from the Bristol
Cross across the Stone Bridge
with the Temple of Apollo and
the Pantheon beyond, 1812–16,
by Francis Nicholson (1753–1844),
watercolour, 404 × 550 mm.
British Museum.

OVERLEAF
The crest of Lily Lake dam and
the pinetum.

storey with an ashlar façade enlivened by hood-mould windows, the lights with trefoil heads. A pierced zig-zag parapet surmounts the porch, copied from the north aisle of the church. In 1844 the 4th baronet enlarged the house to accommodate a gardener while the gatekeeper was moved to Lilliputian quarters in Clock Arch.[46] Censuses in 1851 and 1871 record a woman occupying the latter.[47]

Colt erected Drove Lodge from 1811 to 1812 on the road to Maiden Bradley opposite the house. It is single storey, faced with stone from the nearby Search quarry and capped by a hipped roof.[48] The road façade has Tudor-style windows similar to Clock Arch Lodge. In 1852 the 4th baronet tiled the roof and added a porch.[49]

Terrace Lodge, close to the Obelisk, is also Tudor in flavour. It was designed by Charles Parker (1799–1881), architect of Hoare's Bank. The 3rd baronet began the building and his son completed it in 1841.[50] The lodge is single storey, stone faced, lit by square-headed windows with cusped lights and has the familiar zig-zag parapet. It stands in marked contrast to the Italianate designs for other lodges published by Parker.[51]

The most pretentious lodge, an architectural toy in gleaming ashlar, was never built. Colt had commissioned William Wilkins (1778–1839), architect of the National Gallery, to design this Grecian lodge.[52]

Design for a Grecian Lodge, *c.*1815, by William Wilkins (1778–1839), ink and watercolour, 525 × 856 mm. Stourhead.

New Lake

At the turn of the century Colt Hoare bought the adjoining Manor of Gasper.[53] It lies south-west of Stourton further down the valley of the River Stour as it flows towards Bourton. Within three years he had built a water-powered mill there.[54] But it was not until 1821 that he rebuilt the dam to form an ornamental stretch of water known as New Lake, covering some 14 acres.[55] The lake is memorable for the wrong reason. On the 29 June 1917 the dam broke after a heavy rainstorm.[56] Water surged towards Bourton as *The Western Gazette* reported:

> The estate people living near the spot declare that the noise of the escaping water was like continuous thunder... The sweeping away of the Gaspar bridge left a great chasm some 30 feet deep from the roads on either side. Trees were uprooted and carried away down the stream like so many straws... The great wave proceeded on its destructive course towards Bourton, and ran through and over the lake above Bourton Foundry. Here it apparently made a bed for itself, for it swept through the extensive workshops and caused damage of a most extraordinary character.[57]

The 6th baronet, who enjoyed fishing, rebuilt the dam, bridge and mill (as a dwelling), stocked the lake and later planted the banks with azaleas, dogwood and rhododendrons.[58]

THE VICTORIAN AND EDWARDIAN GARDEN

During the nineteenth century the garden began to assume the character of an arboretum planted with large conifers when new species reached Britain; notably sitka spruce, noble fir and Douglas fir. These experimental trees were clustered close to the Stone Bridge, on the northern shores of the Garden Lake and on the western side of Lily Lake where a small pinetum stands.

The 4th baronet noted in the Stourhead Annals the number of trees planted each year. In the landscape garden he introduced about eighteen new species of conifers, including the first monkey puzzles in the pinetum and below the Temple of Apollo where he also placed a coast redwood. At the entrance to the Grotto and on the path from Lily Lake he established western red cedars. Viewed at close-quarters, the branches dip into the earth and rise mysteriously in massive limbs.

Ainslie, the 5th baronet, gave up the annals after 1860 so there is an element of 'I-spy' to identifying the species he planted, for example, Caucasian fir between the Boathouse and Diana's Basin. Below the Temple of Apollo he placed a tiger-tail spruce, now classed a champion tree, rising to partially obscure the view from

OPPOSITE
Rock Arch.

RIGHT
Stourhead, the entrance to the gardens, 1901. *Country Life*.

the temple. There is no record as to whether the initiative lay with the 5th baronet himself, his agent, Robert Shackleton, or the head forester, James Sinton (d. 1897).[1]

The garden requires constant maintenance to preserve the principal vistas and keep the buildings weather-tight. Succeeding generations of Hoares performed the task, with a lapse in the 1880s when the 5th baronet shut up the house and departed to London and the Continent. The neglect took his successor a decade and more to rectify. Photographs taken around 1900 capture the congestion. The contrast with C. W. Bampfylde's watercolours is stark.

Throughout the nineteenth century the public had access to the grounds. The 4th baronet posted a warning notice to curb vandalism:

> The permission granted to the Public of seeing these Gardens having been so much abused by writing on and otherwise defacing the Temples Statues and Trees therein... it is earnestly hoped that all persons who may visit the Gardens in future, will refrain from such highly objectionable practices otherwise the permission to see them must be withheld. H.R.H. 1842.[2]

Under his successor both house and grounds were open to the public and advertisements placed in local papers gave the days and hours, culminating in a free-for-all in 1869.[3] Societies, learned and otherwise, visited and some published descriptions.[4] From 1894 Stourhead grounds were accessible only by permit from the estate office and after the fire the house was opened on Wednesday afternoons from 2.30 to 6 p. m. from May to October, again by permission from the land agent.[5] George Sweetman reprinted Colt Hoare's guidebook in 1894 and issued his own edition in 1907.The inquisitive public were shown around the house by the butler. Parties of school children received Lady Hoare's personal attention and, if well-behaved, were plied with bonbons. The Hoares made a speciality of Queen Alexandra days when they charged an entrance fee to the grounds which was remitted to charity.[6]

'A Bit in the Gardens, at Stourton', c.1905, post card, 90 ×140 mm. Private Collection.

The landscape garden in the twentieth century

When Sir Henry Hoare, the 6th baronet, moved to Stourton many trees clothing the valley slopes had passed their prime and were toppled by gales. Between 1897 and 1913 he underplanted the hanging woods surrounding the Garden Lake, predominantly with beech saplings.[7] To titivate the lakeside path he planted 'several thousand Narcissus' in 1899–1900 and imported 300 azaleas from Longleat the following year.[8] In 1908–9 he began to blitz the laurels and rhododendrons along the lakeside paths from Watch Cottage to the Pantheon. By 1913–14 he had reached the Stone Bridge and the hillside below the Temple of Apollo.[9] The Great War halted this progress and, with manpower occupied in the commercial woods, the garden suffered.

In the post-war decades variety and experiment became their preoccupation. Along the path bypassing the Grotto Sir Henry planted evergreen trees, for example Sargent's spruce, Momi fir and a Chinese fir. He followed horticultural advances and was eager to excite the 'trippers', as Lady Hoare termed the public. Colour, it is evident, was also important to Lady Hoare who wrote of her pleasure in the scarlet and pink rhododendron blooms.[10] She was delighted that friends admired the early summer blaze.[11] The garden benefitted from Sir Henry's enthusiasm for new varieties of flowering shrubs. He made space by replacing large *Rhododendron*

ponticum with hybrid rhododendrons and azaleas, pungent in early summer. He wrote in the annals for 1923–4:

> The common Rhododendrons were cleared off the Lakeside from Grotto Point to Pantheon Temple and considerable planting of Rhododendron, Escallonias, etc. was done on this site.

And in 1925–6:

> a clearing was also made between the underground arch & the leaf-hole & this was planted with Rhododendrons and 4 Magnolias. A Beech tree overhanging the Flora Temple was felled & the site planted with Rhododendrons.

In 1927–8 Sir Henry was at work on the eastern slopes, 'considerable clearings of laurel was made in the Shades & planting of Rhododendrons commenced.'[12] Four years later, 'upwards of 100 hybrid Rhododendrons were planted in the Shades'.[13] In later entries in the annals he named the plants, so after a tree fell near the Boathouse in 1935–1936:

> the open space on either side planted with Rhododendrons & azaleas.
> The following rhododendrons were also planted:– W. R. Dykes, Mrs
> G. W. Leak, augustinii, cinnabarinum, Cornish Cross, C. B Van Ness.
> Also following flowering shrubs – Magnolia Wilsonii, Magnolia Lennei,
> Eucryphia Nymansay, Liquidambar stryraciflua, Cornus nuttalii,
> Cornus kousa, 12 Std Cherries.

On the eve of the Second World War, Stourhead had never been more colourful in season and more horticulturally diverse.

No buildings of note were added to the garden after Colt Hoare's time but existing structures were repaired. The 3rd baronet rebuilt the Obelisk in Bath stone.[14] The 5th installed the iron bridge next to the Pantheon. The 6th reinstated Diana's Basin, restored Watch Cottage and rebuilt the Pump House.

'Stourton Gardens', c.1910,
post card, 90 × 140 mm.
Private Collection.

Stourton Gardens.

The Iron Bridge

Bampfylde had sketched a horizontal pedestrian bridge, supported by two piers, crossing the backwater between the Pantheon and the dam.[15] In 1811 Colt Hoare replaced this with a similar structure built in stone.[16] Francis Nicholson depicted this resting on three or four piers.[17] The bridge in its turn proved unsatisfactory and was replaced by a second timber version in 1842.[18] The present cast-iron footbridge was supplied in 1860 by Maggs and Hindley of Bourton.[19]

Watch Cottage

In 1895 the 6th baronet repaired the building and converted it as 'a Summer House and furnished as a sitting room.'[20] At the time he was living in the agent's house at the entrance to the garden. That summer Lady Hoare occupied the cottage daily.[21] In 1907 he replaced the roof with stone tiles salvaged from West Knoyle.[22] The National Trust has recently thatched the cottage.

In the little bay separating the cottage from the Pantheon Richard Fenton described 'a fountain trickling from a rocky aperture, through moss intermingled with wild flowers'.[23] The 6th baronet channelled the water into an ornamental well, often visited by Lady Hoare with convalescent soldiers from Mere hospital.[24] It no longer exists.

'Stourton Gardens', *c.*1910, post card, 90 × 140 mm. Private Collection.

The Pump House

The 4th baronet had installed a hydraulic ram beside the Garden Lake dam to supply the house and home farm.[25] There matters rested for fifty years until Sir Henry, the 6th baronet, replaced the ram with pumps powered by a water wheel capable of raising 10,000 gallons a day.[26] The wheel and pump were housed in a shelter whose façade incorporated a stone watering trough made for Colt Hoare in 1824.[27] After fire gutted the house in 1902 he built a reservoir close to Alfred's Tower, fed by new pumps.[28] These were superseded in 1920–1 by the present over-shot wheel, constructed outside the shelter and capable of pumping 11,000 gallons per day.[29] When demand increased a more powerful pump was installed in 1938.[30] This in turn was boosted by a petrol engine in 1945.[31] With the ever-increasing demand from the estate, the problem was solved after the Second World War when Stourton was connected to the main water supply from Mere.

The Iron Bridge, the backwater and Top Wood beyond.

STOURHEAD HOUSE AND PRECINCT

The entrance front of Stourhead faces east. Despite enlargements and alterations it retains some architectural integrity thanks to the consistent (but not exclusive) use of Bath stone and the tactful additions. Campbell's design occupies the centre of the ensemble, a villa rising from a rusticated basement to the *piano nobile* with a bedroom storey above. It is five bays wide with a detached Corinthian portico added in 1838. Almost fifty years previously Colt Hoare had built the flanking pavilions and linking corridors. These tripled the length of the façade and were intended to complement, not compete with, Campbell's elevation. In the mid-nineteenth century the sash windows were replaced with casements.[1]

To appreciate the sophisticated designs for the original Stourhead we turn to Colen Campbell's plan and elevations. Campbell (1676–1729) was appointed Chief Clerk and Deputy Surveyor by William Benson in 1718. The architect was dismissed together with Benson the following year but found a greater patron in the 3rd Earl of Burlington who engaged him to remodel Burlington House in Piccadilly. At about the same time Campbell drew the plans for Stourhead which he published in the third volume of *Vitruvius Britannicus* (1725).[2] These reveal a debt to Palladio in the felicitous proportions and classical detail. Indeed, the east front of Stourhead is a homage to the Villa Emo (*c*.1560) in the Veneto. Palladio's villa was the hub of a working estate and equipped with the necessary service buildings. Campbell's Stourhead was a stand-alone villa, suited to occasional occupancy and entertaining and more akin to Chiswick Villa, that architectural *marron glacé* by Lord Burlington. Stourhead takes its place beside other Paladian villas designed by Campbell: Pembroke House in Whitehall, Mereworth Castle in Kent and Baldersby Park in Yorkshire, originally a near twin to Stourhead.[3]

Good Henry and Benson altered Campbell's ground plan and elevations for Stourhead when building commenced and substituted an engaged portico for the architect's prostyle version.

The south façade is characterised by the banded architraves with exaggerated voussoirs derived from Palladio's Palazzo Thiene in Vicenza. It differs in minor ways from Campbell's drawing: the basement and bedroom-storey windows were heightened and, on the *piano noble*, his balustrade-aprons beneath the penultimate architraves shifted to the central Venetian window. Here Campbell drew a two-leaf door reached by a double flight of steps. If these were ever built, they had disappeared before 1811 (page 235).[4] His long-necked vases on the parapet, again, if

The East front of Stourhead in Wiltshire the Seat of Henry Hoare Esq.ʳ

Co: Campbell Inven.ᵗ   H. Hulfbergh Sculp.

they existed, also disappeared. The swaggering cartouche contains the arms of Good Henry and his wife, Jane (née Benson).

Campbell's proposals for the west and north elevations are lost. The west has been rebuilt; the north is well-proportioned but plain apart from a Venetian window as the centrepiece. It seems unlikely that these were delegated to the builder, Nathaniel Ireson (1686–1769), who came from the Midlands and had served as apprentice to Francis Smith of Warwick. By 1720 Ireson had settled at Stourton. He later moved to Wincanton where he became renowned as a master builder and quarry owner. He was responsible for Crowcombe Court (c.1725) in the Quantock Hills, and Ven (c.1725) at Milborne Port, both red-brick baroque houses.

Work on Stourhead commenced in 1720 and, by March 1723/4, it was habitable and insured.[5] Good Henry paid Ireson over £7,000.[6] Henry himself bought timber, lead and glass, and paid for some labourers from his own pocket. He lavished money on the construction and bequeathed a further £3,000, plus rents from the estate, to complete the house.[7] In 1726/7 Henry the Magnificent paid Campbell £192, presumably for the original designs.[8]

After moving to Stourhead in 1742 Henry the Magnificent engaged Henry Flitcroft to rebuild the centre of the west front one bay forward to accommodate his new Saloon. The façade was dismantled after the 1902 fire but is recorded in

'The East front of Stourhead' by Hendrick Hulsbergh (d.1729), engraving, 250 × 375 mm. From *Vitruvius Britannicus* (London, 1725), vol.III, plate 42. Stourhead.

John Buckler's drawing of 1811 and early photographs (page 117).[9] At the north-west corner of the house Henry added the Skylight Room (a picture gallery) which is discernible in these illustrations and identified on Sir John Parnell's sketch plan.[10]

Colt Hoare's pavilions contain a library and gallery.[11] Thomas Atkinson of Salisbury supervised their construction and fitting out, 1792–1805.[12] From the east they are uninspired but well-behaved as a mark of respect to Campbell's façade. But, on the south side, the Library destroyed the symmetry of the original façade. Colt Hoare further compromised this front by attaching a glasshouse at ground level against the south-west corner.[13]

The 3rd baronet built the projecting portico in 1838–9 to Campbell's original design; the work was supervised by Charles Parker (1799–1881), architect of Hoare's Bank building.[14] He also added the double stone steps replacing the more dramatic single flight which had risen in diminishing steps to the engaged portico.[15]

The 6th baronet began his prolonged residence by removing the conservatory and raising in its place a substantial terrace giving access to the *piano nobile*.[16] After the 1902 fire he rebuilt the core of the house adding further bays on the west side which enabled him to enlarge the Saloon.[17] His architect, Edward Doran Webb, re-edified the west front in Doulting stone but not for the better.[18] To enliven this façade the 6th baronet moved lead sculptures from the Temple of Apollo and purchased a stone figure of *Mars* for the pediment. He distributed the remaining lead figures from the temple along the roofline of the east façade. [19]

Standing at the front door of Stourhead, the visitor today admires the eastward prospect of Salisbury Plain where the chalk ends at the foot of White Sheet Hill as

Stourhead: the south front, c.1860, attr. Frances Annette Hoare (1822–1904), oil on canvas, 72 x 87 cm. Stourhead. On the far left is a glimpse of Colt Hoare's glass house-abutting the south-west corner of the house.

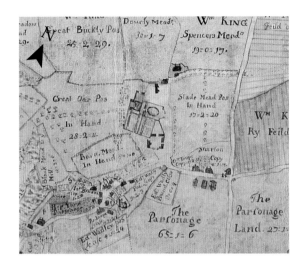

LEFT ABOVE
Detail from 1722 plan of Stourhead,
unknown, ink and tempera on
parchment, 340 × 705 mm. Wiltshire
and Swindon History Centre.

LEFT BELOW
Detail from 'Plan of the Manor
of Stourton in the County of Wilts.
belonging to Richard Colt Hoare
Esqr.' 1785, by John Charlton, ink
and colour wash on parchment,
680 × 965 mm. Wiltshire and
Swindon History Centre.

RIGHT
Detail from 'General plan of the
former banker Henry Hoare's
pleasure park at Stourton in
Wiltshire, near Bristol, drawn 1779
by F. M. Piper', (1746–1824), pencil,
ink and colour wash, 475 × 645 mm.
The Royal Swedish Academy of Fine
Arts, Stockholm.

it dips into arable land. The road from Maiden Bradley to Mere crosses the middle
distance while Slade Mead (or Meadow) occupies the foreground. The view has
scarcely changed since the days of the Stourton family. However, the immediate
surroundings have been altered on two occasions.

Good Henry's villa was flanked by short quadrant walls opening eastwards on a
rectangular forecourt with an oval lawn in the centre. The configuration was plotted
on the 1722 plan of Stourhead and reconstructed in a drawing and watercolour by
Buckler from a lost painting of 1724 (page 35).[20]

Henry the Magnificent replaced the rectangular forecourt with a D-shaped
lawn enclosed by quadrant hedges, punctuated by vases on pedestals.[21] Carriage
drives entering from the north-east and the south met at this lawn. The 1785 plan of
Stourhead shows the southern drive passing through the Stable Yard and descending
steeply to the road from Stourton to Gasper. The east drive curved from the Maiden
Bradley road over flat ground towards the house where a subsidiary track branched
to the service area.

Colt Hoare did away with both approaches. He laid a new service drive in a
straight line from the north. This route is sheltered by an avenue of lime trees planted
in 1896–7.[22] The main drive shadowed the previous route but bypassed the stables.
At the foot of the new drive Colt Hoare re-erected the gateway, known as Clock

Arch. Nearby stand four sweet chestnut trees, now some six hundred years old. Further along this drive is bordered with limes planted in the 1890s.[23] A bank of rhododendrons between the house and stables was established in 1926–7.[24]

The ground extending from the south front has undergone as many alterations as Campbell's façade. The 1722 plan of Stourhead shows a formal arrangement which Buckler reconstructed from a lost painting dated 1724.[25] He drew a level rectangular lawn extending from the house, flanked by brick walls and terminating in an exedra-like hedge.

In 1721 Good Henry paid Stephen Switzer (1682–1745) fifteen guineas 'for making Plans for my Garden'.[26] Switzer had trained with London and Wise and worked on their prestigious commissions at Castle Howard, Cirencester Park, Blenheim Palace and Grimsthorpe Castle. He was a respected author on matters horticultural and hydraulic, and was hired by the 4th Earl of Orrery (1674–1731) to create a garden at Marston, close to Stourhead.

Between the south lawn and the stables, the 1722 plan of Stourhead marked a narrow walk and a second rectangular enclosure, perhaps a kitchen garden, quartered into four beds. The building account lists payments to Mr Whitehead 'for looking after y[e] nursery' for £5–5s.[27] Good Henry kept a note of expenditure on the garden and planting 1721–4; he bought forest and fruit trees, asparagus plants and seeds to the tune of £100.[28]

The 1785 estate plan shows how Henry the Magnificent opened up the south lawn by removing the flanking walls and establishing the Kitchen Garden south of the stables. At the southern end of the lawn stood a circular pond occupied by a cast of the *Apollo Belvedere* acquired by Henry in 1745.[29]

Four years later, the rhymer of 'Stourton Gardens' was effusive:

What shape! what air! What elegance is seen
In yonder statue on that mount of green;
The form how graceful, how divine the mien!
Surely the sculptor sought each grace to find,
Cull'd ev'ry beauty that adorns mankind…
His bosom glow'd, his fancy soar'd on high,
It left the earth, and rang'd the spacious sky,
To find superior models for his plan,
And form'd his god like the most perfect man.[30]

Here are the mount and a statue but no water. Conversely, five years later Richard Pococke ignored the statue but described the pond.[31] The latter was probably fed by the fretful pump installed on the advice of William Benson (page 132).

Colt Hoare took exception to the south lawn which he likened to an avenue.[32] He felled most of the trees, levelled the mount and removed *Apollo*. His single-storey glasshouse stood at ground level and extended from the house, parallel with the Library (page 236).[33] Midway between the two the 5th baronet placed an ornamental stone fountain encircled by flower beds and dubbed the 'Italian Garden'.[34]

The ground between the south lawn and the stables has been variously treated. An ice house is concealed in the shrubbery but no record survives of its construction. In August 1765 Henry the Magnificent wrote, 'we feed on Your Lordship's fat Bounty of Venison & Drink Your Health in Iced Cream.'[35] The ice house is partially sunk below ground level, the roof is domed and the door faces north.[36] The brick-lined chamber is cone-shaped with a drain at the narrow base. The present structure probably dates from Colt Hoare's day and would have remained in use until the advent of domestic ice boxes, again at a date unrecorded at Stourhead. Close to the ice house the 6th baronet recorded in the Stourhead Annals for 1922–3 'a rockery was made at the back of the Stables to replace two fine sycamores that had to be removed owing to their dangerous condition.' As the years passed Lady Hoare became short-sighted and her husband grew lame so they paid greater attention to their immediate surroundings. In 1927–8 they recorded that 'The Old Ponticum bed near Library was grubbed and replanted with good hybrids.' And, in 1934–5:

The following were planted on the [south] Lawn: 1 Prunus Sargentii, Davidia Vilmoriniana, 2 Hibiscus Coelestis & 1 Horse Chestnut (yellow flowering) 1 R[hododendron]. Goldworth crimson 2 R Griersonianum.

Apollo Belvedere, late eighteenth century, unknown, sanguine, 460 × 287 mm. Stourhead.

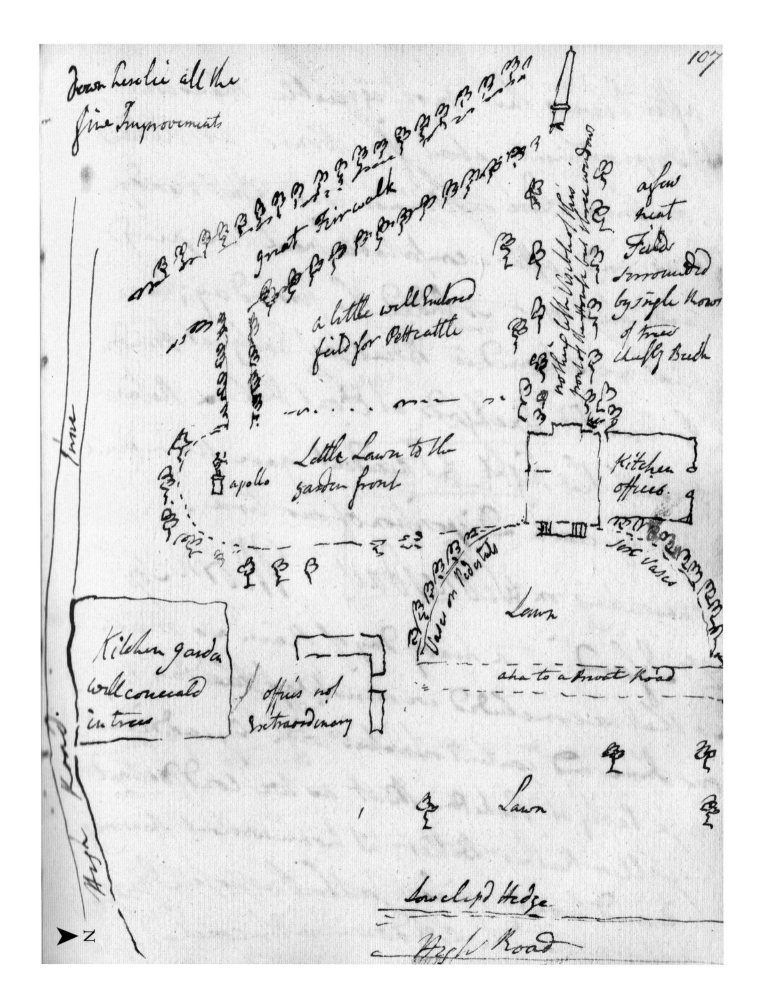

At the opposite end of the lawn an English oak, pre-dating the house, survives to this day as does the nearby tulip tree, planted *c.*1791 by Colt Hoare. The southern skyline is characterised by coast redwoods; the dominant specimen, 130 feet tall, was planted in 1851 by the 4th baronet. Along the park side of the south lawn the 6th baronet commemorated milestones in his life by planting three red oaks:

> A scarlet oak was planted on the Lawn on the occasion of our Golden Wedding & 3 Bronze Tablets were [erected *inserted*] with the dates of this tree, our Silver Wedding tree & Capt Hoare's coming-of-age tree.[37]

The view of the south lawn from the house has changed without resolving its character: formal or informal; garden or recreation ground?

The Saloon windows look westwards to a more satisfactory prospect across the Great Oar, that expanse of park, towards the Obelisk. In 1769 Parnell drew a sketch plan indicating an avenue of trees crossing the field from the house to the Obelisk.[38] So it is a puzzle that the 1785 plan marked a belt of trees lying across this vista.

Colt Hoare opened up this view and dug a ha-ha to separate the Great Oar from an enlarged lawn.[39] The latter now flows around the house and merges with the south garden. However an aerial photo, *c.*1938, shows the west lawn demarcated by a semi-circular gravel path bowed towards the ha-ha.[40]

The 6th baronet undertook the planting. In 1920–1 he recorded in the annals:

> a large beech tree standing on the West side of the house was blown down, doing much damage to the back yard wall and practically demolishing the woodshed. This tree was replaced by planting a number of Rhododendrons & Azaleas.

And in 1932–3, '5 [rhododendrons] from Minterne were also planted in the new Rhododendron bed on the West Front lawn.'

The domestic offices lie to the north of the house. Both the 1722 and 1785 plans indicate a long narrow range extending from the main building but the later plan shows it enlarged by an irregular-shaped service yard along its west flank. In Henry the Magnificent's time the area was screened from the main entrance by a wall which Colt Hoare replaced with the Picture Gallery.

The 4th baronet made a new entrance to the service yard, bypassing the area immediately north of the house which became the north court, reclaimed for polite use.[41] The 6th baronet remodelled the court as a formal garden erecting curved stone walls on the northern perimeter with an ornamental iron gate.[42] An aerial photograph, *c.*1938, shows the court turfed with a central gravel reserve and a path aligned on the gate. A portion of the formal garden survives but the area is now a car park and the service yard has fallen into disrepair.

Close to the north-east corner of the house stood several substantial old buildings. In 1703 Lord Stourton had leased the complex to William King, the principal tenant farmer. The draft lease described a variety of farm buildings.[43] These are conspicuous on the 1722 and 1785 plans but screened by trees from the main house. Colt Hoare demolished the lot in 1799.[44]

Clock Arch

The main drive to Stourhead commences at this castellated archway. In 1799 Colt Hoare moved it from the Stable Yard where it is depicted in two late eighteenth-century sketches.[45] He wrote:

> March. Pulled down a Gateway with two Towers leading from the Village to my Stable Yard. April. Began rebuilding them according to the same plan – at the foot of the Hill – Completed them before the winter.[46]

The origin of the structure is obscure. The twin towers and the pointed arch chime with Leland's description of old Stourton House, 1540–22:

> This maner place hath 2 courtes. The fronte of the inner courte is magnificent, and high embatelid castle lyke. The goodly gate howse and fronte of the Lorde *Stourton*'s howse in *Stourton* was buyldyd *ex spoliis Gallorum*.[47]

The Gateway at Stourhead, *c*.1793, by Hendrik Frans de Cort (1742–1810), pen and grey wash, 240 × 335 mm. The Wiltshire Museum.

Given the gateway is more decorative than defensive, it could have escaped ruination when a Parliamentary army stormed the castle in 1644.[48] But this seems improbable and Aubrey, writing shortly after the Restoration, made no mention of the gateway and omitted it from his sketch.[49] As impecunious Roman Catholics, the Lords Stourton are unlikely to have built or rebuilt the structure after the Civil War. Moreover, in 1762 Horace Walpole described this gateway as 'modern'.[50] The present structure resembles the more elaborate castellated Towers Gate, c.1754–5, attributed to Henry Flitcroft, at nearby Redlynch.[51] Without further evidence Clock Arch remains unvintaged.[52]

The Stable Yard

The 1722 plan marks the stables as a quadrangle between the house and the village with an entrance in the southern wall through which the carriage drive passed towards the house.

Even when Clock Arch formed the entrance to the Stable Yard it was never an architectural show place, rather it represents an accretion of buildings adapted to

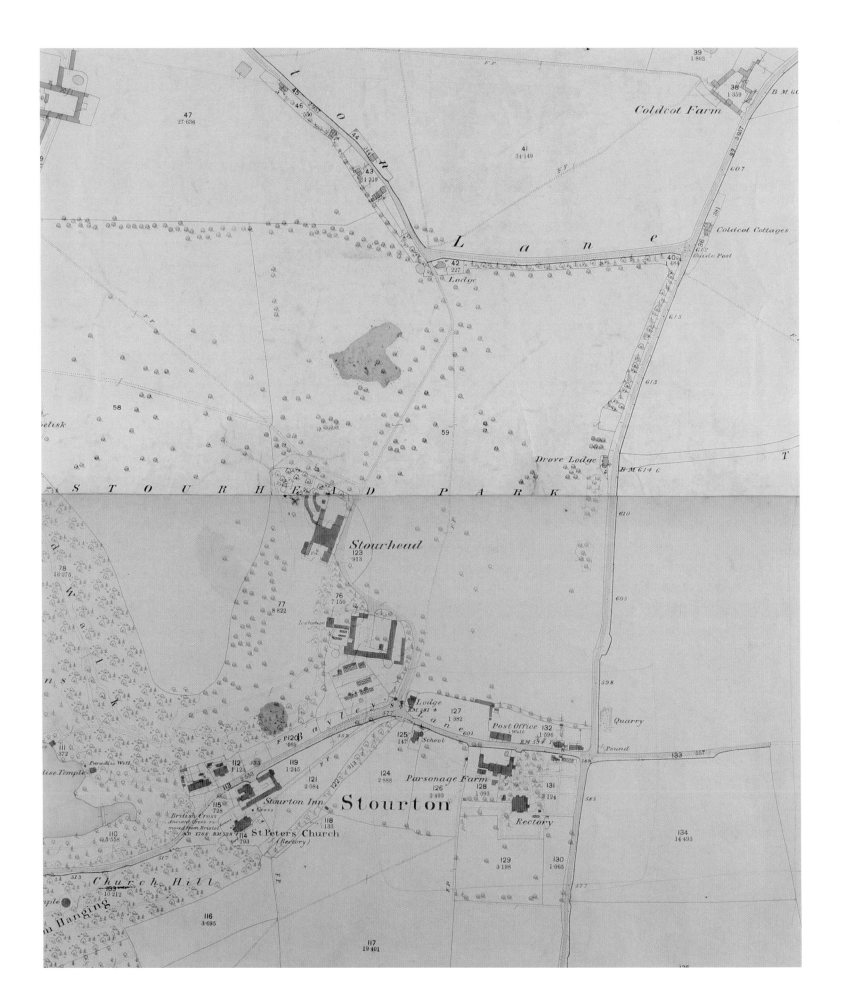

the needs of each generation. Here stone, brick and tiles mingle. This is surprising because the Hoares were horse-proud; Henry the Magnificent was an accomplished rider and delighted in thoroughbreds presented by his son-in-law, Lord Bruce. A hundred and fifty years later the 6th baronet made a name for himself as a breeder of percherons.[53]

Owners kept the Stable Yard in repair and adapted the buildings. The 4th baronet replaced the thatch roofing with tiles and in 1852 installed Diocletian windows.[54] In 1906 the 6th baronet built a motor house on the west side beside the coach house and twenty years later converted the harness room into a garage.[55]

At the north-west corner of the yard stands a detached stone stable with two oval windows and a trefoil-headed doorway. The façade is completed by a large medallion of unknown origin containing a warrior head à *l'antique*, in stone. An equally whimsical doorway leads out of the Stable Yard onto the South Lawn. Are they the antiquarian handiwork of Henry the Magnificent or Colt Hoare?

The Kitchen Garden

Henry the Magnificent probably moved the garden to its present location, south of the stables. The letters to his son-in-law, Lord Bruce, give an inkling of the delicacies provided which included garden peas, strawberries and pineapples.[56]

The 1785 plan showed a second kitchen garden occupying a strip of land on Slade Mead behind the lodge at Clock Arch.[57] The wall remains and the garden is now allotments.

In Colt Hoare's time the kitchen garden reached its zenith.[58] His friend Richard Fenton described:

> the walled gardens occupying the side of a hill which faces south, in a gradation of slopes. In the first range is the green-house, or conservatory, not overgrown, but well furnished with a choice assemblage of plants, including a large collection of heaths [heather], arranged with great taste, and externally covered with the evergreen rose at that time in most luxuriant bloom. In the next are the hot-houses for grapes, peaches, nectarines, &c. seemingly in a most productive state. There are no pines.[59]

In addition to fruit and vegetables for the dinner table, Colt Hoare cultivated geraniums (page 88). The 4th baronet preferred pineapple and melon pits to flowers.[60] The kitchen garden was kept going during the debilitating regime of the 5th baronet.

The 1889 OS 25 inch map of Stourhead recorded the kitchen garden on three terraces with four substantial and five lesser glasshouses.[61] On inheriting in 1894, the 6th baronet rationalised the garden so that the 1900 OS map showed a new configuration of glazed structures.[62] Nevertheless, he maintained the kitchen garden through the two world wars. The National Trust had no use for the walled garden so the terraces declined into a wilderness until a few years ago when they were taken in hand, a geranium house erected, and flower beds dug and planted.

THE PERIMETER DRIVE

'An insolent vale & terrace that has great features'

St Peter's Pump.

Before Henry the Magnificent had completed the landscape garden he had begun a second, equally grand, attraction at Stourhead: a perimeter drive to explore, by horse or carriage, the surrounding woods and to link viewing stations from which to enjoy the country beyond.[1] Henry was keen to win his son-in-law's approval, jesting with him in the words of the chapter heading.[2] He designed this circuit as outward looking and bucolic to contrast with the sequestered, closely manicured lakeside garden. The rhymer of *A ride and a walk through Stourhead* devoted half of his poem to the delights of the drive and the *Salisbury Guide* regretted leaving 'these Elysian Fields'.[3]

Most visitors set out from the Obelisk onto the Terrace which extended in a straight line north along the ridge overlooking Six Wells Bottom. When the Terrace reached Tower Road it swung west towards Alfred's Tower (1762–72) rising at the north-western extremity of the estate. The route then plunged downhill into the woods, emerging at the Convent (1767) and continuing south to join the road from Gasper to Stourton. The 1785 plan of Stourhead shows the route as far as the Terrace and Alfred's Tower, a distance of two and a quarter miles (page 252).[4]

The Terrace

The Terrace survives in decrepit condition. The sequence of views it once commanded are screened by continuous plantation clothing the eastern slopes of Six Wells Bottom, known as Sunny Hanging. So it is worth examining descriptions from its heyday. In 1769 Sir John Parnell wrote:

> [I] had no Idea of its great Extent till I Rode it. It is on the very Virge of the Brow from whence the Hill slopes down... a stripe of ground about forty yards Broad is fenced by a white thorn Hedge from the ground & on the Right hand & thrown into the Brow. This is Planted thickly on the Right and Dressd very smooth like a Race Course and left open but for clumps here and there to the left where the Prospect down the Valley lies. This great walk or Drive is about two miles, nearly straight, and then winds so gently along the Brow still, that the continuance is not Broken by it for about half a mile. The Plantation is on Both sides, this keeps the Eye from being sated with the Prospect & shows it in higher Beauty. Where it Breaks in at the End of this double Plantation on the Right, the Plantation still continues, mostly Beech & firrs.[5]

Tower Road

St Peter's
Pump

SIX WELLS

SUNNY

SHADY

Alfred's Tower

PARK HILL

LITTLE COMBE

Convent

GREAT COMBE

TUCKING MILL

CASTLE WOOD

KILMINGTON COMMON

Stourton Farm

THE PERIMETER DRIVE

······································ National Trust route

- - - - - - - - - - - - - - - - National Trust boundary

HANGING BOTTOM

Terrace Lodge

Obelisk

THE SHADES

Stourhead

Stourton

GARDEN LAKE

St Peter's Church

Rock Arch

BONHAM WOOD

TURNER'S PADDOCK LAKE

Gasper

Bonham

NEW LAKE

N

0   200   400   600

feet

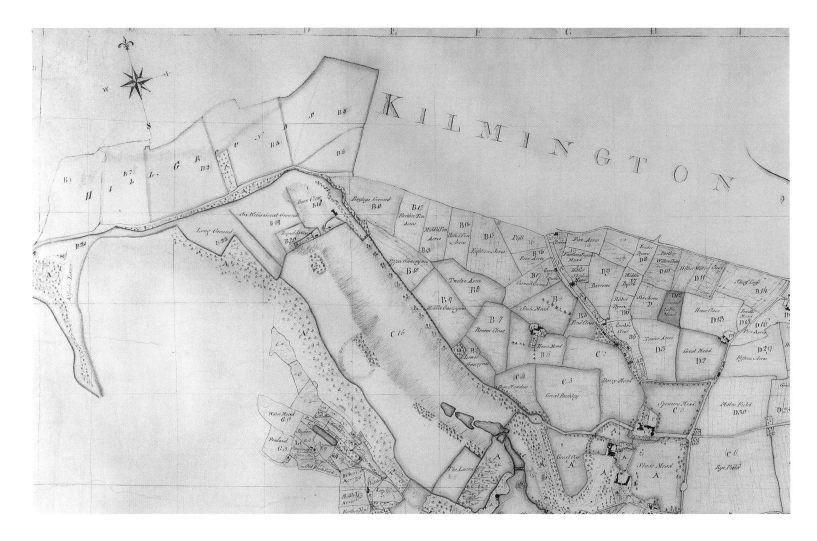

Parnell seems to refer first to a shelter belt of young trees planted along the east side of the Terrace to screen the level fields that lie between Stourhead and Kilmington. F. M. Piper and C. W. Bampfylde depicted the line of young trees and Sunny Hanging bald, apart from isolated clumps.[6]

The quality of turf on the Terrace impressed commentators. Parnell had compared it to a racecourse. In 1807 Richard Fenton admired:

> the most velvety sward I ever trod, extending for some miles, following the summit of a hill that bounds the vales... The surface of this noble terrace is as level and fine as if it was mowed, from being kept constantly fed by a large flock of South-down sheep wandering over it; and so clean, that it will not soil a lady's silk shoe; in short, for a delightful promenade and ride in a carriage, or on horseback, I may venture to say there is nothing to rival it in the kingdom.[7]

Parnell made another comparison, 'this great Drive putt me in mind of Lord Bathurst's'.[8] He was referring to Cirencester Park, famous for its rides, the pride of the 1st Earl Bathurst. Stourhead calls to mind terraces at Duncombe Park in Yorkshire which also take advantage of natural scarps or 'edges' and afford a series of views of the Rye Valley. The second terrace, constructed c.1758, overlooks the ruins of Rievaulx Abbey. Although less than a half a mile long, these terraces begin and finish

at classical temples.[9] The lengthier terrace at Farnborough Hall in Warwickshire, begun in the 1740s, commands views of the Hanwell Valley.[10] It is punctuated by an obelisk and temples. The Stourhead Terrace is about contemporary with the High Ride at Studley Royal, in Yorkshire.[11]

At Stourhead Colt Hoare and his successors planted woods on both hangings of Six Wells Bottom.[12] In 1798 William Gilpin opined, 'The vallies will be more beautiful, as the woods improve; at present they are but unfinished; and yet in their naked state we saw more clearly the peculiarity of the ground'.[13] Today, Sunny and Shady Hanging are densely clothed with conifers hemmed by deciduous trees, predominantly beech.

St Peter's Pump

At the head of Six Wells Bottom stands St Peter's Pump. It commands the valley and comes into sight from the Terrace where the ride swings westwards.

Henry Hoare mentioned the arrival of 'The Cross' at Stourhead in 1767.[14] By then the Bristol Cross was in place so he was referring to St Peter's Pump, another

St Peter's Pump, 1812–16, by Francis Nicholson (1753–1844), watercolour, 404× 552 mm. British Museum.

late medieval monument deemed a liability by the city.[15] Henry perched the Pump on a tall rock-work pedestal over one of the springs. Visitors remarked on it as a landmark, not as a work of art.

In August 1766 Thomas Tyndall had written to Henry enclosing a history of 'St Peter's Cross' and a drawing of the monument (now lost) by Thomas Paty.[16] In the letter Tyndall described it as belonging to the Commission for Building Bristol Bridge (for whom Thomas Paty constructed Bristol Bridge 1763–8). He did not mention the sum that Henry paid, but his reference to the acquisition as 'enter'd in their Books' could suggest the monument was a purchase rather than a gift. Henry's own ledger records 'Thos Patty of Bristol for taking down & pack^g The Cross Paid vide my Fleetst acct'.[17]

Tyndall explained that the monument was rebuilt in 1631 and identified the six dough-like sculptures in niches as Edward VI, Elizabeth I, James I and Anne of Denmark, and Charles I and Henrietta Maria.[18] The stone spire carries the date 1768. Henry surmounted it with a metal cross.[19] The monument was repaired in 1906 under the supervision of Sir Aston Webb, and again in 1986–7.[20]

The 1785 plan of Stourhead showed buildings close to the Pump. Here Colt Hoare either rebuilt, or built anew, two cottages and a barn.[21] Nicholson depicted these in his watercolour.[22] The 1841 Census recorded two families living at Six Wells Bottom: a gamekeeper, his wife and seven children; plus a farm labourer with a family of five. By 1891 the habitation dwindled to a shepherd and family of three.[23] A single remaining cottage was destroyed in 1938.[24]

Alfred's Tower

Tower Road is shadowed by earth banks and gullies demarcating former boundaries and indicating this was the ancient thoroughfare from the west to Salisbury. Today the section of the Terrace running parallel to the road is vestigial until it resumes at Alfred's Tower.

Henry the Magnificent wrote to his daughter, Susanna, on 23 October 1762:

> As I was reading Voltaire's L'Histoire Générale lately in His Character of Alfred the Great He says Je ne sais s'il y a jamais eu sur la terre un homme plus digne des respects de la postérité qu' Alfred le Grand qui rendit ces services à sa patrie.[25] Out of gratitude to Him I propose (if I can find a Quar of Stone in Little Coomb which they tell me I shall) to erect a Tower on Kingsettle Hill where He set up His Standard.[26]

He completed the tower ten years later. It stands at the highest point of the Stourhead Estate and is the culmination of the perimeter drive. Both landmark and belvedere, it rises 160 feet (48.7 metres), almost twice the height of Charles Hamilton's Gothic Tower at Painshill in Surrey. It also topped Horton Tower in Dorset, the brick observatory erected by Humphrey Sturt, c.1750, which reached 140 feet. At Fonthill, 'Alderman' Beckford planned to surpass all others when he began a Brobdingnagian tower on the Beacon which was abandoned after he died in 1770.[27]

Bampfylde depicted Alfred's Tower as a distant prospect from Tucking Mill (page 263).[28] The artist and Henry Hoare were close friends and this sketch, probably made before the tower was commenced, gives an impression of how it would command the landscape.[29] Bampfylde had a say in the design, but Henry Flitcroft was the architect.[30] The triangular ground plan recalls his tower at Wentworth Woodhouse in Yorkshire, c.1748, and his Belvedere in Windsor Park, c.1752.[31]

After some delays Henry Hoare informed Lord Bruce in 1765 that he had found suitable clay on the estate and was making bricks with workmen recommended by Sturt.[32] Colt Hoare described how:

> Much skill and forethought is shown in the structure of this tower, which stands on one of the most exposed spots in our kingdom, being the highest ground between this and the coast of Wales. The triangular form was adopted in order to break the violence of the winds, and brick was selected for its materials, as being more durable than stone, and a more perfect mass of brick-work can no where be found.[33]

Henry calculated that every 20 feet would cost £50 (in bricks?) but the true cost is hard to assess because Faugoin's ledgers do not survive; payments made to him during the construction indicate a greater outlay (Appendix 1).[34] In 1773 Mrs Rishton hazarded the cost was £20,000.[35] Three years later Mrs Powys put the figure 'above £4,000'.[36] In the late nineteenth century George Sweetman wrote:

> According to measurement there were really used 993,384 bricks, the total cost at present prices of material and labour being from £5,000 to £6,000. The bricks were, it is believed, made in the neighbourhood, and a grandparent of the writer was engaged in the making, being a native of Stourton or Kilmington.[37]

At first the tower rose slowly: in April 1770 it stood a mere 15 feet above ground level.[38] Thereafter building speeded up and in the autumn of 1772 *The Bath Chronicle* announced its completion.[39]

Alfred's Tower stands stark and windowless, impregnable as a castle keep, with three cylindrical corner protrusions rising the height of the building. One of these houses a spiral staircase ascending to the viewing gallery and capped by a conical roof. Both were damaged in 1944 when an aeroplane crashed into the Tower.[40] The entrance at ground level is diminutive. An early suggestion to incorporate a statue of *Fame* by Michael Rysbrack came to nothing.[41] But in 1770 Henry Hoare commissioned the over-life-size figure of *King Alfred* and installed him in the gothick niche above this doorway.[42] The Tower carries this inscription:

ALFRED THE GREAT
A.D.879 on this Summit
Erected his Standard
Against Danish Invader
To him We owe The Origin of Juries

The Establishment of a Militia
The Creation of a Naval Force.
ALFRED The Light of a Benighted Age
Was a Philosopher and a Christian
The Father of his People
The Founder of the English
MONARCHY and LIBERTY

Colt Hoare built a pair of single-storey lodges which were enlarged in 1844.[43] These were later demolished.[44]

Both Henry the Magnificent and Colt employed a guardian who conducted visitors to the gallery where the view, through 360 degrees, is breathtaking on a clear day. Mrs Powys remarked somewhat wearily:

> as to the view from yᵉ railing, it does as you may imagine take in an immense tract of prospect, and our Guide inform'd us of Twenty different things he saw or he meant we <u>should</u> see as the Bristol Channel &c. &c.[45]

Louis Simond was also lukewarm about the viewing gallery, 'where you may go and get as giddy as you please, and gaze at an immense prospect like a geographical map'.[46] Beyond the tower the ground falls away steeply to the south-west. Henry Hoare planted the surroundings with Scots pines which his successor felled in 1827–8.[47] Tracks lead down to the Convent. These were in good enough repair in 1789 for

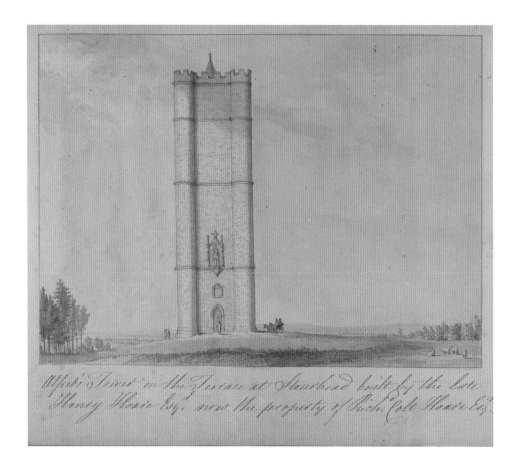

'Alfred's Tower on the Terrace at Stourhead built by the late Henry Hoare Esqre, now the property of Richd Colt Hoare Esqre', c.1780, by Samuel Hieronymus Grimm (1733–94), ink and grey wash, 270 × 330 mm. Stourhead.

George III and Queen Charlotte to venture onto them when driving from Redlynch to Stourhead.[48]

The Convent

The Convent, completed before 1767, is quintessential Horace Walpole gothick and is now embowered in the woods, closed to the public and occupied by tenants.[49] It was otherwise in the eighteenth century. George III and Queen Charlotte paused there in 1789, travelling from Redlynch to Stourhead. The Queen remarked, the Convent was first and foremost a viewing platform from which to enjoy the plantations and farms lying in the valley leading south towards Stourton.[50]

The architect is unknown. The outside walls are faced with jagged, rough-hewn greenstone, the roofs are thatched and the windows set with Y tracery in pointed arches. Squat open-work spires, a bell-cote and miniature obelisks enliven the roofline.[51] Indoors it comprised a large ground floor room, a kitchen and garrets above. Visiting in 1776 Mrs Powys described:

> an elegant Gothic Building painted Glass in the upper part of yᵉ windows, in miniature. Nuns in their different Habbits in pannels round yᵉ room, very pretty Gothick Elbow Chairs painted in mosaic Brown & white, two very Ancient pictures found in the ruins of Glassonbury Abbey, yᵉ wise men's Offerings well painted.[52]

The 1938 *Country Life* photograph recorded most of these features.[53] The nuns were painted by William Hoare of Bath.[54] In 1938 the 6th baronet restored the set which has subsequently disappeared.[55] Count di Rezzònico described the 'very Ancient pictures' as:

> Rescued from Glastonbury Abbey are two rare panel paintings attributed to Andrea Mantegna; they were used as portable altars and when open reveal images on centre panel and doors of the Annunciation and Adoration of the Magi... One is of lesser quality and perhaps French influenced by the work of Goessaert, called Mabuse, the Flemish painter and this could be his work.[56]

They reached the safety of Stourhead by 1898.[57] As did the painting, *Madonna and Child*, attributed to William Hoare and once hung above the chimneypiece in the Convent.[58]

When Parnell visited the building in 1769 he remarked on the residents, 'next Room is a Kitchen; over it a Bed Room for a Man & his wife who takes care of the Room & Breeds fine wild turkeys, Bantam fowle, guinea hens &c. in this wood'.[59] The principal room was used to entertain visitors. In *Columella*, the hero chanced upon the Convent and was regaled by a gentlewoman with a woeful tale.[60] *A Ride and walk through Stourhead* offered an esoteric take on the inmates:

> Within dwells Chastity of loosen'd Zone.
> Happy, cou'd other Convents vie with this

In their Inhabitants! Here social Joy
Connubial Ties enhance. No furtive Kiss
The conscious Bed makes groan: Not Nun and Priest
In Garb religious lustful Pranks repeat:
But Wife and Husband, innocent as Doves![61]

Hester Lyttelton, bride of Colt Hoare, encountered the 'Doves' in 1783 and identified them as 'a Game keeper Lady and Daughter'.[62]

The little folly disappears from family records until Augusta, wife of the 5th baronet, visited during her honeymoon and it later became her favourite picnicking spot.[63] The 1841 census recorded the occupants as a gardener and household of four; by 1891 it was home to a gamekeeper and family of five.[64]

The Convent, 1938. Private Collection.

Tucking Mill

Paths descending from the Convent led to the lost hamlet of Tucking Mill. There the 1722 plan shows a pond and, to the east, a cluster of smallholdings with five cottages (pages 32–3). The pattern is repeated on the 1785 plan; however, the pond is depicted as sausage-shaped (page 252). Here, in 1793, Colt Hoare netted some 270 brace of tench.[65]

A list of tenants compiled shortly after 1782 indicates the settlement flourished although the mill had closed many years before then.[66] Bampfylde drew the cottages in the middle ground with Alfred's Tower on the skyline (see overleaf).[67] Forty years later Nicholson drew the same view when the woods had matured.[68] In 1840 the 3rd baronet built four stone cottages at Tucking Mill.[69] The 1841 census listed nine families in the settlement and by 1891 the number had risen to ten.[70] The 6th baronet converted a double cottage into 'a small farm Homestead' in 1902 but, nevertheless, the settlement dwindled in the twentieth century, the dwellings were demolished, the stone recycled and all that remain are hollows and a single stone ruin.[71]

The round trip from the Obelisk and back to Stourhead measured five and a half miles.[72] Parnell rode while Mrs Powys and a party of four travelled in two phaetons.[73] The author of Defoe's *Tour*, and later Richard Skinner, travelled in chaises.[74] So too did Henry Hoare when accompanying guests.[75] Loudon complained the circuit was too great for those 'like us, [who] travel with only one horse'.[76]

Consolidation

In 1799 Colt Hoare bought the adjoining manor of Gasper, thereby extending his boundary westwards.[77] Fenton wrote:

> yet I hear that the possessor of this fine place, whose taste and spirit keep pace with each other, has it in contemplation to extend his ride in continuation of the terrace, over the summit of his boundary hills, for its whole length, so as to take a circuit of nine or ten miles.[78]

But the scheme was never put in hand.

A survey made in 1829 recorded 1,264 acres of woods on the Stourton Estate and a further 1,558 acres at outlying properties.[79] Colt became an ardent forester with larch as his favourite commercial timber. He replanted Kilmington Common with a mixture of trees, explaining:

> if at the *first* planting a certain proportion of oak is intermixed [with larch], the ground, when deprived of its crop of fir, will be furnished with a second crop of flourishing oak; the space first occupied by the larch can then be filled up with copse-wood.[80]

The western side of his estate remains predominantly wooded. In the annals Colt Hoare recorded the planting accomplished each year, a practice continued by his successors, together accomplishing:

	Total trees planted
Richard Colt Hoare, 2nd Baronet	620,800
Henry Hugh Hoare, 3rd Baronet	unknown
Hugh Richard Hoare, 4th Baronet	452,006
Henry Ainslie Hoare 5th Baronet	(incomplete) 124,278
Henry Hoare, 6th Baronet	1,067,209

The perimeter drive impinges on Stourhead Western Estate which today comprises 2,328 acres (942 hectares) and remains in the ownership of the Hoare family.[81]

In 1833 J. C. Loudon, critical of much at Stourhead, considered that, 'the terrace drive... which is three miles in length, and nearly level, and covered with soft turf, is one of the finest things of the kind in the kingdom'.[82] Subsequently the perimeter drive fell from favour while the woods and monuments along the way were maintained by later baronets. The drive has never regained its éclat although today dog-walkers frequent stretches of the route. By contrast, the landscape garden has remained well-known and popular since the 1760s: it is, above all, Henry the Magnificent's enduring claim to fame. His stone buildings survive to this day but his planting scheme and ephemeral structures, such as the Chinese Alcove and Hermitage, disappeared long ago. By removing the latter Colt Hoare, in one sense, did a good turn to his successors who were spared the cost of maintaining them.

If Colt Hoare took, he also gave, broadening the variety of trees and shrubs planted in the garden so that Stourhead today approximates more closely to his taste than to the vision of his grandfather. The baronets who followed continued to augment the tree collection as the garden gradually transitioned to arboretum.

The house grew with family requirements before it was destroyed by the 1902 fire and bravely reincarnated. This was the achievement of Sir Henry, the 6th Baronet and his wife whose presence insured the sun did not set on their Victorian way of life at Stourhead until 1947.

RIGHT
View towards Alfred's Tower, *c*.1760–70, by C. W. Bampfylde (1720–91), pen and colour wash, 270 × 380 mm. Victoria & Albert Museum.

OVERLEAF
St Peter's Pump and Six Wells Bottom.

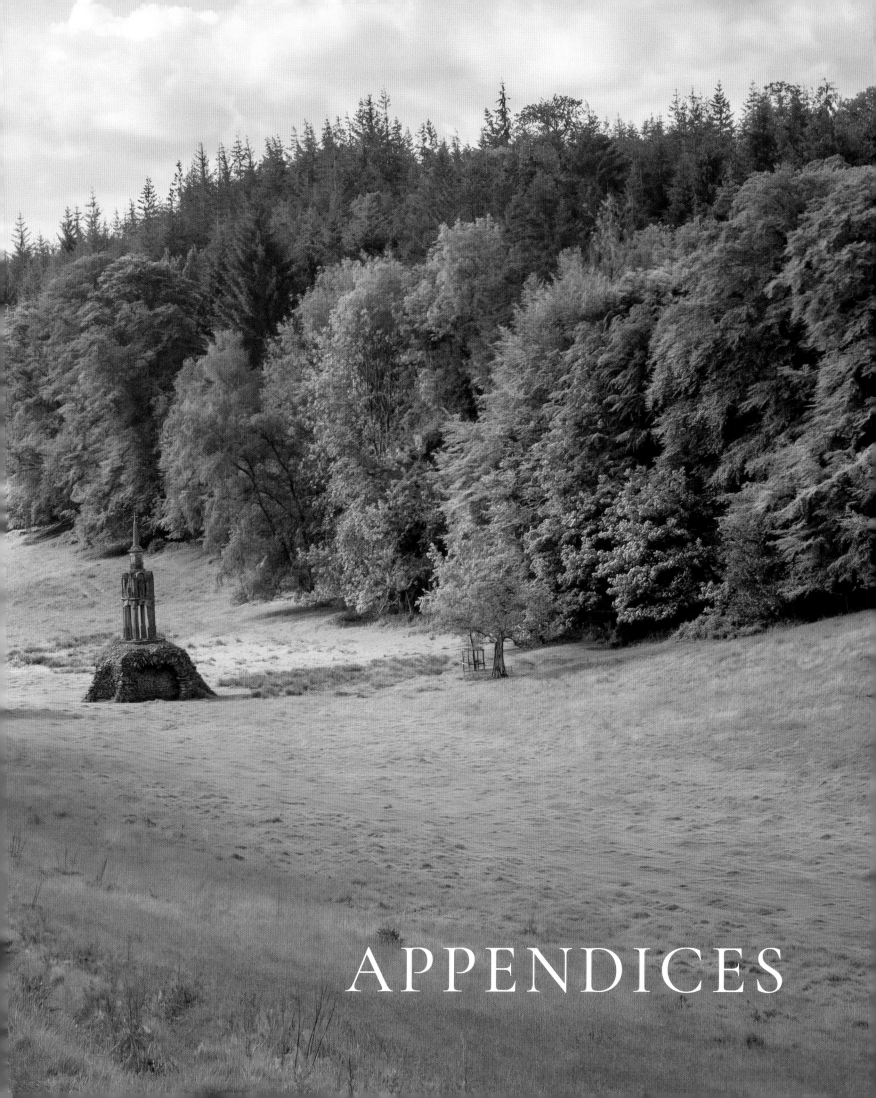

APPENDICES

Appendix I: Henry the Magnificent's payments to Francis Faugoin

Record of Henry the Magnificent's payments to Francis Faugoin at Stourhead from 1 January 1747 to
31 December 1773, as found in:

C. Hoare & Co., HFM/9/1, Henry Hoare Ledger of Personal Accounts 1734–49
WSA, 383/6, Henry Hoare Ledger of Personal Accounts 1749–70
C. Hoare & Co., HFM/9/5, Henry Hoare Ledger of Personal Accounts, 1770–85
HB/5/A/6, Partners' Ledger 1742–51, Henry Hoare's account
HB/5/A/7, Partners' Ledger 1751–64, Henry Hoare's account
HB/5/A/8, Partners' Ledger 1764–83, Henry Hoare's account

Payments are not exclusive to Stourhead because Faugoin managed remote property belonging to both
Henry and Richard Hoare. Henry himself paid artists and senior craftsmen.

Year	Personal ledger £	Partners' ledger £	Annual totals £	Grand totals £	Stourhead garden structures chronology
1747	1,058	-	1,058		Obelisk
1748	1,253	-	1,253		Grotto, Obelisk
1749	200	360	560		Grotto, Obelisk, Chinese Alcove, Wooden Bridge
1750	680	200	880		Grotto, Obelisk
1751	485	200	685		Grotto, Obelisk
1752	664	470	1,134		Obelisk
1753	951	470	1,421		Pantheon
1754	762	293	1,055		Dam, Pantheon
1755	540	228	768		Dam, Pantheon
1756	686	311	997		Pantheon
1757	1,271	548	1,819		Pantheon
1758	230	960	1,190		Pantheon
1759	560	382	942		Pantheon
1760	887	984	1,871		Pantheon
Subtotal				15,633	
1761	700	732	1,432		Pantheon
1762	179	791	970		Pantheon, Stone Bridge, Alfred's Tower
1763	706	948	1,654		Tower
1764	1,995	1,368	3,363		Tower, Temple of Apollo
1765	1,621	3,209	4,830		Tower, Apollo, Bristol Cross, Cascade, Neptune, Rock Arch, Turkish Tent

Year	Personal ledger £	Partners' ledger £	Annual totals £	Grand totals £	Stourhead garden structures chronology
1766	3,650	3,721	7,371		Tower, Apollo, Cross, Cascade
1767	680	3,125	3.805		Tower, Convent, St Peter's Pump
1768	2,390	1,202	3,592		Tower
1769	140	3,414	3,554		Tower
1770	199	2,320	2,519		Tower
1771	400	676	1,076		Tower, Hermitage
1772	10	1,680	1,690		Tower
1773	235	655	890		
Subtotal				36,746	
Total				**52,379**	

Appendix II: Notes on visitors describing Stourhead

Publications and ms sources are found in the bibliography. Structures at Stourhead described by the authors epilogue each biography (features mentioned by name alone in brackets).

Anonymous 1764 (Stourton Gardens 1749)

The author of 'Stourton Gardens. written in June, 1749' remains elusive. So too is the motive for publishing the verses in *The Royal Magazine* some fifteen years after they were written, when the garden had been transformed. This poem of less than two hundred lines describes Stourton before the valley was flooded to form the Garden Lake. The author visited the statue of *Livia Augusta* in the Temple of Ceres/Flora and described the cascade below, then proceeded by boat to the Grotto inhabited by the *Nymph*. He, or she, returned through the Shades encountering the lead statue of *Diana*, the Chinese Seat and the *Apollo Belvedere* on the South Lawn. There is no mention of the Wooden Bridge because it was erected in the year the lines were composed.

The author was interested in the estate for its historical associations, specifically the ancient Britons, the Romans and King Alfred. The comments are contemporary with William Stukeley's archaeological publications. Mention of King Alfred foreshadows a preoccupation of Henry the Magnificent in the 1760s. After the Hanoverian succession Alfred was acclaimed as the model constitutional ruler, beloved by the Whigs, celebrated in Rapin's *History of England* (London, 1725) and lauded interminably by Sir

Richard Blackmore in a twelve-book poem, *Alfred* (London, 1723).

Anonymous 1764 (Stourton Gardens 1749), p. 102, Temple of Ceres/Flora, *Livia Augusta*, Manning's *River God*, Grotto, 'Mr Benson's Ingine'; p. 103, Chinese Alcove, *Diana of Versailles*, Kingsettle Hill, Stourton, *Apollo Belvedere*; p. 104, house.

Anonymous 1765

In 2004 the National Trust received this entertaining manuscript account of Stourhead written in 1765. The notebook was kept by a gentlewoman whose identity is unknown. She did not pretend knowledge of the classics or art but took careful note of the appearance and colour schemes at the house. Outdoors the author admired the Turkish Tent and 'Chinese Temple' complete with the mandarin. The Temple of Apollo was under construction and the Pantheon, she learned, cost £10,000.

Anonymous manuscript 1765: Fir Walk, Obelisk, *Apollo Belvedere*, Gothick Greenhouse, Grotto, Pantheon, Wooden Bridge, Rock Arch, Temple of Apollo, Stone Bridge, Temple of Ceres/Flora, Turkish Tent, Chinese Alcove, house.

Anonymous 1766

James Essex (1722–84), author of the first section in the notebook, was a Cambridge architect and an early admirer of gothic buildings. The second part, which included Stourhead, appears to be in the same handwriting, but is unsigned.[1]

The author set off from Lincolnshire on 26 May 1766 and travelled south to Wiltshire. He was knowledgeable about architecture, paintings and prints. Wilton House, he mentioned by name only. At Longford Castle the author admired paintings by Claude, Poussin and Holbein. *Fonthill Splendens* was incomplete, 'to be intended as magnificent as most in England'. Longleat was 'badly furnish'd but contains some good Family Portraits'. At Stourhead he admired the copies as much as the original paintings. His description of the grounds is competent and spiced by the prices allegedly paid for *Hercules* and *Livia Augusta*.

Anonymous manuscript 1766: fol. 36 verso, art collection, South Lawn, *Apollo Belvedere*, Chinese Alcove; fol. 35 verso, Wooden Bridge, Grotto; fol. 34 verso, Pantheon; fol. 33 verso, Rock Arch, Temple of Apollo, Stone Bridge, Bristol Cross, Temple of Flora, Turkish Tent; fol. 32 verso, Obelisk.

Anonymous 1780

The author of the *Ride and a walk through Stourhead* (London, 1780) described the Perimeter Drive and landscape garden at Stourhead in just under six hundred lines of limping rhyme that rise above doggerel without aspiring to be poetry.

Setting out from the house, the author rode along the Fir Walk, past the Obelisk and Terrace to reach Alfred's Tower. Praise for King Alfred and the view occupy over a hundred lines. Returning through the woods via the Convent, the rider reached the garden at the Cascade whence Francis Faugoin escorted him (or her?) around the lake in a counter-clockwise direction. There is a brief description of the interior of the Pantheon and, fortunately, no attempt to rhyme the art collection in the house.

At first reading the poem seems replete with mythology, yet the author found these associations in the open air, not among the structures: Cybele in the Fir Walk, Daphne and the 'Peneian Nymph' among the woods and dells below Alfred's Tower, Diana and Silenus in the laurel grove at Rock Arch, Nereids and Naiads beside the lake. The poet does not wear this learning lightly: the footnotes contain three acknowledgements to Horace, three to Virgil, two to Terence, two to Ovid and three to Shakespeare.

The author knew Stourhead well, naming the head gardener, gamekeeper and adjoining landowners, Lord Ilchester and Lord Berkeley. Henry the Magnificent's coterie made guest appearances: C. W. Bampfylde, William Hoare of Bath and the Bruce granddaughters. Absent are John Rust (p. 58), John Aislabie Benson and William Benson Earle, each a possible author of the *Ride*.

Anonymous 1780: p. 2/41–49, Obelisk; p. 3/57–69, Fir Walk; p. 3/72–79, Terrace; p. 4/80–94, St Peter's Pump; p. 4/94, *Neptune*

and his prancing horses; p. 5 /117–160, Kingsettle Hill; p. 6/162–232, Alfred's Tower; p. 10/252–283, Convent; p. 14/351–357 Cascade; p. 14/371–374, Rock Arch; p. 15/382–386, Bristol Cross; p. 15/383–394, Temple of Flora; p. 15/395–400 Chinese Alcove; p. 16/401–407, Turkish Tent; p. 16/407–416, Wooden Bridge; p. 18/455–510, Grotto; p. 20/511–538, Pantheon; p. 21/543–555, Hermitage; p. 21/556–566, Temple of Apollo.

Beaufort, Duchess of

Elizabeth Berkeley (d. 1799) was the sister and heir of Norborne Berkeley, Lord Botetourt. In 1740 she married Charles Somerset, the 4th Duke of Beaufort, who died sixteen years later. From her brother she inherited Stoke Gifford in Gloucestershire which became her principal residence.[2]

The duchess was an intelligent and observant commentator, as is apparent from her journal of her Grand Tour, 1769–74. In her *Observations on Places* she recounted her travels in England, from 1750. She wrote about landscape gardening, architecture and interior décor. At Wilton House and Longford Castle she identified the artists and subjects of highlights in the picture collections. The duchess visited Stourhead on 16 July 1762. Her commentary is brisk and objective but without rewarding insights.

Harris 2000 (Beaufort 1762): p. 41, art collection, Fir Walk, Terrace, Pantheon, Temple of Flora, Gothick Greenhouse, Chinese Alcove, Temple on the Terrace, Grotto, Obelisk.

Britton, John

John Britton (1771–1857) was the tireless and prolific author of a shelf-full of architectural and topographical studies. He came from nothing and learned fast how to badger his elders and betters. Unsurprisingly quarrels lay ahead. He was befriended by Colt Hoare who illustrated the second volume of Britton's *The beauties of Wiltshire* (London, 1801); hence the glutinous and florid dedication to Colt, that 'neither pride nor arrogance ever had dominion in your breast'.[3] Britton had also tapped the antiquary and archaeologist, William Cunnington. He fell out with both men in 1804[4]. Britton nevertheless wrote:

> People of all ranks visited Stourhead. The poet sounded its eulogy – the painter delineated its beauties – the architect imitated its ornamental buildings – the connoisseur descanted on its charms in the full glow of admiration and delight... it is more to be admired from having been *one* of the first places laid out in the new style of gardening, and designed by a *country gentleman*, unassisted by any *landscape gardener*.[5]

Britton's assertion 'this celebrated seat never yet accurately described' is disingenuous: his account of the house plundered Colt's guidebook, printed the previous year. His description of the garden is among the best. Britton published the third volume of *The beauties of Wiltshire* in 1825 where he repeated his intention to produce a modern history of north Wiltshire as companion to Sir Richard's volumes on the south. He abandoned the project but his manuscript for the hundreds of Chippenham and North Damerham survive. [6]

Wiltshire was the first county in the topographical survey which Britton, with others, compiled as *The beauties of England and Wales* (London, 1801–21) in twenty-seven volumes. Britton also published the *Architectural antiquities of Great Britain* (London, 1807–27) in five volumes. His magnum opus, the *Cathedral antiquities of England* (London, 1814–35) was well illustrated but remained incomplete in fourteen volumes. [7] Britton was an adept publicist but could not make his ventures profitable.

Britton 1801, vol. II: p. 4, house; p. 13, Garden Lake; p. 14, Wooden Bridge, St Peter's Pump, ferry; p. 15, Grotto; p. 17, Pantheon; p. 18, Rock Arch, Hermitage, Temple of Apollo; p. 19, Temple of Ceres/Flora, Stone Bridge, Bristol Cross; p. 20, St Peter's Church; p. 22, Cascade, Convent; p. 23, Alfred's Tower.

Burlington, Charles

The modern universal British traveller (London, 1779) described Wiltshire in twenty-four pages of double columns. It mentioned the towns, Stonehenge and covered country houses unevenly. Longleat was omitted while Longford Castle, Amesbury Abbey and Stourhead were mentioned briefly. Wilton House occupies eight columns in the *Traveller*, taken from the published guidebook. The account of Stourhead had appeared in *A new display of the beauties of England*. [8]

Burlington 1779: p. 394, art collection, Fir Walk, Obelisk, Wooden Bridge, Grotto.

Clarke, William

The transcript, headed '5 July, Saturday', provides a thoughtful description of Stourhead with nuggets of information, for example, that Henry the Magnificent placed the organ, purchased in 1770, in the Entrance Hall. [9] The text was sent to the National Trust with a photocopy of a letter from one William Clarke to Bartholomew Burton, dated 15 October 1767. The letter refers to Stourhead but not to the text which was evidently written in the 1770s because the author, 'Clarke' visited the Hermitage, which was built in 1771. Given the description named the day and month it may be deduced it was written in 1777.

Clarke 1777, Gothick Greenhouse, Obelisk, Chinese Umbrella,

Temple of Flora, Wooden Bridge, Grotto, Pantheon, Rock Arch, Hermitage, Temple of Apollo, Chinese Alcove, Fir Walk, art collection, Alfred's Tower.

Curwen, Samuel

Samuel Curwen (1715–1802), born in New England, was an Anglophile. He fought the French in America, rose to be a deputy judge in the Admiralty and, at the outbreak of the War of Independence, quit his homeland and travelled to London. His journals describe British towns, institutions and politics. He was often in the South West where he found seaside villages transformed into health resorts. He was less interested in country houses and, on his own admission, was below par on 24 September 1776 when he visited Stourhead. His description is muddled until he climbed Alfred's Tower to delight in the view. A two-volume transcription of his journals was published in 1972. [10]

Oliver 1972 (Curwen 1776), vol. I: p. 229, art collection; p. 230, Turkish Tent, Wooden Bridge, Grotto, Pantheon; p. 231, Cascade, Temple of Apollo, Gothick Greenhouse, Stone Bridge, Bristol Cross, Alfred's Tower.

Defoe, Daniel

Daniel Defoe (*c.*1660–1731), the prolific pamphleteer and author, published *A tour through the island of Great Britain* in 1724, two decades before Henry the Magnificent began Stourhead garden. Samuel Richardson (1689–1761) acquired the title in 1738 and published revised versions, despite his aversion to travel. The ninth and final edition was issued in 1779, 'brought down to the present Time by Gentlemen of Eminence in the Literary World'. The description of Stourhead is perfunctory in the house but thorough around the garden and Perimeter Drive.

Defoe 1779, vol. I: p. 316, house, art collection; p. 317, *Apollo Belvedere*, Fir Walk, Obelisk, Turkish Tent, Wooden Bridge, Grotto; p. 318, Pantheon, Cascade, Rock Arch; p. 319, Hermitage, Temple of Apollo, Stone Bridge, Temple of Ceres/Flora, Bristol Cross, Gothick Greenhouse; p. 320, Alfred's Tower.

Dibdin, Thomas Frognal

Thomas Dibdin (1776–1847) was ordained and held a succession of livings in London. From an early age he was passionate about books. [11] The 2nd Earl Spencer appointed him librarian at Althorp where Dibdin compiled the *Bibliotheca Spenceriana* (London, 1814–15), the first published record of that library. His scholarship has been questioned but not his enthusiasm. In 1812 he founded the Roxburghe Club with the earl as the first president.

Dibdin wrote lighthearted pieces, such as the description of Stourhead in 1822, under the sobriquet of Cuthbert Tonstall (the Tudor scholar and churchman). Dibdin spent the night at the inn at Stourton and was conducted around the garden by 'the fair Gabrielle'. His description is more florid than informative. The following day he was invited to the house where he found Colt Hoare an object of greater fascination than the art. Colt entertained Dibdin well, plying him with venison so that the contented bibliophile wrote, 'the *Cuisine* was as perfect as the *Druidery*'. [12]

Dibdin 1822: p. 389, Pantheon, Grotto, ferry; p. 390, art collection, Bristol Cross, Temple of Flora, Alfred's Tower.

Fenton, Richard

See p. 84

Fenton 1811 (1807): p. 179, house; p. 181, art collection; p. 196, Obelisk, Terrace, Alfred's Tower; p. 204, Kitchen Garden; p. 206, ferry; p. 207, Grotto; p. 208, Pantheon; p. 209, Hermitage, Temple of Apollo; p. 210, Bristol Cross; p. 211, Temple of Flora; p. 213, keeper's house; p. 214, Convent; p. 222, St Peter's Church; p. 220, Sir Richard Colt Hoare.

Gilpin, William

William Gilpin (1724–1804) was a parson, schoolmaster, author and amateur artist.[13] He is renowned for his concept of the picturesque, airily defined in his *Essay on prints* (London, 1768) as 'that peculiar kind of beauty, which is agreeable in a picture'. He evolved the notion in a series of *Observations* published from 1782, chronicling his travels around Britain.

Gilpin arrived at Stourhead in a mood to be critical and did not hold back in the *Observations on the western parts of England* (London, 1798). He referred to 'Mr Hoare' as owner and probably visited Stourhead on a tour made in the mid-1770s.[14] Of the garden he wrote, 'the buildings, in general, are good; but they are too numerous and too sumptuous'. He admired the Pantheon, dismissed the Bristol Cross and criticised the lower garden as too trim and the upper as old-fashioned. He praised the Terrace and plantations as more atuned to his precepts. Gilpin accompanied his description with two of his own aquatints.

Gilpin 1798: p. 120, Wooden Bridge, Grotto; p. 121, Pantheon; p. 122, Bristol Cross; p. 123, Terrace, Perimeter Drive, Alfred's Tower.

Graves, Richard

Richard Graves (1715–1804) was educated at Oxford, ordained and, from 1749, the popular rector of Claverton, near Bath, where he also kept a private school. At university he became friends with William Shenstone whose biography he would publish in 1788.[15]

Graves was always short of money and wrote to swell his income. His range was extensive: from light verse to translations from the Greek. His two-volume novel, *Columella; or, the distressed anchoret* (London, 1779), disparages a life of idleness and solitude. An episode is set at Stourhead, where the protagonists muse over the farrago of architectural styles. An imagined encounter at the Convent played up its rustic charm and would have delighted the master of the genre, George Morland. C. W. Bampfylde provided two frontispieces for the novel, the first evocative of Stourhead.

Graves 1779, vol. II: p. 10, Grotto; p. 12, Pantheon, Convent; p. 30, Alfred's Tower.

Hanway, Jonas

Jonas Hanway (1712–86) made his fortune as a merchant in Europe and Russia and later described his travels in four volumes (London, 1753).[16] After returning to London, Hanway continued to profit from the Russia Company and became a philanthropist, concerned in particular with orphaned city children. He was a prime mover at the Foundling Hospital and Magdalen Hospital, both numbering the Hoare family among their supporters. He lobbied successfully for an Act of Parliament requiring parishes to keep a register of poor children.

In 1756 Hanway published *A journal of eight days journey from Portsmouth to Kingston upon Thames*. The previous year he had visited Wilton House, Longford Castle, Eastbury, Blandford (Bryanston) and Stourhead where he stayed as the guest of Henry the Magnificent. Hanway's account of the place is significant because his *cicerone* was the owner. He described the grounds in transition: the Garden Lake was formed, the Pantheon, incomplete. Hanway took to the water in a boat rowed by two members of the Hoare family and the rector. He rounded off the commentary with a kid-glove character sketch of Henry whom he found, 'liberal without prodigality and charitable without ostentation'.

Samuel Johnson dismissed Hanway's prose, remarking that he had 'acquired some reputation by traveling abroad, but lost it all by traveling at home'.

His account of Stourhead also appeared in *The London Chronicle or Universal Evening Post*, no. 73, 16–18 June 1757, p. 578.

Hanway 1756: p. 87, house, art collection; p. 89, Fir Walk, Obelisk; p. 90, Wooden Bridge, Grotto; p. 91, Pantheon; p. 92, Temple of Ceres/Flora.

Hazlitt, William

William Hazlitt (1778–1830) arrived at Stourhead in a black mood, as he recounted in *Sketches of the principal picture-galleries in England*

(London, 1824). He had been turned away from Longford Castle and talked his way into Wilton House with difficulty. Hazlitt found Fonthill Abbey open but he derived little pleasure from the preponderance of cabinet paintings which he considered too small for the building. He lamented that Beckford had sold the Alteri Claudes.[17] With a few exceptions Hazlitt dismissed the pictures at Stourhead, saving his admiration for Stourton village. Brooding upon Stonehenge, he preferred the monument to remain a mystery.

The contrast between Hazlitt and Colt Hoare appears stark. The former was the son of a dissenting minister, a radical thinker, sometime friend of Coleridge and Wordsworth, supporter of the French Revolution and Napoleon, scourge of reactionary politics and a maverick in his private life.[18] Hazlitt made a precarious living as a journalist and author; fortunately his pen crackled with life and ideas. Unlike Colt he was adept at expressing his emotions and conveying enthusiasm to readers. Nevertheless, in early manhood, both men had pretensions as artists which they later set aside for literary pursuits. In the long perspective both were obsessively hardworking, both at their happiest with an inkwell at their elbow.

Hazlitt 1824: p. 137, Stourton; p. 138 art collection.

Jerningham, Edward

Edward Jerningham (1737–1812) came from an ancient Norfolk family of Catholics.[19] As poet and playwright he was inconsequential but he flourished as a darling of society and friend of the Prince Regent. Jerningham delighted in tittle-tattle and the theatre. In 1777 Sheridan caricatured him as Sir Benjamin Backbite in *The School for Scandal*. He visited Stourhead the same year and pin-pointed the various viewing stations. A selection from his letters, including the description of Stourhead, was published in 1919.[20]

Bettany 1919 (Jerningham 1777): p. 18, Turkish Tent, Wooden Bridge, Grotto, Pantheon, (Temple of Flora, *Neptune and his prancing horses*, Cascade, Stone Bridge) Temple of Apollo, Bristol Cross; p. 19, (Hermitage, Gothick Greenhouse, Alfred's Tower, Perimeter Drive).

Loudon, John Claudius

J. C. Loudon (1783–1843) was a gifted horticultural writer and garden designer.[21] He trained at Edinburgh University before travelling to London in 1803. For income Loudon depended primarily on his publications and is renowned as author of *An encyclopædia of gardening* (London, 1822) and as founder of the *Gardener's Magazine* (1826–43). His *Arboretum et fruticetum Britannicum* (London, 1838) is a magnificent account of native trees and shrubs.

Loudon, although crippled by arthritis, travelled the Continent and Britain. He visited Stourhead during the summer of 1833 and published a description two years later in his magazine. Before reaching Wiltshire he had called at Kingston Lacy in Dorset, where he admired the cedar trees, and nearby Bryanston, where he praised the hothouses and kitchen gardens as commendably weed-free. Loudon spent two days exploring the landscape surrounding Fonthill Abbey relishing the impenetrable woods and absence of gravel walks. At Stourhead he admired the well-tended village as much as the landscape garden in which he found the trees monotonous and the laurels over-abundant. In their place he recommended rhododendrons.

Loudon 1835: p. 335, Stone Bridge; p. 337, Perimeter Drive, Kitchen Garden, Stourton; p. 338, ferry.

Parnell, Sir John

Sir John Parnell, 2nd Baronet (1745–1801) was educated at Eton and Trinity College, Dublin, then studied law at Lincoln's Inn. He sat as an MP in the Irish Parliament and, briefly, at Westminster in 1801. Parnell served as Chancellor of the Exchequer for Ireland, 1785–99.[22]

In May 1769 he embarked on a tour of England, gathering ideas to improve Rathleague, his property in Queen's County, recording his impressions in journals. Parnell was interested in farming, forestry, parks and gardens. He wrote long descriptions, with sketches, of the grounds at Claremont, Hagley, the Leasowes, Painshill, Prior Park and Shugborough. In his second volume, Parnell described a journey from Bath, through Longleat to Stourhead. He devoted thirty-five pages to the latter, delighting in the Perimeter Drive. His account of garden was published in 1982.[23]

Parnell 1769, vol. II, fols 79–113: description of the garden and Perimeter Drive together with notes on the house and art collection.

Piper, Fredrik Magnus

F. M. Piper (1746–1824) is renowned for popularising English gardening in Sweden.[24] He studied mathematics and trained in architecture and hydraulics before he was appointed an architectural overseer at the Royal Palace at Stockholm in 1772. He was dispatched to London for a brief visit under the wing of the Swedish-born architect, Sir William Chambers. In 1774 King Gustav III awarded Piper an allowance to study European gardens. For the next six years he travelled in Italy, France and England. His response to the gardens of Le Nôtre was ambiguous: he recognised the merit of straight avenues, symmetry and formal water as well-suited to royal residences, yet he craved variety and surprise. In England he admired the garden buildings at Kew designed by Chambers for the dowager Princess of Wales and shared the architect's antipathy for the landscapes of Capability Brown.[25] The writings of Thomas Whately caught his imagination and he studied famous gardens including Hagley, Painshill, Stourhead and Stowe.[26] By the time he returned to Sweden he had hit on a style which embraced both French formality and Georgian ornamental gardening. Sadly Piper's architectural designs lack *esprit*: his classical buildings are ungainly while his Chinese and Turkish adventures look derivative.

Gustav III was impatient for Piper's newly acquired expertise and set him to transform the outer grounds at Drottningholm. Piper also landscaped Haga Park and undertook further private commissions. The king interfered and had no qualms about inviting other architects to design buildings that Piper had planned. He fell from favour in the new century. Thereafter he served as president of the Royal Swedish Academy of Fine Arts, in Stockholm, teaching the next generation of architects and composing the idiosyncratic *Description of the idea and general-plan for an English park* (1811–12). Piper wrote in Swedish, French and English. His studies of the hydraulics at Painshill and Stourhead are particularly thorough. [27]

Piper bequeathed his books, manuscripts and drawings to the Royal Swedish Academy including his studies of Stourhead. Pride of place goes to four highly finished plans of the garden, demonstrating for Gustav III the merit of Stourhead.[28] Piper drew what he admired about the garden, omitting utilitarian buildings, adjusting paths and adding islands, to his taste.[29] His preliminary sketches include questions (in English) for the head gardener. Piper may well have had access to Flitcroft's drawings for Stourhead; indeed he seems to have made off with the architect's alternative design for the Pantheon (p. 173). In addition to the general plans, the collection includes an elevation of the Obelisk, thirteen studies of the Grotto, several measured drawings of the Wooden Bridge and one highly finished study of the Hermitage. Piper also made vignettes of Stourhead in a feathery style. If he studied the Temples of Apollo and Flora, the drawings are untraced. He ignored the Perimeter Drive.

Piper's surviving drawings and studies depict the Chinese Umbrella, Grotto, Hermitage, Obelisk, Temple on the Terrace, Wooden Bridge, views and plans of the Garden Lake and dam.

Pococke, Richard

Richard Pococke (1704–65) was an English prelate, adventurer and author. Family connections, notably his uncle, the bishop of Waterford and Lismore, enabled him to rise through the ranks of the Irish church to a bishopric.[30] However he is remembered as an explorer of distant places and as an author. Pococke travelled through Europe in 1733.[31] Four years later he set out to visit Palestine, Syria and Egypt, publishing his experiences as *A Description of the East and some other countries* (London, 1743–5). *The travels through England of Dr. Richard Pococke* were published in two volumes by the Camden Society, 1888–9. As expected from a cosmopolitan observer, his interests were wide-ranging. He responded to ancientness: at Powys Castle, for example, he admired 'fine hanging gardens in the old stile'.[32]

Pococke visited Stourhead in 1754 when the creation of the Garden Lake was imminent. He described the Pantheon under construction and how it would be furnished. In the neighbourhood, he called at Marston and admired improvements which the 5th Earl of Orrery had made to the garden.[33] Redlynch merited only brief mention.

Cartwright 1888 (Pococke 1754), vol. II: p. 43, Fir Walk, Obelisk, house, South Lawn and pool, Temple on the Terrace, Temple of Flora, Grotto, Pantheon.

Polwarth, Lady Amabel Yorke

The daughter of the 2nd Earl of Hardwicke and the Marchioness Grey, Lady Amabel Yorke (1751–1833) is famous as a diarist, author and amateur artist.[34] In 1772 she married Alexander Hume-Campbell, Lord Polwarth, later Baron Hume, who died in 1781. On the death of her mother sixteen years later, Lady Polwarth inherited Wrest Park in Bedfordshire. She was created Countess de Grey of Wrest in 1816. This super bluestocking visited Stourhead in 1776 and described the occasion in a letter to her mother and in her diary.[35] She admired the views and was charmed by the 'elegant simplicity' of the Grotto; the upper garden, however, she considered old-fashioned. Lady Polwarth named pictures in the house that she admired but chided Henry the Magnificent (in his absence) for being 'too fond I think of covering his walls with copies from the famous masters, however they are honestly given as such'.

Polwarth 1776: house, art collection, Fir Walk, Turkish Tent, Wooden Bridge, Grotto, Pantheon, Hermitage, Temple of Apollo, Bristol Cross.

Powys, Caroline

Caroline Girle (1738–1817) married Philip Lybbe Powys of Hardwick House, Whitchurch, Oxfordshire in 1762. From an early age she kept a diary of her social life and visits to country houses. The manuscripts are in the British Library and a selection from her diaries was published in 1899.[36]

Mrs Powys set out from Whitchurch to visit Stourhead on 5 August 1776 with 'M[r] Annesley, my Brother [-in-law], M[r] Powys... in two Phaetons'. Before reaching this destination they called at

Longford Castle, Wilton House and Fonthill. Her description of Stourhead and the grounds is chatty, if breathless.

Powys 1776: fol. 16, Gardener's House, Bristol Cross; fol. 18, Gothick Greenhouse, Wooden Bridge, Pantheon; fol. 19, Cascade, Temple of Apollo, Stone Bridge, Temple of Flora, Turkish Tent; fol. 20, St Peter's Pump, Alfred's Tower; fol. 22, Convent; fol. 23, art collection.

Rezzònico, Count Carlo Gastone della Torre di

Count di Rezzònico (1742–96) was a relative of Pope Clement XIII, a scholar and poet.[37] He was educated in Parma, with interludes studying in Rome and Naples. During the 1760s he immersed himself in the literary life of Palma. After his father died in 1785, he set out on a Grand Tour travelling through Germany and France before reaching England in 1787 where he remained for a year, distilling the experiences in *Viaggio in Inghilterra* published in 1824.[38]

Count di Rezzònico, well-informed and armed with the necessary introductions, explored England thoroughly. At Painshill he complimented Hamilton on his exotic trees, water wheel and grotto but not on the prized statue of *Bacchus* which he considered poorly restored. The count then headed west to Wilton House, Salisbury (for the antique sculpture and Van Dyck's portraits) and on to Stonehenge, Fonthill and Stourhead. Thereafter he travelled to Bath and Bristol, and detoured briefly into Wales. Yorkshire impressed the count; he admired Studley Royal with its magnificent prospect of Fountains Abbey; he called at Newby Hall for the sculpture and at Duncombe Park where he singled out *The Jennings Dog*, now in the British Museum, recalling similar Molossian hounds in the Vatican and at Florence. The count admired Castle Howard although he found the entrance hall over-theatrical. Returning south he called at Chatsworth where the cascade and great fountain pleased him. He praised the Derbyshire alabaster columns at Kedleston and the landscape garden at Stowe.

The count had a perceptive eye for pictures. On occasions he was critical: at Fonthill Splendens he condemned Andrea Casali ('Cristalli') as indifferent. He was less atuned to English artists, although he mentioned Thornhill at Chatsworth and Moreland at Kedleston. Portraits by Reynolds and his rivals did not catch his attention. The *Viaggio* is authoritative and briskly written.[39]

Gamba 1824 (Rezzònico 1787): p. 10, Convent; p. 11, Alfred's Tower; p. 13, Obelisk, house, art collection; p. 17, South Lawn, *Apollo Belvedere*, Turkish Tent; p. 18, Wooden Bridge, Grotto; p. 20, Pantheon, Hermitage; p. 21, Rock Arch, Temple of Apollo; p. 22, Stone Bridge, Temple of Flora; p. 23, Bristol Cross, Gothick Greenhouse, *Neptune and his prancing horses*.

Rishton, Maria

Maria Allen (d. 1820) was the stepsister of Fanny Burney, the celebrated novelist, playwright and diarist. The girls were thrown together after their widowed parents married in 1767. Friendship developed and continued after, in 1772, Maria married Martin Folkes Rishton, from Hillingdon Hall in Norfolk. The following year Maria went to Stourhead and described her visit in a letter to Fanny dated 13 April.[40] She claimed the garden had cost £300,000 to create and, alone among commentators, noted in the Hermitage, 'several inscriptions, there are hundred others disposed about the gardens'.

Ellis 1907 (Fanny Burney 1773), vol. II: p. 322, Grotto, Wooden Bridge, Temple of Apollo, Pantheon, Temple of Flora, Turkish Tent, Hermitage, Perimeter Drive, Alfred's Tower; p. 323, Convent.

Simond, Louis

Louis Simond (1767–1831) was born in Lyons but, shortly before the French Revolution, moved to America. There he prospered in the shipping business and married an English woman, the niece of John Wilkes. They travelled to Britain in 1809 to enjoy twenty-one months touring the country, talking to celebrities and servants, enquiring about the annual income of landowners and forming opinions on the English way of life. Simond attended House of Commons debates, visited Newgate prison and glimpsed the elderly George III at Windsor. Having returned to America briefly in 1811, he sailed once more to England where he remained until the restoration of the monarchy in France. In 1815 he published the *Journal of a tour and residence in Great Britain during the years 1810 and 1811* (Edinburgh, 1817).[41]

Simond visited Stourhead on 6 July 1810, and was dismayed when:

> One of the ladies and myself having sat down a moment to look at a picture more conveniently, a young girl who showed the house, told us as civilly as she could, that it was *the rule of the house not to allow visitors to sit down*. This is a rule of which that gentleman (a rich banker) has the merit of the invention. We have not met with any thing of the sort anywhere else.[42]

He dipped his pen in gall before continuing the description.

Simond 1817 (1810): p. 260, house; p. 261, Grotto; p. 262, Alfred's Tower.

Skinncr, John

The Reverend John Skinner (1772–1839) was an eager attendant at the Stourhead gatherings (p. 97).[43] He began his career as curate to

Richard Graves at Claverton (p. 270). In 1800 an uncle purchased the living at Camerton, in Somerset, for Skinner and there he remained. It was a joyless parish. His family life was blighted by bereavements, none more untimely than the death of his adored wife in 1812. Skinner found solace from his diaries and escape in antiquarian pursuits. The man of God was swallowed up in the scholar.

He described Stourhead for the first time in 1808. On the second occasion, in 1812, he accompanied Peter Hoare as a guest of Colt Hoare. Peter Richard Hoare (1772–1849), half-brother of their host, had taken a house near Camerton and befriended the unhappy rector. Skinner described both occasions in his journal.

Skinner 1808 fol. 158, Clock Arch, house; fol. 161, Temple of Flora; fol. 161 verso, ferry, Grotto Pantheon; fol. 162, Cascade, Temple of Apollo; fol. 162 verso, Perimeter Drive, Convent; fol. 164 Alfred's Tower.

Skurray, Francis

The Reverend Francis Skurray (1774–1848) studied at Oxford, was appointed perpetual curate at Horningsham in Wiltshire, in 1806, and rector of Winterbourne Abbas in Dorset, in 1823. A painting by John Sergeant, *Interior of the parsonage, Horningsham*, c.1840, depicted Skurray in an imposing room close hung with paintings.[44]

Skurray dedicated his best-known work, *Bidcombe Hill* (London, 1824), to Isabella, wife of the 2nd Marquess of Bath. The poem was published in 1808. He prefaced the second edition with a long essay and epilogued it with information he was unable to rhyme. His opening verses describe the hill; thereafter he set out on a journey to Glastonbury, Fonthill, Wardour Castle, Marston, Alfred's Tower, Stourhead and Maiden Bradley. There is charm in his bucolic musings and excursions in local history; his description of Lady Hamilton's 'attitudes' at Fonthill is an unexpected bonus.[45]

Skurray 1824: p. 163, Alfred's Tower; p. 165, Bristol Cross; p. 166, Grotto, Pantheon.

Spence, Joseph

Joseph Spence (1699–1768) was a poet, prelate and travelling companion to the well-born.[46] He is remembered for letters to his patron, Henry Clinton Fiennes, Earl of Lincoln and his posthumous *Anecdotes* (London, 1820), rich in biographies. As a young man Spence was taken up by Alexander Pope and imbued with enthusiasm for gardening as well as verse. He would excel in the former but not the latter. During the 1730s he shepherded gilded youths around the Continent; indeed he coincided with Henry the Magnificent in Italy. His charge at that time was Lord Lincoln who later gave Spence the use of his house at Byfleet in Surrey, where the poet created his *ferme ornée* on a 30-acre site. Spence earned his living from various church preferments secured by influential friends.

Spence's descriptions of Stourhead are perceptive; moreover, his guide in the garden was William Hoare of Bath.

Spence 1765: Wooden Bridge, Grotto, Pantheon, Temple of Apollo (Obelisk, Turkish Tent, Bristol Cross, Gothick Greenhouse).

Sulivan, Richard Joseph

Sir Richard Joseph Sulivan, or Sullivan, (1752–1806) began his career in India.[47] After returning home he was elected MP for New Romney. A loyal supporter of Pitt, Sulivan was rewarded with a baronetcy in 1804.

He described his perambulations in *Observations made during a tour through parts of England, Scotland, and Wales* (London, 1780). Horace Walpole castigated the publication as:

> one of the worst of our many modern books on travels. It is silly, pert, vulgar, ignorant; aims at florid diction, which is no merit, unless when absolutely necessary to description of prospects; it is larded with affectation often and crass sentiment. The blunders & false spellings are numerous; and the whole betrays total want of taste.[48]

Caves were the highlight for Sulivan, notably Wookey Hole in Somerset, and Poole's Hole near Buxton. In 1778 he called at West Country houses including Longford Castle, Stourhead, Wardour Castle and Wilton House. A shortened version of the Stourhead text appeared in *The British tourists; or traveller's pocket companion through England, Wales, Scotland, and Ireland*, by William Mavor (London, 1800).

Sulivan 1780 (1778): p. 53, Convent; p. 54, Alfred's Tower, St Peter's Pump, Obelisk, Fir Walk; p. 55, art collection; p.58, Turkish Tent, Wooden Bridge, Grotto; p. 59, Pantheon, Hermitage, Temple of Apollo; p. 60, Temple of Flora.

Thelwall, John

John Thelwall (1764–1834) was an odd-ball visitor to Stourhead. The son of a silk merchant, he grew into a campaigning journalist for the far left.[49] When London became too hot for him politically he escaped to explore the country and find inspiration for his poetry. He published an account of these travels in *Monthly Magazine*. Before arriving at Stourhead in July 1797, he called at Wardour, where he admired the old castle, Catholic chapel and paintings, in particular those by Vernet. Passing through East and West Knoyle, Thelwall noted the acreage of farms and labourers' wages. His appreciation of Stourhead is unoriginal and it is curious why he singled out copies of *The Death of Dido* and *The Adoration of the Magi* by Cigoli for particular mention (p. 74).[50]

Thelwall 1801 (1797): p. 105, art collection (Cascade, Wooden Bridge, Grotto, Bristol Cross, Borghese Vase, Temple of Apollo) Pantheon, Alfred's Tower.

Van Spaen van Biljoen, Baron Johan Frederik Willem

This Dutch nobleman, Baron van Spaen (1746–1827), visited Britain in July and August 1791. He was proud of the garden at Castle Biljoen, near Arnhem, where J. G. Michael created an English park and alpine garden with a spectacular cascade. Van Spaen travelled with his stepfather-in-law, another baron. His description is written in French.[51] From London, they set out for the Isle of Wight, calling at Kew and Painshill on the way. In Wiltshire they visited Amesbury Abbey, Wilton House, Wardour Castle and Fonthill before reaching Stourhead.

At Longleat the two noblemen admired Capability Brown's landscape park in preference to gardens cluttered with 'tasteless gazebos of trellis-work and a thousand other fancies'. Van Spaen wrote lyrically about Stourhead, dropping in useful details. Quitting Wiltshire they headed north to Chepstow and Tintern Abbey before returning to London, via Oxford, Henley and Windsor. En route the barons, predictably, admired Blenheim and Stowe.

Tromp 1982 (Van Spaen van Biljoen 1791): p. 49, art collection; p. 50, Grotto, Wooden Bridge, Pantheon, Rock Arch, Temple of Apollo; p. 51, Stone Bridge, Temple of Flora, Bristol Cross.

Walpole, Horace

Horace Walpole (1717–97) visited many gardens in the course of his travels and distilled his observations in *The History of the Modern Taste in Gardening* which he wrote during the 1760s and published in the fourth volume of his *Anecdotes of Painting* in 1780. Here he praised the evolution from the formal to the natural approach pioneered by William Kent.[52]

In *Journal of Visits to Country Seats* Walpole recorded, first and foremost, painting collections.[53] As well as listing Old Masters, he included portraits, often with biographical information. He had a taste for genealogy and empathised with ancient families. He described Stourhead in detail, concluding, in the garden, that 'the whole composes one of the most picturesque scenes in the World'. By contrast, he covered the grounds of Chiswick villa in eight

lines, dismissed Painshill in sixteen and savaged Chamber's garden buildings at Kew in twenty-six lines.

Toynbee 1928 (Walpole 1762): p. 41, Clock Arch, house, art collection; p. 43, Fir Walk, Wooden Bridge, Grotto, Pantheon (Temple of Flora, Gothick Greenhouse, Obelisk, Terrace).

Warner, Richard

After the Reverend Richard Warner (1763–1857) was ordained he served as curate to William Gilpin in Hampshire.[54] The latter became a mentor although the young Warner was attracted to antiquarian pursuits rather than analysis of the picturesque. In 1794 he moved to Bath and secured a number of church appointments in the neighbourhood. He became a prolific author, his publications being commercial rather than scholarly. He seldom discovered new information and his easy-reading style riled Joseph Hunter.[55]

Excursions from Bath (Bath, 1801) recount three itineraries undertaken by Warner in September 1800. The first, to the south, included Fonthill, Longleat, Marston, Wardour Castle and Wilton House. The account of Stourhead is a good example of his cursory research, quoting verbatim from Colt Hoare's guidebook of 1800.

Warner 1801 (1800): p. 92, house; p. 93, art collection; p. 195, ferry; p. 106, Stone Bridge, Temple of Flora; p. 106, Grotto; p. 108, Pantheon; p. 111, Rock Arch; p. 112, Hermitage, Temple of Apollo; p. 113, Bristol Cross; p. 115, Terrace, Alfred's Tower; p. 116, St Peter's Church.

Woodforde, James

The Reverend James Woodforde (1740–1803) was the son of the rector of Ansford in Somerset.[56] He attended Winchester and New College, Oxford before serving as curate to his father. His old college found him a lucrative living at Weston Longville in Norfolk from where he returned frequently to Wiltshire, often calling at Stourhead. His nephew, the artist Samuel Woodforde RA (1763–1817), was taken up by the Hoare family (page 100).

Parson Woodforde is famous for his diaries where he recorded the minutiae of daily life: his travels, food and lodgings, the tips proffered to servants and so on. Woodforde was more interested in human exhibits than art objects and gave few insights into Stourhead. Between 1763 and 1776 he paid several visits with friends when their favourite excursion was to Alfred's Tower. He described meeting Henry Hoare in 1768.[57] Woodforde succeeds in making the reader one of his company. He frequented the inn at Stourton where he found the food variable: we can share his disappointment when the bread was musty.

Appendix III: Stourhead Planting 1741–1946

As compiled by Kenneth Woodbridge in *The Stourhead Landscape* (London, 2001)

Serial numbers in the final column derived from *Mature Trees in the Stourhead Landscape* (National Trust, 1981) which is no longer available. The current *Stourhead Tree List* (2013) quotes the numeric codes selectively and omits the alphabet prefixes which locate the trees. Labels on individual specimens are found infrequently in the garden today.

1720–1785
There are no records of trees planted by Henry Hoare II [Henry the Magnificent] apart from notes on F. M. Piper's sketches (1778–9), Colt Hoare's *Memoirs*, and some references by visitors. On the whole his range was restricted.

His thoughts on planting, reported by Joseph Spence, were:

> The greens should be ranged together in large masses as the shades are in painting, to contrast the dark masses with the *light* ones, and to relieve each dark mass itself with little sprinklings of lighter greens here and there.

His difficulty was in finding evergreens for the dark accents. Colt Hoare said that the wood-land was a mixture of beech and fir, which in the nomenclature of the time included the spruce family. Piper refers to American silver pine ('Americanske silvera furar') in the Fir Walk, which could be *Picea glauca* (white spruce) introduced from North America in 1700. On the other hand, Sir John Parnell (1768) identified them as 'Spruce Fir'. Weeping willow was planted on the shore near the Grotto; and common laurel was used as underplanting.

List 1. *Trees existing in 1741 or planted by Henry Hoare II*

Genus	Species	Common name	Introduced England	Stourhead	Reference
BROAD-LEAVED TREES					
ACER	campestre	Field maple	N		S654
	platanoides	Norway maple	N		F441, M559, Z708
	pseudoplatanus	Sycamore	N		Q
ALNUS	glutinosa	Alder	N		H480, K534
CASTANEA	sativa	Spanish chestnut	N		A995, B759, I497, J514
FAGUS	sylvatica	Common beech	N		Q
FRAXINUS	excelsior	Common ash	N		
QUERCUS	robur	Common oak	N		Q
	ilex	Holm oak	16th C		C812, G435
CONIFEROUS TREES					
CEDRUS	libani	Cedar of Lebanon	c.1645		E376, W561, Z574
LARIX	decidua (europaea)	Common larch	c.1620		O502
PICEA	abies (excelsa)	Common or Norway spruce	c.1500		N461
TAXUS	baccata	Yew	N		Q

(N = Native Q= Quantity)

1785–1838

Many of Sir Richard Colt Hoare's nurserymen's bills have been preserved; and he recorded some of his planting in the *Stourhead Annals.* He introduced new ornamental species, but many are not now represented; for instance only three of the eight species of maple, and four out of some dozen species of oak. He favoured broad-leaved trees, especially in the woodland, from which he removed Henry Hoare's conifers, cutting down the Fir Walk. He introduced *Rhododendron ponticum* in 1791, and in 1828 planted a large number of an unspecified species (possibly *R. catawbiense*

which had been introduced into England in 1809). Two *R. arboreum* were ordered in 1834. He greatly increased the amount of common laurel as underplanting; and some fifty species of hardy or half hardy shrubs are listed in nurserymen's bills. (See Woodbridge, *Garden History,* IV, No. 1, 1976.) At least half were probably intended for the conservatory. The gardener's house, remodelled in 1808–9, and shown in Francis Nicholson's painting, has a verandah covered with some climbing plant; the Gothic Watch Cottage too. Those listed are clematis (eight varieties), honeysuckle, ivy, jasmine, *Rosa banksiae* and *Rosa multiflora.*

List 2. *Trees introduced by Sir Richard Colt Hoare 1791–1838*

Genus	Species	Common name	Introduced England	Stourhead	Reference
ACER	negundo	Box elder	c.1688	1791	I499
	rubrum	Red maple	1656		436
	saccharinum	Silver maple	1735	1791	G433, O573, Q594, W690
	pseudoplatanus 'Variegatum'	Variegated sycamore	1730	1791	C443, N566, Y701
AESCULUS	hippocastanum	Horse chestnut	E 17th C		J519
	carnea	Pink horse chesnut	E 17th C	1833	Y695
	octandra (flavia)	Sweet buckeye	1764	1791	F456
BETULA	pendula	Silver or common birch	N		K537, L531, Q597
CATALPA	bignonioides	Indian bean tree	1726	1791	B821
CELTIS	occidentalis	Hackberry (Nettle tree)	1656	1791	
CRATAEGUS	mollis	Red hawthorn		1811	F462
FRAXINUS	excelsior 'Pendula'	Weeping ash		1791	G415
	ornus	Manna ash	17th C	1791	E403, E477, S630, S642, S644, S645, T656, U675, Y697
ILEX	aquifolium	Common holly	N		
LIRIODENDRON	tulipifera	Tulip tree	c.1688	1791	B765, B769, B770, B763, G429, K536, Q600, S630, S665, U677, V676, V683
LIQUIDAMBAR	styraciflua	Sweet gum	17th C	1791	C795, C784, Q605
PHILLYREA	latifolia		1597	1791	003

Genus	Species	Common name	Introduced England	Stourhead	Reference
PLATANUS	*hispanica*	London plane	c.1663	1791	H469, R622
	orientalis	Oriental plane	E 16th C	1817	719
PRUNUS	*avium*	Wild cherry	N	1791	L543, N568, O575
	avium 'Plena'	Double gean	since 1700	1791	969
QUERCUS	*cerris*	Turkey oak	1735	1807	B820, J509, P592
	coccinea	Scarlet oak	1691	1791	837
	palustris	Pin oak	1800	1813	741
	phellos	Willow oak	1723	1813	C790
ROBINIA	*pseudoacacia*	Locust tree or false acacia	17th C	1791	L548
TILIA	*americana*	American lime	1752	1791	R620, W690
	europea	Common lime	N		J956, R617
	platyphyllos	Broad-leaved lime	N	1791	F439
CONIFEROUS TREES					
TAXODIUM	*distichum*	Deciduous or swamp cypress	c.1640		Q528

(N = Native Q = Quantity)

1838–1894

The lifetime of the 3rd, 4th and 5th Baronets, covering most of Queen Victoria's reign, was a period when many new species of trees were introduced into England. Discoveries by Archibald Menzies, David Douglas and William Lobb gave a new character to many parts of the English landscape, nowhere more than at Stourhead. From 1838 to 1857 about twenty new species of conifer were added to the collections, including the first specimens of Douglas fir and hemlock spruce, which were later widely used in commercial plantations. Giant species such as *Thuja plicata* (western red cedar) made their appearance; as well as strange trees like the monkey puzzle (*Araucaria araucana*) introduced by Lobb from Chile in 1844. Although the *Stourhead Annals* were discontinued from 1860 to 1894, it is evident from the estimated age of existing trees that at least fourteen varieties were added in that period, including Lawson cypress, Wellingtonia and Sitka spruce.

List 3. *Conifers: Nineteenth-century introductions now represented at Stourhead*

Genus	Species	Common name	Introduced England	Stourhead	Reference
ABIES	*nordmanniana*	Caucasian fir	1840	c.1872	F398, M453, N464
	procera	Noble fir	1830	1850–60	G387, G388, N463, O509, P518, P525
	procera 'Glauca'		1863		H402

Genus	Species	Common name	Introduced England	Stourhead	Reference
ARAUCARIA	*araucana*	Monkey Puzzle	1844	1852–3	I418, N485, N462, N510, W562
CALOCEDRUS	*decurrens*	Incense cedar	1853		459
CEDRUS	*atlantica*	Atlas cedar	c.1840	1854–5	J429
	atlantica 'Glauca'	Blue cedar	c.1840	c.1872	F394
	deodara	Deodar	1831	1852–3	R534
CHAMAECYPARIS	*lawsoniana*	Lawson cypress	1854	c.1872	H404, L441, L443, L444, N486, Q531, Z572
	nootkatensis	Nootka cypress	1853	1855–60	F377, H413, I416, N466, O501
	pisifera 'Filifera'	Sawara cypress	1861	c.1872	
	pisifera 'Squarrosa Aurea'		1889		U550
CRYPTOMERIA	*japonica*	Japanese cedar	1842	c.1882	F397, P524, V579
PICEA	*polita*	Tiger-tail spruce	1861	c.1872	W558
	sitchensis	Sitka spruce	1831	1862	H408, I415, N469
PINUS	*parviflora*	Japanese white pine	1861	c.1861–4	I419, N476
	peuce	Macedonian pine	1864		H405, N495
	pinaster	Maritime pine	16th C		N479
	wallichiana (excelsa)	Bhutan pine	c.1823	1851–3	K435
PSEUDOTSUGA	*menziesii*	Douglas fir	1827	1854–5	J424, J428, N490, Y567
SEQUOIA	*sempervirens*	Coast redwood	1843	1852–3	H514, P564, Y564
SEQUOIADENDRON	*giganteum*	Wellingtonia	1853	c.1862	H412, K439, W555
THUJA	*plicata*	Western red cedar	1853	c.1854–60	F379, O500, Q530, Y565, Y566
THUJOPSIS	*dolobrata*	Hiba	1853	c.1882	S539
TSUGA	*heterophylla*	Western hemlock	1851	1852–5	B961, F396, K434, N483, R537, W554

1894–1946

The 6th baronet added enormously to the ornamental planting, particularly in the collection of conifers. He cleared much of the laurel, substituting new flowering shrubs; substantial introductions were made in 1901–3, 1906–9, 1912–14, and every year from 1920 to 1933. Three hundred azaleas were brought from Longleat in 1901–2; and in 1913–14 the south side of the lake, below the Temple of Apollo, was cleared and planted with new varieties of rhododendron and azalea from Messers Vuyk and Sons of Holland. It was not until 1922 that a systematic substitution of 'good hybrids' for 'common rhododendron' was recorded in the *Annals*. This went on yearly round the lake until 1938; in the Shades from 1927–33; also in the drive in 1926–7; and on the west and south lawns 1920–1, 1927–8, 1930–5.

List 4. *Trees at Stourhead introduced by the 6th Baronet*

Genus	Species	Common name	Introduced England	Stourhead	Reference
BROAD-LEAVED TREES					
ACER	griseum	Paper-bark maple	1901	1941	E401, G424, F425
	grosseri var. hersii	Snake-bark maple	c.1923		F463
	negundo californicum	Box elder		1927	
	palmatum	Japanese maple	1820	1927	B818, C800, C818, F449, G426, G434, I500, T664
	palmatum purpureum			1927	
	pseudoplatanus 'Purpureum'			1927	W686
	rufinerve	Grey budded snake-bark maple	1879	1927	570, 574
AILANTHUS	altissima	Tree of Heaven	1751		H479, S635, T657
BETULA	pendula 'Youngii'		c.1900	1931	
CERCIDIPHYLLUM	japonicum		1881	1925	B757, B768, F466, G423, T658, T659
CLADRASTIS	sinensis	Chinese yellow-wood	1901		Q606
CORNUS	nuttallii		1835	1935	406, 407, 455
DAVIDIA	involucrata (vilmoriniana)	Dove tree (Handkerchief tree)	1897	1935	F409, I489, Z720
FAGUS	sylvatica heterophylla 'Aspleniifolia'	Fern-leaved beech	1820		R625
HAMAMELIS	mollis	Wych-hazel	1879	1927	
IDESIA	polycarpa		c.1864		D839
LABURNUM	alpinum	Scotch laburnum	1877		506, 525, 824
MAGNOLIA	hypoleuca	Japanese big-leaf maple	1865	1931	
	soulangiana		E 19th C	1927	

Genus	Species	Common name	Introduced England	Stourhead	Reference
x	soulangiana 'Alexandrina'		E 19th C	c.1945	
	soulangiana 'Lennei'			1935	
	tripetala		1752	1931	
MALUS	floribunda	Japanese crab	1862	c.1920	G432
	tschonoskii		1892		
POPULUS	canadensis robusta		1895		Q611
	canadensis 'Serotina Aurea'	Golden poplar	1871	1927	Y704
	canescens	Grey poplar	N	c.1905	L539, L540
	szechuanica		1908	1927	
	trichocarpa	Black cottonwood (Western balsam poplar)	1892	c.1905	L542
PRUNUS	cerasifera 'Pissardii'		1880	1927	
	sargentii		1890	1935	
	yedoensis chidare yoshino				693
QUERCUS	canariensis (mirbeckii)	Algerian oak (Mirbeck's oak)	c.1845		Q610
	coccinea splendens			1940	
	rubra (borealis maxima)	Red oak	1720	1934	C787, C788, C792, J517, K532, L553, O581, S631, X728
SALIX	alba	White willow	N	c.1900	Q603
	alba 'Britzensis'	Scarlet willow		c.1900	
SORBUS	aria 'Decaisneana' ('Majestica')	Whitebeam	N		B778
TRACHYCARPUS	fortunei	Chusan palm	1836		R615
CONIFEROUS TREES					
ABIES	amabilis	Red fir	1830	1935	
	delavayi 'Fabri'	Delavay's silver fir	1901	c.1905	F395
	delavayi 'Forestii'		1844	c.1925	H411
	firma	Momi fir	1861	1935	L451
	koreana	Korean fir	1905	1938	P522
	nephrolepis	East Siberian fir	1851		
	spectabilis	Himalayan fir	1822	1935	N497
	veitchii	Veitch's silver fir	1879	c.1894	N480

Genus	Species	Common name	Introduced England	Stourhead	Reference
CEPHALOTAXUS	harringtonia 'Fastigiata'	Cow's tail pine	1861	c.1900	W552
CHAMAECYPARIS	lawsoniana 'Erecta'	Lawson cypress	1855		L440
	lawsoniana 'Fraseri'	Lawson cypress	1893	c.1900	T542
	lawsoniana 'Intertexta'	Lawson cypress	c.1869	1930	N482
	lawsoniana 'Stewartii'	Lawson cypress	1920	c.1920	P519
	lawsoniana 'Triomphe de Boskoop'	Lawson cypress	c.1890	1906–7	M452
	lawsoniana 'Westermannii'	Lawson cypress	c.1880		M457
	lawsoniana 'Wisselii'	Lawson cypress	1888	1919	I422, P520, Z573
CRYPTOMERIA	japonica 'Lobbii'	Japanese red cedar	c.1850	c.1930	M454
CUNNINGHAMIA	lanceolata	Chinese fir	1804	1931	N481, O506
CUPRESSUS	macrocarpa 'Lutea'	Monterey cypress	1892	1906–7	Y563
GINKGO	biloba	Maidenhair tree	1727	c.1900	J430
JUNIPERUS	squamata 'Meyeri'	Flaky juniper	1914	1934	F393
LARIX	decidua 'Pendula'		1836		U549
PICEA	abies 'Nana Compacta'	Norway spruce	c.1855		H401
	abies 'Pendula Inversa'	Norway spruce	1855	c.1930	Z571
	brachytyla	Sargent spruce	1901		P523
	jezoensis var. hondoensis	Hondo spruce	1861	c.1890	O499
	omorika	Serbian spruce	1889	c.1922	N538
	orientalis	Oriental spruce	1839		N477, N581
	pungens 'Glaucea'	Blue spruce	c.1885	1906–7	P513
	pungens 'Specki' (Glauca group)			1930	
	smithiana	West Himalayan spruce	1818		M456, N575
PINUS	cembra	Arolla pine	c.1746	c.1930	U548
	ponderosa	Western yellow pine	1826		
TAXUS	baccata aurea	Golden Yew	c.1855		H403
THUJA	plicata 'Zebrina'	Western red cedar	1868	1907	G389

(N = Native)

Acknowledgements

Fifty years have elapsed since Kenneth Woodbridge wrote *Landscape and Antiquity: Aspects of English Culture at Stourhead 1718 to 1838*, the seminal study of Stourhead. His research was impeccable and frequently I found my supposed discoveries lurking in his footnotes. The book is long out of print and illustrated in monochrome. This was my pretext to venture into his king-sized footprints, re-examining the archive material and, occasionally, challenging his conclusions. I am grateful to Tim Woodbridge for permission to include as Appendix III, *Stourhead Planting 1741–1946*, compiled by his father, Kenneth.

The following have kindly given permission to quote from their archives and publications: the partners at C. Hoare & Co; London School of Economics and Political Science; National Trust, Stourhead; Royal Academy of Fine Arts, Stockholm; West Sussex Record Office; Wiltshire Museum, Devizes; Wiltshire & Swindon History Centre.

Chapters on Henry the Magnificent draw on my research published by the Wiltshire Record Society as *The Letters of Henry Hoare 1760–1781* and I am grateful for the society's permission to quote from them.

These historians, archivists and friends have gone out of their way to help me: Pamela Hunter, Victoria Hutchings and William Acton at C. Hoare & Co; Helen Taylor at Wiltshire and Swindon History Centre and Eva-Lena Bengtsson at the Royal Academy of Fine Arts, Stockholm. Julian Orbach quizzed me minutely and in return plied me with fresh ideas and information. John Harrison introduced me to 'Stourton Gardens, written in 1749' and *Viaggio in Inghilterra di Carlo Gastone della Torre di Rezzònico*. Julia Mottershaw explored lost garden features at Stourhead and, with Jean Booth, began the search for Faugoin, the great head gardener.

I would have been lost without encouragement from Audrey Hoare who suggested I write the book and lobbied for its publication. My thanks also go to Caromy Hoare, Henry Cadogan Hoare, Nick Hoare, Michael Cousins, Gill Harris and Sandy Haynes. I am grateful to Emily and Mike MacCormack and the National Trust staff at Stourhead who have given me their willing assistance over a long period. Alan Power, former head gardener, facilitated Marianne Majerus's visits and polished the garden sections of my text. James Stourton complimented me by writing the foreword.

Jancis Williams corrected my first draft. David Adshead read the second and helped reshape it. Veronica Clare James translated F. M. Piper from the Swedish. At Head of Zeus I am grateful to Clémence Jacquinet for her expert guidance and to Georgina Blackwell who made the book a reality: seldom can an editor have nurtured an author with greater care. At the pit-head, Greg Walker encouraged the project and has given me unstinting support for which I am forever grateful.

Dudley Dodd, May 2021

Endnotes

Author's note

Paintings, drawings and prints have their titles in single quotes when inscribed; in italics when generally recognised; in roman when the author has supplied these.

Annotations within the quotations are in square brackets in italics when found in the original ms, in roman when inserted by the author.

Abbreviations

attr. for attributions

fl. flourished i.e. working years of the artist

HH for Henry Hoare (1705–85)

nd. not dated

RCH for Sir Richard Colt Hoare, 2nd Baronet (1758–1838)

BA Bedfordshire Archives & Record Service, Riverside Building Borough Hall, Cauldwell Street, Bedford, MK42 9AD

BL The British Library, 96 Euston Road, London, NW1 2DB

BM The British Museum, Great Russell Street, Bloomsbury, London, WC1B 3DG

C. Hoare & Co. C. Hoare & Co., 37 Fleet Street, London, EC4P 4DQ

Christie's Christie's London, 8 King Street, SW1Y 6QT

DZSWS The Wiltshire Museum, 41 Long Street, Devizes SN10 1NS

NAL National Art Library, Victoria and Albert Museum.

NAS Nautical Archaeological Society, Fort Cumberland, Fort Cumberland Road, Portsmouth, PO4 9LD

NT Prefix to the National Trust's collection management system coding. (http://www.nationaltrustcollections.org.uk/ has individual photographs of the contents of National Trust houses.)

NT archive records National Trust Archive Records Management, Heelis, Kemble Drive, Swindon, Wiltshire, SN2 2NA

ODNB 2004 Oxford Dictionary of National Biography (Oxford, 2004)

SHC Somerset Heritage Centre, Brunel Way, Norton Fitzwarren, Taunton, TA2 6SF

RAS The Royal Academy of Fine Arts, Jakobsgatan 27C, 111 52 Stockholm, Sweden

Stourhead Archive The National Trust, Stourhead, Stourton, Warminster, Wilts, BA12 6QH

TNA The National Archives, Bessant Drive, Richmond, Surrey, TW9 4DU

V&A Victoria and Albert Museum, Cromwell Road, London, SW7 2RL

WANHS Wiltshire Archaeological and Natural History Society which runs the Wiltshire Museum and owns the collections

WSA Wiltshire and Swindon Archives at the Wiltshire and Swindon History Centre, Cocklebury Road, Chippenham, Wilts, SN15 3QN

WSRO West Sussex Record Office, 1DB, Record Office, 3 Orchard Street, Chichester, PO19 1DD

On the Map

1   Barron 1976, p. 155.
2   Clay 1994, p. 117. There are various methods to calculate the equivalent price today. Floud 2019, pp. 9–14, explains the choices. Readers may consult these websites to compare and contrast, taking £14,000 in 1720: https://www.nationalarchives.gov.uk/currency-converter in 2017, £1,625,505. https://www.measuringworth.com/calculators/ukcompare in 2017, measured as 'income or wealth' under 'real value', £1,989,000 or under 'labour earnings', £27,450,000. (accessed 21 September 2020).
3   Clay 1994, p. 116.
4   WSA, 383/20, Henry Tylee to Julia Hoare, 18 August 1883.
5   *The three eldest children of King Charles I, c.1745*, attn Jeremiah Davison (c.1695–1745), after Sir Anthony Van Dyck, oil on canvas, 147.3 × 147.3 cm (lent to Montacute House NT 598023).
6   C. Hoare & Co., HFM/9/19, memorandum from HH to Richard Hoare, nephew, undated. www.nationalarchives.gov.uk/currency-converter equivalent of £20,000 in 2017, £2,322,150 (accessed 21 September 2020). Ellis 1913 (Fanny Burney 1773), vol. II, p. 322.
7   Llandower 1862, p. 140, Mrs Boscawen to Mrs Delany, 25 September 1783.
8   Skurray 1824, pp. 165–6.
9   Sweetman 1913, pp. 29–30, citing John Wesley's *Journal* for 12 September 1776.

How the Hoare Family Acquired Stourhead

1   Hutchings 2005, pp. 8–31; Woodbridge 1969.
2   Hutchings 2005, pp. 230–231.
3   'Good Henry' and 'Henry the Magnificent', sobriquets first published in Hoare 1932, Hoare 1955, pp. 32 and 35.
4   TNA, Prob 11/602/173, will of Henry Hoare (d.1724/5).
5   Clay 1994, p. 117.
6   Stourhead Archive, C.9.21, letters of Sir Richard Hoare (d. 1718/19), p. 67, Richard to Tom Hoare, 5 August 1709, 'Your Brother Hoare & Brother Henry, with your two Sisters... are gone to your Cozon Benson's in Wiltshire'.
7   Eavis 2002, p. 13.
8   Campbell 1717, vol. I, pls 51–52.
9   WSA, 383/253 and 383/254, 2 surveys of 1703.
10 Jackson 1862, pp. 389–390.
11 WSA, 383/ 255, valuation of Stourton and Stourton Caundle 1704.

12 WSA, 383/366, Chancery action, Lord Stourton's estate 1713. Raymond 2019, pp. 11–12.
13 Hutchins 1868, pp. 666–667.
14 Stourhead Annals, vol. III, 1911–12.
15 Jackson 1862, pp. 390–391.
16 WSA, 383/58, account book for Stourhead 1717–28, Farmer King's account, 1718, 'Money he craveth to be allowd or pd by Order of Mr Benson to Mr Johnson for pulling down ye house', £114–18s–7d.
17 Observed by the author in 1975 at cornice level on the north façade.
18 Campbell, vol. III, p. 8 'Stourhead Castle'; pl. 41 'Stourhead'.
19 Clay 1994, p. 135.
20 TNA, Prob 11/602/173, will of Henry Hoare (d. 1724/5).
21 Dodd 2017.
22 C. Hoare & Co, HFM/4/7, 'An Account of Money paid for House Hold Goods & furniture &c att Stourton' May 1720–February 1724/5.
23 Ibid., 27 July 1722, 'Lady Kingston for a Mohair Bed & Hangings' £60–18s–6d; 13 July 1723, 'Rob. North Upholsterer on Acct' £150; 19 December 1723, 'Mr North in full' £36–13s–3d; 15 January 1724/5, 'Robert North Upholsterer' £40; C. Hoare & Co., HB/5/A/4, Partners' Ledger 1725–34, Henry Hoare (d. 1724/5) Executors' Account, 17 March 1725/6, 'Mr Coxe's [Henry Hoare's agent] note to Robert North' £150; 31 March 1727, 'Mr North for Cloath &c' £61–6s.
24 Ibid., 'An Account of Money paid for House Hold Goods & furniture &c att Stourton', May 1720–February 1724/5, 18 June 1720, 'Eliz. Gratnick for a Bust of King Charls Head in Copper & a Picture' £31–10s. Avery 1979.
25 *Henry Hoare on horseback* (1705–85), 1726, by Michael Dahl (1659–1743) and John Wootton (1682–1764), oil on canvas, 330.2 × 304.8 cm (NT 732232); *The Bloody Shouldered Arabian*, c.1728, by John Wootton (1682–1764), oil on canvas, 115.6 × 115.6 cm (NT 732306); the pair of *Still Life of Flowers* by Philip van Kouwenbergh (1671–1729), oil on canvas, 48.3 × 42.5 cm (NT 732166 and 732167).
26 *Elijah raising the widow's son* is recorded in the 1742 Stourhead Inventory. From 1754 onwards the painting was attributed to Rembrandt. The first printed guidebook to Stourhead (Hoare 1800, p. 11, no. 12) stated that Bishop Atterbury (1663–1732), a declared Jacobite and a friend of Good Henry, gave the painting to the family. Christie's 1883, lot 69, the painting was auctioned in 1883 and bought in. In 1768 Richard Earlom (1743–1822) made a mezzotint, published by John Boydell, 503 × 354 mm, inscribed, 'From the Original Picture painted by Rembrandt; in the Collection of Henry Hoare Esqr at Stourhead, Wilts'. Sumowski 1983, vol. IV, p. 2596, no. 1723, the Earlom mezzotint; the painting, neither illustrated nor located, is attributed to Jan Victors (1619–76). However the first Old Master acquired by Good Henry was the *Madonna and child with St John*, after Andrea del Sarto, oil on canvas, 69.9 × 55.2 cm (NT 724306), which Robert Nelson (1656–1714/15) bequeathed to his

executor, Good Henry. Information kindly supplied by Victoria Hutchings.

27 A wine cistern with gadrooned sides and the Hoare coat of arms, marble, 21.5 × 79 × 58 cm (NT 732931). A pair of console tables with carved foxes and *Rosso di Verona* marble tops, English, *c.*1730, 90.5 × 91.5 × 56.5 cm (NT 731596).

28 'East Front Stourhead house, Wilts. AD 1724' and 'South Front', 1817, by John Buckler (1770–1851), pencil, each 152 × 228 mm. BL (Add MS 36.392, Buckler Architectural Drawings, vol. XXXVII, fol. 148) annotated 'Sketched from two old Paintings at Stourhead October 1817. Traced Jan 7. 1823.' From these derive two watercolours, 'East View of Stourhead House AD' and 'South View of Stourhead House', both by John Buckler in Stourhead Archive (NT 3204200); Hoare 1819. A second version of 'South View of Stourhead House 1724', 1817, watercolour, 155 × 233 mm. (DZSWS 1990.590). WSA 383/4/3, Buckler's bill, 8 October 1817, '2 Drawings Old Stourhead House'.

Henry the Magnificent

1 Hutchings 2005, p. 49.
2 *Henry the Magnificent on horseback (1705–85)*, 1726, by Michael Dahl (1656/9–43) and John Wootton (*c.*1682–1764), oil on canvas, 330.2 × 304.8 cm (NT 732232).
3 Clay 1994, pp. 123–124. C. Hoare & Co., HFM/9/19, '1774 Freehold Lands purchased by me [HH] & old Rents since The death of my Hond Father', West Knoyle, £31,360.
4 Hutchings 2005, p. 56.
5 Clay 1994, pp. 135–7.
6 WSA, 1300/2950, HH to Lady Bruce, 28 May 1776.
7 C. Hoare & Co., Customer Ledgers, HH building account 1727–33, ledgers/folios nos: 29/17, 30/303, 30/1, 33/293; furnishing account 1727–33, ledgers/folios nos: 29/318, 33/113.
8 Ibid., HB/5/A/4, Partners' Ledger 1725–34, HH paid John Wootton, 13 July 1726, £53–14s; ibid., Benjamin Hoare paid Wootton, 27 November 1732, £105.
9 Ibid, HB/5/A/4, Partners' Ledger 1725–34, Benjamin Hoare paid Jeremiah Davison, 3 December 1725, £18–18s; Customer Ledger, HH furnishing account, ledger/folio no: 29/ 318, HH paid Davison, 19 September 1728, £10–10s.
10 Ibid., Customer Ledger, HH furnishing account, ledger/folio no: 29/318, HH paid Arthur Pond, 13 January 1727/8, £94–10s. HB/5/A/4, Partners' Ledger 1725–34, Benjamin Hoare paid Pond, 25 May 1728, £21.
11 HH Ledger 1734–49, 5 December 1746, 'Mr Wootton for a Picture a Compn to my Claude L' £36–15s. The Stourhead Catalogue of 1754 lists both paintings in the best bedroom (South Apartment) at Stourhead. The Claude, of doubtful authenticity, was sold by Christie's 1883, lot 67, 'Peasants driving cattle', at £262–10s. The fate of Wootton's companion piece is unknown.
12 Ibid., John Wootton, account opened 1708, Customer Ledgers, ledgers/folios nos: 10/244+303+370+422, 29/184, 30/163, 34/3, 37/313, 39/60, 44/55, 50/313, 57/202. Closed 1764. Ibid., Customer Ledgers, HH building and furnishing accounts, ledgers/folios nos: 29/318, 30/1, 30/303,

payments to Wootton for the years 1728–30 totalling £417–5s. HH Ledgers 1734–49 and 1749–70 payments to Wootton, 1746–62 totalling £381–5s.

13 Stourhead Catalogue 1784 listed nine paintings by Wootton but omitted *Henry the Magnificent on horseback* (NT 732232). There are three paintings by Wootton at Stourhead today and a fourth, lent to C. Hoare & Co., none of which are landscapes. The latter were relegated to the Staircase Hall at Stourhead and probably perished in the 1902 fire.
14 HH Ledger 1734–49, 27 November 1742, 'Mr Pond prints pd by Mr Adams' £1–7s–6d.
15 WSA, 383/4(1), Arthur Pond's receipted 15 January 1727/8 and annotated by RCH, 'I remember these pictures in H Hoares Villa at Clapham'.
16 *A classical landscape with sportsmen*, *c.*1658, oil on canvas, 152.4 × 222.3 cm (NT 732125) and *Mountainous landscape with Eurydice*, *c.*1658, oil on canvas, 152.4 × 222.2 cm (NT 732126). Both by Gaspard Dughet (1615–75).
17 HH Ledger 1770–85: 10 May 1774, 'Mr Boydell No 1 & 2 of Claude's prints /40/' £3–3s; 24 December 1774, 'Mr Boydell No 3 & 4 of Devonse Claudes' £3–3s.
13 June 1775, 'Mr Boydell, 5th Book of Devons Draws Claud Lorrain' £1–11s–6d.
18 October 1777, 'Mr Boydell 5 last book of Claude in full' £7–17s–6d.
18 WSA, 1300/4280, HH to Lady Bruce, 23 October 1762.
19 Osborn 1966, vol. I, Spence's anecdotes, p. 418, no. 1105, *c.*1752; Spence's observations of Pope on gardening, pp. 250–252, nos 603, 606.
20 Defoe 1779, p. 319.
21 Tromp 1982 (van Spaen van Biljoen 1791), p. 50.
22 Skinner 1808, fol. 162 verso.
23 Woodbridge 1965; Malins 1966, pp. 50–51; Woodbridge 1968.
24 I am grateful to David Adshead who drew my attention to, *Sophia Anne Delaval, Mrs John Jadis (1755–93), holding a 'Claude glass' or 'landscape mirror' to the landscape*, attr. Edward Alcock (fl. 1757–78), oil on canvas, 91.4 × 55.9 cm (Seaton Delaval Hall, NT 1276770).
25 Gilpin 1798, pp. 117 and 121.
26 Acton 2019.
27 Clay 1994, p. 124.
28 Eavis 2002, pp. 19–20.
29 C. Hoare & Co., HFM/9/10, HH to his nephew, Richard Hoare, nd.
30 Eavis 2002, p. 25. In 1796 Benson's grandson, William Benson Earle, bequeathed the busts to RCH who placed them in the Library at Stourhead (NT 732892 and 732893).
31 *The London Evening Post*, 3–6 March 1739, 'Henry Hoare Esq, Member for Parliament for Salisbury, being in a Consumption, is set out for the South of France by the Advice of his Physicians'.
32 C. Hoare & Co., HB/5/A/5, Partnership Ledger, 1734–42, HH account; WSA, 383/28, HH pocket account books, 28 June 1738–6 September 1739 and 25 June 1739–29 August 1740. Jervis 2015, pp. 130–143.
33 WSA, 383/28, HH pocket account book, 1738–39, 9 June 1739, 'Jos Smith' £102–9s–6d. C. Hoare &

Co., Partnership Ledger HB/5/A/5, 1734–42, HH account, 20 January 1740/1, 'Custom & Charges on two Cases of Pictures from Mr Smith of Venice' £11–7s.
34 C. Hoare & Co., HB/8/M/8, Girolamo Belloni's letters to Hoare's Bank, 5 September and 3 October 1739 and a copy of the receipt from Parker: 'I have received of Mr Girolamo Belloni Six hundred Crowns ['£142–17s–2d quoted in first letter] in Mony paid me on Account by Order of a larger Sum by Order given in my Favour by Mr Henry Hoare at Florence by his 'n[ote] of the 4th past'.
35 Ibid., HB/5/A/5, the Partnership Ledger 1734–42, HH account, recorded frequent payments to Susan Hoare up to 10 September 1739 and these recommenced on 15 June 1741. *Daily Gazetteer*, 3 October 1741, 'Henry Hoare Esq; the Banker and late a Member of Parliament for Salisbury, who has been for a Year or more in the South Parts of France for his Health, is return'd to England with a very good Share of it, and is since gone to his Seat at Quarley in Hampshire'.
36 C. Hoare & Co., HE/5/A/7, Partnership Ledger 1751–64, HH account, payments to Sir Horace Mann, 20 July 1758 for £48–18s–5d and 2 August 1758 for £238–14s–3d. *Marchese Niccolò Maria Pallavicini (1650–1714) guided to the temple of Virtù by Apollo*, 1705, by Carlo Maratti (1625–1713), oil on canvas, 299.7 × 212 cm (NT 732098). *A classical landscape with sportsmen*, *c.*1658, oil on canvas, 152.4 × 222.3 cm (NT 732125) and *Mountainous landscape with Eurydice*, *c.*1658, oil on canvas, 152.4 × 222.2 cm (NT 732126). Both by Gaspard Dughet (1615–75).
37 Lewis 1960, pp. 208–209, Sir Horace Mann to Horace Walpole, 3 June 1758.
38 WSA, 383/907/1, John Plimmer [for Thomas Jenkins] to HH, 9 June 1759.
39 *The Judgment of Midas*, *c.*1630, by Sébastien Bourdon (1616–71). WSA, 383/907, Sir John Lambert to HH, 1 February 1743/4, reporting the purchase and dispatch of this painting from Paris for 976 *livres* [about £46]. It was rescued from the fire at Stourhead in 1902 but was subsequently mislaid.
40 C. Hoare & Co., HB/5/A/5, Partnership Ledger, 1734–42, HH account, payments to Edward Fowler, 3 November 1739, 'Custom & Charges on Pictures' £19–2s–6d; 19 June 1740, 'Customs & Charges on Figures &c for Leghorne' £9–15s–6d. Ibid., HB/5/A/6, Partnership Ledger 1742–51, HH account, payments to Edward Fowler, 4 August 1742, 'Do [*Customs & Charges*] 10 Cases of Cabinetts from Leghorn' £37–1s–6d; 2 March 1742/3, 'Custom & Charges of 2 figures fr Livourno' £13–5s–6d.
41 *Zeus* and *Hera*, first or second century AD, Roman, marble, H 81 and H 70 cm (NT 732925 and 732926).
42 Jervis 2015.
43 HH Ledger 1734–49, 30 May 1743, 'Expences in seeing Windsor Castle & ye Dukes Isle' £2–9s–6d; WSA, 9/35/165(1)/2408, HH to Lord Bruce, 30 June 1763, his visit to Strawberry Hill.
44 WSA, 383/909, narrative written in 1756 and

circulated by Margaret, Countess of Cork and Orrery.

45 Cartwright 1888 (Pococke 1754), vol. II, pp. 40–41, 'The [5th] Earl is improving the place [Marston] in very elegant taste. There is a lawn with a statue of Minerva at the end of it; then to the right another lawn with a plantation of wood adorned with busts, and an open temple with an altar in it, and ancient statues. To the left of the first lawn is a winding walk to the cottage... At the other end of the garden in a corner is a little Hermitage nearly finished for my Lord's youngest son: there is a deep way cut down to it with wood on each side, a seat or two in it – one is made in the hollow of a tree; it leads to a little irregular court, with a fence of horses' heads and bones... Two or three fields below the house is a cold bath, as in an enclosure of an ancient Cemitery, with several old inscriptions made for it, and at the end is a small room very elegantly furnished, this I take to be Lady Orrery's place of retirement'.

46 WSA 9/35/165(1)/2406, HH to Lord Bruce, 15 December 1763.

47 C. Hoare & Co., Alan Bathurst, Baron Bathurst (1684–1775), account opened 1728/9. Customer Ledger/folio no: 30/351; 1729–32/3, Customer Ledger/folio no: 31/264; 1735–37, Customer Ledger/folio no: 36/47; Money Lent Ledger 1718–43/95; joint account with brother 1754, Customer Ledger/folio no: 55/242; with Lord Vernon, 1767–70, Customer Ledger/folio no: 77/193.

48 Ibid.,The Honourable Charles Hamilton, account opened June 1747. Customer Ledger/folio no: 47/411. Closed November 1748. Account re-opened July 1766, Customer Ledger/folio nos: 74/384, 84/22. Closed July 1773. Money Lent ledger: 1743–73/113.

49 Ibid., Richard Boyle, 3rd Earl of Burlington, account opened in 1717, Customer Ledgers/folios nos: 20/16+221, 21/334, 22/423, 23/373, 24/92+428, 25/12+51+276+381, 26/2+178+400, 27/213, 28/176, 31/286, 36/262 (1736), H/378+415+437+438, I/3+232, P/352, R/141, S/205, T/163, U, W/430, X/278, Y/445, 63/76, 76/452. Irish account, ledger/folio nos: N/406+407, O/152+153. English account: ledger/folio no: N/410. Money Lent Ledger 1718–43/33. English account closed in 1737; Irish, in name of executors, in 1771.

50 Hutchings 2005, pp. 63–66. C. Hoare & Co., Thomas Pelham, 1st Duke of Newcastle upon Tyne, account opened August 1714, closed in 1730. Transferred to Little Ledger November 1730. Re-opened in 1734. Customer Ledgers/folios nos: /203+206+212+227+234–236+268+270, M/223+317+320, N/79+400, O/85, Q/277–278, R/220–222, S/131+132+383, T/94–96+442–443, V/151+251–253, W/331, X/259–260, Y/35–38, Z/304–307+360, A/63, B/277–279+437, C/78–80+263–266, Exors D/116–121+70. Money Lent ledger: 1696–1718: 137+153; Money Lent ledger: 1718–43: 6+141+162; Money Lent ledger: 1743–73: 16+64; Misc Record Book pages 216, 219, 227 (as Duke of Newcastle); Misc Record Book pages 65, 205, 210, 217, 241 (as Thomas Pelham Esq); Separate Account: 60, 73. Account in name of executors closed in 1770.

51 C. Hoare & Co., George Lyttelton, 1st Baron Lyttelton, account opened 1745/6, Customer Ledger/folio no: 46/271 with deposit (£400) by himself. Closed January 1750. Opened October 1751, closed May 1774. Customer Ledgers/folios nos: W/71, X/162, Y/396, A/16, 62/133, 64/334+326, 67/78, 69/159+160, 71/394, 73/172+173, 75/330+331, 77/249–251, 84/126; Money Lent ledger: 1743–73/17,125. Money Lent ledger: 1773–83/131. Separate Account opened December 1771. Closed December 1773. Re annuity payments to Lady Lyttelton. Customer Ledger/folio no: 85/175. WSA 9/35/165(2)/-, HH to Lord Bruce, 28 August 1773, 'I grieve at the Loss of my amiable Friend Lord Littelton'.

52 Clay 1994, p. 136.

53 Hoare 1819, pp. 26, 29.

54 WSRO, Parham papers, 2/2/2/6, letter 4/80, the Honourable Hester Hoare to Harriet Anne, Lady Bisshopp, 'Stourhead, Sun the 14th' [1783].

55 C. Hoare & Co., HFM/9/19, HH ms list of gifts, c. 1774, 'To Dear Lady Dungarvan £25,000 | To Ditto £1,000 | To Do In Jewells £3,000 | To Furniture of L.I. F. [Lincoln's Inn Fields] House £1,000 | To the Value of the House sold at £6,000'.

56 Hoare 1819, p. 27, 'I have heard him say that he never thought seriously of enriching his grounds by plantations, until he had attained the age of forty years; but when he once began, he proceeded, con spirito, upon a widely extended scale, covering a barren waste with wood'.

57 Cartwright 1888, (Pococke 1754), vol. II, p. 43.

58 C. Hoare & Co., Henry Flitcroft account opened in 1724, Customer Ledgers/folios nos: 27/3, 40/280, 42/103, 44/382, 52/375, 56/284, 60/367, 67/215, 71, 72, 74/238. Account closed 1769.

59 Roberts, pp. 47, 356, 435–436; figs 365, 366.

60 WSA, 383/907(1), Henry Flitcroft to HH, 7 September 1744.

61 Ibid., Henry Flitcroft to HH, 18 August 1744.

62 Ibid., Henry Flitcroft to HH, 25 August 1744.

63 Miller 2010, p. 208; The temple at Barn Elms, 1817, after J. C. Nattes (1765–1839), ink and sepia wash. Richmond upon Thames Local Studies (LCP/2540).

64 HH Ledger 1734–49: 16 May 1745, 'Mr Flitcroft in full & till all Buildings are finish'd (Vide ye Voucher)' £100; 10 August 1748, 'Mr Flitcroft for all designs & works in full' £100.
HH Ledger 1749–70: 17 July 1752, 'Mr Flitcroft in full' £100; 7 November 1752, 'Mr Couch Mr Flitcrofts Clerk' £5–5s; 30 July 1753, 'Mr Couch Flitcrofts Clerk for His trouble at Clapham & L.I.F [Lincoln's Inn Fields].' £5–5s; 24 November 1753, 'Mr Flitcroft for His trouble in Clapham House in full' £200; 4 May 1754, 'Mr Couch, Clerk to Mr Flitcroft a Gratuity' £10–10s; 25 April 1755, 'Mr Flitcroft for The Pantheon &c and Subterrn Arch' £100; 29 October 1757, 'Mr Flitcroft as pd for a Model of the pantheon Dome' £7–11s–3d; 4 November 1757, 'Mr Flitcroft's rect for Clapham, Pantheon Stourhd &c in full' £100; 21 June 1764, 'Mr Flitcroft in full & on further accot' £100; 19 June 1766, 'H. Flitcroft Esqr for Temple of Apollo Alfreds Tower &c in full' £100; 16 June 1769, 'Mr Flitcroft Exr in full of all demands' £20. C. Hoare & Co., HB/5/A/6–8,

Partners' Ledgers 1742–51, 1751–64 and 1764–83 HH account: 19 June 1745, 'Henry Flitcroft in full for Surveyg at Stourhead' £100 (see payment 16 May 1745 above); 10 August 1748, 'Mr Flitcroft for survey &c at Stourhd in full' £100 (see payment on 10 August 1748 above); 18 November 1752, 'Heny Flitcroft Esqr' £100; 13 August 1755, 'Henry Flitcroft Esqr for Himself £100. Sir Rd £20' £120; 21 December 1757, 'Mr Flitcroft in full' £100 (perhaps payment 4 November 1757 above); 15 November 1764, Henry Flitcroft Esqr' £100 (perhaps payment 21 June 1764 above); 28 July 1766, 'His Draft to H Flitcroft 19 June' £100 (perhaps payment 19 June 1766 above). WSA, 383/907, deed signed by William Privett, 6 September 1746, annotated by HH 'also all Their Bills & Mr Flitcrofts remarks on Them as pd Decr 11th 1750'.

65 Adshead 2007, pp. 42–43.

66 Sketch for a three-storey octagonal temple, with the Obelisk and Wooden Bridge at Stourhead, c.1744, unknown, pencil, 305 × 375 mm. Bodleian Library (MS.top. gen.a.4, fol. 4).

67 White 1995, p. 6.

68 Pheasant and Lapwing and Yellowhammer Still Life, 1771, by Mary Bampfylde (d. 1806), silk and wool, 68 × 81 cm (NT 730920). WSA, 9/35/165(2)/1478, HH to Henrietta Boyle, 30 November 1771, 'Mrs Bampfield has sent me some of Her work, a Pheasant & Lapwing & Yellow Hamr still Life most wonderfully fine, a Gold frame & plate [glass inserted] is orderd for it'.

69 The Temple of Flora, 1753, by C. W. Bampfylde (1720–91), pen and colour wash, 280 × 470 mm. BM (1970,0919.20).

70 Somerset Heritage Centre, SHC/DD/SAS/C795/FA/42, HH to C. W. Bampfylde, 4 June 1782, with a warm invitation to join HH and William Benson Earle at Stourhead.

71 In 1786 C. W. Bampfylde dedicated his 'Friendship Urn' at Hestercombe to HH and Sir Charles Kemeys-Tynte. Shephard 2003.

72 A bay with a temple and tower, 1766, by C. W. Bampfylde (1720–91), oil on canvas, oval, 69.2 × 94 cm (NT 732182). The watercolours, NT 730868–730871.
WSA, 9/35/165(1)/1421, HH to Lord Bruce, 13 December 1765, 'Mr Bampfield has brought me a Sweet picture of His own painting a Delightfull Sea & Land view'.

73 Anstey 1776; Graves 1779, the frontispiece to vol. I nods towards Stourhead.

74 Stourhead Pleasure Grounds, Wiltshire, view to the Pantheon (NT 730729) and View to the Bristol Cross and village (NT 730732). Both c.1775, by C. W. Bampfylde (1720–91), watercolour, 360 × 546 mm.

75 HH 1734–49, 24 July 1736, 'Francs The Gardener' £5–5s.

76 Ibid., 23 June 1743, 'Mary Faugoin for Nanny's [Anne Hoare] Gloves &c' 16s 9d'; 24 June 1743, 'Mrs Faugoin for Miss Nanny for Do to Do [Wages Board Wage in full to Midsr 1743]' £5–12s; 6 January 1743/4, 'Mary Faugoin for 15 Weeks board of Nanny pd ye 23d of Decr & all Disbursements' £15–9s–9d; 19 May 1744, 'Mary Faugoin in full of all Demands for Nanny' £12–13s–9d and 'Do as

Given Her £1–16 to Mr Godolphin's Servts £2–2s' £3–18s. William Godolphin lived at East Colston close to Westbury in Wiltshire. www.British-history.ac.uk/vch/wilts/vol8 (accessed 14 February 2017).

77 HH Ledger 1734–49, 21 March 1745/6, 'Do [Rogr Helliker] given Him on Accot of extraordy trouble during the Building &c' £10–10s; the final settlement: 2 June 1747, Rogr Helliker ye ballce of His accot & all demds' £16.

78 Anonymous ms 1766, fol. 32 verso, 'the whole circuit of the Gardens is near 3 Miles – it is thought 4000gs per Ann: is laid out in adorning them, and keeping them in repair'.

79 Powys 1776, fol. 16.

80 C. Hoare & Co., HFM/9/7–9, Francis Faugoin to HH, 2 March 1782.

81 Anonymous 1780, p. 15, lines 388–389.

82 Parnell 1769, vol. II, fol. 99.

83 Dodd 2017.

84 WSA, 383/907(1), Henry Flitcroft to HH, 18 August 1744, 'I am Glad you go on so well with the Decorations of your Salon & hope it will be executed to our wishes'.

85 WSA, 383/5/47, Francis Cartwright 'The measurements of the Saloon 1744' bill for £366–13s–6d, signed. 'Frs Cartwright'.

86 Toynbee 1928 (Walpole 1762), p. 41.

87 NT 732232, 732098, and 732099.

88 Hanway 1756, p. 87.

89 Parnell 1769, vol. II, fol. 102.

90 WSA, 383/4(1), agreement with HH dated 10 October 1727 and receipted by Rysbrack on 21 April 1729, 'For a Bustow of Inigo Jones in Statuary Marble' £35 | 'For a Pedestall' £2–10s | 'For two Figures of Inigo Jones an[d] Palladio in Plaester' £1–10s.

91 Sir Anthony Van Dyck and Sir Peter Paul Rubens, c.1743, by Michael Rysbrack (1694–1770), plaster statuettes painted black, H 60 cm. (NT 732895.1 and .2). The third, Duquesnoy, is no longer at Stourhead. HH Ledger 1734–49, 15 June 1744, 'Mr Risbreck for 3 figures Bronzed in full' £9–9s. Vertue 1934, p. 135, February 1747, 'Mr Van Aken had bought three Models most excellently done by M. Rysbracke Sculptor – & paid for them freely – one the portrait of Rubens at lenght. Vandyke. & Quesnoy fiamingo the Sculptor. of these three figures. molds were made & casts. at seaven guineas the three sold'.

92 Bacchus, 1751, by Michael Rysbrack (1694–1770), marble, H 115 cm. The Calouste Gulbenkian Foundation Museum, Lisbon (2216). C. Hoare & Co., HB/5/A/7, Partners' Ledger 1751–64, HH account, 3 October 1751, 'Mr Rysbrack in full for a Bacchus' £71–18s–10d. Christie's 1883 (a), lot 49 'The Youthful Bacchus, a fine statuette in marble, by M. Rysbrack – 46 in. high. Executed for H. Hoare, Esq., 1751' annotated £65–2s.

93 Webb 1954, p. 137.

94 Alfred the Great, 1764, by Michael Rysbrack. HH Ledger 1749–70, 12 May 1764, 'Mr Rysbrack in full for a Bust & pedesl of Alfred' £100. After a destroyed terracotta bust of King Alfred, c.1736, formerly at Windsor Castle. Terracotta reliefs by Rysbrack (NT 732913–732916). HH Ledger 1749–70, 19 Feb 1767, 'Mr Rysbracks sale 5 Drawgs

& 3 Bass Relievo's' £41–9s–6d.

95 TNA, Prob 11/954/263, will of Michael Rysbrack (d. 1770) who bequeathed to HH, 'the model of Hercules I made for him and the Drawing by me of Judas's last Kiss to our Saviour'. The drawing is untraced.

96 Langford 1764, Rysbrack's sale.

97 Langford 1989, p. 346.

98 WSA, 9/35/165(1)/-, HH to Lord Bruce, 2 February 1765.

99 WSA, 383/909, narrative written in 1756 and circulated by Margaret Countess of Cork and Orrery describing the circumstances of an estrangement between HH and the 5th Earl of Cork and Orrery annotated by HH.

100 HH Ledger 1749–70, 16 June 1760, 'Mr Rivets fee for His opinion on Duke of Somersets Marge articles' £10–10s.

101 Lewis 1967, p. 218, Horace Walpole to Sir Horace Mann, 5 June 1776.

102 Ibid., p. 218, n. 27.

103 Winstanley 1988 (Woodforde 1773), p. 146, 13 July 1773, Woodforde dined at Stourhead with HH and guests, including John Rust whom he dubbed 'a coxcomical Chap'.

104 WSA, 1300/4119, Frances Bruce to George Bruce, nd.

105 WSA, 9/35/165(2)/2692, HH to Lord Ailesbury, 12 June 1778.

106 Hunter 2018, pp. 106–109 'Portrait of Henry Hoare jnr by an unknown artist, c.1775'.

107 WSA, 1300/2948, HH to Lord Bruce, 11 May 1776. Acton 2015.

108 WSA, 9/35/165(2)/1777, HH to Lord Ailesbury, 25 August 1778.

109 WSA, 1300/2947, HH to Lord Ailesbury, 7 August 1776.

110 WSA, 9/35/165(2)/238, HH to Lord Ailesbury, 18 June 1776, 'The Barnes Family set out for Wales tomorrow'; ibid., 9/35/165(2)/1775, HH to Lord Ailesbury 19 August 1778, 'The Welch [sic] Travelers are just gone for London'; ibid., /35/165(2)/1783, HH to Lord Ailesbury, 26 September 1778, 'The Barnes Family & Young Harry &c are gone this morng which lours for Rain'.

111 WSA, 1300/2947, HH to Lord Ailesbury, 7 August 1776.

112 The Public Advertiser, 10 October 1778.

113 WSA, 1300/2877, HH to Lord Bruce, 20 August 1763; WSA, 90/35/165(1)/1412, HH to Lord Bruce, 9 March 1765.

114 WSA, 1300/2878, HH to Lord Bruce, 8 February 1770.

115 HH Ledger 1770–1785, 6 November 1770, 'Mr Chs Green for an Organ in full' £65. WSA, 1300/2941, HH to Lord Bruce, 6 May 1776, 'the Organ is kept going by the charming Musicians [the Bruce children] alternately'.

116 WSA, 1300/2882. HH to Lord Ailesbury, 22 August 1778.

117 HH Ledger 1749–70, 3 July 1754, 'Mr Hoare for Picture Glass & frame of Mary Qn of Scots' £15–15s.

118 WSA, 383/907(3), William Hoare to HH, 5 June 1760.

119 Entries in HH Ledgers 1749–70 and 1770–85; C. Hoare & Co, HB/5/A/7, 1751–64 and HB/5/A/8,

1764–83, Partners' Ledgers. Newby 1990. Stourhead Catalogue 1784, pictures by William Hoare of Bath RA: 'A View of the Gardens at Stourhead'; 'Portraits of the two Mrs Hoares in Crayons'; 'Four Children after Rubens and two Venus's'; 'Two Drawings of Happy Spirits'; and 'The Honourable Mrs O'Neill'.

120 TNA, Prob 11/1842, will of Prince Hoare (d. 1834), 'I also give and bequeath unto the said Sir Richard Colt Hoare all my family portraits painted in Crayon by my father and now hanging in my parlor in New Norfolk Street'.

121 WSA, 383/907(1), A. R. Mengs to HH, 27 June 1761 and HH to Mengs, 27 July 1761.

122 A view of Florence and A view of the Mole at Naples, with Mount Versuvius, by William Marlow (1740–1813). HH Ledger 1749–70, 13 October 1767, 'Mr Marlow a Picture of Vesuvius &c' £12–12s; 27 May 1768, 'Mr Marlow for a Little picture of Florence' £6–6s. Christie's 1883, lot 1, Florence, annotated £43–1s and, lot 2, Naples, £15–15s.
A Sun shine and Moon light, 1766, by Claude-Joseph Vernet (1714–89). C. Hoare & Co., HB/5/A/8, Partners' Ledger 1764–83, HH account, 25 April 1767, 'Rd Foley &c bill to T Selwyn as pd Monsr Vernet' £108–9s–3d. Stourhead Catalogue 1784, Christie's 1883, lots 36 and 37 annotated £99–15s the pair.
The Lake of Nemi, with Diana and Callisto, c.1758, by Richard Wilson RA (1714–82), 76.6 × 97.2 cm (Trustees of Jane, Lucy and Charles Hoare). C. Hoare & Co., HB/5/A/7, Partners' Ledger, 1751–64, HH account, 8 January 1760, 'Rd Wilson for a Landscape of Avernus' £30. Christie's 1883, lot 11 annotated £98–14s.
Diana and her nymphs, 1765, by Francesco Zuccarelli, RA (1702–88), HH Ledger 1749–70, 23 May 1765, 'Zuccarelli for Diana & Her Nymphs' £26–5s; Christie's 1883, lot 10 annotated £84.
Procession to the Temple of Apollo at Delos, 1759–60, by John Plimmer (1722–60), after Claude Lorrain, oil on canvas, 149.8 × 200.6 cm (NT 732178). WSA, 383/907, John Plimmer's letter to HH 12 July 1760, 'the thirty pounds you was pleased to give me for the Copy of Claud'.

123 HH Ledger 1770–85, 15 March 1771, '100 Louis d'or carry'd abroad' £105. Thereafter the ledger is kept in another hand and regular entries by HH resume from 2 August 1771.

124 C. Hoare & Co., HB/8/T/11, letter from Samuel Harding of Mere to the bank, 9 March 1771, he has received HH's letter 'of the 5th instant: advising me of his Ill state of health, from the severe Winter we have had, that he is going to France to try the change of Air, which I hope will have the desired effect, & reestablish his health'.

125 Ibid., HB/5/A/8, Partners' Ledger 1764–83, HH account, 6 April to 10 August 1771.

126 Ibid., HFM/M/9/7–9, statement 'Henry Hoare Esqr his Account Curt wth Sr Jn Lambert Bart', dated 19 July 1771 to 2 July 1772, entry 30 September 1771, 'Msr Poirier for 2. brass Levretts 157.10 [livres, about £7] | 'Mr Vernet 2 Pictures for Lord Bruce 720 [about £32]'.
A pair of Greyhounds, French, c.1771, bronze, 12.7 × 19 × 9 cm (NT 731854). One greyhound is depicted

in the portrait of *Sir Richard Hoare, 1st Baronet of Barn Elms (1734/5–87)*, c.1780, by Samuel Woodforde RA (1763–1817), oil on canvas, 52 × 41.9 cm (NT 732218).

127 Sandoz 1961, pp. 392–395; Sandoz 1964, pp. 510–513.Seven paintings by Jean Louis François Lagrenée, the elder (1725–1805) remain at Stourhead and one replica by Samuel Woodforde:
La Lacédémonienne (The Spartan mother), 1770, oil on canvas, 110.5 × 86.4 cm (NT 732110).
Telemachus and Termosiris, 1770, oil on canvas, 109.2 × 86.4 cm (NT 732111).
Philosophy unveiling Truth, 1771, oil on copper, 15.2 × 18.1 cm (NT 732248).
Susannah and the Elders, 1771, oil on copper, 41.3 × 31.1 cm (NT 732290).
La mère complaisante (The indulgent mother), 1771, oil on copper 40.6 × 33 cm (NT 732293).
'L'heureuse vieillesse' (Happy old age), 1771, oil on copper, 40.6 × 33 cm (NT 732294).
Charity, 1771, oil on copper, 15.9 × 18.7 cm (NT 732366).
Lot and his daughters, 1782–1785, by Samuel Woodforde RA (1763–1817), after Lagrenée, oil on canvas, 40.6 × 33 cm (NT 732291).

128 HH Ledger 1770–85, 27 April 1773, 'Signra Angelica a Greek Lady & Penelope' £63; Christie's 1883, lot 3, 'A. Kauffman, R.A., Penelope and Euricle[i]a' annotated £7–7s
and [ms addendum] 'lot 6* A. Kauffman, R.A., A Lady in Oriental Dress' annotated £23–2s.

129 *Frances Anne Acland, Lady Hoare (1735/6–1800)*, c.1773, by Angelica Kauffman RA (1741–1807), oil on canvas, 125.7 × 100.3 cm (NT 732283). *Penelope sacrificing to Minerva for the safe return of her son, Telemachus*, 1774, by Angelica Kauffman RA, oil on canvas, 149.9 × 126.4 cm (NT 732292).

130 *Peasants going to market: early morning*, c.1773, by Thomas Gainsborough RA (1727–88), oil on canvas, 121.8 × 147.2 cm. C. Hoare & Co., HB/5/A/8, Partners' Ledger 1764–83, HH Account, 6 July 1773, 'Willm Hoare's Bill Gainsh Picture' £84. Christie's 1883, lot 16, T. Gainsborough, R.A., 'Peasants and colliers going to market: early morning', annotated £2,835. Sothebys sold in 2019 for £7,961,000.

131 WSA, 383/907, Sir John Lambert to HH, 20 August 1772, Sir John offered two paintings by Claude, 'a Marine and a Paysage', for 15,000 *livres* [about £700].
HH Ledger 1749–70, 22 March 1770, 'Mr Devis for Picture of D Neeffs' £21. HH Ledger 1770–85, 8 April 1773, 'Mr Christi[e] a Picture of Cuyp of Cattle' £25–14s–6d; Christie's 1883, lot 50, 'Cuyp, A female peasant, with cattle and sheep in a ford', annotated £21. *Jonah and the whale*, 1745–72, by William Taverner (1703–72), after Gaspard Dughet, oil on canvas, 97.8 × 134.6 cm (NT 732144); HH Ledger 1770–85, 26 Feb 1774, 'Mr Langford a Picture at Taveners, Storm & Jonas' £12–1s–6d.

132 WSA, 9/35/165(1)/2353, HH to Lady Bruce, July 1765.

133 WSA, 9/35/165(1)/2408, HH to Lord Bruce, 30 June 1763.

134 WSA, 1300/4280.

135 WSA, 9/35/165(1)/1426, HH to Lord Bruce, 9 December 1765.

136 WSA, 9/35/165(1)/1421, HH to Lord Bruce, 13 December 1765.

137 WSA, 9/35/165(1)/1109, HH to Lord Bruce, 23 December 1765.

138 WSA, 9/35/165(2)/-, HH to Lord Bruce, 13 September 1770.

139 WSA, 1300/2948, HH to Lord Bruce, 11 May 1776.

140 Powys 1776, fol. 16.

141 *The New Bath Guide*, 1762, p. 57.

142 WSA, 9/35/165(1)/2353, HH to Lady Bruce, July 1765.
Landscape with, in the foreground, two figures walking and a herd of goats, hills and forest in background, 1747, by James Mason (1710–c.1780), after Claude Lorrain, engraving, 398 × 523 mm. Inscribed 'in the collection of Henry Hoare Esq.'
A Firelight (The rest on the flight into Egypt), 1752, by Joseph Wood (fl. 1720–63/4), after Rembrandt, etching and engraving, 362 × 483 mm. Inscribed, 'From the Original Picture of the same size, in the Collection of Henry Hoare Esqr.' (NT 730949).
The Choice of Hercules, 1759, by Sir Robert Strange (1721–92), after Nicolas Poussin, etching and engraving, 507 × 394 mm. Inscribed, 'in the Collection of Henry Hoare Esqr...'
Lake of Nemi or Speculum Dianæ, 1764, by Joseph Wood (b. 1720), after Richard Wilson RA, engraving, 471 × 418 mm. Inscribed, 'in the Collection of Hen. Hoare Esqr.'
Elijah raising the widow's son, 1768, by Richard Earlom (1743–1822), after Rembrandt.
Two views of Stourhead garden, 1777, by Francis Vivares (1709–80), after C. W. Bampfylde, etchings and engravings, 445 × 555 mm. Both inscribed 'The Seat of Henry Hoare Esqr.' (NT 731088 and 731090).
Morning Amusement, 1784, by William Wynne Ryland (1733–83), after Angelica Kauffman RA, stipple etching, 390 × 296 mm. Inscribed, 'in the Possession of Henry Hoare Esqr' (NT 730756 and 732722).

143 C. Hoare & Co., HFM/9/19, '1774 Freehold Lands purchased by me [HH] & old Rents since The death of my Hond Father'.

144 Ibid.

145 WSA, 383/417, abstract of title for the manor of Bruton, 1777; Clay 1994, p. 132.

146 WSA, 383/912, ms by 'Fat Harry' revealing his uncle's intentions for Stourhead.

147 Ibid.

148 Hunter 2018, pp. 40–43, 'Settlement on the marriage of Richard Colt Hoare and Hon Hester Lyttelton, 1783'. *Sir William Henry Lyttelton, 1st Baron Westcote, 1st Baron Lyttleton (1724–1808)*, 1801, by Samuel Woodforde RA (1763–1817), oil on canvas, 124.5 × 87.6 cm (NT 732349).

149 WSA, 383/912.

150 Hutchings 2005, pp. 84–85.

151 WSRO, Parham papers, 2/2/2/6, letter 4/80, the Honourable Hester Lyttelton to Harriet Anne, Lady Bisshopp, 'Stourhead, Sun the 14th' [1783].

152 HH Ledger 1770–85, 23 October 1783.

153 WSA, 383/714, copy deed of the settlement. HH renounced his own interest in Stourhead in favour of his grandson by a separate deed dated 30 September 1784.

154 HH Ledger 1770–85, 3 March 1784, 'Lloyd & Co Wine Merchant' £40–2s–6d; 18 October 1784, 'Lloyd & Thackeray Wine Merchants Bill' £198–6s.

155 TNA, Prob 11/1133/354, will of HH.

Sir Richard Colt Hoare

1 *Sir Richard Colt Hoare, 2nd Baronet (1758–1838)*, 1841, by Richard Cockle Lucas (1800–83) marble, figure H c.183 cm. The memorial was commissioned by Sir Henry Hugh Hoare, 3rd Baronet.

2 BL, Add MS 36527, Joseph Hunter, notices of contemporaries, fols 150 and 152 verso.

3 Benson 1843, p. 18, RCH to Robert Benson, 30 July 1836.

4 WSA, 1412/1, RCH to France & Banting, 27 October 1823.

5 C. Hoare & Co., HFM/11/13, RCH ms memoir, p. 28.

6 BL, Add MS 36527, Joseph Hunter, notices of contemporaries, fol. 150 verso.

7 C. Hoare & Co., HFM/11/13, RCH ms memoir, pp. 5–6.

8 TNA, Prob, 11/1898, RCH codicil of 9 December 1837.

9 Stourhead Archive, C.9.38, RCH ms 'My Life, no. I, to 1795'.

10 WSA, 9/35/165(2)/667, HH to Lord Ailesbury, 28 September 1779.

11 Hutchings 2005, pp. 82.

12 Dodd 2011, pp. 49–50.

13 C. Hoare & Co., HFM/9/10, HH to Sir Richard Hoare Kt, 8 September 1754.

14 Miller 2010, pp. 201–202.

15 Two surveys of the garden at Barn Elms, c.1755, anonymous, ink and colour wash, 570 × 785 mm and 482 × 717 mm (NT 730838 and 730839).

16 Hutchings 2005, p. 82.

17 TNA, Prob, 11/1133/354, will of HH (d. 1785).

18 Hutchings 2005, p. 86.

19 Hoare 1824, pp. 103 and 124.

20 C. Hoare & Co., HFM//11/5, RCH to his father, 19 September 1786.

21 Woodbridge 1970, pp. 72–4.

22 WSA, 383/911, loose accounts, RCH, 'Mrs Hoare's Chair Man's Bill' January to May 1784, logged fifteen visits to the opera.

23 NT 731559; Dodd 2011, pp. 53–71.

24 216 WSRO, Parham papers, 2/2/2/6, letter 4/92, 14 May 1785, Hester Hoare to Harriet Anne, Lady Bisshopp.

25 Hoare 1815 (I), p.iv.

26 C. Hoare & Co., HFM//11/5, RCH to Henry Hugh Hoare, 21 February 1787.

27 DZSWS. MSS 4255, RCH travel journal, 1785–87.

28 C. Hoare & Co., HFM//11/5, RCH to Henry Hugh Hoare, 13 February 1786.

29 Ibid.,HFM/11/13, RCH ms memoir, p. 9.

30 Ibid.,HFM//11/5, RCH to Henry Hugh Hoare, 21 February 1787.

31 Stourhead Annals, vol. I, 1834–35.

32 WSA, 383/919, RCH notebook 1785–87, nd,

payments to Davis and Giro and one payment to the latter's wife.

33 Hoare 1815 (I), p. 266.

34 C. Hoare & Co., HFM//11/5, RCH to Henry Hugh Hoare, 5 January 1787.

35 WSA, 383/919, RCH notebook 1785–87, nd, 'won at Cards £100' and 'Lost at cards [scudi ?] 60' [about £14].

36 C. Hoare & Co., HFM//11/5, RCH to Henry Hugh Hoare, 21 February 1787.

37 WSA, 383/919, RCH notebook 1785–87.

38 Hoare 1822, p. 75.

39 WSA, 383/4/1, Fratelli Pisani's receipted bill March 1787, 'Avuta noi Sig Pisani da Monsieur Hor da Consegnare al Sigre Orsi in una Sola Cassa | Un gran paro Urne di prezzo di Zecchini dodici 12 | Un Solo Vaso da metterlo in mezzo a dette Urne 6 | Un paro Vasi con manichi, e fogle nella gola 8 | Un Urna con manichi da mettere in mezzo a detti vasi 6 | Due putti, ho Sia Amorini che dorme 8 | [further items omitted total 43 zecchini, about £20]. Ibid.,'Accot of Sir Richard Hoare Bart to Colin Morison', nd, 'For a Vase of black & white Oriental Granite put on the monument instead of the intended Vase of Alabaster as paid to the Scalpellino 15 sequins [zecchini] or £7' | 'N.B. The Vase of Alabaster cost 5 the other twenty sequins'. Ibid., estimate in Colin Morison's handwriting, nd, 'Remain to be paid | Paid To the Carpenter for four Cases 25 | For packing & forwarding paid 35 | To Extraordinary expenses for the Granite Sarcophagus instead of the black & yellow as ordered 125 | To 3 Cases for the different pieces of the monument 30 | The Packing & forwarding may come to about 25 | For the Urn of granite 40 | In all, scudi 300 or £68' [amounts in scudi with two scudi to a zecchino].

40 Ibid. Pietro Pisani's bill for RCH and receipt dated 5 October [1787] for 225 zecchini [about £105], specifying the *Niobe group*, three statuettes (NT 732934), *Venus de' Medici* (NT 732922), *Callipygian Venus (*NT 732923), *Arrotino* (NT 732938) and three vases. C. Hoare & Co., HFM//11/5, RCH to Henry Hugh Hoare, 5 January 1787, 'I bought three beautiful Italian Alabaster Vases for you'.

41 BL, Add MS 36496, fol. 333, Christopher Hewetson to George Cumberland, 4 May 1792, 'I have heard Sir Rd Hoare severely abused because he only employ'd Artists in the branch he is fondest of, Landskip, instead of Sculpture &c'.

42 WSA, 383/919, RCH notebook 1785–87.

43 TNA, Prob, 11/1158, will and codicils of Sir Richard Hoare, 1st Baronet (d. 1787). Hutchings 2005, p. 88.

44 C. Hoare & Co., HB/5/H/6, Money Lent Ledger 1783–94, RCH, 25 April 1788, money lent on mortgage, £14,000; 13 November 1788, repaid £5,000; 9 January 1789, repaid £9,000.

45 Hoare 1815 (II), p. 109.

46 Ibid.,p. 8.

47 WSA, 383/919, RCH notebook 'Journal no. I, 1789, Holland, Flanders, Germany Italy', diary entries for April 1789.

48 Woodbridge 1970, p. 128.

49 Hoare 1817 (III), p. 151.

50 Brydone 1773; Saint-Non 1781; Paterno 1781; Swinburne 1783; Houel 1782.

51 Hoare 1817 (III), p. 3.

52 Hoare 1815 (II), p. 204.

53 Ibid.,pp. 119–120.

54 Clifford 1977.

55 WSA, 383/919, RCH notebooks, Journal no. II, 1789 Italy, 14–21 February 1791 in Florence.

56 WSA, 383/4/1, RCH miscellaneous bills, receipt for *The Adoration of Magi* by Cigoli from Giovanni Battista Cassana, 19 February 1791.

57 Woodbridge 1970, p. 144.

58 C. Hoare & Co., HFM/11/1, RCH, private account book.

59 Umbria: NT 730805, 730806, 730811, 730815, 730816. Tivoli: NT 730807, 730810, 730817, 730808. Rome: NT 730809✻, 730812, 730814, 730818✻. Asterisks denote omissions in Hoare 1822, pp. 82–83.

60 WSA, 383/919, RCH notebook 1785–87, nd. 'Modern Pictures [*purchased*]: 1 do [*landscape*] by 'Hackart' £20 and '4 Do [*drawings*] by 'Hackart'. Probably *Rocky landscape with anglers*, 1776, by J. P. Hackert (1737–1807), oil on canvas, 686 × 546 mm. (NT 732270) and drawings 1770–72, NT 730746, 730747, 730752, 730753.

61 Hoare 1818 (IV), pp. 14–28 and 31–32.

62 *Vallone dell' Inferno Piedimonte Matese*, 1790, by J. P. Hackert (1737–1807), pencil and sepia wash on paper, 572 × 705 mm. (NT 730724). And also perhaps *Landscape with a Bridge, and a View of Monte Sarchio (Alife)*, 1790, by J. P. Hackert, pencil and sepia wash on paper, 572 × 705 mm (NT 730723).

63 WSA, 383/919, RCH notebook 1785–87, nd, modern pictures bought, '1 Do [*landscape*] Labruzzi £50' also '2 drawings Labruzzi £4' and 'C. Labruzzi £30'.

64 Hoare 1815 (II), pp. 269–331.

65 Ibid.,pp. 300–301. RCH admired the relief on the *cratere di Salpion*, today in the National Archaeological Museum, Naples (6673). He copied this for the frieze of the marble chimneypiece in the Picture Gallery at Stourhead. It represents the birth and infancy of Bacchus, a counterpoint to *The Adoration of the Magi* by Cigoli hung above.

66 Jatta 2013, pp. 518–522; Watson 1960.

67 Sotheby 1883, lot 1170, 'Labruzzi, (Carlo), *Via Appia illustra* ..., 5 vols, 226 Magnificent Drawings in Sepia by the Artist', annotated £17–17s.

68 Jatta 2013, pp. 518–522.

69 WSA, 383/4/3/556, 'Subscribers to the Antiquities of the Via Appia', by bookseller Charles Smith, nd, included Colt's half-brothers and friends. WSA, 383/4/3/555, executors of Smith sent a bill January 1803–September 1804 with a credit for sales of six *Via Appia illustrata*. Remaining copies of the publication were sold in Sotheby 1887, lots 943–953, *Via Appia*, nd, pts I and II, 43 copies and 24 further copies of pt I.

70 Ingamells 1997, pp. 824–825.

71 Hoare 1822, p. 84.

72 'A catalogue of books relating to the history and topography of Italy, collected during the years 1786, 1787, 1788, 1789, 1790 by Sir Richard Colt Hoare, Bart' (London, 1812). British Library (C.61.B.12). He donated 1,493 volumes in 1825 and 453 in 1828.

73 Hoare 1815 (I), pp. 13–14.

74 Ibid.,p. 384, Versailles and p. 301, the Boboli Garden, Florence.

75 Hoare 1817 (III), p. 242 and pp. 227–228, the Capuchin convent at Nicosia.

76 Stourhead Annals, vol. I, 1799–1800; C. Hoare & Co., HFM/11/13, RCH ms Memoir, p. 17.

77 C. Hoare & Co., HB/2/E/1, fol. 74, Partners' memorandum book 1793–99, agreement to lend RCH £10,000 paid in 1799 and 1800 and lent at standard 5%.

78 WSA, 383/108, 'Particulars of Woods & Plantations in Hand Jany 1803'.

79 Jameson 2003 (Woodforde 1791), p. 284. James Woodforde, 11 September 1793, 'I don't think that the Gardens or House are kept so neat as in old Mr Hoare's time'.

80 Hoare 1822, pp. 65–66.

81 WSA, 383/66, 'Sundry Building Accounts for Sir Richd C. Hoare Bart. at Stourhead', 1792–1805, by Thomas Atkinson.

82 WSA, 383/924, RCH annual engagement diaries, folder 2, 1796.

83 Ibid.

84 WSA, 1300/4675, RCH to Lord Ailesbury, 9 August 1791.

85 RCH Journals of travels in Britain and Ireland 1793–1810 comprise six quarto and five folio notebooks. The former written during the journeys, the latter. These sold in 1883 and 1887 and are now at the South Glamorgan County Library (MS.3.127 and 4.302). Extracts were published in Thompson 1983. WSA, 383/924, RCH appointment diaries 1794–1816.

86 Coxe 1801.

87 Mitchell 2012, pp. 61–68.

88 Cave 1978, vol. XI, p. 4052, 17 December 1811.

89 Thompson 1983, pp. 18–19.

90 Hunter 2018, pp. 32–33, 'Drawing of Neath Abbey by Sir Richard Colt Hoare Bt, 1802'.

91 Hoare 1806, vol. II, p. 406.

92 Sotheby 1883, lots 791, 792, 794, 796, 799, 949, 803–805 and 951; Sotheby 1887, lots 586, 587, 589, 590 and 599.

93 *A mill near Llangollen, North Wales*, 1811–12, by Sir Augustus Wall Callcott, RA (1779–1844), oil on canvas, 65.4 × 94.6 cm (NT 732269).

94 Fenton 1811 (1807), pp. 171–232.

95 WSA, 383/924, RCH diary, April 1798.

96 Thompson 1983, p. 148, Fountains Abbey, 21 July 1800. Hoare 1806, vol. I, pp. 153–154 for general comment.

97 Thompson 1983, p. 211, Margam, 14 June 1802; p. 267, Beaumaris, 10 August 1810.

98 Ibid., p. 159, Kedleston, 2 August 1800; p. 124, Harewood, 21 May 1800.

99 Ibid., pp. 157–158, Chatsworth, 30 July 1800. Hoare 1806, vol. II, pp. 400–401, Powis Castle, 'it should be made into a *Villa d'Este* in miniature'.

100 Thompson 1983, pp. 148–151, Studley Royal, 21 July 1800.

101 Ibid., pp. 118–119, Burleigh, 14 May 1800.

102 Ibid., pp. 108–109, Downton, 2 June 1799; pp. 200–201, Foxley, 24 May 1802.

103 WSA, 383/924, RCH annual engagement diaries.

104 Stourhead Annals, vol. I, 1805–6.

105 Anne Rushout's diary (location unknown), 6 July 1798, at Stourhead, 'There are two large rooms lately added, but they are not furnished & many of the pictures were not hung up. The whole furniture looked so old fashioned and shabby'. Hoare 1800.

106 WSA, 383/57, Thomas Atkinson to RCH, 23 October 1806, enclosing final statement of accounts.

107 Stourhead Inventory 1838.

108 WSA, 383/4A, Thomas Chippendale the younger, bills. Goodison 2005 and 2017.

109 WSA, 383/4/217, Josiah Wedgwood & Byerley, 2 June 1806, '1 Egyptian tea pot' 7s–6d; ibid., 19 February 1808, 'Red with black Egyptian Ornaments: 1 tripod Incense Vase' £1–1s; 2 Canopus Vases' £2–10s; 1 Pentray 7s; 4 Paper holders 12s; 2 Pint Jugs 6s (NT 730562).

110 Montfaucon 1719, vol. II, pt II, figs 107 and 129.

111 Goodison 2017, pp. 44–45; Piranesi, 1769.

112 WSA, 383/4A and 383/911; Goodison 2005.

113 Woodbridge 1970, p. 238.

114 Sweet 1820, vol. I, nos 18, 38, 72, 73, 80, 91. 115.

115 Hoare 1821.

116 *The Gentleman's Magazine* (London, 1822), vol. XCII, pt II, p. 517 attr. Reverend Thomas Dudley Fosbroke.

117 Douglas 1793.

118 Simpson 1975, pp. 15–16.

119 DZSWS, MSS 2597.5.62, RCH to William Cunnington, nd [1809].

120 Annable 1964, p. 5.

121 Hoare 1828; Nichols 1840, pp. 723–732, reprinted the text.

122 Dibdin 1822, p. 390.

123 *The Quarterly Review*, vols V and VI, nos 9 and 12, 1811, pp. 111–120, 440–448.

124 Simpson 1975, p. 15.

125 Woodbridge 1970. p. 230.

126 Hoare 1812, vol. I, p. 240, verses composed after sheltering from a storm with RCH at a barrow near Woodyates.

127 Kassler 2015 (Queen Charlotte 1789), vol. IV, p. 22, 14 September 1789.

128 *Henry Hoare (1784–1836) as a boy*, c.1795, by Samuel Woodforde RA (1763–1817), oil on canvas 73.7 × 61 cm (NT 732202); *Sir Richard Colt Hoare, 2nd Baronet (1758–1838), and his son Henry*, 1795/6, by Samuel Woodforde, oil on canvas, 254 × 167.6 cm (NT 732213); *Henry Hoare*, 1829, by Margaret Carpenter (1793–1872), oil on canvas, 127 × 101.6 cm (NT 732210).

129 Hoare 1807.

130 C. Hoare & Co., HFM/11/13, RCH ms memoir, p. 25. Sir Abraham Hume was married to Amelia Egerton, sister of the 8th, and last, Earl of Bridgewater. Her younger daughter, Sophia, married John Cust, 1st Earl of Brownlow and their elder son inherited the extensive Bridgewater estates.

131 WSA, 383/714, volume of copies of wills and indentures, 'Settlement on the marriage of Henry Hoare Esqre and Miss Dering', 3 February 1808.

132 WSA, 9/35/166/222, RCH to Lord Ailesbury, 2 April 1809, Henry and Charlotte Hoare are 'not very well satisfied with their residence at Donhead which is very damp. They have luckily the option to quit it after a months trial'.

133 C. Hoare & Co., HFM/11/21, correspondence concerning mental health of Henry Hoare, 1811–13.

134 Ibid., HB/8/T/11, Henry Hoare to Hoare's Bank, Paris, 27 February and 6 April 1819.

135 WSA, 383/931, RCH cash account with Messrs Messiter at Wincanton, 1805–24.

136 Ibid., 383/72, Steward's books, order book, 1822, listing rooms at Stourhead when replacing window panes including 'Henry's Room & Column Room' (i.e., South and North Apartments).

137 BL, Add MS 36527, Joseph Hunter, notices of contemporaries, fol. 151.

138 C. Hoare & Co., HFM /11/14, RCH draft will 1729.

139 WSA, 383/14, list of creditors to the late Henry Hoare, 1836.

140 C. Hoare & Co., HFM/11/14, Messiter's bank, Wincanton, to Sir Henry Hugh Hoare, 3rd Baronet, 1838, claiming payment of Henry Hoare's overdraft.

141 WSA, 383/11, RCH book of expenses 1818.

142 Stourhead Annals, vol.I, 1818–19.

143 Fenton 1811 (1807), p. 213, 'The dwelling-house over the door has this inscription: *Venatoribus atq. amicis*: and is decorated with prints representing the sports of the field, exhibiting within and without every thing that can render it picturesque, comfortable, and appropriate.'

144 WSA, 383/926, RCH journal from 1797 to 1814, 19 January 1801; Goodison 2005, p. 84.

145 Woodbridge 1970, p. 228.

146 WSA, 383/937, RCH diary, 1–6 January 1816.

147 Cave 1978, vol. XIII, p. 4506.

148 Dibdin 1822, p. 390.

149 *Quarterly Review*, vol. CLXIII, December 1847, p. 12.

150 C. Hoare & Co., HFM/11/17, letters and papers re the publication of *Modern Wiltshire*.

151 Benson 1843, pp. 9–10.

152 Hunter 1851.

153 BL, Add MS 36527, Joseph Hunter, notices of contemporaries, fol. 150.

154 Hunter 1851, p. 25.

155 BL, Add MS 36527, Joseph Hunter, notices of contemporaries, fol. 211, Hunter considered Cassan 'singularly unpleasing' for his high church pretensions.

156 NT 730727, 730730, 730745, 730751, 730829, 730830.

157 Nichols 1840, pp. 477 and 543–544.

158 Skinner 1808, fol. 156 verso. Perhaps Nicholson used the device to draw the panorama of the Garden Lake (NT 730725).

159 Sotheby 1883, lots 416 and 417.

160 Ibid., lot 459.

161 Ibid., lots 237–242.

162 Nichols 1840, p. 412. Sotheby 1883, lot 1415.

163 BM 1944,1014.124–148; sketches, 1956,1114.1–47.

164 Bell 2012, p. 126.

165 Ibid., pp. 45–47.

166 WSA, 383/4/1, misc. bills, 'Drawings made by Mr Nicholson for Sir Richard Hoare for the year 1813...

8 Views of Stourhead... 15 views at Stourhead in forwardness for 1814' at £7–7s each.

167 Hazlitt 1824, p. 139.

168 Cave 1978, vol. VIII, p. 2888, 16 October 1806.

169 Rowell 2012, p. 68.

170 *Stourhead*, 1811, by John Constable RA (1776–1837), pencil, 860 × 149 mm. Fogg Museum, Harvard (1943.686).

171 *Distress by sea*, 1804, (NT 732138) and *Distress by land*, 1811, both by Henry Thomson RA (1773–1843), oil on canvas, 237.5 × 145.4 cm (NT 732137).

172 *Master Henry Hoare (1784–1836) as a boy gardening*, 1788, by Sir Joshua Reynolds PRA (1723–92), oil on canvas, 127 × 102 cm. Toledo Museum of Art, Ohio (1955.31). At the time of sale, the dealer, Asher Wertheimer, commissioned a replica (NT 732329).

173 *Sleeping nymph and cupid*, 1806, by John Hoppner RA (1758–1810), oil on canvas, 132 x 167.6 cm, Petworth House (NT 486138). *The Dumb Alphabet*, by James Northcote RA (1746–1831), sold Christie's 1883, lot 13.

174 Smith 1860, p. 1.

175 *Annals of the Fine Arts for 1817*, vol. II pt 4 (London, 1818), pp. 1–19, RCH letter to the editor, 'On the Conduct of the Directors of the British Institution...'

176 Cave 1978, vol. VIII, pp. 2940–2941.

177 WSRO, Parham papers, 2/2/2/6, letter 4/78, Hester Hoare to Harriet Anne, Lady Bisshopp, Saturday 1783.

178 TNA, Prob, 11/1133/354, will of Henry Hoare (d. 1785).

179 WSA, 383/944, transcript of 'Extracts from Note Book belonging to the late Samuel Woodforde Esqr. R.A.', 3 February 1786.

180 NT 732278 and NT 732279.

181 Warrell 2015, pp. 27–28. *Landscape with the rest on the flight into Egypt*, 1647, by Rembrandt (1606–69), oil on panel, 34 × 48 cm. National Gallery of Ireland Dublin (NGI. 215). Christie's 1883, lot 68.

182 Warrell 2015, pp. 28–31; Tate Britain (DO1907/TB XLIV e, DO1908/TB XLIV f and DO1909/TB XLIV g).

183 Ibid., pp. 42–75.

184 Ibid., p. 64.

185 Warrell 2015, pp. 35–8.

186 Ibid., p. 39.

187 WSA, 383/936, RCH journal 1815–33, logging visits to Weymouth, 1822–30.

188 Woodbridge 1970, pp. 263–266.

189 RCH, 'Roman villa at Littleton, Somersetshire', *The Gentleman's Magazine*, vol. XCVII, pt II (London, 1827), p. 113 and 'Roman villa at Pitney', *The Gentleman's Magazine*, vol. C, pt I (London, 1830), pp. 17–18.

190 Benson 1843, p. 15, RCH to Robert Benson, 13 May 1835.

191 WSA, 383/12, RCH, housekeeper's monthly accounts and annual summaries, vol. I, 1827–34.

192 TNA, Prob, 11/1898, will of RCH (d. 1838).

The Later Baronets

1 Hutchings 2005, p. 103.

2 *The Gentleman's Magazine*, vol. CLXXI (London, 1841), pp. 425–426.

3 *Henry Hugh Hoare (1762–1841) as Mercury*, c.1770, by William Hoare RA (1707–92), pastel, oval, 57

× 47 cm (NT 730777); *Sir Henry Hugh Hoare 3rd Baronet*, by Prince Hoare (1755–1834), c.1780, oil on canvas, 127 × 101.6 cm (NT 732215); *Sir Henry Hugh Hoare, 3rd Baronet*, attr. John Rising (1753–1817), oil on canvas, 75 × 70 cm (NT 732207).

4 WSA, 383/16, 'Inventory of Heir Looms the Property of the late Sir Henry Hugh Hoare Bart deceased at Wavenden House, Wavenden, St James's Square and Fleet Street', 1841.

5 TNA, Prob 11/1952/235, will of Sir Henry Hugh Hoare, 3rd Baronet (d. 1841).

6 Portrait also engraved NT 731031 and NT 732687.

7 Hutchings 2005, p. 231.

8 Ibid., p. 126. Woodbridge 1981, p. 49.

9 Stourhead Archive, Augusta, Lady Hoare's Diaries, 1845–57, 15–23 April 1845.

10 Ibid., 29 April 1848.

11 www.stourtonhistory.org/census_1851 (accessed 30 August 2018).

12 Stourhead Annals, vol. I, 1844.

13 Ibid., vol. I, 1842.

14 Hunter 2018, pp. 18–19, 'Primrose League diploma awarded to Sir Henry Ainslie Hoare Bt, 1892'.

15 *Sir Henry Ainslie Hoare, 5th Baronet (1824–94)*, c.1860, by John Prescott Knight RA (1803–81), oil on canvas, 110.4 × 85 cm (NT 732212); *Sir Henry Ainslie Hoare, 5th Baronet*, c.1880, by Paul-Albert Besnard (1849–1934), oil on canvas, 53.3 × 44.5 cm (NT 732362).

16 Stourhead Archive, Augusta, Lady Hoare's Diaries, 1845–57, 3 November 1845 and 10 May 1848.

17 C. Hoare & Co., HFM/16/1, letters from Sir Henry Ainslie Hoare, 5th Baronet, to his mother, Anne Penelope Hoare (née Ainslie).

18 Hunter 2018, pp. 112–114, 'Chelsea Election: The Final Contest, 1868'.

19 *Shepton Mallet Journal*, 4 December 1885.

20 Stourhead Annals, vol. I, 1857–59.

21 Stourhead Archive, 'Directions for Sweeping the Chimneys... November 1863' printed notice, 329 × 275 mm. (NT 732032).

22 Stourhead Annals, vol. II, 1857, 1857–58, 1859–60.

23 Stourhead Archive, Augusta, Lady Hoare's Diaries, 1857–66 and 1867–78, chimney fires on 6 and 24 October 1863, 31 October 1876. WSA, 383/127, daily diaries of Robert Shackleton, Stourhead roof leaking, 10–16 June and 9–11 October 1882, 4 May and 4 September 1883.

24 WSA, 383/127, daily diaries of Robert Shackleton, 1863–87.

25 Stourhead Annals, vol. II, 1857–60.

26 WSA, 383/89, Stourhead estate accounts 1870–80; Stourhead Settled Estates Act 1882, 45 & 46 Victoria, Chapter 5, p. 9. *Salisbury and Winchester Journal*, 19 August 1882, reported the fall in income from £23,000 to £20,000.

27 *Western Gazette*, 24 September 1880.

28 *The Field*, 15 August 1885.

29 WSA, 383/20, sale of heirlooms correspondence 1881–86, Thomas Stevens of Messrs Longbourne, Longbourne & Stevens at 7 Lincoln's Inn Fields (for Sir Ainslie Hoare, 5th Baronet) and Henry Tylee of Messrs Tylee, Wickham, Moberly & Tylee at 14 Essex Street, Strand (for the guardians of Henry Hugh Arthur Hoare). C. Hoare & Co., HE/1/B/16, three letters, 1882–83.

30 WSA, 383/20, Stevens to Tylee, 9 March 1883.

31 WSA, 383/21, 'List of Articles in Stourhead Heir Loom Catalogue referred to in Mr Henry Tylee's letter to Mrs Henry Arthur Hoare of November 1882'.

32 WSA, 383/20, 'Stourhead Heirlooms Schedule of Pictures [and China] which it is proposed to sell in 1883', nd.

33 Christie's 1883 (a); Christie's 1883. WSA 383/20, Christie's statement June 1883.

34 Christie's 1883, lot 16.

35 WSA, 383/20, Tylee to Stevens, 20 July 1883.

36 Ibid., Stevens to Tylee, 24 July 1883.

37 Sotheby 1883.

38 WSA, 383/20, Tylee to Julia Hoare, 11 August, 1883.

39 Ibid., Tylee to Julia Hoare, 21 August 1882.

40 Ibid., Stevens to Tylee, 24 July 1883.

41 Ibid., Tylee to Stevens, 20 July 1883. Stourhead Inventory 1838, pp. 12–13, no. 115, 'Henry only Son of Sir Rd Colt Hoare Bart by Sir J Reynolds'; no. 127, 'Two Children and a Cat by Gainsborough'.

42 WSA, 383/20, Tylee to Julia Hoare, 18 August 1883.

43 Christie's 1884. Stourhead Archive, copy annotated with prices and totalling £1524–12s–5d (without commission).

44 WSA, 1617/1/2, Abstract of title, 10 September 1953, reciting agreement between Sir Henry Ainslie and H. H. A. Hoare to create a mortgage of £45,000 on the Stourhead Estate.

45 Stourhead Archive, Augusta, Lady Hoare's Diaries show Leighton first visited Stourhead in September 1858. He remained friends with Lady Hoare until his death. She recorded visiting his studio on several occasions and entertaining him frequently at her London houses.

46 Ibid., 1878–86.

47 Ibid., Wavendon visitors' book 1889.

48 Dodd 1979.

49 Stourhead Annals, vol. II, July 1902–July 1903; Ibid, July 1904–July 1905, Trask & Co. proved unsatisfactory and the 6th baronet took the firm to court in October 1904. Doran Webb had used the firm in 1900–1, to build a chapel for the Royal Masonic School at Bushey in Hertfordshire where their shoddy work had also resulted in a court case. Information kindly supplied by Julian Orbach.

50 Ibid., July 1904–July 1905.

51 WSA, 383/131, Lady Hoare to Thomas Stevens, 23 March 1905.

52 WSA, 383/131, nd memorandum by Lady Hoare describing meeting Doran Webb on 28 March 1905.

53 Ibid., Mrs Doran Webb to Lady Hoare, 4 April 1905

54 Ibid., Doran Webb to Stevens, 23 April 1905.

55 Ibid., Stevens to Lady Hoare, 25 April 1905; ibid., 1617, uncatalogued drawings, mostly from 1902–6 by Doran Webb and Sir Aston Webb.

56 Stourhead Annals, vol. II, 1906–7, rebuilding and equipping house at £35,000 | salvage £1,090 | reservoir and pumping station £3,880 | repair of contents £3,360 | total £43,330. The insurers paid £47,200.

57 Stourhead Annals, vol. III, 1944–5.

58 Ibid.

59 Lees-Milne 1992, p. 74.

60 Jose Billing, *Blackmoor Vale Magazine*, 3 September 2004 p. 90.

61 Booth, Jean, *Alda: the last Lady Hoare of Stourhead* (privately printed, 2020), pp. 3–6.

62 Stourhead Archive, Alda, Lady Hoare's Diaries, 27 February 1917.

63 Lees-Milne 1992, p. 71.

64 Alma 1979, p. 105.

65 Information kindly provided by Christopher Myles Jenkins 2014.

66 Stourhead Archive, Alda, Lady Hoare's Diaries, 24 July 1923; Visitors' Book, October 1923, Ralph Edwards; Macquoid 1924.

67 WSA, 383/944, Mrs Esdaile to Lady Hoare, 14 June 1924.

68 Stourhead Archive, Alda, Lady Hoare's Diaries, Clouds, 26 January 1921; Wardour, 11 February 1921; Bryanston, 18 February 1923; Brympton, 17 October 1923.

69 WSA, 383/106, *Terræ Hoaresnæ in com. Wilts, Dorset, Somerset* (Frome, 1829).

70 Stourhead Annals, vol. III, for sums raised in sales.

71 *Exeter and Plymouth Gazette*, 15 June 1911.

72 *Bath Chronicle and Weekly Gazette*, 15 June 1911

73 WSA, 383/106, *Terræ Hoaresnæ in com. Wilts, Dorset, Somerset* (Frome, 1829).

74 *Western Times*, 12 September 1913.

75 *Western Gazette*, 14 June 1918

76 *Bedfordshire Times and Independent*, 17 May 1918

77 Stourhead Archive, Alda, Lady Hoare's Diaries, 21 July 1920.

78 Ibid., Stourhead Annals, vol. II, 1895–96.

79 Ibid., vol. III, 1915–16.

80 Ibid., vol. III, 1927–8.

81 Ibid., vol. III, 1917–18.

82 Ibid., vol. III, 1938–9; 1944–5.

83 www.stourtonhistory.org/population.html (accessed 30 August 2018).

84 Ibid., vol. III, 1911–12.

85 Stourhead Archive (mislaid), Alda, Lady Hoare's 'Short Sketch of the life of our Son'.

86 Ibid., Alda, Lady Hoare's Diaries, 26 October 1923.

87 Ibid., Alda, Lady Hoare's Diaries, 9–12 July 1920.

88 Ibid., 20 August 1920.

89 Ibid., Alda, Lady Hoare's Diaries, 26 October 1923 and 11 January 1924.

90 Hutchings 2005, pp. 198–203.

91 Fedden 1968, pp. 118–120.

92 Stourhead Annals, vol. III, 1946–7.

93 Ibid., transcribing Sir Henry's memorandum of wishes dated 7 March 1946, 'It is my wish that the management of the two parts of the Estate which are the subjects of the gifts to the National Trust should so far as practicable continue as heretofore and that favourable consideration should be given to any tenants or employees on the property transferred to the National Trust who express a wish to continue in their tenancies or employment as the case may be.' An additional request that Home Farm 'would be carried on either with the co-operation or by arrangement with the person in occupation of the Mansion House.'

94 Ibid. and Lees-Milne 1992, p. 73.

95 *Western Gazette*, 19 September 1947.

96 Ibid., 10 October 1947.

The Stourton Demesne 1700–42

1 Raymond 2019.
2 WSA, 383/253, survey of Stourton 1703.
3 C. Hoare & Co., HFM/4/7, 'An account of money paid for Gardning & Planting att Stourton', April 1721–February 1723/4, 13 November 1722, '[money paid] Mason in full for trees sent' £24.
4 Calland 2010.
5 C. Hoare & Co., HFM/4/7, 'An Account of House Hold Expenses att Stourton', March 1723–October 1724, 27 January 1724/5, 'Communion plate for the Church' £50–0–9d.
6 Skinner 1808, fol. 12.
7 Hoare 1822, p. 42.
8 WSA, 383/724, indenture for lease of Stourton Grist Mill, 20 July 1651 between William Lord Stourton and Emanuell Swetnam. Ibid., indenture for lease of 'water grist mill & mills in Stourton' to Philip Pittman, 18 November 1699.
9 WSA, 383/748, agreement of 2 August 1735 between HH and Robert Turner for 'Stourton Mills', leased for 21 years at £22 p. a. 'Mill and Mill House called Cascade Mill beside Black Mead'.
10 Hoare 1822, p. 64, 'a mill formerly stood near the present stately imitation of Agrippa's Pantheon'.
11 WSA, 383/117, 'John Humphry's agreemt to raise the withy bed pond', 30 September 1724.
12 www.mapapps.bgs.ac.uk/geologyofbritain3d/index.html (accessed 29.08.19)
13 TNA, Prob 11/602/173, will of Henry Hoare (d. 1724/5), 'I will that there shall be laid out by my Executors when required by my said Wife or my Son Henry Hoare in Building, ffinishing, and ffurnishing the house and out houses at Stourton in the County of Wilts in laying and bringing water to it and making a Garden there the Sume of three thousand pounds'.
14 Switzer 1729, vol. II, pp. 313–343.
15 WSA, 383/57, 'Mr Andrews Estimte of an Engine' September 1724, for £262–6s.
16 Ibid., 'Mr Bensons Ingine with Repairing ye same and ye Wheel to do with ye thorrow and every other Charge to Rais to sett up ye same to do its office in ye best and Most Workmanlike mannor for ye sum of £70 | The house for Setting ye Ingine in £35'.
17 Desaguliers 1744, vol. II, pp. 431–436.
18 WSA, 383/57, Joseph Andrews to HH, 3 June 1724.
19 Prosser, Richard B., 'A List of Wiltshire Patentees', *Wiltshire Notes and Queries* (Devizes, 1896), vol. I, pp. 3–6, no. 410, 8 November 1716, Thomas Holland, Amesbury, clerk, 'New-invented engine for raising a continual flux of water with two barrels, only in much greater quantity, with more ease and certainty, by locks and chain works, than by any other engine hitherto invented. '
20 1722 plan of Stourhead.
21 C. Hoare & Co., HB/5/A/4, Partners' Ledger 1725–34, HH account, payments to Joseph Andrews for unspecified work: 16 June 1732, £30; 8 May 1733, £60; 5 June 1733, £100; 22 February 1734/5, £30. HH Ledger 1734–49, 17 April 1744, 'Mr Audr Benson being ye Ballce of His Accot & Jos: Andrews's for Pipe ye Engine &c' £44–1s.
22 Anonymous 1764 (Stourton Gardens 1749), p. 102.
23 Cartwright 1888, (Pococke 1754), vol. II, p. 43 'To the South of the house is a lawn with a piece of water, and from that a winding descent over the above-mentioned valley'.
24 WSA, 383/57, Joseph Andrews to HH, 3 June 1724.
25 Fenton 1811 (1807), p. 211.

The First Landscape Garden 1742–54

1 Piper general plan 1779.
2 McKewan 2006, p. 34.
3 Spence 1765, 'The Obelisk, & Turkish Tent, in the old (Bridgman) part of the Gardens'.
4 Anonymous 1764 (Stourton Gardens 1749), p. 103.
5 HH Ledger 1734–49, 2 May 1745, 'Mr Cheere for Apollo & Diana & ye 2 Packing Cases in full' £51–5s.
6 'A View from the Mount of Diana in Mr Hoare's Garden at Stourton in Wiltshire', c.1773, unknown, etching and engraving, 115 × 198 mm. Anonymous 1774, vol. II, opposite p. 304.
7 Clark 2013.
8 'Passage through the Wood, approaching the Grotto', 1779, by F. M. Piper, ink and sepia wash, 200 × 158 mm. RAS (Pi - e 6, 6 bok [24]). A vase at Stourhead, c.1800, by Samuel Woodforde RA (1764–1817), ink and colour wash, 295 × 170 mm. Olympia Auctions, British & Continental pictures and prints, 23 October 2019, lot 22.
9 Anonymous 1764 (Stourton Gardens 1749), p. 102. Graves 1779, vol. II, p. 10, 'They now came down to the grotto, which is situated at the side of the lake, amidst weeping willows and other wild aquatic shrubs, and shaded by a rising bank of ancient oaks which hang over it'.
10 'Plan of Grotto complex at Stourton's Pleasure Park in Wiltshire, near Bristol', c.1779, by F. M. Piper (1746–1824), pencil, ink and colour wash, 205 × 325 mm, annotation translates '[at the entrance]... here is [?] of ash and [*alder* inserted] mixed with Babylon willow along the shore, with bushes underneath and in front of [?] underwood [?] laurels' and 'Open place between the Main Cave and Cavern A, overshadowed by laurels and sweet chestnuts, which form a bower with their very extensive branches'. RAS (Pi - e 6, 5 bok [7]).
11 Fenton 1811 (1807), p. 206.
12 Cartwright 1888, (Pococke 1754), vol. II, p. 43.
13 Parnell 1769, vol. II, fol. 94. Hanway 1756, p. 89, 'On the brow of this hill is a walk, of considerable extent, of the softest mossy turf, bordered on each side by stately Scotch firs of Mr H.****'s own planting about four-and-twenty years since; they seem to be too thick set, as the wood behind them'.
14 Anonymous 1764 (Stourton Gardens 1749), p. 103.
15 Parnell 1769, vol. II, fol. 97.
16 Annotation of Piper general plan 1779. Woodbridge 2001, p. 61.
17 Polwarth 1776.
18 Stourhead Annals, vol. I, 1792, 'Began to cut down the Fir Walk' and completed the following year; 1794, 'Planted up the Avenue in the Old Fir Walk'.
19 'Plan and cross section of the Obelisk in Stourton Park', c.1779, by F. M. Piper (1746–1824), pencil and ink, 445 × 322 mm. Recording the dimensions. RAS (Pi - e 6, 4 bok [21]).
20 WSA, 383/907, deed signed by William Privett, 6 September 1746.
21 WSA, 383/4(1), 'Mr Privets Estimate or Bill of ye Obelisk', nd; HH Ledger 1734–49, payments for the Obelisk: in 18 June 1747, 'Mr Privet on Accot of ye Obelisk pd' £70; HH Ledger 1749–70, 29 November 1752, 'Mr Privet being an extra allwce on Obelisk Accot' £20.
22 HH Ledger 1734–49, 17 October 1748,' Mr Norris for the Mithras of Capr for ye Obelisk' £57–11s. HH Ledger 1749–70, 19 March 1750/1, 'Thos Spinks … his Journey to set up ye Mithras &c in full of all Demds' £2–2s. Hanway 1756, p. 89.
23 Hoare 1822, pp. 69–70; Sweetman 1925, p. 50, translated.
24 Stourhead Annals, vol. I, 1839; Hoare 1844, p. 16. Ibid., vol. I, 1854, 'Finished restoring the Obelisk from effects of Lightning – Expense £70'.
25 Cartwright 1888, (Pococke 1754), vol. II, p. 43. Alone among visiting authors Pococke mentions the temple.
26 Piper general plan 1779; 'Lit A. plan of the nearest portion of the grounds surrounding the former banker Hoare's Casino at Stourton, not far from Bristol, drawn on the spot in 1779 by F. M. Piper', ink and colourwash, 336 × 422 mm. RAS (Pi - e 6 bok [18]). Both plans rely on the more accurate 'Stourton', a preliminary plan of the eastern portion of the garden also showing the Temple on the Terrace facing south-west, pencil, 210 × 335 mm. RAS (Pi - e 6, 5 bok [3]).
27 Ibid.
28 Langley 1736, vol. II, pl. 79, fig. 3, after Serlio.
29 Gibbs 1728, pl. 70, a pavilion with a comparable façade surmounted by a facetted dome.
30 WSA, 383/907(1), Henry Flitcroft to HH, 18 August 1744, 'I have sent ye Cornice at Large for ye Venetian seat, as to the Price Mr Ireson demands of 1:10:0 p Rodd I should be glad to have the Work worth that money, which I think it may if he will take pains about it'.
31 Hoare 1822, p. 66.
32 WSA, 383/907(1), Henry Flitcroft to HH, 25 August 1744, 'My Next shall bring you... the Temple of Ceres with the Rocky Arch in which I propose to place the River God, & a Sketch how I conceive the head of ye lake'; Henry Flitcroft to HH, 7 September 1744, 'I have inclosd to you the Plan & Elevation of ye Temple of Ceres with a Sketch of ye Entablature showing how the Tryglyphs & Metops should be proportioned with the Skuls &c introduced therein... I have also sent a plan & Section for the Manner of Laying the Foundations... a Section of ye inside of this Building shall be soon sent, with particular drawing of ye Doorcase & pedestal Mouldings'. Payments to William Privett which may relate to the Temple of Flora: HH Ledger 1734–49; 27 September 1745, 'on accot of ye Temple' £40; 3 November 1746, 'in full of all Demands' £28–8s–1d; 30 March 1747, 'on accot of Buildg' £30. C. Hoare & Co., HB/5/A/6, Partners' Ledger 1742–51, HH account, 5 October 1745, 'His Bill to Willm Privet (Mason)' £40; 30 December 1745, 'Willm Privet of Chillmark's Bill' £30.
33 Stourhead Annals, vol. I, 1842, 'the Temple of Flora new roofed and new leaded, and the entire Building repaired and painted'; vol. II, 1894–5.

34 Gamba 1824 (Rezzònico 1787), p. 22. Virgil, *Aeneid*, bk VI, line 258.

35 Hanway 1756, p. 92.

36 McKewan 2006, pp. 94–104.

37 HH Ledger 1734–49, 28 January 1743/44, 'Thos Manning for a River God &c' £18–15s. Anonymous 1764 (Stourton Gardens 1749), p. 102, 'For yonder silver god they sigh, they burn, | And pour their tears incessant thro' his urn; | But cold as lead, and deaf when they complain, | Supine he lies, and they but weep in vain. | See from beneath him (tinctur'd by the sun | With colours radiant) sheets of water run'.

38 The Temple of Flora, 1753, by C. W. Bampfylde (1720–91), pen and colour wash, 280 × 470 mm. BM (1970,0919.20).

39 WSA, 383/907(1), Henry Flitcroft to HH, 25 August 1744, 'My Next shall bring ... a Sketch how I conceive the head of ye lake should be formd twill make a most Agreeable Scene'.

40 McKewan 2006, p. 34.

41 Vermeule 1956, p. 343.

42 C. Hoare & Co., HB/5/A/5, Partners' Ledger 1734–42, HH account, 19 June 1740, 'Edmond Fowlers for Customs & Charges on Figures &cc for Leghorne' £9–15s–6d and HB/5/A/6, Partners' Ledger 1742–51, HH account, 2 March 1742/3, 'Edmd Fowler Custom & Charges of 2 figures fr Livourno' £13–3s–6d.

43 Bertolotti 1880, pp. 79–80, Parker's export licences (no reference to HH as the customer), 13 December 1740, 'una statua antica di marmo al naturale di mediocre scultura figurante una donna in parte ristorata' [an antique marble statue, mediocre in quality, representing a woman in part restored].

44 Anonymous 1766, fol. 33 verso, describing the Pantheon, 'a charming Antique Statue of Livia Augusta, from the Collection of Cardinal Ottoboni, and the cost 1000gs.' Harrison 2017, p. 88, n.252.

45 Oliver 1972 (Curwen 1776), vol. I, p. 231, Curwen asserted that *Livia Augusta* was purchased in Rome for £700; Warner 1801 (1800), p. 111, quoted two thousand guineas.

46 Britton, 1801, vol. II, p. 17. Tromp 1982 (van Spaen van Biljoen 1791), p. 50. Repeated in Sweetman 1907, p. 26.

47 Anonymous ms 1766, fol. 33 verso.

48 Dallaway 1816, p. 314. Langford 1755, second day, 12 March 1755, p. 7, lot 73, 'Statue of *Flora*, white marble' [ms annotation *Wild 18.-18*] and p. 218, 'Flora stans, tunicata et velata; dextra corollam tenet, sinistra pateram. *Ex marmore albo: alt. duos pedes cum semisse*, Stylobatae *ex Mahogony* imposita. *Alt. tres pedes*', i.e., a diminutive sculpture.

49 Gamba 1824 (Rezzònico 1787), p. 22.

50 Warner 1801 (1800), p. 113.

51 *Bust of Vibia Sabina*, Italian, eighteenth century, marble, H 91.5 cm (NT 562908); *Bust of Faustina Minore*, Italian, eighteenth century, marble, H 91.5 cm (NT 562907).

52 *Bust of the Young Marcus Aurelius*, Italian, eighteenth century, marble, H 89 cm (NT 562905); *Bust of Alexander the Great*, Italian, eighteenth century, marble, H 86.5 cm (NT 562906).

53 Hanway 1756, p. 92.

54 Gamba 1824 (Rezzònico 1787), p. 22. Did the count mis-count? Four *pulvinaria* survive.

55 NT 562863. Dodd 2007. Montfaucon 1724, vol. II, bk V, pp. 98–99, pl. 29.2, engraved plate, 328 × 188 mm.

56 NT 562861. Unlike the *pulvinaria*, these altars are not cut away at the back to accommodate the skirting of the temple.

57 Bodleian Library, ms. top. gen. a 4, fol. 3, interior elevation of Temple of Flora, inscribed and dated 23 January 1748/9 by Thomas Spinks (active 1743–55), ink, 215 × 205 mm; fol. 5, interior elevations of the Temple of Flora, anonymous, pencil, 325 × 415 mm; fol. 6, interior elevations of the Temple of Flora with four relief panels, pilasters and further embellishments, annotated 'by Sr R. C. Hoare' and 'Stourhead', pencil, 325 × 415 mm.

58 *The Borghese Vase*, Kelly 1980, p. 97. HH Ledger 1770–85, 8 October 1770, 'Do[Pincot] my subn to ye Borghese Vase in pt' £5–5s; 7 May 1772, 'Elenr Coade for a Borghese Vase & packg' £12–14s–6d.

59 Bath Record Office, B731.7 PAR, 'A collection of vases terms &c'. by Thomas Parsons (1744–90), bound collection of drawings, no. 92, 'Antique', ink, 220 × 134 mm.
HH Ledger 1749–70, payments to Parsons:
14 April 1750 'Mr Parsons of Bath for ye Vases in part' £21.
26 May 1750, 'Mr Parsons of Bath on acct' £30.
25 September 1750 'Mr Parsons of Bath for ye Vases in pt' £40.
17 June 1751, 'Mr Parsons of Bath for ye Vases Pedestls &c in full' £49–8s.
Parsons also supplied the vases for the Wooden Bridge and evidently elsewhere at Stourhead. Bryant 2014, p. 552, fig. 20.5, *Entrance front of Chiswick House*, c.1728, by William Kent (1685–1748), pencil, ink and wash. Trustees of Chatsworth Settlement (26A.13).

60 Montfaucon, 1719, vol. V, pt I, pl. 21.

61 Temple of Flora, 1812–16, by Francis Nicholson (1753–1844), watercolour, 411 × 568 mm. BM (1944,1014.133).

62 Stourhead Annals, vol. II, 1894–5, 'The Urn over Diana's Well in front of the Temple of Flora was restored'.

63 Harris 2000 (Beaufort 1762), p. 41, 'a Gothic Temple'; Toynbee 1928 (Walpole 1762), p. 43, 'a greenhouse of false gothic'.

64 Parnell 1769, vol. II, fols 86–87.

65 Powys 1776, fols 17–18.

66 Wrighte 1767, p. 14 notes on pl. 28, 'Plan and Elevation for a Green-house'.

67 View from the Temple of Apollo, c.1770–80, by C. W. Bampfylde (1720–91), pencil, 340 × 940 mm. V&A (E.387–1949).

68 Defoe 1779 vol. I, p. 319.

69 Hirschfeld 1779, vol. V, p. 43, 'on arrive par une allée couverte à une petite orangerie champêtre; devant l'entrée sont quelques lits de fleurs & des ronces odorantes...' [one arrives by a shady path at the little rustic orangery at whose entrance are flower-beds and fragrant brambles].

70 *The flower garden at Nuneham Courtenay*, 1777, by Paul Sandby (1730/1–1809), watercolour and engraving.

71 Hoare 1822, pp. 65–66.

72 Anonymous 1764 (Stourton Gardens 1749), p. 103; Harrison 2015, p. 128.

73 Harris 2000 (Beaufort 1762), p. 41.

74 Symes 2010, p. 103.

75 Miller 2010, pp. 204–205. HH Ledger 1749–70, 14 August 1751, 'Mr Harding for Sr Richd Chinese Temple in full' £39–12s–6d.

76 BL, Add MS 51373A, correspondence of 1st Earl of Ilchester, fols 39–40, 'Work done for the Rt H'ble Lord Ilchester 1751–1755 by Nathl Ireson', fol. 40 verso, 5 June 1755, 'To Building the Chinese Seat' £6–5½ d.

77 Hoare 1822, p. 66. Piper 1812.

78 HH Ledger 1734–49, 2 May 1745, ''Mr Cheere for Apollo & Diana & ye 2 Packing Cases in full' £51–5s.

79 Anonymous 1764 (Stourton Gardens 1749), p. 103, described *Diana* immediately after the Chinese Alcove.

80 Bieber 1961, p. 63. *Diane de Versailles*, The Louvre Museum, Paris (Ma 589).

81 Toynbee 1928 (Walpole 1762), p. 43, Pantheon, 'Next to him [Hercules], Lord Leicester's Diana'.

82 See also View of the Wooden Bridge and Obelisk, c.1770–80, by C. W. Bampfylde (1720–91), pen and colour wash, 315 × 545 mm. V&A (E359–1949) and Wooden Bridge and Temple of Apollo, 1770s, by C. W. Bampfylde, pen and ink. Private Collection.

83 Toynbee 1928 (Walpole 1762), p. 43. Nichols 1840, p. 624. Leoni 1721, bk III, p. 19; pl. 6, 'The height of the Bridge, in which are the rails or braces that go from one pillar to another, will be the eleventh part of the breadth of the River. All the *radii* or lines of the pillars must correspond to the center, which will make the work very strong; and the pillars will bear up the beams laid athwart and along the Bridge, as in the foregoing ones. The Bridges of these four kinds may be made as much in length as occasion shall require but all their parts must be made proportionately greater'.

84 Shields 2016, p. 199. The Wotton bridge was reconstructed in 1990s.

85 HH Ledger 1749–70, 4 December 1749, 'Mr Privet in full for ye Bridge & other work' £34–9s.

86 Roberts 1997, pp. 435–437.

87 Miller 2010, p. 201.

88 Bath Record Office, B731.7 PAR, 'A collection of vases terms &c.' by Thomas Parsons (1744–90), bound collection of drawings, no. 51, ink, 220 × 134 mm, credited to Charles Errard. Recueil de divers vases antiques, vase with vine motif, Errard, c.1680, inscribed, 'Romæ in horta private iuxta Templum Ste Petri ad Vincule', engraving, 330 × 225 mm. See also Parsons, no. 102, a plain pedestal, ink, 220 × 134 mm. The drawing by F. M. Piper, p. 152 corresponds with Parsons's designs for the vase and pedestal.

89 Eight pencil studies of the Wooden Bridge, c.1779, by F. M. Piper (1746–1824). RAS (Pi - e, 6, 5 bok).

90 Powys 1776, fol. 18.

91 Toynbee 1928 (Walpole 1762), p. 43; Ellis 1907 (Fanny Burney 1773), vol. II, p. 322; Powys 1776, fol. 18; Defoe 1779, vol. I, p. 317; Anonymous 1780, p. 16, line 407; Gamba 1824 (Rezzònico 1787), p. 18.

92 Anonymous ms 1765; Anonymous ms 1766, fol. 35

verso; Tromp 1982 (van Spaen van Biljoen 1791), p. 50; Thelwall 1801 (1797), p. 105; Hoare, 1800, p. 45; Britton 1801, vol. I, pp. 14; Hoare 1818, p. 23; Hoare 1822, p. 65; Neale 1823, vol. V. Stourhead Annals, vol. I, 1797–8, 'In the Summer 1798, 'I took down the Palladian Bridge – placed a ferry on the same spot.' Dibdin 1822, p. 389, 'We enter the wherry. The fair Gabrielle accompanies us. The cord runs smoothly through the pulleys, and the boat, feeling no "unusual weight", we alight on the thick soft grass on the opposite side in a trice'.

93 Spence 1765.

94 WSA, 1300/2944. HH to Lady Bruce, May 1776, 'I am upon the entrance into The Grotto to get it finish'd before You arrive.'

95 Virgil, Aeneid, bk I, lines 167–168, the passage as translated by Dryden, 'A grot is form'd beneath, with mossy seats | To rest the Nereids, and exclude the heats.' Woodbridge 2001, p. 47, comparing a stone seat with the same Latin inscription at William Shenstone's garden, The Leasowes.

96 WSA, 1300/2948, HH to Lord Bruce, 11 May 1776.

97 WSA, 9/35/165(1)/2353, HH to Lady Bruce, July 1765.

98 WSA, 1300/3264, HH to Lord Bruce, August 1765.

99 Anonymous 1764 (Stourton Gardens 1749), p. 102, described the grotto but without Cheere's River God. The poet had previously mentioned Manning's River God below the Temple of Flora.

100 WSA, 383/4(1), William Privett's bill dated 1748 specifying coping round the cupola, ribs, pediments, '37 Days work at Quarr ... 935 Days worke my men ... at 2[s] 6[d per day], Laborour 110 days at 14d, Myself 101 days at 3sh' totalling £186–17s-6d.

101 HH Ledger 1734–1749, 21 October 1747, 'Mr Merewether for Grotto Stones & Carriage' £10–4s-6d; 23 April 1748, 'G: Macey of Sarum for a Black Marble Slab for the Nymph & an Old Bill for Willberry in full' £2–11s-16d; 23 July 1748, 'Revd Mr Merrywether for Stones &c in full' £11.17s. Symes 2010, p. 97.

102 Anonymous 1764 (Stourton Gardens 1749), p. 102.

103 Parnell 1769, vol. II, fol. 85.

104 Ellis 1907 (Fanny Burney 1773), vol. II, p. 322.

105 Polwarth 1776.

106 Symes 2010, pp. 97–98. Thacker 1979, p. 197.

107 Nine plans and cross-sections of the Stourhead Grotto, c.1779, by F. M. Piper (1746–1824). RAS (Pi-e, 6, 2; 6,5 bok; 6,6 bok); Preliminary plan and sections of the Grotto, by F. M. Piper, pencil and four in ms booklet 'Änglelske Banquierens Henry Hoares superbe Grottanläggning... 1779' [the English Banker Henry Hoare's superb Grotto... measured in situ 1779]. RAS (Pi-e, 6,7).

108 'Plan of the Grotto in Stourhead Pleasure Park', 1779, by F. M. Piper (1746–1824), ink and colour wash, 215 × 280 mm. RAS (Pi - e 6, 6 bok [25]).

109 McKewan 2006, pp. 46–47.

110 Stourhead Annals vols I and II.

111 The Nymph was first mentioned in Anonymous 1764 (Stourton Gardens 1749), p. 102.

112 Nymph of the Grotto, by Michael Rysbrack, c.1762, pencil and ink, 252 × 267 mm. Inscribed 'M.

Rysbrack, Sculptor'. City Museum and Art Gallery Plymouth. Eustace 1982, pp. 179–180.

113 Ariadne, Roman copy of Greek marble of second century BC, 162 × 195 cm. The Museo Pio-Clementino, Musei Vaticani (548).

114 Gamba 1824 (Rezzònico 1787), pp. 18–19.

115 Ariadne, lead, 73 × 186 cm, at West Wycombe Park resembles more closely the Vatican marble (NT 807677).

116 Ariadne, Roman copy of Greek marble of second century BC , marble, 129 × 226 cm. Uffizi (MAF n.13728); the deposed sixteenth century head and arm (MAF n. 13727).

117 The Gentleman's Magazine, vol. LXXXIX, pt I, (London, 1819), p. 116, with the Latin text, incorrectly attributed to Cardinal Bembo: 'Hujus Nympha loci, sacri custodia fontis | Dormio, dum placidæ sentio murmur aquæ | Parce, precor, quisquis tangis cava marmora, somnum | Rumpere, sive bibas, sive, lavere tace.' Anonymous, The Salisbury Guide (1799), p. 78, 'a perpetual pellucid Spring, that murmuring falls over her rocky bed, has quite effaced the following well applied charming lines, formerly legible on the pedestal: "Huius Nympha..." Mr Pope's translation is now on the marble margin of the bason'.

118 MacDougall 1975, p. 358.

119 Montfaucon 1719, vol. I, pt II, pl. 220, fig.3; Kurz 1953, p. 173.

120 HH Ledger 1749–70, 7 August 1751, 'Mr Cheere in full for ye River God Sr Richd figures &c' £98.

121 The dream of Aeneas. Virgil, Aeneid, bk VIII, lines 31–35.

122 Langford 1764, Rysbrack's sale, p. 10, 18 February, lot 55, 'Works of Salvator Rosa'.

123 'Lit. D. Cross section of the length of the Grotto in Stourton Pleasure Park', c.1779, by F. M. Piper (1746–1824), ink and colour wash, 210 × 334 mm. RAS (Pi - e 6, 6 bok [26]), annotation.

124 'Part of the Grotto at Stourhead, showing the exterior of that part of the same called The Rivergod's Cavern', c.1779, by F. M. Piper (1746–1824), ink and sepia wash, 204 × 155 mm. RAS (Pi - e 6 [26a]). Dibdin 1822, p. 389, also noted a paddle.

125 Hoare 1822, p. 66.

126 Hanway 1756, p. 91, 'From the grotto of the nymph, we proceeded to that adjoining, which is sacred to the river god Stour, and to him inscribed by some latin verses'; Anonymous ms 1766, fol. 34; Parnell 1769, vol. II, fol. 85; Tromp 1982 (van Spaen van Biljoen 1791), p. 50; Warner 1801 (1800), p. 107; Hoare 1822, p. 66.

127 Warner 1801 (1800), p. 108, 'Over the arch in front of this recess [for the River God] hangs a wooden tablet, with some lines allusive to this aquatic deity'. Ovid, Metamorphoses, bk I, lines 574–576, in translation, 'This was the home, the dwelling, the most secret haunt of the great river. Sitting here, in a cave hewn out of the cliffs, he was dispensing justice to the waves and to the nymphs who inhabited his stream'.

128 Hanway 1756, p. 91; Harris 2000 (Beaufort 1762), p. 41; Toynbee 1928 (Walpole 1762), p. 43; Spence 1765; Anonymous ms 1766, fol. 34; Anonymous 1780, p. 19, line 502; Warner 1801 (1800), p. 107;

Fenton 1811 (1807), p. 208; Dibdin 1822, p. 389.

129 Clarke (1777); Ellis 1907 (Fanny Burney 1773), vol. II, p. 322; Tromp 1982 (van Spaen van Biljoen 1791), p. 50; Sweetman 1907, p. 28.

130 Anonymous 1780, p. 18, lines 471–473.

131 Britton 1801, vol. II, p. 15.

132 The interior of the Grotto with the Nymph and River God, 1812–16, by Francis Nicholson (1753–44), watercolour, 410 × 469 mm. BM (1944,1014.127).

133 Skurray 1824, p. 166.

The Garden Lake and Pantheon 1754–62

1 The dates suggested by descriptions written in 1754 and 1755: Cartwright 1888, (Pococke 1754), vol. II, p. 43, 'below this [Temple of Flora] are two large pieces of water, which are to be made into one and much enlarged, for which a head is making at great expence'; Hanway 1756, p. 90, describing his visit in 1755, found 'a very large piece of water at the bottom... We made a coasting voyage on the little enchanting ocean, where we discovered several little islands'.

2 NT archive records, 624950, Wx 15:47, 'Report on Garden Lake, Stourhead' by Ian Charles Carter, 2003, pp. 2–3.

3 Ibid.

4 F. M. Piper, 'Beskrifning öfwer Lustparkerne uti Stourton ... 1778–79, 1780', p. 2. RAS (Pi - e 6, 7 bok).

5 NT archive records, 45821.511, Wx 02:67, Stourhead Lakes, Watson Hawksley drawing U16401/0/2/T1, amended February 1988.

6 Roberts 1997, pp. 356, 393, 470.

7 Ibid, p. 473.

8 C. Hoare & Co., HFM/9/10, HH to Richard Hoare (nephew), nd, the letter also referred to the Great Lisbon Earthquake of 1755, Information kindly provided by Jean Booth and Julia Mottershaw.

9 Skempton 2002, pp. 341, 279, 591, 83.

10 Rutton 1903, pp. 81–91, 184.

11 Binnie 1987, pp. 68–70.

12 Skempton 2002, pp. 278–285.

13 Ibid., pp. 83–84.

14 'A View from the Mount of Diana in Mr Hoare's Garden at Stourton in Wiltshire' and 'A View from the Pantheon in Mr Hoare's Garden at Stourton in Wiltshire', c.1773, unknown, etching and engravings, 115 × 198 mm. Anonymous 1774, vol. II, opposite pp. 304 and 305.

15 Earlier estimates include, Parnell 1769, fol. 81, 'The water covers twenty four acres'; Warner 1801 (1800), p. 105, 20 acres; 1792 low-water plan of the Garden Lake, 19 acres.

16 F. M. Piper, 'Beskrifning öfwer Lustparkerne uti Stourton... 1778–9, 1780', p. 3. RAS (Pi - e 6, 7 bok).

17 McKewan 2006, p. 34.

18 NT archive records, 45805, Wx 02:65, Stourhead Garden buildings, Henry Cadogan Hoare to John Cripwell, 2 December 1974.

19 McKewan 2006, p. 98.

20 WSA, 1300/4280, HH to Lady Bruce, 23 October 1762.

21 Stourhead Annals, vol. II, 1902, 'the two Islands were cleared out and the ground raised and turfed'. Woodbridge 1978, p. 24.

22 'Lit. B. Approximate appearance of the lake pent up between three hills in Banker Hoare's pleasure park at Stourton near Bristol, drawn on the spot in 1779 by F.M. Piper', pencil, ink and colourwash, 333 × 422 mm. RAS (Pi - e 6, 1 bok [19]) shows four islands: the Pantheon island divided in two, the supposed Temple of Apollo island and Bird island.

23 Anonymous 1780, p. 16, lines 420–421.

24 Stourhead Annals, vol. I, 1792.

25 Fenton 1811 (1807), p. 206.

26 Simond 1817 (1810), vol. I, pp. 261–262.

27 Stourhead Annals, vol. I, 1824–5, recording 620 carp netted.

28 Stourhead Archive, diaries of Augusta, Lady Hoare, 21 August 1856 and 11 August 1759.

29 McKewan 2006, p. 29.

30 Hanway 1756, p. 90.

31 'A View from the Mount of Diana in Mr Hoare's Garden at Stourton in Wiltshire' and 'A View from the Pantheon in Mr Hoare's Garden at Stourton in Wiltshire', c.1773, unknown, etching and engravings, 115 × 198 mm. Anonymous 1774, vol. II, opposite pp. 304 and 305.

32 Burlington 1779, p. 394.

33 WSRO, Parham papers, 2/2/2/6 letter 4/91, Hester Hoare to Harriet Anne, Lady Bisshopp, Stourhead, 4 April 1785.

34 Stourhead Archive, Augusta, Lady Hoare's Diaries, 22 April 1845 and 27 June 1857. Ibid., Alda, Lady Hoare's Diaries 1895.

35 Architectural capriccio with the Pantheon and the Maison Carrée, c.1745, attr. Francis Harding (fl. c.1730–60) oil on canvas, 72.4 × 47 cm (NT 732275), includes the Stourhead Pantheon in the distance. But the Pantheon was not built in 1745. If the approximate date of the painting is correct Harding either had access to Flitcroft's design or amended the capriccio in the 1750s.

36 Parnell 1769, vol. II, fol. 80.

37 Defoe 1779, vol. I, p. 318.

38 WSA, 1300/4280, HH to Lady Bruce, 23 October 1762.

39 Symes 2010, pp. 78–81; Laing 2018. Colossal Bacchus with a panther, Roman, first or second century AD and eighteenth century, marble, H 241.3 cm (NT 516675).

40 HH Ledger 1749–70, 25 April 1755, 'Mr Flitcroft for The Pantheon &c and Subterrn Arch' £100; 4 November 1757, 'Mr Flitcroft's rect for Clapham, Pantheon Stourhd &c in full' £100.

41 'Section of Squire Hoare's Temple call'd Pantheon at Stourton in Wiltshe', c.1754, attr. Henry Flitcroft (1697–1769), ink and grey wash, 355 × 485 mm. RAS (Pi - e 6, 3 [113]).

42 Hoare Ledger 1749–70, 16 June 1753, 'Mr Privet on Acct of The Temple of Hercules' £100; 29 September 1753, 'Mr Privet on Accot of Temple of Hercules' £200; 20 February 1755, 'Mr Privet for the Palladn Temple &c all Demds in full' £226–2s.

43 C. Hoare & Co., HB/5/A/7, Partners' Ledger 1751–64, HH Account, 10 October 1754, 'Heny Jordans bill to Geo: Cannick for Lead' £223–3s. IIII Ledger 1749–70, 1 April 1755, 'Mr Jordan Plumr of Blandford for ye Pantheon in full' £56–2s–8d; 20 December 1761, 'Mr Jelfe for Pantheon pavemt' £106–2s; 20 December 1761, 'Mr Holmes for

Pantheon Iron Gates' £33–3s.

44 Piper general plan 1779, annotation stated the Pantheon cost £12,000.

45 Callipygian Venus, 1767, lead, H 157.5 cm. (NT 562878); Bacchus, 1767, lead, H 158 cm. (NT 562879). Both by John Cheere (1709–87).

46 Gamba 1824 (Rezzònico 1787), p. 20.

47 Toynbee1928 (Walpole 1762), p. 43.

48 Warner 1801 (1800), p. 109.

49 Sweetman 1907, p. 26.

50 NT 562909 and 562910.

51 Leoni 1721, bk IV, pl. 61.

52 Warner 1801 (1800), p. 109, 'A circular opening in the dome admits the light, which receives a rich golden tinge from some yellow glass introduced in the aperture'. C. Hoare & Co., HB/5/A/8, Partners' Ledger 1764–83, HH Account, 5 May 1772, 'Willm Pickett's Bill for seven staind' Glass Stars' £25–18–6d.

53 The entablature derived from Robert Wood's engraving of the great temple at Balbec (Wood 1757, pl. 20). The stuccatori stretched the design. WSA, 383.6, HH Ledger 1749–70, 26 April 1757, 'Plans &c. of Balbeck pd Lord Dungarvan' £3–15s.

54 Spence 1765, 'The Walls are of a Blossom, or rather light broken-purple, color. The Dome, Entablature; & Ornaments generally, white'. Warner 1801 (1800), p. 109, 'The walls are stained of a deep purple colour'.

55 Interior of the Pantheon, c.1784, by Samuel Woodforde RA (1763–1817), oil on canvas, 121.9 × 91.4 cm. (NT 732271). Woodforde, however, depicted the statues correctly placed in his preliminary drawing (NT 731023). The Pantheon interior, 1812–16, by Francis Nicholson (1753–1844), watercolour, 548 × 422 mm. British Museum (1944,1014.131).

56 Meleager, 1762, by John Cheere (1709–87), plaster, H 208 cm. (NT 562914). HH Ledger 1749–70, 12 November 1762, 'Mr Cheere for The Meleager &c in full' £23–15s. Marble version is a Roman copy of a Greek original of the mid-fourth century BC, H 210 cm. The Museo Pio-Clementino, Musei Vaticani (490).

57 Kenworthy-Browne, 1993, pp. 248–252.

58 A Priestess of Isis, attr. John Cheere (1709–87), plaster, H 188 cm (NT 562916). The antique marble Priestess, 117–138 AD, Musei Capitolini, Rome (Albani Col. MC0744). Santa Susanna, attr. John Cheere, plaster, H 203.5 cm (NT 562915). The marble saint is in the church of S. Maria di Loreto, Rome.

59 WSA, 383/4/1, agreement dated 1 July 1747 between Rysbrack and HH witnessed by John Wootton, 'in Consideration of the summ of three Hundred pounds, the said Michael Rysbrack shall make a Hercules in Statuary marble Six feet three Inches high and the plint five Inches and the same shall be finish'd according to the model agreed on within the space of two years and Half...' receipt for £300 dated 9 July 1752.

60 HH Ledger 1734–49, payments to Rysbrack: 3 July 1747, 'in part for ye Figure of Hercules, Vide His agremt & Rect July ye 1st' £150; HH Ledger 1749–70, 9 July 1752, 'for The Statue of Hercules in full' £150; 16 July 1757, 'a Gratuity for ye

Hercules beyond ye contract' £50. C. Hoare & Co., HE/5/A/7, Partners' Ledger 1751–64, HH account, 18 February 1757, 'Mr Rysbrack for a Pedestal to Hercules in full' £83–14s–6d. Anonymous ms 1766, fol. 33 verso, put the cost at 700 guineas.

61 Hercules, by Michael Rysbrack (1694–1770), signed and dated 1744, painted terracotta, H 60 cm (NT 732894). TNA, PROB, 11/954/263, will of Michael Rysbrack (d. 1770).

62 Vertue 1934, pp. 121–122.

63 Farnese Hercules, third century AD by Glykon, marble, 317 cm. Museo Nazionale, Naples (277).

64 Kenworthy-Browne 1983, pp. 216–219. 'Hercules in the garden of the Hesperides', published as the frontispiece to Ferrari 1646. Rysbrack owned this book (Langford 1764, 17 February, p. 8, lot 54, 'Hesperides, sive Malorum Cultura, &c.').

65 Walpole 1786, vol. IV, p. 210. Bust of Hercules, 1745–52, by Michael Rysbrack (1694–1770), terracotta, H 57.2 cm, Yale Center for British Art, New Haven (B1977.14.28).

66 WSA, 383/4/1, agreement between Rysbrack and HH, 14 March 1759. HH Accounts 1749–70, 11 December 1760, 'Mr Rysbrach for The Flora in part' £200; 14 December 1761, 'Mr Rysbrach for The Statue of Flora in full' £200.

67 Farnese Flora, Roman, second century AD, marble, H 335 cm. Museo Nazionale, Naples (6409).

68 Eustace 1982, pp. 164–166.

69 Webb 1954, pp. 201–202, Michael Rysbrack to Sir Edward Littleton, 4th Baronet, 14 December 1758. HH's aunt, Mary, had married Sir Edward's cousin, the 3rd Baronet.

70 Flora, 1759, by Michael Rysbrack (1694–1770), terracotta, H 57.3 cm. V&A (A9–1961).

71 Friedman 1974, no. 33.

72 Toynbee 1928 (Walpole 1762), p. 43. Kenworthy-Browne 1983, p. 219.

73 WSA, 9/35/165/2411, HH to Lord Bruce, 17 July 1762. Walpole's letter not found.

74 Eight relief panels, c.1760, by Benjamin Carter (1719–66), plaster, 113.1 × 180 cm. (NT 562961–562968). WSA, 1300/4280, HH to Lady Bruce, 23 October 1762.

75 HH Ledger 1749–70, payments to Mr Carter: 9 May 1761, 'in part for 8 Alto Relievo's £16 each' £100; 3 November 1761, 'Rect in further paymt for Alto Relievos' £50; 20 December 1761, 'for 8 Bass Relievos, all Demds' £12–9s.

76 Montfaucon 1719, vol. I, pt. I, pl. 15, 'Jupiter et Autres Dieux'; ibid., pl. 33, 'Neptune'; vol. II, pt. I, pl. 86, 'Pompe Bacchique'; ibid., pl. 89, 'Fête de Bacchus'; vol. III, pt. II, pl. 133, 'Mariage'; ibid., pl. 161, 'Course de Cirque'; ibid., pl. 179, 'Chasse au Sanglier'. Bartoli 1693, the corresponding pls 27, 29, 46–47, 43, 82, 23, 25. The eighth relief is taken from The Triumph of Bacchus, c.1635–6, attr. Nicolas Poussin (1594–1665), oil on canvas, 128 × 152 cm. The Atkins Museum, Kansas City (31–94).

77 Hoare 1818, p. 24, attributing the reliefs to Rysbrack. For the latter's library, see Langford 1764, 25 February, lot 55, 'Montfaucon's Antiquities with the Supplement, 15 vol.' (Montfaucon 1719 and 1724).

78 Four benches made for the Pantheon, the backs painted by William Hoare RA (1707–92), pine and

oil on board, 110.5 × 122 × 54.5 cm (NT 562867). Dodd 2007, citing Montfaucon 1719, vol. I, pt I, bk II, pl. 15. Toynbee 1928 (Walpole 1762), p. 43, 'round are four benches in beautifull Classic style, invented by Mr Hoare of Bath, & painted with the history of Cupid & Psyche'; Spence 1765, 'the very backs of ye Seats are painted with other relievo's in Chiaro scuro, by Mr Hoar'; Oliver 1972 (Curwen 1776), vol. I, p. 231, Curwen noted the seats had cushions.

79 Toynbee 1928 (Walpole 1762), p. 43, 'Behind the Hercules, is a large grate of brass to admit heat from a stove, and looking like a grate for Nuns in a catholic chapel'.

80 Piper 1812, prefaced by three ink and colour wash sketches of the Pantheon at Stourhead in elevation, section and plan. RAS (Pi - 6 mm).

81 'The Pantheon at Stourhead', c 1793, by Hendrik Frans de Cort (1742–1810), pencil, 130 × 205 mm. (DZSWS:1991.513).

82 WSA, 383/4/1, William Hopkins of Greek Street Soho, bill to RCH, 2 February 1804, 'by order of Mr Chippendale 1 large strong square second hand cast Iron Pedestal & Obelisk Warming Machine with large Antique Vase on top & altering do agreeable to Mr Chippendale's design ...' £49–8s. WSA, 383/4A, Thomas Chippendale the younger's account for RCH, 11 January 1804, 'Mens time packing the large Iron Stove and funnels for pantheon loading Carts &c' £1–12s plus incidentals.

83 WSRO, Parham papers, 2/2/2/6 letter 4/91, Hester Hoare to Harriet Anne, Lady Bisshopp, Stourhead, 4 April 1785.

84 Magleby 2009.

85 Piper general plan 1779, marked 'B'.

86 Anonymous ms 1765.

87 Parnell 1769, vol. II, fol. 82.

88 Symes 2010, pp. 105–107.

89 Raeburn 1995, p. 362, no. 962.

90 WSA, 9/35/165(2)/3192, HH to Henrietta [Harriot] Boyle, 18 July 1776. Powys 1776, fol. 19.

91 Anonymous 1780, p. 16, lines 401–405, Mussulman, an archaic term for a Muslim.

92 Stourhead Annals, vol. I, 1792.

The Garden 1762–72

1 View of the Temple of Flora, Stone Bridge, Stourton village and Temple of Apollo, pen and colour wash, 270 × 515 mm; 'Gardens at Stourhead from ye Pantheon', view of the Temple of Flora, *Neptune and his horses*, Stone Bridge, Stourton village and Temple of Apollo, pencil and grey wash, 275 × 752 mm. Both c. 1770–80, by C. W. Bampfylde (1720–91). V&A (E 360–1949 and E.382–1949).

2 WSA, 1300/4280, HH to Lady Bruce, 23 October 1762.

3 Leoni 1721, bk III, pl. 12, 'Bridge of *Vicenza* that is over the *Rerone*', engraving, 310 × 225 mm.

4 WSA. 1300/4280, HH to Lady Bruce, 23 October 1762.

5 Loudon 1833, p. 335.

6 *The Bristol Cross*, c.1400, by unknown masons, H 13 metres (NT 562952).

7 Parnell 1769, vol. II, fol. 86.

8 Liversidge 1978, p. 2.

9 *Bristol High Cross*, 1734, by Samuel (1696–1779) and Nathaniel (fl. 1724–59) Buck, engraving, 475 × 300 mm. (NT 73310).

10 HH Ledger 1734–49, 14 May 1747, 'Revd Cutts Barton for a Black Geldin' £21.

11 Parnell 1769, vol. II, fol. 86.

12 Liversidge 1978, p. 4, citing J. Evans, *A Chronological Outline of the History of Bristol, Bristol*, 1825, n.281.

13 WSA, 9/35/165(1)/1426, HH to Lord Bruce, 9 December 1765.

14 WSA, 9/35/165(1)/1109, HH to Lord Bruce, 23 December 1765.

15 WSA, 1300/2948, HH to Lord Bruce, 11 May 1776; WSA, 1300/4671, HH to Lord Ailesbury, 16 June 1781.

16 Powys 1776, fols 15–16.

17 Gamba 1824 (Rezzònico 1787), p. 23, 'over sceptres and crowns raise your skirt'.

18 Gilpin 1798, p. 122.

19 The Bristol Cross, 1812–16, by Francis Nicholson (1753–1844), pencil and watercolour, 360 × 210 mm. BM (1872,1012.3377).

20 Britton 1801, vol. II, p. 19, claiming the Cross to be 'the most interesting building here; and for richness of execution, and fine preservation, is probably unequalled by any now remaining in England'.

21 *Southern Times and Dorset County Herald*, 10 May 1879.

22 NT archive records, 45805, Wx.02:65, Stourhead Garden file, National Trust Solicitor to Wessex Regional Agent, 3 March 1975, concerning request from Bristol City Council to return the Cross.

23 Stourhead Annals, vol. II, 1894–95, 'The Bristol Cross being in a most dangerous condition and in imminent danger of falling down was restored by Messrs Harry Hems of Exeter at the cost of £500. The work was carried out under the superintendence of Mr Ponting as Architect and was completed in February 1895'; WSA 383/944, report on condition of the Cross by C. E. Ponting, 7 September 1894.

24 Dodd 1980.

25 WSA, 9/35/165(1)/1109, HH to Lord Bruce, 23 December 1765.

26 WSA, 9/35/165(1)/1421, HH to Lord Bruce, 13 December 1765.

27 View from the Temple of Apollo, 1770–80, by C. W. Bampfylde (1720–91), pencil, 340 × 940 mm. V&A (E.387–1949).

28 'Gardens at Stourhead from ye Pantheon', view of the Temple of Flora, *Neptune and his horses*, Stone Bridge, Stourton village and Temple of Apollo, 1770–80, by C. W. Bampfylde (1720–91), pencil and grey wash, 275 × 752 mm. V&A (E.382–1949).

29 HH Ledger 1749–70, 30 April 1766.

30 Parnell 1769, vol. II, fols 82–83.

31 Gamba 1824 (Rezzònico 1787), p. 23.

32 McKewan 2006, pp. 58–62.

33 'A View from the Mount of Diana in Mr Hoare's Garden at Stourton in Wiltshire', c.1773, unknown, etching and engraving, 115 × 198 mm. Anonymous 1774, vol. II, opposite p. 304.

34 Stourhead Annals, vol. II, 1907–8. The name

'Turner's Paddock' probably originated from the tenant of the mill. WSA, 383/748, agreement of 2 August 1735 between HH and Robert Turner for 'Stourton Mills', leased for 21 years at £22 p. a. 'Mill and Mill House called Cascade Mill beside Black Mead'.

35 'Lit B. Approximate appearance of the lake pent up between three hills in Banker Hoare's pleasure park at Stourton near Bristol, drawn on the spot in 1779 by F. M. Piper', pencil, ink and colourwash, 333 × 422 mm, annotated, 'K. Lower water that, in olden times, received the little stream that ran through the dale'. RAS (Pi - e 6, 1 bok [19]). 'Lit C. Part of Stourton Park at the dammed up Lake', by F. M. Piper (1746–1824), ink, colour wash and pencil, 336 × 422 mm, identified Turner's Paddock Lake as, 'low water in olden times'. RAS (Pi - e 6, 2).

36 Parnell 1769, fol. 93.

37 1785 plan of Stourhead.

38 Piper general plan 1779. Cascade, Turner's Paddock Lake and mill at Stourhead, 1793, by Lancelot-Henri Roland Turpin de Crissé (1754–c.1800), pencil, 230 × 370 mm. Musées d'Angers. (MTC 226).

39 Stourhead Annals, vol. I. 1811–12.

40 WSA, 9/35/165(1)/1109, HH to Lord Bruce, 23 December 1765, 'Messrs Bampfield & Hoare have made me an ingenious model for the Cascade like Mr Bampfields & as I have a Stone Quarr on the Hill just above it, I hope to finish it soon in the Summer'.

41 *The Cascade at Hestercombe, Somerset*, 1769–70, by John Inigo Richards, RA (1731–1810), oil on canvas, 53.3 × 63.5 cm (NT 732169). HH Ledger 1770–85, 11 October 1770, 'Mr Richards a Picture Mr Bame Cascade' £15–15s.

42 Tromp 1982 (van Spaen van Biljoen 1791), p. 50.

43 Skinner 1797, fol. 162.

44 Thelwall 1801 (1797), p. 105.

45 'Lit. C. Part of Stourton Park at the dammed up Lake', c. 1779, by F. M. Piper (1746–1824), ink, colour wash and pencil, 336 × 422 mm. RAS (Pi - e 6, 2[20]).

46 Parnell 1769, vol. II, fol. 90.

47 Anonymous ms 1765; Spence 1765, 'You go from hence [the Pantheon], by the side of the Lake & between the two waters, to an odd sort of ruinous Building, which hides the road; & over which you wind by roughish steps, toward the Walk of the Muses, & the temple of Apollo'.

48 The Dam, Rock Arch and Temple of Apollo, 1770–80, by C. W. Bampfylde (1720–91), black chalk, 250 × 470 mm. V&A (E.384–1949).

49 Parnell 1769, vol. II, fol. 90.

50 Anonymous 1780, pp. 14–15, lines 371–374.

51 Tromp 1982 (van Spaen van Biljoen 1791), p. 50.

52 HH Ledger 1749–70, 25 April 1755, 'Mr Flitcroft for The Pantheon &c and Subterrn Arch' £100.

53 WSA, 9/35/165(1)/1109, HH to Lord Bruce, 23 December 1765. The quotation is from Virgil, *Aeneid*, bk VI, line 126, 'easy is the descent to Avernus'.

54 Spence 1765. 'Lit. C. Part of Stourton Park at the dammed up Lake', c.1779, by F. M. Piper (1746–1824), ink, colour wash and pencil, 336 × 422 mm. RAS (Pi - e 6, 2[20]).

55 'Gardens at Stourhead from ye Pantheon', view of the Temple of Flora, *Neptune and his horses*, Stone Bridge, Stourton village and Temple of Apollo, 1770–80, by C. W. Bampfylde, pencil and grey wash, 275 × 752 mm. V&A (E.382–1949); also 'Part of the Pleasure grounds at Stourhead, Wiltsh. Augt. 1790', by S. H. Grimm (1733–94), ink, 190 × 270 mm. BL (Add MS 15,547, fol. 210).

56 Stourhead Annals, vol. I, 1792, 'Planted the Hill on which the Temple of Apollo stands'; ibid., 1794 and 1797–8. View from the dam towards the Temple of Flora and Stourton village, watercolour, 399 × 555 mm: View across the Stone Bridge with the Temple of Apollo and the Pantheon beyond, watercolour, 404 × 554 mm, both 1812–16, by Francis Nicholson (1753–1844). BM (1944,1014.134 and 137). For the distant prospect, View of the Obelisk, Temple of Apollo and the Garden Lake, 1812–16, by Francis Nicholson, watercolour, 403 × 557 mm. BM (1944,1014.148).

57 View from the Temple of Apollo, *c*.1770, by C. W. Bampfylde (1720–91), pencil, 340 × 940 mm. V&A (E.387–1949).

58 Spence 1765, 'The Obelisk, & Turkish Tent, in the old (Bridgman) part of the Gardens; – the Palladian Bridge; – the Grotto; – the Pantheon; – the Parish Church, Bristol Cross, & Gothic Temple; & the Lake, & Woods all round it'.

59 Tromp 1982 (van Spaen van Biljoen 1791), p. 50.

60 HH Ledger 1749–70, 19 June 1766, 'H Flitcroft Esqr for Temple of Apollo Alfreds Tower &c in full vide' £100. WSA, 9/35/165(1)/1426, HH to Lord Bruce, 9 December 1765. 'The Temple of Apollo was finishd last Week & the Scaffolds are now taking down & it charms every body'. Fitting out the temple occupied another year and more: Anonymous ms 1766, fol. 33, 'the Temple of Apollo, an elegant building (unfinished 1766)'.

61 Ware 1738, bk IV, pls 34–36 and 65–68, for the Temples of Vesta in Rome and at Tivoli. Wood 1757, pl. 44 for Baalbek. HH Ledger 1749–70, 26 April 1757, 'Plans &c of Balbeck pd Lord Dungarvan' £3–15s.

62 Polwarth 1776. Woodbridge 2001, p. 55. Chambers 1763, p. 3; pls 5 and 6.

63 Warner 1801 (1800), p. 112.

64 Stourhead Annals, vol. I, 1835–7; Hoare 1844, vol. V, p. 16. 'On 22d of July 1837, the Temple of the Sun was set on fire by the incautious use of fire applied to dislodge a swarm of bees. The roof was entirely destroyed, but the damage was shortly after repaired'. Stourhead Annals, vol. I, 1853.

65 The Stone Bridge and Temple of Apollo, 1901. *Country Life* photographic archive (Stourhead L2622_2).

66 Stourhead Annals, vol. III, 1926–7, 1928–9, 1938–9.

67 Spence 1765.

68 WSA, 383/4/1, bill to HH from John Cheere, 1766, total with packing £233–2s–11d. Receipted 19 January 1767.

69 Oliver 1972 (Curwen 1776), vol. I, p. 231.

70 Gamba 1824 (Rezzònico 1787), pp. 21–22.

71 Stourhead Annals, vol. II, July 1903 to July 1904, 'Three lead Statues by Rysbrack were moved from the Pantheon and Sun Temples and placed on each corner and top of the Portico [east] at my wife's suggestion'; ibid., vol. II, 1905–6, 'four lead statues by Rysbrack were placed there [Saloon French window] which had been removed for that purpose from the Sun Temple'. Taken in the order of Cheere's bill: *Vestal Virgin*, west front of Stourhead (NT 562884); *Ceres*, east pediment (NT 731879); *Pomona/Flora*, east pediment (NT 731880); *Minerva*, east pediment (NT 731878); *Venus*, Pantheon exterior (NT 562878); *Urania*, west front (NT 562883); *Mercury*, west front (NT 562881); *Apollino*, west front (NT 562882); *Bacchus*, Pantheon exterior (NT 562879).

72 Stourhead Annals, vol. II, July 1907 to July 1908, 'Two copies of the lead Statues in front of big Dining room were executed by Thos Rudge, Sculptor, and put in the niches of the Sun Temple.' *Urania* 1907–8, by Thomas Rudge (1868–1942), after John Cheere, stone, H 157.5 cm (NT 562918) the right arm placed against the body to fit the niche; *Vestal Virgin*, 1907–8, by Thomas Rudge, after John Cheere, stone, H 158 cm (NT 562917).

73 Spence 1765, 'It is to be lighted from the top of the Dome [*which wou'd not admit of a Statue, in the middle, Mr Hoar* inserted]. In the context this is William Hoare of Bath.

74 Warner 1801 (1800), p. 112, 'A large cast statue of the Belvedere Apollo occupies the interior'. Tromp 1982 (van Spaen van Biljoen 1791), p. 50.

75 Woodbridge 1978, p. 53, citing DZSWS MSS (mislaid February 2020), Sir Richard Colt Hoare, 1834, 'On succeeding to this Estate... The South front... where there was a spacious lawn... terminated by the colossal statue of Apollo raised on an artificial mount... I have succeeded... by the removal of the magnus Apollo'.

76 Spence 1765.

77 A large curved bench, the back panel painted with the *Aurora*, *c*.1765, by William Hoare RA (1707–92), pine and oil on board, 132 × 222.5 × 67.5 cm (NT 562873). The painting derived from *Aurora* by Guido Reni and *Dance to the Music of Time* by Nicolas Poussin. Dodd 2007. Perhaps HH Ledger 1749–70, 9 May 1765 'Mr Wm Hoare for 4 Aura, Nymphs, Busto Draw'gs &c' £300.

78 Hoare 1822, p. 67.

79 WSA 9/35/165(1)/1423, HH to Lord Bruce, 6 July 1765.

80 Bettany 1919 (Jerningham 1777), pp. 18–19.

81 'Lit. C. Part of Stourton Park at the dammed up Lake', *c*. 1779, by F. M. Piper (1746–1824), ink, colour wash and pencil, 336 × 422 mm. RAS (Pi - e 6, 2[20].

82 Warner 1801 (1800), p. 112.

83 Miller 2010, p. 207; *The hermitage at Barn Elms*, 1817, after J. C. Nattes (1765–1839), ink and sepia wash. Richmond upon Thames Local Studies Library (LCP/2541).

84 Cartwright 1888 (Pococke 1754), vol. II, pp. 40–41.

85 WSA, 9/35/165(2)/1478, HH to Henrietta (Harriot) Boyle, 30 November 1771.

86 Ellis 1907 (Fanny Burney 1773), vol. II, p. 322.

87 Gamba 1824 (Rezzònico 1787), p. 20.

88 Piper 1812, p. 133. 'Plan and profile of the Hermitage called the Druid's Cell in Stourton Park, Hermitage ', *c*.1779, by F. M. Piper (1746–1824), watercolour, pencil, ink and colourwash, 432 × 280 mm. RAS (Pi - e 6, 6 bok [23]).

89 'Interior of the Hermitage' and 'the innermost part of the retreat, called The Druid's Cell; 'Entrance to the Druid's Cell, or Hermitage, in the Park at Stourton'. All *c*.1779, by F. M. Piper (1746–1824), ink and sepia wash, each 200 × 158 mm. RAS (Pi - e 6, 6 a tergo (3) [24] and (Pi - e 6, 6 bok (4) [24]).

90 Wrighte 1767, pp. 3–4, description of pl. 3 'elevation of an Hermit's Cell'.

91 Fenton 1811 (1807), p. 209. Stourhead Annals, vol.I, 1814–15.

92 Dodd 2007.

93 Clarke (1777).

94 WSA, 1300/4283, HH to Lord Ailesbury, 6 September 1778.

95 'Parasol entourné d'un Siege', 1812, by F. M. Piper (1746–1824), ink and colour wash, 210 × 215 mm, a comparable design. From Piper 1812 p. 48. The illustration opposite p. 45 is an ornate version. RAS (Pi-6 mm).

96 *Stourhead Pleasure Grounds, Wiltshire, view to the Pantheon*, *c*.1775, by C. W. Bampfylde (1720–91), watercolour, 360 × 546 mm. (NT 730729).

97 Parnell 1769, vol. II, fols 88–89.

98 Hardy 1979, p. 119, fig.3.

99 Powys 1776, fol. 18. 'Druidical Seat at Stourhead. Wilts Aug 1790', by S. H. Grimm (1733–94), ink, 265 × 182 mm. BL (Add. MS. 15,547/212); 'Druidical Seat in the Pleasure Ground of Stourhead. Wilts Augt [1790]', by S.H. Grimm (1733–94), ink, 262 × 185 mm. BL (Add. MS.15,547/213).

100 Ellis 1907 (Fanny Burney 1773), vol. II, p. 322.

The Regency Garden

1 The Temple of Apollo from the north end of the lake with the Wooden Bridge, 1792, by Amos Green (1735–1807), pencil and watercolour, 190 × 267 mm. Annotated 'Stourhead Augst 1792. The trees are in general rather formal, the water trim, & artificial in its appearance. The whole scene wants the simple grace of nature, but it is a highly decorated & amusing piece of art.' (NT 732386).

2 Polwarth 1776, 'From the garden front [lawn] you turn on your right hand through some old-fashion'd avenues which are still left'. Stourhead Annals, vol. I, 1793; Hoare 1822, p. 64.

3 Woodbridge 1970, p. 146; Woodbridge 1976.

4 Loudon 1835, p. 336.

5 Woodbridge 1976, p. 100; WSA, 383/57 Miller & Sweet, St Michaels Hill, Bristol, 22 November 1791, '1 Rhododendron ponticum' 3s 6d; Stourhead Annals, vol. I, 1830–1, Completed the plantation of rhododendrons in the Gardens round the Lake (North Side)'.

6 Stourhead Annals, vol. I, 1792, 'Made the New Gravel Walk from the upper part of the Gardens, to the side of the Lake & Palladian Bridge'; 1793, 'Made a Gravel Walk from the Temple of Flora to the Village by the Cross. Another from the Stone Bridge to the Rock Arch'; 1794, 'Laid out the New Gravel Walk on the Pond Head leading to the Grotto'; 1796, 'New Walk formed along the Terrace where the Turkish Tent formerly stood, and leading down to the Park Bottom'.

7 Ibid., vol. I, 1797–8, 'In the Summer 1798 I

took down the Palladian Bridge... made a new walk round the Water - NB this upper part of the Garden was before unconnected with the rest'; 1792, listed 'Diana's Bason' as fished and restocked.

8   Fenton 1811 (1807) p. 206.
9   Simond 1817 (1810), pp. 261–262.
10 Graves 1779, vol. II, pp. 8–9.
11 Hoare 1822, pp. 65–66.
12 Woodbridge 1978, p. 53, citing WANHS MSS (mislaid February 2020), RCH 1834, 'I have succeeded ... by the removal of the magnus Apollo'.
13 Hoare 1822, p. 66.
14 WSA, 383/4/144, Charles Harcourt Masters [architect] to RCH, 14 September 1799, 'For a plan and Elevations of the old Conduit at Wells with an Estimate of taking down & rebuilding the same – Carriage &c Also attendance at Stourton to find a Situation for the said Conduit &c &c And Expences for two Days £4–4s'; Britton 1830, pp. 70–71.
15 Stourhead Annals, vol. I, 1794.
16 McKewan 2006, p. 99, fig. 86.
17 WSA, 383/57/1, bill for replacement craft dated 3 January 1822, 'James Hill & Co. Nova Scotia Yd, Bristol | New Boat 17 feet long Built of Oak & Copper fastned with 3 Coats of Paint & 2 Ash Sculls at 25s pr foot' £27–5s | 'New Fishing Boat at 14 feet long Built of Oak & Copper fastned with 3 Coats of Paint 2 Ash Sculls & Boat hook at 25s pr foot' £17–10s.
18 WSA, 9/35/165(1)/2353, HH to Lady Bruce, July 1765.
19 Fenton 1811 (1807), p. 206.
20 C. Hoare & Co., HFM/9/7–9, Francis Faugoin to HH, 2 March 1782.
21 Graves 1779, vol. II, pp. 11–12.
22 The Pantheon and Watch Cottage, c.1770–80, by C. W. Bampfylde (1720–91), black chalk and Chinese white, 540 × 510 mm. V&A (E.390–1949). 1785 plan of Stourhead.
23 Hoare 1818, p. 24. Stourhead Annals, vol. I, 1806–7, 'Added a Gothic porch to the Garden Cottage and turned the walk to it'. WSA, 383/907/3, John Carter to RCH, 1806, 'I doubt I do not sufficiently understand your instructions about the Cottage and Porch... It is possible to do the Porch in town under my eye, and then sent down by the waggon'. The porch was perhaps designed for the Gardener's House, not the cottage. Woodbridge 1978, p. 32. The Pantheon and Watch Cottage, watercolour, 401 × 550 mm and Watch Cottage, watercolour, 531 × 429 mm. Both 1812–16, by Francis Nicholson (1753–1844). BM (1944,1014.129 and 130).
24 Skinner 1808, fol. 161 verso.
25 WSA, 1300/2944, HH to Lady Bruce, 24 May 1776, 'The Dear Charles [his three-year old grandson, Charles Brudenell-Bruce] is as stout as a Buck has shook off his Cold & trudges down to Mary Faugoins with His Wagon twice a Day & has found out The easy path to & from it'.
26 Powys 1776, fol. 16.
27 Skinner 1808, fol. 161.
28 Stourhead Annals, vol. I, 1813–14.

29 Ibid., vol. I, 1808–9.
30 'View of Stourhead Wilts 1811', by John Buckler (1770–1851), pencil, 257 × 368 mm. BL, (Add MS 36.392, Buckler Architectural Drawings, vol. XXXVII /164). The Gardener's House, 1812–16, by Francis Nicholson (1753–1844), watercolour, 400 × 552 mm. BM (1944,1014.128).
31 Stourhead Annals, vol. I, 1813–14.
32 St Peter's Church, Stourton, 1793, by Lancelot-Henri Roland Turpin de Crissé (1754–c.1800), pencil, 210 × 340 mm. Musées d'Angers. (MTC 221). Clark 2013. St Peter's Church, Stourton, signed 'F.R.G', pencil sketch, 134 × 168 mm (NT 730698).
33 Stourhead Annals, vol. I, 1812–13, 'Pulled down a lot of Cottages that stood very disadvantageously between the Church and the Cross and Gardens'.
34 WSA, 383/911, George Ashley bill for RCH, 2 December 1814 for erecting at St Peter's Church a stone cross and railing, £45–4s–½ d. WSA, 383/4/3, George Ashley bill, September 1815, at the church, a stone seat and coat of arms for the Spread Eagle Inn, £136–2s–10d. Stourhead Annals, vol. I, 1815–16, 'Put up a new Cross on the pedestal of the old one in the parish Church Yard – also a gothic stone seat for the people assembled on Sundays to rest upon.'; 1817–18, 'My Masons were employed in erecting a chapel over the tombs of my honor'd Grandfather, Henry Hoare, and Jane Benson his mother'; 1819–20. 'A large Sepulchral Vault decorated with a Gothic Porch [Note The structure of this vault & Mausoleum cost about £50 inserted]'. Colvin 2008, pp. 804–805. I am grateful to Julian Orbach for drawing Pinch to my attention.
35 Stourhead Annals, vol. I, 1812–13, 'Began to build a new range of Stabling and Coach houses at Stourton Inn'. 'North West View of the Inn at Stourton Oct 4th 1817', by John Buckler (1770–1851), pencil, 260 × 355 mm. BL (Add MS 36.392, Buckler Architectural Drawings, vol. XXXVII, fol. 190).
36 Ibid., vol. I, 1815–16, 'Altered the sign of Stourton Inn, from that of the river Stour, to the Spread Eagle – the family arms – put up the same cut in stone on one of the inn buildings – also two Eagle heads – on the gate piers'.
37 Ibid., vol. I, 1832–3, 'Commenced a new room at the Spread eagle Inn'.
38 WSA, 383/57, George Ashley bill to RCH included, on 10 May 1824 for a 'Stone Seat' £25 which could refer to the seat drawn by Buckler.
39 Stourhead Annals, vol. I, 1825–6, 'Laid out a new flower garden near the Cross'.
40 Neale 1823, vol. V, 'Stourton village, adjoining Stourhead, is seated in a low dell, the fronts of most of the houses are covered with roses, jessamines, and varieties of the clematis'.
41 Loudon, vol. XI, 1835, pp. 336–337.
42 Hazlitt 1824, pp. 137–138.
43 Stourhead Annals, vol. I, chronological list of lodges built: the Terrace, two (1792), Hilcomb, two (1792), North Drive (1799–1800), Turnpike (1799–1800), Alfred's Tower two (1800–1), Clock Arch (1802–3), Penn (1805–6), Whitesheet (1805–6), Drove (1811–12), Kingswood (1829–30),

Terrace (1841). WSA, 383/250, Sir RCH list of lodges, 1833: 'Alfreds Lodge – late Coy's, Tower Lodges, Stourton Lodge, Drove Lodge, Whitesheet Lodge, Penn Lodge, Hilcomb Lodge, Kilmington Lodge, Kingswood Lodge – [built inserted], Terrace Lodge – intended'.
44 Woodbridge 1970, p. 131.
45 WSA, 383/907, Willey Reveley to RCH, 25 February 1793, alterations to design for lodge. The Exhibition of the Royal Academy, 1793, catalogue, p. 22, no. 774, 'Lodges at Stourhead' by W. Reveley.
46 Stourhead Annals, vol. I.1844.
47 www.stourtonhistory.org/census_1851 - 1871 (accessed 30 August 2018).
48 Stourhead Annals, vol. I, 1811–12.
49 Ibid., vol. I, 1852.
50 Ibid., vol. I, 1841.
51 Parker 1848.
52 WSA, 383/4 /225, William Wilkins's letter to RCH and bill, 1815, 'Design for a Grecian lodge in No 4 finished drawings viz. Plan two Elevations and perspective view – time 10 days 5 Gs per diem £52–10s' | 'paid Mr Feilding for the Landscape to the perfection £8–8s', total £60–18s.
53 Stourhead Annals, vol. I, 1799–1800.
54 Ibid., vol. I, 1802–3.
55 Ibid., vol. I, 1821–2, 'Commenced a new piece of Water at Gasper, of 14 acres on ground truly adapted by nature for the purpose'.
56 Ibid., vol. III, 1916–17.
57 Western Gazette, 6 July 1917.
58 Stourhead Annals, vol. III, 1917–18; Ibid., 1918–20. 'After careful consideration it was decided to restore the dam head with the object of enabling the road to be renewed to Gasper as the District Council [declined inserted] to do anything beyond restoring the surface of the road. The lake will of course greatly add to the beauty of the valley besides being a reservoir for trout fishing and a preventative to sudden floods'; ibid., 1921–2 and 1924–5.

The Victorian and Edwardian Garden

1   Stourhead Annals, vol. II, 1897–8, named Sinton, aged 88, as the forester for thirty-six years.
2   Stourhead Archive, painted noticeboard.
3   Salisbury and Winchester Journal, advertisements from May 1857 to 1864 and on 22 May 1869: 'We understand that Sir Henry Hoare has given instructions that the mansion at Stourhead and the beautiful grounds shall be opened to the visitors on any day when the family is not at home. The rhododendrons are now in beautiful bloom.'
4   Salisbury and Winchester Journal, 13 June 1868, account of Wincanton Grand Masonic fete at Stourhead; Taunton Courier, 21 August 1878, Somerset Archaeological and Natural History Society; Bristol Mercury, 19 July 1883, Canynge Druidic Independent Society; Central Somerset Gazette, 22 September 1883, Glastonbury volunteer fire brigade.
5   Western Gazette, 6 September 1907, advertisement.
6   Stourhead Annals, vol. III, 1933–44, £67–19s–6d sent to the Queen's Institute of District Nursing. The annual charity openings continued up to the Second World War.

7 Ibid., vol. II, 1895–6, 67 beech trees planted; 1897–8, 187; 1899–1900, 86; 1902–3, 300; 1903–4, 1,000; 1905–6, 450; 1907–8, 6,700; ibid., vol. III, 1908–9, 7,000; 1910–1911, 5,800.

8 Ibid., vol. II, 1899–1900 and 1901–2.

9 Ibid., vol. III, 1908–9, 'A large rhododendron was cleared out in front of the Pantheon and the lawn which had always existed there re-instated. Also other large rhododendrons were cut between the Pantheon and the Grotto. The laurels at the back of the Pantheon, extending from there to the Watch Cottage were also cut.'; ibid., 1913–14, 'On each side of the stone bridge huge clumps of Rhododendrons, which had greatly overgrown and blocked the view, were removed; also several Conifers from the lawn in front of the bridge. On the Sun Temple [of Apollo] side of the grounds clumps of laurel and Rhododendrons were removed, greatly improving the appearance, which had become overgrown'.

10 Stourhead Archive, Alda, Lady Hoare's Diaries, 3 June 1917.

11 Ibid., 27 May 1923.

12 Stourhead Annals, vol. III, 1927–8.

13 Ibid., vol. III, 1932–3

14 Ibid, vol. I, 1839; Hoare 1844, p. 16.

15 *Stourhead Pleasure Grounds, Wiltshire, view to the Pantheon*, c.1775, by C. W. Bampfylde (1720–91), watercolour, 360 × 546 mm. (NT 730729).

16 Stourhead Annals, vol. I, 1811–12, 'New bridge of Stone in the Gardens near the Pantheon'.

17 *The Pantheon and Gothic Cottage*, 1812–16, by Francis Nicholson (1753–1844), watercolour, 401 × 550 mm. BM (1944,1014.129).

18 Stourhead Annals, vol. I, 1842, 'The old Foot Bridge in the Garden by the Pantheon taken up, and a new one of Oak laid down'.

19 Ibid., vol. II, 1859–60, 'A new Iron Bridge erected in the Gardens (Lower) cast by Messrs Maggs and Hindley July 1860'.

20 Ibid., vol. II, 1894–5.

21 Stourhead Archive, Alda, Lady Hoare's Diaries, July 1895.

22 Stourhead Annals, vol. II, 1907–8.

23 Fenton 1811 (1807), p. 208.

24 Stourhead Annals, vol. II, 1895–6, 'the Spring near the Pantheon was converted into a small ornamental Well'. Stourhead Archive, Alda, Lady Hoare's Diaries, 21 November 1916, 26 February, 14 June 1917.

25 Stourhead Annals, vol. I, 1848, 'An Hydraulic Ram, by Roe of London was this year erected below the Cascade at the Rock Arch, to supply with water the Mansion and Stourton Farm'.

26 Ibid., vol. II, 1897–8, 'a new Turbine Water Wheel... pumped to the amount of 10,000 gallons a day... executed in a very satisfactory manner by Mr Lauder [?] of Mere was about £400'.

27 WSA, 383/57, perhaps the bill from George Ashley, 1 March 1824, 'Working one Stone Watering Trough £11-0-0; Trough, lined with Lead £2-10s'.

28 Stourhead Annals, vol. II, 1903–4, 'A contract was entered into for a 150,000 gallon reservoir to supply the house and insure protection from fire'; ibid., 1906–7, 'A new and more powerful Water Wheel was put up in the place of the existing one,

by Messrs Hindley at a cost of £136 guaranteed to deliver 10,000 gallon a day to the reservoir near Alfreds Tower'.

29 Ibid., vol. III, 1920–1, 'a new over shot water wheel and [a] three throw pump were erected on the lower side of the road by the Rock Arch, giving an additional supply of 11,000 gallons per diem to the Reservoir – This work was executed by Messrs Hindley & Sons of Bourton under the direction of Messrs Hal Williams & Co, as Engineers, at a total cost of £1,400'.

30 Ibid., vol. III, 1938–9, 'Though the breaking of the crankshaft the upper set of Pumps at Rock Arch were smashed & new Pumps made by Green & Carter, guaranteed to pump 12,000 gallons per 24 hours, were installed by J. Wallis Titt[?] & Co. at a cost of £150. After installation the pumps did not deliver the above quantity of water it was found that the power pipe had become corroded & was not supplying the necessary flow to drive the wheel. A new power pipe was fixed at a cost of £14–15[s]–0'.

31 Ibid., vol. III, 1945–6, 'The installation of the Hathorn Davey Pump and the Engine at the Rock Arch pumping station was carried out during the Autumn of 1945. The pump proved satisfactory in its work and was able to raise a greater quantity of water then could be gathered in the present collecting chamber... The total cost of the above work including that to the Reservoir and the new pump house and laying the new main & collecting chamber was £915–4[s]–4[d]'.

Stourhead House and Precinct

1 Stourhead Annals, vol. II, 1857–59, probably part of the renovations by the 5th Baronet.

2 Campbell 1725, vol. III, pls 41–43.

3 Ibid, pl. 48, Pembroke House; pls 35–38, Mereworth; pl. 46, Baldersby.

4 'South West View of Stourhead, Wilts. July 1811', by John Buckler (1770–1851), pencil, 260 × 365 mm. BL (Add MS 36.392, Buckler Architectural Drawings, vol. XXXVII, fol. 149).

5 C. Hoare & Co., HFM/4/7, 'An Account of House Hold Expenses att Stourton', March 1723–October 1724, 6 March 1723/4, 'Insuring Stourton House' £16–17s–6d.

6 WSA, 383/58, account book for Stourhead 1717–28, payments to Ireson £1,060; C. Hoare & Co., 'An Account... for Building my House &c att Stourton', April 1720–January 1723/4 payments to Ireson, £7,000.

7 TNA, Prob 11/602/173, will of Henry Hoare (d. 1724/5).

8 C. Hoare & co., HB/5/A/4, Partners' Ledger, 1725–34, HH account, 28 January 1726/7, 'Collen Campbell' £192–6s.

9 WSA, 383/907(1), Henry Flitcroft to HH, 18 August 1744.

10 Parnell 1769, vol. II, fol. 106, a sketch plan of the house.

11 Stourhead Annals, vol. I, 'Quid feci? In the year 1792 I commenced adding two wings to my house: the Southern one intended for a library; the Northern for a Picture Gallery'.

12 WSA 383/66, RCH, sundry building accounts

1792–1805; 383/57, Thomas Atkinson to RCH, 23 October 1806.

13 Stourhead Annals, vol. I, 1814–15, 'Began to build a new conservatory adjoining the house'; ibid., 1816–17, 'Removed the Conservatory from the Kitchen garden to the vicinity of my house, and made a communication from on to the other'. The 1889 OS 25 inch map, LXII/4, marked a narrow glasshouse.

14 Stourhead Annals, vol. I, 1838, 'In August was commenced the building of the Corinthian Portico at the House, Mr Parker being the Architect'; ibid., 1839, 'The building of the Portico finished'. 'Mansion house at Stourhead Wiltshire JB 1840', by John Buckler (1770–1851), pencil, 237 × 333 mm. BL (Add MS 36.392, Buckler Architectural Drawings, vol. XXXVII, fol 154).

15 'Stourhead House. Wiltshire The Seat of Sir Richard Colt Hoare Bart. Oct 1st 1817', by John Buckler (1770–1851), pencil, 260 × 355 mm. BL (Add MS 36.392, Buckler Architectural Drawings, vol. XXXVII, fol. 151).

16 Stourhead Annals, vol. II, 1895–6, 'The large Conservatory running from the West corner of the House parallel with the Library was pulled down it being very much out of repair and in my opinion a great eyesore'; ibid., 1896–7, 'Mr Doran Webb of Salisbury drew out the Plan of the Terrace which was completed July/97. The stone doorway leading out of the House being removed from the passage leading along the North Court towards the Larders & placed where it now stands leading out on to the Terrace. The work being executed by Avery of Mere at a cost of about £200'.

17 Dodd 1979.

18 Stourhead Annals, vol. II, July 1902 to July 1903, 'The old West Front consisted of green sandstone which was much damaged by the fire, so it was pulled down to the level of the basement floor and rebuilt, using the green sandstone [sic]. From the basement to the ground floor level and above the work was executed to Mr Webb's design in Doulting Stone'.

19 Ibid., 1903–4, 'a statue of Mars from Dijon (*by Jean Goujon* inserted) 16th century moved from an old Palace in Dijon was placed on the top of the new [west] front of the large Dining room'; ibid., 1905–6, on the west front, 'In the spring of this year the new approach to the big Dining room was designed by Sir Aston Webb and executed by Messrs Avery of Mere at a cost of £340 and four lead statues by Rysbrack were placed there which had been removed for that purpose from the Sun Temple'; ibid., July 1902 to July 1903, 'Three lead Statues by Rysbrack were moved from the Pantheon and Sun Temples and placed on each corner and top of the [east] Portico at my wife's suggestion'.

20 'East Front Stourhead house, Wilts. AD 1724', pencil, 152 × 228 mm; 'South Front. Sketched from two old Paintings at Stourhead. October 1817. Traced Jan 7 1823', pencil, 152 × 228 mm, both by John Buckler (1770–1851). BL (Add MS 36.392, Buckler Architectural Drawings, vol. XXXVII, fol. 148) annotated 'Sketched from two old Paintings at Stourhead October 1817. Traced Jan 7. 1823.' From these derive two watercolours,

'East View of Stourhead House AD' and 'South View of Stourhead House', both by John Buckler in Stourhead Archive (NT 3204200); Hoare 1819. A second version of 'South View of Stourhead House 1724', 1817, watercolour, 155 × 233 mm. (DZSWS 1990.590). WSA 383/4/3, Buckler's bill, 8 October 1817, '2 Drawings Old Stourhead House'.

21 Parnell 1769, vol. II, fol. 107, sketch plan; fol. 100, 'The Lawn is but small till the Road crosses, but its Reassumed beyond the Road'.

22 Stourhead Annals, vol. II, 1896–7, 'The whole of the Carriage Drive from the Kilmington Lodge was re-gravelled, and an avenue of Lime Trees planted where necessary along it'.

23 Hoare 1822, p. 63, the trees described as of 'very great age'. NT Gardens Survey 1981, pp. 28–29 and 31–32.

24 Stourhead Annals, vol. III, 1926–7.

25 'East Front Stourhead house, Wilts. AD 1724', 1817, by John Buckler (1770–1851), pencil, 152 × 228 mm BL (Add MS 36.392, Buckler Architectural Drawings, vol. XXXVII, fol. 148); Stourhead Archive, Hoare 1819, with a watercolour taken from this drawing. WSA 383/4/3, Buckler's bill 8 October 1817, '2 Drawings Old Stourhead House'.

26 C. Hoare & Co., HFM/4/7, 'An Account... for Building my House &c att Stourton', April 1720–January 1723/4, payment on 19 April 1721. WSA, 383/58, account book for Stourhead 1717–28, Joshua Cox's account, logs further payments to Switzer, 31 March 1724, 'Mr Switzer upon Accot' £4–4s and, 27 August 1724, 'Cash pd Switzar in full' £2–2s.

27 C. Hoare & Co., HFM/4/7, 'An Account... for Building my House &c att Stourton', payment on 19 April 1721.

28 Ibid., HFM/4/7, Good Henry Hoare 'An Account of money paid for Gardning & Planting att Stourton', 18 February 1721/2, 'Nich. Parker for Plain trees & fruit trees' £12–15s; 2 March 1721/2, 'Obadiah Lowe for 1000 Asparaguss plan[ts]' £1–2s; 6 July 1722, 'Mr Bernard for fruit trees' £7–11s–2d.

29 HH Ledger 1734–49, 2 May 1745, 'Mr Cheere for Apollo & Diana & ye 2 Packing Cases in full' £51–5s. Apollo Belvedere, marble version is a Roman copy of a Greek bronze of the mid-fourth century BC at the Museo Pio-Clementino, Musei Vaticani (1015).

30 Anonymous 1764 (Stourton Gardens 1749), p. 103.

31 Cartwright 1888, (Pococke 1754), vol. II, p. 43, 'To the South of the house is a lawn with a piece of water, and from that a winding descent'.

32 Woodbridge 1978, p. 53, citing DZSWS MSS (mislaid February 2020), RCH 1834, 'On succeeding to this Estate... The South front... where there was a spacious lawn... terminated by the colossal statue of Apollo raised on an artificial mount... I have succeeded... by the removal of the magnus Apollo'.

33 Stourhead: the South Front, c.1860, attr. Frances Annette Hoare (1822–1904), oil on canvas, 72 × 87 cm. (NT 732307).

34 Stourhead Annals, vol. II, 1859–60, 'Fountain erected by G. P. White Pimlico on the Lawn in front of Lady Hoare['s] window May 1860'; ibid., 1896–7, 'the two windows looking onto the Italian Garden were opened in the Library'.

35 WSA, 1300/3264, HH to Lord Bruce, August 1765.

36 Beamon 1990, pp. 5 and 452–453.

37 Stourhead Annals, vol. III, 1937–8.

38 Parnell 1769, vol. II, fol. 107, sketch plan.

39 Stourhead Annals, vol. I, 1796, '[dug a] Stone Ha ha against [the Great] Oar'.

40 Ordnance Survey, Air Survey Branch, Stourhead (CK090).

41 Stourhead Annals, vol. I, 1842, 'A new Wall built, a new Gate-way made, and various alterations affected in the Back-yard and Offices at the Mansion'.

42 Woodbridge 1978, p. 12.

43 WSA, 383/737.

44 Stourhead Annals, vol. I, 1799, 'At the commencement of this Year, I began pulling down a large farm house and offices, situated at a short distance N.E. of my house – behind a large row of Beech trees'.

45 The Gatehouse at Stourhead, c.1770, by C. W. Bampfylde (1720–91), ink and watercolour, 157 × 220 mm. (Private Collection, illustrated White 1995, fig. 24).

46 Stourhead Annals, vol. I, 1799–1800.

47 Jackson 1854, p. 194.

48 Stourton 1899, vol. I, p. 495.

49 Jackson 1862, p. 390 and pl. 37.

50 Toynbee 1928 (Walpole 1762), p. 41.

51 Orbach 2014, p. 541.

52 Skinner, fol. 157 verso; Fenton 1811 (1807), p. 204; Hoare 1822, p. 63.

53 Stourhead Annals, vol. II, 1904–5, 'Four loose boxes were erected in the [back inserted] Park at a cost of £80 and the [back inserted] Park was divided into four Paddocks'.

54 Ibid., vol. I, 1849, 'The Coach House, Stabling, and Garden Wall at Stourhead were stripped of their thatch, new roofed and tiled'; ibid., 1852, 'Stable Yard. The lower [or South inserted] range of buildings newly Tiled. New Stalls erected, the Saddle room and the other Offices connected with the Stables improved and lighted by Semicircular windows'.

55 Ibid., vol. II, 1906–7, 'In the Stableyard the Granary was re-roofed and reconstructed, a fresh room for Stablemen was made and a New Motor house built adjacent to the present coach houses'; ibid., vol. III, 1925–6, 'Improvements to Stables were carried out, including the conversion of the Harness Room into Garage and two loose boxes into three'.

56 WSA, 9/35/165(1)/1423, HH to Lord Bruce, 6 July 1765, 'We have strawberrys here, 20 of each sort of which I wish were in H. F. Bs [Henrietta (Harriot) Boyle] merry mouth with a piece of Ice Cream at the Heals of Them, that's all the harm I wish Her'; ibid, 9/35/165(2)/1478, HH to Henrietta (Harriot) Boyle, 30 November 1771, 'I shall on Tuesday next send over to Tottenham Park 35 strong good Fruiting pine plants & each will have a Pot in case they should be sick in their Journey'; ibid., 1300/4292, HH to Lord Bruce, 15 May 1779, 'We are to have Green Peas for the first time today & Charles [Brudenell-Bruce] begins the feast, pepper proof'.

57 Stourhead Annals, vol. I, 1806–7.

58 NT Gardens Survey 1981, appendices 4–6 list trees and seeds purchased by RCH.

59 Fenton 1811 (1807), p. 204.

60 Stourhead Annals, vol. I, 1842, 'A double Pine House built, and a double Vinery formed from the old Geranium House and both fitted up and heated with Rogers' Patent Conical Boilers'.

61 OS 25 inch map, 1889, LXII/ 4.

62 OS 25 inch map, 1900, LXII/4. Stourhead Annals, vol. II, 1895–6, 'The following Works were carried out this year in the Kitchen Gardens and Stable Yard by Messrs Clarke of Bruton'. 'The whole of the Kitchen Garden walls were re-pointed and repaired throughout. The old Pine House and Vinery adjoining converted into a cold Peach House the whole being re-glazed, repainted and renewed. The Vinery was shortened and converted into 3 Forcing pits repaired, repainted and re-glazed throughout. The Green House Vinery and Plant Houses were re-glazed, repainted and repaired. New Boilers Pipe and Heating Apparatus were put in by Messrs Messenger of Loughborough to heat the Green houses and forcing pits. The Gardens were entirely replanted with 118 various Fruit trees, and new Vines put into the large Vinery'.

The Perimeter Drive

1 Hanway 1756, p. 92, 'Mr H**** has formed his plan for extending his walks upon the brow of the hill, through his park for near five miles. By this means he will take in the delightful views which Dorsetshire, Wiltshire and Somersetshire afford: these counties all meet in his grounds. Part of Hampshire is also to be seen, and contributes its share to heighten the charms of this august and captivating scene'.

2 WSA 1300/4298, HH to Lord Bruce, nd [1762].

3 Anonymous 1799, p. 79.

4 WSA, 383/907, ms note of distances, 12 September 1812, annotated by RCH.

5 Parnell 1769, vol. II, fols 109–110.

6 View of the Wooden Bridge and Obelisk, c.1770–80, by C. W. Bampfylde (1720–91), pen and grey wash, 280 × 760 mm. V&A (E.383–1949).

7 Fenton 1811 (1807), p. 196.

8 Parnell 1769, vol. II, fol. 111.

9 https//historicengland.org.uk/listing/the-list/list-entry/1001072 (accessed 2 May 2018).

10 https://historicengland.org.uk/listing/the-list/list-entry/1000110 (accessed 2 May 2018).

11 https//historicengland. org.uk/listing/the-list/list-entry/1000410 (accessed 28 July 2018).

12 Stourhead Annals, vol. I, 1796, 'A Plantation of Scotch Fir & Larch on the right & left hand of the Hills on each side of the Valley leading up to the Terras behind the new Barn at Six Wells'; 1797–8, 'Continued the plantations along the Park hanging. The one facing North was finished early in 1798 with Beech and Fir. The opposite one to the South with copse wood, was completed at the end of the year 1798'.

13 Gilpin 1798, p. 123.

14 WSA, 9/35/165(1)/1604, HH to Lord Bruce, 16 May 1767.

15 Bristol Streets Act 1765, 6 Geo III c.34, an act 'for widening several streets... within the city

of Bristol... St. Peter's cross and pump to be removed: Persons liable for repair of same, are to repair the new'.

16 WSA, 383/907(1), Thomas Tyndall to HH, 7 August 1766.

17 HH Ledger 1749–70, 14 March 1769, 'Thos Patty of Bristol for taking down & packg the Cross Paid – Vide my Fleet St act' £00. C. Hoare & Co., HB/5/A/8, Partners' Ledger, HH account, has no entry with a matching date; the closest being 20 December 1768, 'Thos Paty's bill to Jn Devall' £14–1s–10d. John Devall, the mason-sculptor had previously worked for HH.

18 WSA, 383/907(1), ms, 'At the Northwest part of the Church of St Peter in Bristol was from the earliest Times a fine Spring of Water & a Well sunk there for the accommodation of ye people & an Old Cross erected over. But in the Year 1631 the Old Cross was taken down, and... was repaird and new built'.

19 HH Ledger 1749–70, 21 March 1770, 'Mr Norris for the Copper Cross at 6 Wells' £6–10s.

20 Sweetman 1907, p. 33; NT archive records, 45520, Wx.02.67, Stourhead garden buildings, Caroe & Martin specification June 1986.

21 Stourhead Annals, vol. I, 1795, 'May. Began to a new cottage at Six Wells'; 'May Began building a Double Cottage at the Six Wells'; 'June. Began building a Barn at the same Spot. also formed a new Road on the side of the Hill leading from the Obelisk to the Six Wells'.

22 St Peter's Pump, 1812–16, by Francis Nicholson (1753–1844), watercolour, 404 × 552 mm. BM (1944,1014.139).

23 www.stourtonhistory.org/census_1841/1891 (accessed 30 August 2018).

24 Mayes 1996, p. 31.

25 Voltaire 1761, vol. I, p. 223, 'I do not know of a man more worthy of the respect by posterity than Alfred the Great who devoted himself wholeheartedly to his fatherland'.

26 WSA, 1300/4280.

27 Storer 1812, p. 4.

28 View towards Alfred's Tower, c.1760–70, by C. W. Bampfylde (1720–91), pen and colour wash, 270 × 380 mm. V&A (E.352–1949). In the watercolour Alfred's Tower is loosely drawn and is unlike the completed structure; indeed it resembles church towers for which Somerset is famous. White 1995, p. 10.

29 Worcestershire Archives and Archaeology Service, 899:310/BA10470/20, HH to Edward Knight the younger, Wolverley, near Kidderminster, 4 February 1766, 'Mr Flitcroft has drawn mine 50 feet Square [tower] & 150 high, according to Mr Bampfields opinion, the Angles being took off in the inside turns it into an Octagon there & one Corner is a Circular Staircase to go up to the Battlements... every body now are for Mass, & Bulk & a square Shape rather than one that diminishes as it will be seen all round at such a distance'. I am grateful to Michael Cousins for this reference.

30 HH Ledger 1749–70, 19 June 1766, 'H. Flitcroft Esqre for Temple of Apollo Alfreds Tower &c in full vide' £100.

31 Roberts 1997, p. 451, fig. 480, the first design for the Windsor Belvedere, c.1752. The Royal Collection

(RL17938B). Woodbridge 2001, p. 60.

32 WSA, 9/35/165(1)/1109, HH to Lord Bruce, 23 December 1765, 'if Your Lordship makes any Bricks near You I wish You could learn how much They fairly cost pr Thousand, Mr Sturt sent me 2 Brick-makers & they are now at work & I luckily found some excellent good Earth very handy'.

33 Hoare 1822, p. 68.

34 WSA, 1300/4280, HH to Lady Bruce, 23 October 1762, 'every 20 feet high will cost 50£ & it will be 4 years in hand about 75£ or £80 pr annm'.

35 Ellis 1907 (Fanny Burney 1773), p. 323.

36 Powys 1776, fol. 20.

37 Sweetman 1894, p. iv.

38 WSA, 9/35/165(2)/-, HH to Lady Bruce, 28 April 1770; WSA, 9/35/53, Francis Faugoin to Lord Bruce, 16 March 1771, 'if Your Lordship is not Provided with a Workman, the Bricklayer [here]... will not have much Business this Summer as we do not go on with Building Alfreds tower therefore could wait on you Lordship'.

39 The Bath Chronicle and Weekly Gazette, 22 October 1772.

40 'Alfred's Tower on the Terrace at Stourhead built by the late Henry Hoare Esqre, now the property of Richd Colt Hoare Esqre', c.1780, by Samuel Hieronymus Grimm (1733–94), ink and grey wash, 270 × 330 mm. (NT 733100) inscription on the backboard: '1944 (July) American Transport Plane flew into the Pinnacle of the Tower & demolished it. One wing of the Plane was cut off & plane crashed into Woods below Tower & caught fire. The two occupants were killed'.

41 WSA, 1300/4281, HH to Lord Bruce, 18 November 1762.

42 WSA, 9/35/165(2)/-, HH to Lady Bruce, 28 April 1770, 'A Young lad of 18 Mr Hoare sent from Bath has in 7 Weeks finishd the Figure of Alfred The Great 10 feet high from a Model given him to The admiration of all the Spectators'. Possibly C. Hoare & Co., HB/5/A/8, Partners Ledger 1764–83, HH Account, 3 September 1770, 'Mr Wm Hoare for Charles of Bath' £30.

43 Stourhead Annals, vol. I, 1827–8.

44 Mayes 1996, p.33.

45 Powys 1776, fol. 21.

46 Simond 1817 (1810), vol. I, p. 262.

47 Stourhead Annals, vol. I, 1827–8.

48 Kassler 2015 (Queen Charlotte 1789), vol. IV, p. 22.

49 WSA, 9/35/165(1)/1604, HH to Lord Bruce, 16 May 1767, '2 Saints are also arrived with the Virgin & 12 more', referring to the decoration of the Convent.

50 Kassler 2015 (Queen Charlotte 1789), vol. IV, p. 22.

51 The Convent, 1812–16, by Francis Nicholson (1753–1844), watercolour, 400 × 547 mm. BM (1944,1014.142).

52 Powys 1776, fol. 22.

53 Interior of Convent, 1938, Country Life photographic archive. (Stourhead 11577_8).

54 Graves 1779, vol. II, p. 13, 'pictures of the several orders of nuns and of saints, painted by that respectable artist Mr. Hoare of Bath'.

55 137 Stourhead Annals, vol. III, 1937–8, '15 Figures of Nuns at the Convent... restored by Mr Cecil Lawson and replaced during this year'.

56 Gamba 1824 (Rezzònico 1787), pp. 10–11.

57 Stourhead Archive, 'Catalogue of the principal Paintings & Drawings at Stourhead July 6th 1898', p. 21, Picture Gallery, 'Two "Triptych"; by Memling'. Triptych of the adoration of the Magi, c.1500, by Jan Provost (1462/5–1529), oil on panel, centre, 86.4 × 71.1 cm (NT 730686); Triptych of the adoration of the Magi, c.1518, attr. Jan van Dornicke (c.1470–1527), oil on panel, centre 87.6 × 55.2 cm (NT 732308).

58 The Madonna and Child, c.1767, attr. William Hoare RA (1707–92), after Raphael, oil on canvas, 76.2 × 63.5 cm. (NT 732334). Anonymous 1780, p. 11, lines 267–272, 'The Virgin-Parent and her human Son | Divine, masterly, placid, lib'ral ✳Hoare, | With tender, filial, and parental Looks | Has fill'd: His soft and feeling Heart humane | To Touches delicate his Pencil guides: | And Nature follows as his Hand directs.' The footnote ✳ identified the artist as 'Mr. Hoare of Bath'.

59 Parnell 1769, vol. II, fol. 112.

60 Graves 1779, vol. II, pp. 17–29, chapters III and IV, 'Love in a Cottage'.

61 Anonymous 1780, pp. 10–11, lines 253–259.

62 WSRO, Parham papers, 2/2/2/6, letter 4/78, Hester Hoare to Harriet Anne, Lady Bisshopp, Stourhead, Saturday 1783.

63 Stourhead Archive, Diaries of Augusta, Lady Hoare, 1845–57, 1857–66, 1867–78, 1878–86.

64 www.stourtonhistory.org/census_1841 & 1891 (accessed 30 August 2018).

65 Stourhead Annals, vol. I, 1793.

66 WSA, 383/716, list of tenants, c.1782, 'A Messuage and Plott of Meadow Ground where Tucking Mill formerly stood'. WSA, 383/99, survey of Stourton, 1745, 'Turking Mill has been taken down time out of mind'.

67 View towards Alfred's Tower, c.1760–70, by C. W. Bampfylde (1720–91), pen and colour wash, 270 × 380 mm. V&A (E.352–1949).

68 Distant view towards Alfred's Tower, 1812–16, by Francis Nicholson (1753–1844), watercolour, 404 × 555 mm. BM (1944,1014.144).

69 Stourhead Annals, vol. I, 1840, 'Two new stone Cottages built in Stourton Lane and four new ones, similar in structure, erected at Tucking Mill, all with iron casements'.

70 www.stourtonhistory.org/census_1841 &1891 (accessed 30 August 2018)

71 Ibid., vol. II, 1902–3, Tucking Mill, 'A double Cottage was converted into a small farm Homestead at a cost of £72–16s–10d'.

72 WSA, 383/907, ms note of distances, 12 September 1812, annotated by RCH.

73 Powys 1776, fol. 11.

74 Defoe 1779, vol. I, p. 320; Skinner 1808, fol. 164.

75 WSA, 9/35/165(2)/1605, HH to Lord Bruce, 29 August 1774.

76 Loudon 1833, p. 337.

77 Stourhead Annals, vol. I, 1799–1800.

78 Fenton 1811 (1807), p. 198.

79 WSA, 383/106, Terræ Hoaresnæ in com. Wilts, Dorset, Somerset (Frome, 1829).

80 Hoare 1822, p. 88.

81 Information kindly supplied by Nick Hoare.

82 Loudon 1833, p. 337.

Appendix II: Notes on Visitors Describing Stourhead

1 ODNB 2004.
2 Harris 2000.
3 Britton 1801, p. iv.
4 Woodbridge 1970, pp. 207–209.
5 Britton 1801, p. 3.
6 Chandler 2017.
7 ODNB 2004.
8 Anonymous 1774, vol. II, p. 304–305.
9 Henry Hoare Ledger 1770–85, 6 November 1770, 'Mr Chs Green for an Organ in full' £65.
10 Oliver 1972.
11 ODNB 2004.
12 Dibdin 1822, p. 390.
13 ODNB 2004.
14 Jackson 1879, p. 141.
15 ODNB 2004.
16 Ibid.
17 Anglesey Abbey, NT 515654 and 515656.
18 ODNB 2004.
19 Ibid.
20 Bettany 1919.
21 ODNB 2004.
22 Ibid.
23 Woodbridge 1982.
24 Karling 1981, pp. 79–80.
25 Harris, John, 'F.M. Piper, his English garden studies', Piper 2004, vol. I, pp. 113–119.
26 Whately 1770.
27 F. M. Piper, 'Beskrifning öfwer Lustparkerne uti Stourton och Payneshill... 1778–9 1780,' pp. 1–3. RAS (Pi - e 6, 7 bok).
28 Olausson, Magnus, 'Fredrik Magnus Piper, the man and his work', Piper 1812, vol. II, p. 172. The author noted that Gustav III copied the drawing of the Stourhead Hermitage.
29 Olausson, Magnus, 'A practitioner becomes a theorist', Piper 1812, vol. II, p. 200.
30 ODNB 2004.
31 Ingamells 1997, pp. 779–780.
32 Cartwright 1888 (Pococke 1754), vol. II, p. 17.
33 Ibid., vol. II, pp. 40–41.
34 ODNB 2004.
35 Harrison 2017 p. 46, n. 99, citing *Diaries of Lady Amabel Yorke*, vol. V.
36 Climenson 1899, pp. 168–173.
37 www.treccani.it/enciclopedia/della-torre-di-rezzonico-carlo-gastone_(Dizionario-Biografico) (accessed 9 December 2019).
38 Gamba 1824 (Rezzònico 1787).
39 Harrison 2015.
40 Ellis 1907 (Fanny Burney 1773), pp. 321–323.
41 Hibbert 1968.
42 Simond 1817, vol. I, pp. 260–261.
43 ODNB 2004.
44 V&A E.407:1,2–2005.
45 Skurray 1824, pp. 160–161 and 210–221.
46 ODNB 2004.
47 Ibid.
48 Horace Walpole's annotation in Sullivan 1780, NAL (Dyce T 4to 9578).
49 ODNB 2004.
50 *The death of Dido*, after Guercino, *c.* 1740, oil on canvas, 264 × 327 cm Victoria Art Gallery, Bath, (P:1907.4), the gift of Sir Henry Hoare, 6th Baronet. *The Adoration of the Magi*, 1605, by Lodovico Cardi, called Il Cigoli, (1559–1613), oil on canvas, 345.4 × 233.7 cm. (NT 732100).
51 Tromp 1982 (van Spaen van Biljoen 1791).
52 ODNB 2004.
53 Toynbee 1928 (Walpole 1762).
54 ODNB 2004.
55 BL, Add. MS 36527, Joseph Hunter, notices of contemporaries, fols 134–143 verso.
56 ODNB 2004.
57 Winstanley 2008 (Woodforde 1766), p. 187, 6 August 1768.

Archives

Abbreviations

1722 plan of Stourhead

WSA 383/316, plan of Stourhead, 1722, unknown, ink and tempera on parchment, 340 × 705 mm.

1785 plan of Stourhead

WSA/135/4, 'A Plan of the Manor of Stourton in the County of Wilts. belonging to Richard Colt Hoare Esqʳ.' 1785, by John Charlton, ink and colour wash on parchment, 680 × 965 mm.

1792 low-water plan of the Garden Lake

DZSWS, M908, 'Ground plan of the Lake at Stourhead when empty. Anno 1792.' attr. Philip Crocker, ink and watercolour, 460 × 495 mm.

Anonymous ms 1765

Stourhead Archive, anonymous, transcript description of Stourhead on 10 August 1765.

Anonymous ms 1766

British Library, Add. MS 6767, James Essex architectural collections 'Tour through the Peak, by Winchester, Salisbury &c into Wales by – ', 26 May 1766. Stourhead, fols 33–37 verso.

Clarke 1777

Stourhead Archive, William Clarke ms diary transcript headed '5 July Saturday' [1777], description of Stourhead.

HH Ledger 1734–49

C. Hoare & Co., HFM/9/1, Henry Hoare's Ledger of Personal Accounts, 1734–49; the so-called 'Wilberry' ledger.

HH Ledger 1749–70
WSA, 383/6, Henry Hoare's Ledger of Personal Accounts, 1749–70.

HH Ledger 1770–85
C. Hoare & Co., HFM/9/5, Henry Hoare's Ledger of Personal Accounts, 1770–85.

Mayes 1996
National Trust Estate Office, Stourton, Ian Mayes, 'Proposals for restoration of parkland, terrace ride, Park Hill on the Stourhead Estate by the National Trust, June 1996', unpublished report.

NT Gardens Survey 1981
National Trust Estate Office, Stourton, B. J. Woods et al., 'Survey of Stourhead Gardens, Wiltshire, 1981–2', unpublished report.

Parnell 1769
The London School of Economics and Political Science, archives coll. misc. 0038, 'Journal of a tour thro' Wales and England, anno. 1769', by Sir John Parnell, 2nd Baronet, 4 vols, vol. II, fols 79–113.

Piper general plan 1779
RAS (Pi - e 6, 1 bok [17]). 'General plan of the former banker Henry Hoare's pleasure park at Stourton in Wiltshire, near Bristol, drawn 1779', by Fredrik Magnus Piper (1746–1824), pencil, ink and colour wash, 475 × 645 mm.

Polwarth 1776
Bedfordshire Archives & Record Service, Lucas MSS, L30/9/60/84, Amabel Yorke, Lady Polwarth, to her mother, Marchioness Grey, 27 August 1776.

Powys 1776
British Library, Add. MS 42168, Caroline Powys, Journals and recipe-book of

Caroline Powys, 'Journal of a Five days Tour in a Letter to a Friend 1776', vols 14, Stourhead, vol. IX, fols 15–27.

Skinner 1808
British Library, Add. MS 33635, Reverend John Skinner, 'Journals of tours in the South of England, Sketches in Somerset, Devon and Cornwall', Stourhead, fols 154 verso–166.

Spence 1765
The Beinecke Rare Book & Manuscript Library, Yale University, Joseph Spence Papers, OSB MSS 4 Box 6, folder 202 – Series V. 'Mr Hoar's at Stourton: Wiltshire', copied into a letter to the 9th Earl of Lincoln, 17 September 1765.

Stourhead Annals
Stourhead Archive, (NT 3027141) Stourhead Annals commencing in the year 1792, 3 vols.

Stourhead Catalogue 1754
Longleat House Archives, North Muniment Room 8963.9, ms catalogue headed 'In the Hall at Stourton' and endorsed with the date 1754.

Stourhead Catalogue 1784
WSA, 383/715, copy deed, fols 57–64, 'The Catalogue or Particulars of the Pictures Prints Statues and other Things in… Stourhead… mentioned in the Indenture whereunto the same is annexed.' The catalogue is attached to the Settlement of 27 January 1784.

Stourhead Inventory 1742
C. Hoare & Co., HB/l/B/4, 'An Inventory of Goods and ffurniture in the House at Stourhead belonging to Henry Hoare Esq taken the 24th day of June 1742'.

Stourhead Inventory 1838
WSA, 383/16, '1838 Inventory of Heir-Looms at Stourhead directed to be taken by the Will of the late Sir Rich[d] Colt Hoare Bar[t]. with the state and condition thereof'.

Stourhead Inventory 1908
Stourhead Archive, 'Stourhead. Wilts. Inventory of Furniture, Bedding, Carpets, China, Plate, Pictures, Curios, and other effects on the premises of the Mansion the property of Sir Henry Hugh Arthur Hoare Bart., January 1908. John Walton & Co: Ltd. Mere, Wilts.'

Bibliography

Acton 2019
Acton, Will, 'Descendants of Sir Richard Hoare', 2019 (Hoare family website).

Adshead 2007
Adshead, David, *Wimpole, Architectural drawings and topographical views* (London, 2007).

Alma 1979
Alma, Roger, 'Thomas Hardy and Stourhead', *National Trust Studies 1979* (London, 1978), pp. 99–111.

Annable 1964
Annable, F. K. and D. D. A. Simpson, *Guide catalogue of the Neolithic and Bronze Age collections in Devizes Museum* (Devizes, 1964).

Anonymous 1764 (Stourton Gardens 1749)
Anonymous, 'Stourton Gardens, written in 1749', *The Royal Magazine or Gentleman's Monthly Companion*, London, vol. X, 'Poetical Essays in February, 1764', pp. 102–104.

Anonymous 1774
Anonymous, *A new display of the beauties of England; or, a description of the most elegant or magnificent public edifices... in different parts of the kingdom*, 2 vols (London, 1774).

Anonymous 1780
Anonymous, *A ride and a walk through Stourhead a poem* (London, 1780).

Anonymous 1799
Anonymous, *The Salisbury Guide* (Salisbury, 1799) pp. 77–79.

Anstey 1776
Anstey, Christopher, *An election ball* (Bath, 1776).

Avery 1979
Avery, Charles, 'Hubert le Sueur's Portraits of King Charles I in Bronze, at Stourhead, Ickworth and elsewhere', *National Trust Studies 1979* (London, 1978), pp. 128–147.

Barron 1976
Barron, R. S., *The geology of Wiltshire* (Bradford-on-Avon, 1976).

Bartoli 1693
Bartoli, P. S., *Admiranda romanarum antiquitatum ac veteris sculpturæ vestigia anaglyphtico opere elaborata, ex marmoreis exemplaribus... à P. Sancte Bartolo delineata, incis ... notis J. P. Bellorii illustrata.* (Rome, 1693).

Beamon 1990
Beamon, Sylvia and Susan Roaf, *The ice-houses of Britain* (New York/London, 1990).

Bell 2012
Bell, Gordon et al, *Francis Nicholson (1753-1844)* (Pickering, 2012).

Benson 1843
Benson, Robert, *Facts and observations touching Mr. Hatcher and the History of Salisbury* (London, 1843).

Bertolotti 1880
Bertolotti, A., 'Esportazione di Oggetti di belle arti da Roma per l'Inghilterra', Fabio Gori (ed.), *Archivio storico, artistico, archeologico e letterario della città e provincia di Roma*, vol. IV, anno VI, f. 2, (Spoleto, 1880).

Bettany 1919 (Jerningham 1777)
Bettany, Lewis (ed.) *Edward Jerningham and his friends, a series of eighteenth-century letters* (London, 1919).

Bieber 1961
Bieber, Margarete, *The sculpture of the Hellenistic age* (New York, 1961).

Binnie 1987
Binnie, G. M., *Early dam builders in Britain* (London, 1987).

Britton 1801
Britton, John, *The beauties of Wiltshire*, 3 vols, vol. II (London, 1801–25).

Britton 1830
Britton, John, *Picturesque antiquities of the English cities* (London, 1830).

Bryant 2014
Bryant, Julius, 'Exempla Vertutis: designs for sculpture', Susan Weber (ed.), *William Kent: designing Georgian Britain* (New Haven/London, 2014), pp. 549–587.

Brydone 1773
Brydone, P., *A tour through Sicily and Malta*, 2 vols (London, 1773).

Burlington 1779
Burlington, Charles, David Llewellyn Rees and Alexander Murray, *The modern universal British traveller* (London, 1779).

Calland 2010
Calland, Gary, *St Peter's Stourton, a tour and history of the church* (Bath, 2010).

Campbell 1725
Campbell, Colen, *Vitruvius Britannicus, or the British architect*, 3 vols (London, 1717–25).

Cartwright 1888 (Pococke 1754)
Cartwright, J. J., (ed.), *The travels through*

England of Dr. Richard Pococke, 2 vols (London, 1888–9).

Cave 1978
Cave, Kathryn and Kenneth Garlick, *The Diary of Joseph Farington*, 15 vols (New Haven/London, 1978 onwards).

Chambers 1763
Chambers, William, *Plans, elevations, sections and perspective views of the gardens and buildings at Kew, in Surry* (London, 1763).

Chandler 2017
Chandler, John, 'A Neglected Britton Manuscript', *The Recorder, the annual newsletter of the Wiltshire Record Society*, no. 16, February 2017, pp. 14–15.

Christie's 1883 (a)
Stourhead heirlooms catalogue of old Sevres, Chelsea, Worcester and oriental porcelain, Wedgwood ware, Italian cabinets and caskets and a fine statue by Rysbrack which (by order of Sir Henry Hoare, Bart.,) will be sold by auction by Messrs. Christie, Manson & Woods... on Friday, 1 June, 1883.

Christie's 1883
Stourhead heirlooms catalogue of the pictures, by Old Masters of the Italian, French, and Dutch schools; fine works of the Early English School, and drawings by A. Canaletti and J. M. W. Turner, R.A. which (by Order of Sir Henry Hoare, Bart.,) will be sold by auction by Messrs. Christie, Manson & Woods... on Saturday, 2 June, 1883.

Christie's 1884
Catalogue of handsome jewels, the property of Thomas Gee, Esq... handsome silver plate, being a portion of the Stourhead heirlooms, sold by order of Sir Henry Hoare, Bart... which will be sold by auction by Messrs. Christie, Manson & Woods... on Wednesday, 2 July, 1884.

Clark 2013
Clark, Jan, 'An amateur artist's sketching tour of late eighteenth-century English gardens' (Lancelot-Henri Roland Turpin de Crissé in 1793), *Garden History*, vol. XLI, no. 2, 2013, pp. 209–223.

Clay 1994
Clay, C. G. A., 'Henry Hoare, banker, his family, and the Stourhead estate', F. M. L. Thompson (ed.), *Landowners, capitalists and entrepreneurs, essays for Sir John Habakkuk* (Oxford, 1994), pp. 113–138.

Clifford 1977
Clifford, Timothy, 'Cigoli's Adoration of the Magi at Stourhead', *The National Trust Year Book 1977-78* (London, 1977), pp. 1–17.

Climenson 1899
Climenson, Emily J. (ed.), *Passages from the diaries of Mrs Philip Lybbe Powys of Hardwick House, Oxon. A.D. 1756–1808* (London, 1899).

Colvin 2008
Colvin, Howard, *A biographical dictionary of British architects* (New Haven/London, 2008).

Coxe 1801
Coxe, William, *An historical tour in Monmouthshire*, 2 vols (London, 1801).

Dallaway 1816
Dallaway, James, *Of statuary and sculpture among the antients. with some account of specimens preserved in England* (London, 1816).

Decker 1759
Decker, Paul, *Chinese architecture civil and ornamental* (London, 1759).

Defoe 1779
Defoe, Daniel and Samuel Richardson (ed.), *A tour through the island of Great Britain*, ninth edition, 4 vols (Dublin, 1779).

Desaguliers 1744
Desaguliers, J. T., *A course of experimental philosophy*, 2 vols (London, 1744).

Dibdin 1822
Dibdin, T. F. 'Cuthbert Tonstall', 'Visit to Stourhead Wilts.', *The Gentleman's Magazine*, vol. XCII, pt. II, June to December, 1822, pp. 388–391.

Dodd 1979
Dodd, Dudley, 'Rebuilding Stourhead 1902–1906', *National Trust Studies 1979* (London, 1978), pp. 113–127.

Dodd 1980
Dodd, Dudley, 'Repairing the Bristol High Cross', *National Trust Wessex Region Newsletter*, Spring, 1980.

Dodd 2007
Dodd, Dudley, 'Fit for the Gods, Furniture from Stourhead's Temples', *Apollo: The National Trust Annual 2007*, pp. 14–22.

Dodd 2011
Dodd, Dudley and Lucy Wood, 'The "Weeping Women" commode and other orphaned furniture at   Stourhead by the Chippendales, senior and junior', *Furniture History*, vol. XLVII, 2011, pp. 47–124.

Dodd 2016
Dodd, Dudley, 'Mr Studio's Hand-Coloured Prints at Stourhead' *Print*

Quarterly, vol. XXXIII, no. 3 (September, 2016), pp. 263–277.

Dodd 2017
Dodd, Dudley, 'The 1742 inventory of Stourhead: contemplating a transient house', *Furniture History*, vol. LIII, 2017, pp. 51–89.

Dodd 2018
Dodd, Dudley (ed.), *The letters of Henry Hoare 1760–1781*, WRS, vol. LXXI (Chippenham, 2018).

Douglas 1793
Douglas, James, *Nenia Britannica: or, a sepulchral history of Great Britain; from the earliest period to its general conversion to Christianity* (London, 1793).

Eavis 2002
Eavis, Anna, 'The avarice and ambition of William Benson', *Georgian Group Journal*, vol. XII (2002), pp. 8–37.

Ellis 1907 (Fanny Burney 1773)
Ellis, A. R., *The early diary of Fanny Burney 1768–1778*, 2 vols (London, 1907).

Eustace 1982
Eustace, Katherine, *Michael Rysbrack, sculptor 1694–1770* (Bristol, 1982).

Fedden 1968
Fedden, Robin, *The continuing purpose: a history of the National Trust its aims and work* (London, 1968).

Fenton 1811 (1807)
A Barrister [Richard Fenton], *A tour in quest of genealogy, through several parts of Wales, Somersetshire, and Wiltshire... with a description of Stourhead and Stonehenge* (London, 1811).

Ferrari 1646
Ferrari, G. B. *Hesperides, sive, de malorum aureorum cultura et usu libri quatuor* (Rome, 1646).

Fisher 1917
Fisher, John (ed.), *Tours in Wales (1804–1813) by Richard Fenton from his ms journals...* (London, 1917).

Floud 2019
Floud, Roderick, *An economic history of the English garden* (London, 2019).

Friedman 1974
Friedman, Terry and Timothy Clifford, *The man at Hyde Park Corner, sculpture by John Cheere, 1709–1787* (Leeds, 1974).

Gamba 1824 (Rezzònico 1787)
Gamba, B. (ed.), *Viaggio in Inghilterra di Carlo Gastone della Torre di Rezzònico Comasco* (Venice, 1824).

Gibbs 1728
Gibbs, James, *A book of architecture* (London, 1728).

Gilpin 1798
Gilpin, William, *Observations on the western parts of England, relative chiefly to picturesque beauty*, second edition (London, 1798).

Goodison 2005
Goodison, Judith, 'Thomas Chippendale the Younger at Stourhead', *Furniture History*, vol. XLI, 2005, pp. 57–116.

Goodison 2017
Goodison, Judith, *The life and work of Thomas Chippendale Junior* (London, 2017).

Graves 1779
Graves, Richard, *Columella; or, the distressed anchoret*, 2 vols (London, 1779).

Hadot 2004
Hadot, Pierre, *Le voile d'Isis: essai sur l'histoire de l'idée de nature* (Paris, 2004).

Halfpenny 1752
Halfpenny, W. and J. Halfpenny, *Rural architecture in the Chinese taste*, second edition (London, 1752).

Hanway 1756
anway, Jonas, *A journal of eight days journey from Portsmouth to Kingston upon Thames... in a series of sixty-four letters: addressed to two ladies of the partie... by a gentleman of the partie* (London, 1756).

Hardy 1979
Hardy, John, 'The Garden Seat 1650–1850', *The Connoisseur*, vol. CC, no. 808, June 1979, pp. 118–123.

Harris 2000 (Beaufort 1762)
Harris, John, 'The Duchess of Beaufort's Observations on Places', *Georgian Group Journal*, vol. X, 2000, pp. 36–41.

Harrison 2015
Harrison, J. E., 'The development and content of Stourhead gardens: recent findings, insights from an eighteenth-century poem and the visit of Carlo Gastone della Torre di Rezzònico in 1787', *Garden History*, vol. XLIII no. 1, 2015, pp. 126–143.

Harrison 2017
Harrison, J. E., 'Myth in reception: insights from Stourhead gardens,' unpublished thesis 2017. http://oro.open.ac.uk/55678/ (accessed 10.10.19)

Hazlitt 1824
Hazlitt, William, *Sketches of the principal picture-galleries in England* (London, 1824).

Hibbert 1968
Hibbert, Christopher (ed.), *Louis Simond: an American in Regency England* (London, 1968).

Hirschfeld 1779
Hirschfeld, C. C. L., *Théorie de l'art des jardins*, 5 vols (Leipzig, 1779–1785).

Hoare 1800
Hoare, Sir Richard Colt, Bt, *A description of the house and gardens at Stourhead... with a catalogue of the pictures &c.* (Salisbury, 1800).

Hoare 1806
Hoare, Sir Richard Colt, Bt, *The itinerary of Archbishop Baldwin through Wales AD MCLXXXVIII, by Giraldus de Barri*, 2 vols (London, 1806).

Hoare 1807
Hoare, Sir Richard Colt, Bt, *Journal of a tour in Ireland. A.D. 1806* (London, 1807).

Hoare 1812
Hoare, Sir Richard Colt, Bt, *The ancient history of Wiltshire*, 3 vols (London, 1812–1821).

Hoare 1815 (I)
Hoare, Sir Richard Colt Hoare, Bt, *Recollections abroad, during the years 1785, 1786, 1787*, vol. I (Bath, 1815).

Hoare 1815 (II)
Hoare, Sir Richard Colt Hoare, Bt, *Recollections abroad, during the years 1788, 1789, 1790*, vol. II (Bath, 1815).

Hoare 1817 (III)
Hoare, Sir Richard Colt Hoare, Bt, *Recollections abroad, during the year 1790. Sicily and Malta*, vol. III (Bath, 1817).

Hoare 1818 (IV)
Hoare, Sir Richard Colt Hoare, Bt, *Recollections abroad during the years 1790 and 1791*, vol. IV (Bath, 1818).

Hoare 1818
Hoare, Sir Richard Colt, Bt, *A description of the house and gardens at Stourhead* (Bath, 1818).

Hoare 1819
Hoare, Sir Richard Colt, Bt, *Pedigrees and memoirs of the families of Hore* (Bath, 1819).

Hoare 1821
Hoare, Sir Richard Colt Bt, 'A list of geraniums in the conservatories... at Stourhead' (Bath, 1821).

Hoare 1822
Hoare, Sir Richard Colt, Bt, 'The Hundred of Mere', *The modern history of South Wiltshire*, (London, 1822) vol. I. A complete list of hundreds is found on pp. 93–4.

Hoare 1824
Hoare, Sir Richard Colt, Bt, *Monastic remains of the religious houses at Witham, Bruton, & Stavordale, com. Somerset* (Frome, 1824).

Hoare 1828
Hoare, Sir Richard Colt, Bt, *Antiquitates Wiltunenses* (Shaftesbury, 1828).

Hoare 1844
Hoare, Sir Richard Colt, Bt, 'Addenda to Hundred of Mere', *The modern history of South Wiltshire*, vol. V (London, 1844).

Hoare 1932
Hoare, H. P. R, *Hoare's Bank, a record 1672–1955* (London, 1932 and 1955).

Houel 1782
Houel, Jean-Pierre-Laurent, *Voyage pittoresque des isles de Sicile...*, 4 vols (Paris, 1782).

Hunter 1851
Hunter, Joseph, 'The topographical gatherings at Stourhead 1825–1833' *Memoirs illustrative of the history and antiquities of Wiltshire and the city of Salisbury* (London, 1851).

Hunter 2018
Hunter, Pamela, *Through the years, tales from Hoare's Bank archive*, vol. II (London, 2018).

Hutchings 2005
Hutchings, Victoria, *Messrs Hoare Bankers: a history of the Hoare banking dynasty* (London, 2005).

Hutchins 1868
Hutchins, John, *The history and antiquities of the county of Dorset*, 4 vols, vol. III (London, 1868).

Ingamells 1997
Ingamells, John, *A dictionary of British and Irish travellers in Italy 1701-1800, compiled from the Brinsley Ford archive* (New Haven/London, 1997).

Jackson 1854
Jackson, J. E. (ed.) 'Leland's Journey through Wiltshire: A.D. 1540–42', *The Wiltshire Archaeological and Natural History Magazine* vol. I (Devizes, 1854), pp. 193–195.

Jackson 1862
Jackson, J. E. (ed.) Wiltshire. *The topographical collections of John Aubrey F.R.S., A.D. 1659–70* (Devizes, 1862).

Jackson 1879
Jackson, William (ed.), *Memoirs of Dr. Richard Gilpin* (London, 1879).

Jameson 2003 (Woodforde 1791)
Jameson, Peter (ed.), *The Diary of James Woodforde* (The Parson Woodforde Society, 2003), vol. XIII, 1791–3.

Jatta 2013
Jatta, Barbara, 'The drawings of the Appian Way', P. A. Rosa and B. Jattta (ed.), *La Via Appia: nei disegni di Carlo Labruzzi alla Biblioteca Apostolica Vaticana* (Rome, 2013).

Jervis 2015
Jervis, Simon Swynfen and Dudley Dodd, *Roman Splendour English Arcadia: the English taste for Pietre Dure and the Sixtus Cabinet at Stourhead* (London, 2015).

Karling 1981
Karling, Sten, et al., *Fredrik Magnus Piper and the landscape garden* (Stockholm, 1981).

Kassler 2015 (Queen Charlotte 1789)
Kassler, Michael (ed.), 'The Diary of Queen Charlotte, 1789 and 1794', *Memoirs of the Court of George III*, vol. IV (London, 2015).

Kelly 1980
Kelly, Alison, 'Coade Stone at National Trust Houses', *National Trust Studies* (London, 1980), pp. 95–112.

Kenworthy-Browne 1983
Kenworthy-Browne, John, 'Rysbrack, "Hercules", and Pietro da Cortona', *The Burlington Magazine*, Vol. CXXV, no. 961, April 1983 pp. 216–219.

Kenworthy-Browne 1993
Kenworthy-Browne, John. 'Designing around the statues: Matthew Brettingham's casts at Kedleston', *Apollo, The National Trust Historic Houses and Collections Annual, April 1993*, pp. 248–252.

Kurz 1953
Kurz, Otto, 'Huius Nympha loci: a pseudo-classical inscription and a drawing by Dürer', *Journal of the Warburg and Courtauld Institutes*, vol. XVI, no.3/4, 1953, pp. 171–177.

Laing 2018
Laing, Alastair. 'Bacchus the wanderer: the peregrinations of an antique statue between Painshill Park and Anglesey Abbey', *Apollo: The National Trust Annual 2008*, pp. 22–29.

Langford 1755
A catalogue of the... collection of valuable gems, bronzes, marble and other busts and antiquities of the late Doctor Mead... will be sold by auction, by Mr. Langford... on Tuesday, the 11th of this instant March 1755.

Langford 1764
A catalogue of the capital and entire collection of prints, drawings, and books of prints, of Mr. Michael Rysbrack... will be sold by auction, by Mr. Langford and son... 15th of this instant February 1764, and the nine following evenings.

Langley 1736
Langley, Batty, *Ancient Masonry*, 2 vols (London, 1736).

Langford 1989
Langford, Paul, *A Polite and Commercial People England 1727–1783* (Oxford, 1989).

Lees-Milne 1992
Lees-Milne, James, *People and places: country house donors and the National Trust* (London, 1992).

Leoni 1721
Leoni, Giacomo, *The architecture of A. Palladio*, 2 vols (London, 1721).

Lewis 1960
Lewis, W. S. et al. (ed.), *Horace Walpole's correspondence with Sir Horace Mann*, vol. XXI (New Haven/London, 1960).

Lewis 1967
Lewis, W. S. et al. (ed.), *Horace Walpole's correspondence with Sir Horace Mann*, vol. XXIV (New Haven/London, 1967).

Liversidge 1978
Liversidge, M. J. H., *The Bristol High Cross* (Dursley, 1978).

Llanover 1862
Llanover, Augusta Hall, Baroness (ed.), *The autobiography and correspondence of Mary Granville, Mrs Delany*, second series, 3 vols, vol. III (London, 1862), pp. 140–141.

Loudon 1835
Loudon, J. C., 'Notes on gardens and country seats visited from July 27 to September 16 1833', *The Gardener's Magazine*, vol. XI, 1835, pp. 335–337.

MacDougall 1975
MacDougall, Elisabeth, 'The Sleeping Nymph: Origins of a Humanist Fountain Type', *The Art Bulletin*, vol. LVII, no. 3, 1975, pp. 357–365.

McKewan 2006
McKewan, Colin (ed.), *Stourhead lake project 2005, survey and excavation of the lakes at Stourhead House* (NAS, 2006).

Macquoid 1924
Macquoid, Percy and Ralph Edwards, *The dictionary of English furniture*, 3 vols (London, 1924–7).

Magleby 2009
Magleby, M. A, *Reviewing the Mount of Diana: Henry Hoare's Turkish Tent at Stourhead* (Columbus, Ohio, 2009).

Malins 1966
Malins, Edward, *English landscaping and literature, 1660–1840* (London, 1966).

Miller 2010
Miller, Sally, '"The Fruits of Industry": the garden of Sir Richard Hoare at Barn Elms, Surrey, 1750–54', *Garden History*, vol. XXXVIII, no. 2, 2010, pp. 194–212.

Mitchell 2012
Mitchell, Julian, 'A new look at Richard Colt Hoare', *The British Art Journal*, vol. XIII, no. 3, December 2012, pp. 61–68.

Montfaucon 1719
Montfaucon, Bernard de, *L'antiquité expliquée et représentée en figures*, 5 vols, (Paris, 1719).

Montfaucon 1724
Montfaucon, Bernard de, *Supplément au livre de l'antiquité expliquée et représentée en figures*, 5 vols (Paris, 1724).

Neale 1823
Neale, J. P., *Views of the seats of noblemen and gentlemen in England, Wales, Scotland and Ireland*, 6 vols, vol. V (London, 1823).

Newby 1990
Newby, Evelyn, *William Hoare of Bath R.A. 1707–1792* (Bath, 1990).

Nichols 1840
Nichols, J. B., *Catalogue of the Hoare library at Stourhead* (London, 1840).

Oliver 1972 (Curwen 1776)
Oliver, Andrew (ed.), *The journal of Samuel Curwen loyalist*, 2 vols (Massachusetts, 1972).

Orbach 2014
Orbach, Julian and Nikolaus Pevsner, *Somerset: South and West* (New Haven/ London, 2014).

Osborn 1966
Osborn, James M., *Joseph Spence: observations, anecdotes and characters of books and men*, 2 vols (Oxford, 1966).

Parker 1848
Parker, Charles, *Villa Rustica: selected from buildings and scenes in the vicinity of Rome and Florence*, second edition (London, 1848).

Paternò 1781
Paternò-Castello, Ignazio, principe di Biscari, *Viaggio per tutte le antichità della Sicilia* (Naples, 1781).

Piper 1812
Piper, Fredrik Magnus, *Description of the idea and general-plan for an English park written during the years 1811 and 1812*, Royal Swedish Academy of Fine Arts, no. IX, 2 vols (Stockholm, 2004).

Piranesi 1769
Piranesi, G. B., *Diverse maniere d'adornare i cammini* (Rome, 1769).

Prosser 1896
Prosser, Richard B., 'A List of Wiltshire Patentees', *Wiltshire Notes and Queries*, vol. I (Devizes, 1896), pp. 3–6.

Raeburn 1995
Raeburn, Michael, et al. (eds), *The Green Frog service* (London, 1995).

Rapin 1725
Thoyras de Rapin, Paul, *The history of Great Britain and Ireland*, 10 vols (London, 1725).

Raymond 2019
Raymond, Stuart A., *Stourton before Stourhead* (Gloucester, 2019).

Roberts 1997
Roberts, Jane, *Royal landscape the garden and parks of Windsor* (New Haven/ London, 1997).

Rowell 2012
Rowell, Christopher, *Petworth: the people and the place*, National Trust guidebook (London, 2012).

Rutton 1903
Rutton, W. L., 'The Making of the Serpentine', *The Home Counties Magazine*, vol. V, 1903, pp. 81–91, 183–195.

Saint-Non 1781
Saint-Non, Richard de, *Voyage pittoresque ou description des royaumes de Naples et de Sicile*, 5 vols (Paris, 1781–1786).

Sandoz 1961
Sandoz, Marc, 'Paintings by Jean-Louis-François Lagrenée the Elder at Stourhead', *The Burlington Magazine*, vol. CIII, no. 702, September 1961, pp. 392–395.

Sandoz 1964
Sandoz, Marc, 'Lagrenée's 'Charity' returned to Stourhead House', *The Burlington Magazine*, vol. CVI, no. 740, November 1964, pp. 510–513.

Shields 2016
Shields, Steffie, *Moving heaven & earth: Capability Brown's gift of landscape* (London, 2016).

Simond 1817 (1810)
Simond, Louis, *Journal of a tour and residence in Great Britain during the years 1810 and 1811*, 2 vols, (Edinburgh, 1817).

Simpson 1975
Simpson, D. D. A., 'Ancient Wiltshire', *The ancient history of Wiltshire by Sir Richard Colt Hoare*, 2 vols (Wakefield, 1975), pp. 11–16.

Shephard 2003
Shephard, Sue, 'Three gentlemen in arcadia' Halswell, Hestercombe and Stourhead (dissertation 2003) https://halswellpark.files.wordpress.com/2016/03/arcadia.pdf. (accessed 7 March 2020).

Skempton 2002
Skempton, A. W. et al. (eds) *A biographical dictionary of civil engineers in Great Britain and Ireland*, 3 vols, vol. I (London, 2002).

Skurray 1824
Skurray, Francis, *Bidcombe Hill* (London, 1824).

Smith 1860
Smith, Thomas, *Recollections of the British Institution... 1805-1859* (London, 1860).

Sotheby 1883
Sotheby, Wilkinson and Hodge, The Stourhead heirlooms. Catalogue of the library, removed from Stourhead, 30 July–8 August 1883.

Sotheby 1887
Sotheby, Wilkinson and Hodge, The Stourhead heirlooms. Catalogue of the remaining portion of the library, removed from Stourhead, 30 July–8 August 1883, 9–13 December 1887.

Storer 1812
Storer, James, *A description of Fonthill Abbey, Wiltshire* (London, 1812).

Stourton 1899
Stourton, C. B. J., Baron Mowbray, Segrave and Stourton, *The history of the noble house of Stourton*, 2 vols (London, 1899).

Sulivan 1780 (1778)
Sulivan, Sir Richard Joseph, *Observations made during a tour through parts of England, Scotland, and Wales, in a series of letters* (London, 1780).

Sumowski 1983
Sumowski, Werner, *Gemälde der Rembrandt-Schüler*, 6 vols, vol. V (Landau, 1983–1994).

Sweet 1820
Sweet, Robert, *Geraniaceæ, the natural order of gerania*, 5 vols (London 1820–30).

Sweetman 1894
Sweetman, George, *Stourhead: mansion, gardens, church* (Wincanton, 1894).

Sweetman 1907
Sweetman, George, *Guide to Stourhead, Wilts* (Wincanton, 1907).

Sweetman 1913
Sweetman, George, *Guide to Stourhead, Wilts* (Wincanton, 1913).

Sweetman 1925
Sweetman, George, *Guide to Stourhead* (London, 1925).

Swinburne 1783
Swinburne, Henry, *Travels in the two Sicilies*, 2 vols (London, 1783).

Switzer 1729
Switzer, Stephen, *An introduction to a general system of hydrostaticks and hydraulicks, philosophical and practical*, 2 vols (London, 1729).

Symes 2010
Symes, Michael, *Mr Hamilton's Elysium: the gardens of Painshill*, (London, 2010).

Thacker 1979
Thacker, Christopher, *The history of gardens* (London, 1979).

Thelwall 1801 (1797)
Thelwall, John, 'A pedestrian excursion through England and Wales, during the summer of 1797', *Monthly Magazine*, vol. XII, 1801, p. 105.

Thompson 1983
Thompson, M. W. (ed.), *The journeys of Sir Richard Colt Hoare through Wales and England 1793–1810* (Gloucester, 1983).

Toynbee 1928 (Walpole 1762)
Toynbee, Paget (ed.), 'Horace Walpole's journals of visits to country seats &c.', *The Walpole Society*, vol. XVI, 1928, pp. 41–44.

Tromp 1982 (van Spaen van Biljoen 1791)
Tromp, Heimerick, 'A Dutchman's Visits to Some English Gardens in 1791', *Journal of Garden History*, vol. II, no. 1, 1982, pp. 49–51.

Vertue 1934
'Vertue note-books, volume III ', *The Walpole Society*, vol. XXII, 1934.

Vermeule 1956
Vermeule, C. and D. von Bothmer, 'Notes on a New Edition of Michaelis: Ancient Marbles of Great Britain, Part Two', *American Journal of Archaeology*, vol. LX, 1956, pp. 343–344.

Voltaire 1761
Voltaire, François-Marie, Arouet, *Essai sur l'histoire générale... des nations*, 8 vols, (Geneva, 1761–3).

Walpole 1786
Walpole, Horace, *Anecdotes of painting in England*, 4 vols, vol. IV (London, 1786).

Ware 1738
Ware, Isaac, *The four books of Andrea Palladio's architecture* (London, 1738).

Warner 1801 (1800)
Warner, Reverend Richard, *Excursions from Bath* (Bath, 1801).

Warrell 2015
Warrell, Ian, *Turner's Wessex: architecture and ambition* (London, 2015).

Watson 1960
Watson, F. J. B., et al., *Carlo Labruzzi (1748–1817): an exhibition of fine watercolour drawings of the Appian Way, 9 June–16 July 1960* (London, 1960).

Webb 1954
Webb, M. I, *Michael Rysbrack, sculptor* (London, 1954).

Whately 1770
Whately, Thomas, *Observations on modern gardening* (London, 1770).

White 1995
White, Philip, *A gentleman of fine taste: the watercolours of Coplestone Warre Bampfylde 1720–1791* (Taunton, *c.*1995).

Winstanley 1988 (Woodforde 1773)
Winstanley, R .L. (ed.), *The Ansford diary of James Woodforde*, vol. V, 1772–3 (the Parson Woodforde Society, 1988).

Winstanley 1998 (Woodforde 1778)
Winstanley, R. L. (ed.) *The diary of James Woodforde,*, vol. VIII, 1778–9 (the Parson Woodforde Society, 1998).

Winstanley 2008 (Woodforde 1766)
Winstanley, R. L. (ed.), *The diary of James Woodforde,* vol. III, 1766–8 (the Parson Woodforde Society,2008).

Wood 1757
Wood, Robert, *The ruins of Balbec* (London, 1757).

Woodbridge 1965
Woodbridge, Kenneth, 'Henry Hoare's paradise', *The Art Bulletin*, vol. XLVII, no..1, March 1965, pp. 83–116.

Woodbridge 1968
Woodbridge, Kenneth, 'The sacred landscape. Painters and the Lake-garden of Stourhead', *Apollo*, vol. LXXXVIII, September 1968, pp. 210–214.

Woodbridge 1969
Woodbridge, Kenneth, 'Accounts rendered, 1700–1714: the letters of Sir Richard Hoare, banker, goldsmith and lord mayor of London, to his sons', *History Today*, vol. XIX, November 1969, pp. 793–791.

Woodbridge 1970
Woodbridge, Kenneth, *Landscape and antiquity: aspects of English culture at Stourhead 1718 to 1838* (Oxford, 1970).

Woodbridge 1976
Woodbridge, Kenneth, 'The planting of ornamental shrubs at Stourhead: A history, 1746 to 1946', *Garden History*, vol. IV, no. I, 1976, pp. 88–109.

Woodbridge 1978
Woodbridge, Kenneth, et al., *The conservation of the garden at Stourhead... report and recommendations of the committee appointed by the National Trust* (Bath, 1978).

Woodbridge 1981
Woodbridge, Kenneth et al., *Stourhead, Wiltshire*, National Trust guidebook (London, 1981).

Woodbridge 1982
Woodbridge, Kenneth, 'Stourhead in 1768: Extracts from an unpublished journal by Sir John Parnell', *Journal of Garden History*, vol. II, no. 1, January–March 1982, pp. 59–70.

Woodbridge 2001
Woodbridge, Kenneth, *The Stourhead Landscape, Wiltshire* (London, 2001).

Wrighte 1767
Wrighte, William, *Grotesque architecture, or rural amusement...* (London, 1767).

Further Reading

Bevington, M. J., 'Henry Hoare and the creation of his "demy-paradise"', *Studies in Iconography*, vol. XII, 1988, pp. 121–147.

Charlesworth, Michael, 'On meeting Hercules in Stourhead garden', *Journal of Garden History*, vol. IX, no. 2, 1989, pp. 71–75.

Charlesworth, Michael, 'Movement, intersubjectivity, and mercantile morality at Stourhead', Michel Conan (ed.), *Landscape design and the experience of motion* (Washington DC, 2003), pp. 263–286.

Cox, Oliver, 'A mistaken iconography? Eighteenth-century visitor accounts of Stourhead', *Garden History*, vol. XL, no. 1, 2012, pp. 98–116.

Gillette, Jane, 'Can gardens mean?' *Landscape Journal*, vol. XXIV, no. 1, 2005, pp. 85–97.

Harrison, J. E., 'From Rome to Stourhead and thence to Rome again: the phenomenon of the eighteenth-century English landscape garden', Jon Stobart (ed.), *Travel and the British country house* (Manchester, 2017), pp. 42–62.

Hunt, J. D., 'Stourhead revisited & the pursuit of meaning in gardens', *Studies in the history of gardens & designed landscapes*, vol. XXVI, no. 4, 2006, pp. 328–341.

Kelsall, Malcolm, 'The iconography of Stourhead', *Journal of the Warburg and Courtauld Institutes*, vol. XLVI, 1983, pp. 133–143.

Olin, Laurie, *Across the open field, essays drawn from English landscapes* (Philadelphia, 2000), pp. 257–276.

Paulson, Ronald, *Emblem and expression: meaning in English art of the eighteenth century* (London, 1975), pp. 28–32.

Schulz, M. F, 'The circuit walk of the eighteenth-century landscape garden and pilgrim's circuitous progress', *Eighteenth-Century Studies*, vol. XV, no. 1, 1981 pp. 1–25.

Turner, James, 'The structure of Henry Hoare's Stourhead', *The Art Bulletin*, vol. LXI, no. 1, 1979, pp. 68–77.

Woodbridge, Tim, *The Choice* (Wiltshire, 2017).

Publications on Stourhead mentioned neither above nor in the bibliography may be found in National Trust Bibliography (nt.global.ssl.fastly.net).

Photography and Picture Credits

Marianne Majerus is one of Europe's finest garden photographers. Her artistic and sensitive images are widely sought after by publishers and private clients across Europe. She has been commissioned by the Highgrove Estate to photograph HRH The Prince of Wales and his garden. She has won many awards, including International Garden Photographer of the Year, European Garden Photographer of the Year, and has been named Photographer of the Year by the Garden Media Guild on several occasions.

Marianne's images, in addition to those images captioned as from 'Stourhead',

Index

Page numbers in *italics* refer to figures; ordinal numerals preceding titles denote the order of succession.

Chafyn Grove, William, 59

Chambers, William, Sir, 196

Charles I, King of England, Scotland, and Ireland: bust of, 19, 34, *34*

Charlotte, Queen of Great Britain and Ireland, 90, 259

Charlton, John: 'A Plan of the Manor of Stourton in the County of Wilts. belonging to Richard Colt Hoare Esqr.', *48*, 135, *168*, 237, *237*, 239, 249, *252*, 255

Charlton, Thomas, 71

Chatsworth (Derbyshire), 86

Cheapside (London), 31

Cheere, John, 173, 177, 190, 197; *Diane de Versailles*, 150, *150*; *Nymph of the Grotto* (attr.), 156, *156*; Pantheon, 173; *River God*, *158*, 159

Child, Francis, 31

Chinese Alcove (Stourhead), 10, 135, 137, 149–50, *149*, 262, 267

Chippendale, Thomas, the younger, 11, 69, 70, 87–8, 92, *99*, 123, 178; library armchair, *87*; satinwood commode (attr.), 70, *71*

Chiswick Villa (London), 48, 55, 233, 275

Christie's auctions, 115

Cigoli (Lodovico Cardi): *The Adoration of the Magi*, *74*, 76–7, 275; *The death of Dido* (after Guercino), 275

Cirencester Park (Gloucestershire), 46, 252

Clapham Villa (London), 39, 49, 51, 58, 59, *64*, 65

Claremont (Surrey), 48

Clarke, John, 108

Clarke, William, 204, 269

Clock Arch (Stourhead), 51, 82, 217, 222, 237–8, 242–3, *242*, *243*

Coade, Eleanor: *Borghese Vase*, 148

Collinson, John: *The History and Antiquities of the County of Somerset*, 93

Colocci, Angelo, 157

Colt, Susanna, *see* Hoare, Susanna (Susanna Colt, 2nd wife of Henry The Magnificent)

Constable, John, 98

Convent (Stourhead), 63, 249, 258, 259–60, *260*, *261*

Cork, Lady (Margaret Countess of Cork and Orrery), 56–7, 58

Cork, Lord (5th Earl of Cork and Orrery), 45, 49, 56–7, 272

Cort, Hendrik Frans de: The Gateway at Stourhead, *242*; 'The Pantheon at Stour Head', *174*, 178

Cotes, Francis: *Anne Hoare, Mrs Richard Hoare (1737–59) playing a cittern*, 69; *Sir Richard Hoare, 1st Baronet*, 69

Country Life (1938), 259

Coxe, William, Archdeacon, 82–3, 88, 89, 94; *Historical tour in Monmouthshire*, 83

Cozens, John Robert: *The Lake of Nemi looking towards Genzano*, 89

Crocker, John, 89

Crocker, Philip, 88, 89–90, 94, 97, 104; Gold hoard from a barrow at Normanton, *95*; 'Ground plan of the Lake at Stourhead when empty. Anno 1792' (attr.), *138*

Cumberland, Duke of, 49, 51, 150, 164

Cunnington, William, 87, 88–90, 93, 268

Curwen, Samuel, 197, 269

Dahl, Michael: *Henry Hoare on horseback*, 35, 55

Dallaway, James, 145

Davis, Robert, 72, 105

Davison, Jeremiah, 38

Defoe, Daniel, 269; *Tour through the island of Great Britain*, 148, 171, 261, 269

Devis, Arthur, 53

Diana (sculpture, Stourhead), 135, 150, *150*, 267

Diana's Basin (Stourhead), 210, *213*, 225, 229

Diana's Mount (Stourhead), 135, *140*, 150, 161, *179*, 207, 210

Dibdin, Thomas Frognal, 89, 93, 269–70; *Bibliotheca Spenceriana*, 269

Dodd, Dudley, 9, 10, 11

Domesday Book, 131

Doran Webb, Edward, 11, 117–19, 236

Dorset, 15

Douglas, James, Reverend, 88; *Nenia Britannica*, 88

Downton Castle (Herefordshire), 86

Drake, John (of Amersham), 108

Ducros, Abraham Louis, 11, 73, 77, 81, 87, 97, 100; *The Falls of Tivoli*, *76*; *View of Civita Castellana*, *77*

Dugdale, William: *The Antiquities of Warwickshire*, 93

Dughet, Claude, 39

Dughet, Gaspard, 25, 39, 40, 44

Duncombe, Charles, 31

Duncombe Park (Yorkshire), 252, 273

Dungarvan, Lady, *see* Hoare, Susanna (daughter of Henry The Magnificent...)

Dungarvan, Lord (Charles Boyle, Viscount Dungarvan, Susanna Hoare's 1st husband), 10, *20*, 49, 50, 56–7

Earle, Joseph, 32

East, Augusta, *see* Hoare, Augusta Frances

East, George Clayton, Sir (1st Baronet), 115

Edington, Battle of, 10

Edwards, Ralph, 123; *Dictionary of English Furniture*, 123

Egremont, Lord (3rd Earl of), 98, 100

Elizabeth I, Queen of England and Ireland, 19

Ellis, J. A., 101

Ellisfield Manor (Hampshire), 125

Esdaile, Katharine, 123

Essex, James, 267

Farnborough Hall (Warwickshire), 254

Farnese Flora (sculpture), 177

'Fat Harry' Hoare, *21*, *57*, 58–9, 63–5, 100; Hoare's Bank, 59, 64, 70

Faugoin, Francis, 25, 50, 52–3, 65, 161, 164, 171, 215, 216; head gardener at Stourhead, 53

Faugoin, Mary, 52

Fenton, Richard, 84, 133, 138, 168–9, 203, 210, 215, 230, 252, 261, 270; *Historical tour through Pembrokeshire*, 84; *A tour in quest of genealogy*, 84

ferry (Stourhead), 140, 153, 210

Fir Walk (Stourhead), *133*, 137, *139*, 140–1, 268; Hoare, Henry The Magnificent, 135, 140; Hoare, Richard Colt, 141, 207

Fleet Street (London), 31, 37, 41, 108

Flitcroft, Henry, 45, 50–1, 148, 243, 272; Alfred's Tower, 51, 256; 'Chinese' bridge (Barn Elms), 152; Garden Lake dam, 51, 164; Grotto, 51, 135, 155; Obelisk, 51; Pantheon, 51, 171, 172; *Rocky Arch* (attr.), *144*, 145; 'Section of Squire Hoare's Temple call'd Pantheon at Stourton in Wiltshe' (attr.), *173*; Stourhead house, 234; Temple of Apollo, 51, 181, 194, 196; Temple of Flora, 51, 135, 142, 164; Temple on the Terrace, 51, 135, 141; Wooden Bridge, 51, 150; work at Stourhead, 51, 53, 55, 135

Fonthill Abbey (Wiltshire), 271, 273, 275

Fortescue, Matthew, Captain, 98

Fortescue, Henrietta Anne, *see* Hoare, Henrietta Anne

Fountains Abbey (Yorkshire), 86, 273

Fowler, Edward, 44

Fox, Stephen (1st Earl of Ilchester), 45, 56, 150, 268

Fox family, 58

Foxley (Herefordshire), 86

French Revolution, 75, 82, 271, 273

Gainsborough, Thomas, 61; *Peasants going to Market*, 114; *Two children and a cat*, 115

garden (Stourhead), *see* Italian Garden; Kitchen Garden; landscape garden; plants

Garden Lake (Stourhead), 10, 24, 25, 49–50, *166*, 167–71, *193*, 207, 272; 1792 drainage, 168; boat trips, 169, 171, 270; Crocker, Philip: 'Ground plan of the Lake at Stourhead when empty. Anno 1792' (attr.), *138*, 168; as dominant feature in the landscape garden, 161; eastern shore, *106*, *146–7*, *185*, *188–9*; fish, 168, 169, 215; geology, 161; Hoare, Henry The Magnificent, 140, 161, 168, 193; Hoare, Richard Colt, 168, 169; islands, 168; north end, *66*, *198–9*, 210; paths, 82; Piper, Frederik Magnus, 167, 168, *169*; southern shore, 193; springs, 161; trees around the shores, 210; western shore, *22–3*, *160*, *180*, 210

Garden Lake dam (Stourhead), 24, *36*, 49, 133, 137, *162–3*, *166*, *167*, 181; backwater, 164, *231*; comparison with other ornamental lakes, 166–7; construction, 161, 164; Flitcroft, Henry, 51, 164; footpath, 161; Hoare, Henry The Magnificent, 161; Piper, Frederik Magnus, 161, 164, *164*, *165*

garden seats (Stourhead), 203–205, *203*, *204*; barrel seat, 204–205; 'Chinese parasol', 204, *205*; Convent, 203; Hermitage, 203; Pantheon, bench backs, 177, 178; stone seat, 216, *217*; Temple of Apollo, 197; X-frame chairs, 203, 205

gardener's house (Stourhead), 216

Garrick, David, 19, 59, 159

Gasper (Wiltshire), 15, 193; New Lake, 104, 223; Richard Colt Hoare and Gasper Manor, 81–2, 223, 261; road from Stourton to Gasper, 193, *195*, 237, 249

Gateway (Stourhead), *see* Clock Arch

George I, King of Great Britain and Ireland, 31

George III, King of Great Britain and Ireland, 56, 57, 61, 90, 259, 273

Gibbs, James, 141

Gifford, William, 90

Gilpin, William, 41, 186, 254, 270, 275; *Essay on prints*, 270; *Observations*, 270; *Observations on the western parts of England*, 270

Giraldus de Barri, 84, 87

Goodison, Judith, 87

Gothick Greenhouse (Stourhead), *139*, 148–9, 212

pp. 20–1 Coat of arms of Henry Hoare, engraving, 80 × 63 mm,
from the book plate of *Persian letters*, (by Montesquieu)
translated by Mr Ozell, vol. I (London, 1736).
Stourhead library (V.2.20). Reproduced by kind permission
of the National Trust.

First published in the UK in 2021 by Head of Zeus Ltd
An Apollo book

A CIP catalogue record for this book is available from
the British Library.

ISBN [HB] 9781788543620
ISBN [E] 9781788543613

Designed by Heather Bowen
Maps by Jamie Whyte
Colour reproduction by DawkinsColour
Printed and bound in Latvia by Livonia Print

Head of Zeus Ltd
5–8 Hardwick Street
London EC1R 4RG
www.headofzeus.com

An Apollo Book